PRESIDENT

AND

CONGRESS

PRESIDENT
AND
CONGRESS

Power and Policy

BY LOUIS FISHER

THE FREE PRESS
A Division of Macmillan Publishing Co., Inc.
NEW YORK

Collier Macmillan Publishers
LONDON

Copyright © 1972 by The Free Press
A Division of Macmillan Publishing Co., Inc.
Printed in the United States of America
All rights reserved. No part of this book may be
reproduced or transmitted in any form or by any means,
electronic or mechanical, including photocopying, recording,
or by any information storage and retrieval system,
without permission in writing from the Publisher.

The Free Press
A Division of Macmillan Publishing Co., Inc.
866 Third Avenue, New York, New York 10022

Collier-Macmillan Canada Ltd.

First Free Press Paperback Edition 1973

Library of Congress Catalog Card Number: 78–142362

printing number

2   3   4   5   6   7   8   9   10

To PAUL H. DOUGLAS
for setting and satisfying
high standards,
personal and public

PREFACE

This is a book about how the President and Congress share four types of power: legislative power, spending power, taxing power, and the war power. Admittedly, any of these topics could fill a volume several times the size of this one. To tackle all four powers at once entails considerable risk.

It is a risk I choose to take for the sake of perspective, and I mean that in several senses. I want perspective first as to subject area, since there is considerable advantage in being able to compare executive-legislative relationships in different areas. An understanding of their sharing of the war power, for example, can be balanced by an understanding of how they share the spending power or the taxing power.

We also need perspective as to time. Judgments of the President and Congress vary, depending on what decade or period you have in mind. Such judgments are improved by broadening the time factor. To make that possible, I have placed the discussion of executive-legislative relationships within the framework of two centuries of constitutional development.

Lastly, I want the kind of perspective that comes from different approaches. Certain questions have helped define the scope of this book. How have the four powers shifted between the President and Congress? *Why* have they shifted? What impact have these shifts of power had on policy? What are the constitutional implications? To answer these ques-

tions, I have necessarily drawn material from a wide variety
of disciplines. The questions are partly philosophic, political, economic, and legal.

I have taken several liberties in writing this book. First,
I concentrate on conflicts and struggles between the President and Congress; one could just as easily have written
about their cooperation, or about conflict and cooperation.
The latter is indispensable in any political order, but I
decided not to dwell on it here. Second, it is an obvious
simplification to speak of the President and Congress as
though they are two separate entities. I do so for the sake
of convenience, with the warning of David Truman very
much in mind: "The political process rarely, if ever, involves a conflict between the legislature and the executive
viewed as two monolithic and unified institutions. The
actual competing structures on each side are made up of
elements in the legislature and in the executive, reflecting
and supported by organized and unorganized interests"
(*The Governmental Process*, p. 433).

The main emphasis of the book is on power and policy,
not on process. For instance, in the chapter on legislative
power, I examine the general scope and growth of executive
power, as well as the different types of administrative legislation. The next chapter explores why Congress delegates
power to the executive branch and it cites some of the methods that are used to check arbitrary executive action. The
focus is not so much on the legislative process itself (tactics,
strategies, "how a bill becomes a law") but rather on the actual exercise of legislative power and its impact on policy.

In the area of the spending power, I want to show the
political and economic factors that prompted Congress to
delegate budgetary responsibilities to the President in 1921.
What caused Congress to give up part of its "power of the
purse"? Again, I am not so much interested in the budget
process (how the President formulates the budget, the techniques of program budgeting, the details of the unified budget, etc.) but rather the reasons for shifting budgetary responsibilities to the President. Also of interest: what is the

scope and range of Presidential discretion over the expenditure of funds? how does this discretion affect public policy? Although of vital importance, there is little in the literature to tell us much about executive spending power.

The chapter on the taxing power allows me to study executive-legislative relationships in two areas: international trade and domestic fiscal policy. Existing studies on the President make passing reference to the flexible tariff act, the reciprocal trade acts and the Kennedy Round, but not much else is said about executive responsibilities in foreign trade. I develop these topics in considerable detail, trying to understand the shifting back and forth of power. As for fiscal policy, I review the factors that led up to the Employment Act of 1946; trace the postwar countercyclical record and the performance of the Truman and Eisenhower Administrations; and follow that with a discussion of President Kennedy's request in 1962 for standby tax and spending powers as part of his anti-recession program. His request was rejected, but the topic of Presidential tax discretion remains current.

The last two chapters are on the war power. One chapter covers the general scope of Presidential power: the constitutional and extraconstitutional sources of power, the ill-defined boundaries of the "war period" (stretched in both directions to include the prewar and the postwar periods), and the increasingly generous definitions of "defensive war" that allow the President to dispatch troops abroad under a wide variety of circumstances. Because it is so customary to speak of "judicial acquiescence" in the war power, I decided to broaden the definition of war power to include actions taken by the President and executive officials in the name of national security, and then show where the Court has and has not been silent.

The final chapter deals with Congress' effort to reassert its role in foreign policy-making and thereby exercise greater influence over the commitment of troops and financial assistance to other nations. Legislative assertion has been particularly conspicuous in the spirited debate over the Safeguard ABM system; for that reason I have a lengthy section showing how Congress challenged the Administration's rationale. I also reexamine many of the traditional properties attributed to the executive branch (such as "unity" and "expertise") and suggest what Congress will have to do in the way of procedural and organizational reform to increase its influence.

All of these subjects inevitably raise constitutional questions. What is the purpose of the separation of power doctrine? How did it originate? What did it mean to the framers? What has it come to mean in the decisions of the Supreme Court? Textbooks and scholarly works promote all sorts of misconceptions about the separation doctrine. We are told that the framers borrowed it from Montesquieu, that they held executive power in distrust, and that they deliberately adopted a separation of power—not for efficiency—but to preclude the arbitrary exercise of power and to slow down the process of government.

Whatever the topic, be it Presidential tax discretion, congressional reassertion of its war powers, or some other contest for power between the two branches, the debate has a way of revolving around the purpose of separated powers and the "framers' intent." I therefore feel an obligation to present my own views on the subject, and do so fully sensitive to the obstacles before me. A history of the 1774–1787 period is widely regarded as tedious, musty, and of little relevance to contemporary political problems. Curiously, those who adopt such an attitude nevertheless feel free, when it is to their advantage, to expound on the "intentions" of the framers and the "real meaning" of the Constitution. One spots this time and again in congressional hearings, where experts inject mistaken political and legal assumptions into their policy recommendations.

To minimize interruptions and distractions, I have omitted footnotes from the text. As a substitute, the reference section is keyed to the text by chapter and by section title. The purpose of the reference section is twofold: to document what I have said, and to provide a starting-point for more ambitious studies by students and colleagues.

ACKNOWLEDGMENTS

The temptation is great, upon finishing a book, to believe that somehow you did it on your own. Errors of fact and judgment are indeed our own creations; for those I properly take credit. But for portions of the book with more lasting value, credit must be shared.

My first debt is to the New School for Social Research, where I developed my interest in politics, law, and economics. My doctoral thesis, supported by a two-year fellowship grant from the National Science Foundation, provided an early test run for this book. One of the first to stimulate my work in political economy was Robert L. Heilbroner, who has since remained available for advice and encouragement. I have benefited greatly from that. To another former professor of mine at the New School—Paul H. Douglas—the book is dedicated.

Harvey C. Mansfield read the manuscript in its entirety, offering a detailed list of criticisms and suggestions. Stephen Jay Wayne also read the complete manuscript, focusing more on general questions of content and organization. The manuscript was markedly improved as a result of their close readings. Other specialists, who read portions of the manuscript, also recommended valuable ideas and perspectives: Felicia J. Deyrup and Howard S. Piquet on tariff policy; John H. E. Fried and Erich Hula on war powers; John F. Campbell and Samuel P. Huntington on Congress and the war power; and William B. Gwyn on the "intent" of the framers on separated powers. Three of my colleagues at the Congressional Research Service of the Library of Congress read sections of the book and offered many helpful suggestions: Walter Kravitz, Walter Oleszek, and William Tansill.

A paper of mine on "Presidential Spending Discretion and Congressional Controls" was read by Samuel M. Cohn, Paul O'Neill, and Carl Tiller of the Office of Management and Budget; by Paul M. Wilson, Ralph Preston, and Eugene Wilhelm of the House Appropriations Committee; and by William Woodruff of the Senate Appropriations Committee. The latter paper was presented at the 1971 annual convention of the American Political Science Association, held in Chicago from September 6 to September 11, 1971. Another paper, on "Congress and the War Power," was presented to the Center for the Study of Democratic Institutions, Santa Barbara, California, on July 28, 1971.

A large part of this book has already appeared in article form in the following magazines and journals: *The New Leader, George Washington Law Review, The Progressive, Administrative Science Quarterly, Western Political Quarterly, Journal of Public Law,* and *Journal of American Studies.* Another article will appear in *Law and Contemporary Problems* in 1972. The careful review and editing performed by these publications helped produce a better book.

I am grateful to David C. Harrop, formerly of The Free Press, for understanding, at our first meeting, the need for this kind of book. That meant very much to me. I am indebted also to my wife, Alice, for bearing up through all the drafts and all the rewritings. Without her perseverance the obscurities would have been more numerous.

CONTENTS

1

PRINCIPLE OF
SEPARATED POWERS

The President and Congress frequently collide when exercising the legislative, spending, tax, and war powers. When they do, it is customary to charge one another with having violated a central tenet of American government: the separation of powers. Although this principle is considered the cornerstone of our system and an article of political faith for the Founding Fathers, there are wide differences of opinion as to what the framers of the Constitution meant by it. We are told that they embraced the doctrine of Montesquieu, yet there is a good deal of doubt as to what *he* meant, or whether they borrowed from him in the first place. Moreover, there remains the question: how should one apply a principle, adopted in 1787, to the situations facing us today?

SEPARATED POWERS: ORIGIN AND PURPOSE

The pitfalls of communication are nowhere more evident than in the concept of separated powers. It seems as though we cannot avoid one misinterpretation without simultaneously committing another. If we fail to insist on separation, then one branch might accumulate too much influence and either mismanage or abuse its powers. On the other hand, if separation is interpreted in a literal and strict sense, this encourages each branch to spin independently and freely in its own orbit. That too can lead to mismanagement and abuse.

Separated Powers and Liberty

Students are often taught that powers are separated as a means of preserving liberties; yet it is equally true that too much stress on separation can *destroy* liberties. The historic antagonism in France between executive and legislature, characterized by an oscillation between administrative and representative forms of government, is a classic example of the danger of extreme separation. The constitutions of 1791 and 1848 represented the most ambitious attempts in France to establish a pure separation of powers. The consequence, in the first case, was the Committee of Public Safety, the Directory, and the reign of Napoleon Bonaparte, while the second experiment led to Louis Napoleon, reaction, and the Second Empire. "It is hardly surprising," Professor Vile has observed, "that this last flirtation with the pure doctrine ended in the same way as others had ended in France—in absolutism."

It was just this kind of political fragmentation and paralysis of power that the framers of the American Constitution wanted to avoid. Justice Story explained that the framers accepted a separation of power, but "endeavored to prove that a rigid adherence to it in all cases would be subversive of the efficiency of the government, and result in the destruction of the public liberties."

Separated Powers and Efficiency

That raises a second issue: the relationship between separated powers and governmental efficiency. In *United States*

v. *Brown* (1965), Chief Justice Warren declared that a separation of powers was "obviously not instituted with the idea
that it would promote governmental efficiency. It was, on
the contrary, looked to as a bulwark against tyranny." A
more famous dictum by Justice Brandeis, in the 1926 *Myers*
case, asserts: "The doctrine of the separation of powers was
adopted by the Convention of 1787, not to promote efficiency but to preclude the exercise of arbitrary power."

According to this view, the framers adopted a separation
of powers essentially to obstruct the process of government
—to slow it down and to frustrate whatever designs one
branch might have on another, or on the citizens. This impression pervades not merely college textbooks but professional journals as well.

It is curious that we still identify the framers with a
doctrinaire view of separated powers, instead of placing our
emphasis on the practical considerations that gave rise to
three branches. I would not go so far as to claim that the
framers' search for administrative efficiency, and their adoption of a separate executive for that purpose, represents the
whole truth. Still, it is at least half the truth, and since this
side of the story receives so little attention it should be told.
The evolution of separate branches from 1774 to 1789 will
be traced in detail in this chapter.

Influence of Montesquieu

Although the Articles of Confederation did not provide
for a separate executive and judiciary in 1777, only a decade
later the Federal Constitution included the office of the
Presidency and the Supreme Court. In this interval of ten
years, the political theory of Montesquieu is said to have
gained greater acceptance. Under his influence, the Founding Fathers supposedly agreed upon the need for a separation of powers. We have it from Woodrow Wilson that the
makers of the Constitution "followed the scheme as they
found it expounded in Montesquieu, followed it with genu-
ine scientific enthusiasm." James Bryce, whose *American*

Commonwealth is regarded as one of the great works on the United States, said that the Constitution was created "*de novo,* on the most slender basis of pre-existing national institutions. . . ." The framers, he argued, "had for their oracle of political philosophy the treatise of Montesquieu on the Spirit of Laws. . . . No general principle of politics laid such hold on the constitution-makers and statesmen of America as the dogma that the separation of these three functions is essential to freedom."

It would seem as if delegates at the Philadelphia Convention took turns exploring the merits and subtleties of abstract theories, arguing the fine points of political power and human nature. There is, indeed, some evidence to support that picture. Montesquieu was mentioned several times at the Federal Convention and at the state ratifying conventions. He was praised in the *Federalist Papers* as "the celebrated Montesquieu" and the "oracle" who was always cited on the separation doctrine. The idea that the Constitution was the product of mental gymnastics, derived more from theoretical principles than from experience and practice, gained wide currency when William Gladstone described it as "the most wonderful work ever struck off at a given time by the brain and purpose of man." One of the most perceptive students of representative government, John Stuart Mill, maintained that the whole edifice of the Constitution was "constructed within the memory of man, upon abstract principles."

All of this puts the emphasis more on borrowed theory than on first-hand experience. It implies that Madison and the other leading figures used an essentially scriptural approach to the construction of government, first adopting Montesquieu's *The Spirit of the Laws* as the authoritative text and then extracting from it to fashion their arguments. The framers did refer to such foreign writers as Montesquieu, Hume, and Blackstone, but they did so to embellish an argument, not to prove it. The argument itself was grounded on what had been learned at home. Theory played

a role, but it was always circumscribed and tested by experience.

To assert that the framers accepted Montesquieu's work
as the "Bible of political wisdom" is to overlook their intellectual debt to earlier writers who had urged that government be stabilized by distributing power and by a system of
mixed government. It overlooks also the experiences of colonial government in America prior to the appearance of *The
Spirit of the Laws* in 1748, as well as the evolving nature of a
separate executive and judiciary under the Articles of Confederation. Finally, it ignores the very significant differences
between Montesquieu's conception of tripartite government
and the form it took in our own Constitution.

These are important points, but to develop all of them
here, I think, would prove to be too much of a diversion. If
you are interested in the historical and philosophical background of the principle of separated powers, and want to
know what this principle actually meant to six of the Founding Fathers, I invite you to read the material in the Appendix.

What I want to do at this point is trace the evolution of
a separation of powers under the Articles of Confederation.
During that period, the Continental Congress demonstrated
its inability to discharge legislative duties and at the same
time tend to administrative and judicial matters. This history will help undercut the notion that the framers were in-
fluenced primarily by Montesquieu. More important, it will
show that the shift of power away from Congress began long
before the drafting of the Constitution or the appearance of
our more assertive Presidents.

In the years before the Philadelphia Convention, fundamental economic and political forces were at work. The existing governmental structure was gradually discredited, and
in its place there appeared new forms and new distributions
of power. Shortly after the Constitution had set up the three
departments of government, George Washington observed
that it was "unnecessary to be insisted upon, because it is

well known, that the impotence of Congress under the former confederation, and the inexpediency of trusting more ample prerogatives to a single Body, gave birth to the different branches which constitute the present general government."

NATIONAL EXECUTIVES, 1774–1789

The Articles of Confederation (1777) did not provide for a national executive. There was a President of Congress, but he was merely a presiding officer, without executive power. Thus the Continental Congress had to handle both legislative and executive duties. Congress first delegated administrative responsibilities to a number of committees. That failed to work, and so did the subsequent system of boards staffed by men outside Congress. When departments run by single executives were finally established, in 1781, it was not until delays and makeshift arrangements had imperiled the war effort. "It is positively pathetic," wrote Jay Caesar Guggenheimer, "to follow Congress through its aimless wanderings in search of a system for the satisfactory management of its executive departments."

Administration by Committee

Instead of setting up a separate executive body, the Articles of Confederation authorized the Continental Congress to appoint a committee to sit during a recess of Congress. In addition, Article 9 permitted Congress to appoint "such other committees and civil officers as may be necessary for managing the general affairs of the United States." Committees of that character had been operating for several years prior to the drafting of the Articles. In 1774, for instance, committees were established to petition the King, to examine matters relating to trade and manufacture, and to prepare addresses to the people of Great Britain and Quebec.

After the battles at Lexington and Concord in April 1775, Congress appointed a committee to consider ways and means of securing ammunition and military supplies. A committee was also appointed to maintain regular correspondence with friends in Great Britain, Ireland, and other countries. First called the Committee of Secret Correspondence, it later became the Committee for Foreign Affairs. With the outbreak of the war of independence, Congress formed other committees to handle military preparedness: the Committee of Commerce, to oversee the importation of gunpowder and munitions; the Marine Committee, to construct armed vessels; and the Board of War and Ordnance. In a technical sense these were legislative committees; but in the context of what actually took place, they are best remembered as forerunners of the executive departments of state, commerce, navy, and war.

A rapid proliferation of committees prevented members of Congress from carrying out their deliberative functions. John Adams was kept busy from four in the morning until ten at night, serving, by his own count, on close to ninety recorded committees, as well as on a great number of others that were unrecorded. The appearance of literally hundreds of committees was in part a reflection of factional struggles within Congress. When members failed to gain dominance over one committee, they were often successful in setting up special committees which they could control. Matters having to do with foreign affairs, for instance, were sometimes referred to special committees. The Committee for Foreign Affairs was periodically reduced to the status of an investigating body, or "a mere burial vault for questions which the parent body did not care to face."

Committee work was further hampered by a failure to select members on the basis of special ability. According to one contemporary, most committee members owed their appointment more to zeal and patriotism than to ability: "Competent merchants, therefore, are placed on the Committee for Foreign Affairs. Many colonels and generals are in Congress, but none of them are on the Board of War." Of the Marine Committee, John Jay said that "few members understand even the state of our naval affairs, or have time or inclination to attend to them." Furthermore, fluctuations in the membership of Congress would produce comparable shifts in committee policy. Under these conditions, it was impossible to achieve any coherence or consistency in committee work.

A System of Boards

As a compromise between the committee system and a single executive, Congress tried to relieve delegates of managerial details by establishing boards composed of men from outside Congress. In March 1776, one of the delegates suggested setting up a Board of Treasury, a War Office, a Board of Public Accounts, and others boards. When nothing came of this idea, members of Congress continued to press for better means of execution.

Early in November 1776, Congress authorized the appointment of three commissioners to execute the business of the navy, subject to the direction of the Marine Committee. This body came to be known as the Navy Board. On December 26, Congress appointed a committee to look into the plan of establishing executive boards composed of persons who were not members of Congress. Delays set in again, despite the belief of some members of Congress that the country's safety required immediate reform. William Hooper wrote Robert Morris in February 1777 that the country would be ruined unless competent officers were appointed to manage the nation's funds: "from a false parsimony in saving hundreds in salaries of proper Officers we are sporting away millions in the want of them."

A plan was reported in April 1777 for a board of war and ordnance. Deliberation was postponed and the motion sent back to committee. Another plan appeared in July. Appointments for the board were shelved several times and the matter eventually lost in the shuffle of congressional business. Action finally came in October. The committee report in favor of a board composed of members outside Congress was adopted with some amendments, and appointments to the Board of War were announced the following month.

The introduction of outside personnel helped relieve legislators of some committee work, but it did not noticeably improve the efficiency and dispatch of the war effort. A new Board of War and Ordnance was reconstituted to include members of Congress. Financial administration was divided between a Board of Treasury and the Committee of Finance. When mistakes by the boards occurred, or when the work proceeded at too slow a pace, no single party could be held responsible. Moreover, the boards could not execute legislative business unless Congress disciplined its own activities and expedited matters. There is ample evidence that much of the time saved by delegating matters to the boards was subsequently lost in trifling debate. Members of Congress were especially irritated by proceedings during 1778.

A delegate from Maryland reported that "The Congress do worse than ever: We murder time, and chat it away in idle impertinent talk." Washington learned from Gouverneur Morris that legislative business could have been completed, except that "our superior Abilities or the Desire of appearing to possess them lead us to such exquisite Tediousness of Debate that the most precious Moments pass unheeded away like vulgar Things." One delegate begged to be relieved of his legislative duties, exclaiming that "I'll be dam'd if you ever catch me here again. Those who have dispositions for Jangling, and are fond of displaying their Rhetorical abilities, let them come. I never was so sick of anything in my life." Other letters, equally caustic of congressional behavior, could be cited.

Not until 1781 did Congress take the next step in efficient administration: the appointment of single officers. In the meantime, power fell into the hands of the more energetic and able public officials.

"Democratical Forms, Monarchical Substance"

The reluctance of Congress to entrust power to single executives might seem understandable in view of the lingering enmity toward colonial governors. But when Samuel Adams praised the standing committees of Congress for their democratic qualities, the compliment applied more to appearances than to the existing state of affairs. On an informal level, committee chairmen found that the actual work necessarily fell into their hands, regardless of the number of men on the committee who officially shared power with them.

Gouverneur Morris explained how the lion's share of the work fell on him: "You must not imagine that the members of these committees took any share or burden of the affairs. Necessity, preserving the democratical forms, assumed the monarchical substance of business. The Chairman received and answered all letters and other applications, took every step which he deemed essential, prepared reports, gave orders, and the like, and merely took the members of a committee into a chamber and for form's sake made the needful communications, and received their approbation which was given of course."

Robert Morris became a single executive, in effect, as early as December 1776. He had informed Congress that his powers on the Marine Committee fell short of his responsibilities. Congress subsequently authorized him, in conjunction with his two associates, to adopt whatever measures he deemed proper, not only in marine matters but "in all others, as you shall think necessary, and most conducive to the public Good. . . ." Thus, Morris used his discretionary authority to execute matters specifically related to the navy, as well as to other areas touched by the Marine Committee.

A single executive also emerged in the Committee of Foreign Affairs—not as a result of congressional policy, but because of attrition. Originally staffed with five members of Congress, by the summer of 1779 it had dwindled to one man: James Lovell. To explain why things were not cared for promptly, he wrote to Arthur Lee that "there is really no such Thing as a *Com'tee* of foreign affairs existing—no Secretary or Clerk—further than that I persevere to be one and the other."

The powers of Benjamin Franklin were of formidable dimensions. In seeking new sources of funds in Europe, as the fiscal agent of Congress, he exercised the duties of a secretary of state and a secretary of the treasury. He also had to function as a secretary of war in selecting and forwarding supplies, as a secretary of the navy in supervising a system of privateers in the European waters, and as a supreme admiralty judge in settling the prize questions that arose from privateering.

Though Gouverneur Morris, Robert Morris, Lovell, and Franklin all possessed the responsibilities of single executives, other duties prevented them from discharging their administrative workloads with the proper speed and attention. Gouverneur Morris described the war years as unimaginably laborious: "Not to mention the attendance from 11 to 4 in the house, which was common to all, and the appointments to committees, of which I had a full share, I was at the same time Chairman, and of course did the business, of the Standing Committees; viz., on the commissary's, quartermaster's and medical Departments."

The strain of discharging both legislative and executive duties, and the inevitable delays associated in carrying this double burden, produced strong demands for administrative reform. A delegate from Maryland wrote to his Governor, in the spring of 1779, that "If we talked less, and thought more than we do in Congress, our business in my opinion would be better conducted. I wish with all my heart that we had an Executive." During the fall of 1780 James Madison heard from Joseph Jones of the reforms being contemplated for the civil departments. Jones hoped that single executives would be chosen: "We shall never have these great departments well managed untill something of this kind is done."

Single Executive Officers

Congress had meanwhile taken some cautious steps toward the creation of executive bodies. Early in 1779, American representatives in Europe were instructed to obtain copies of the "arrangements and forms of conducting the business of the treasury, war office, marine, and other offices of government" in France or Great Britain, and in any other kingdoms and republics to which they were accredited. In May 1780, James Duane proposed that a committee be appointed to consider improvements in the Department of Foreign Affairs. The committee report was submitted to Congress the following month. Robert Livingston made a similar motion on August 29 to bring about reform in the other civil departments.

Finally, on January 10, 1781, Congress heard the committee on the Department of Foreign Affairs recommend the establishment of a permanent office "as a remedy against the fluctuation, the delay and indecision to which the present mode of managing our foreign affairs must be exposed." Responsibility for the overall direction of the Department was to fall on a Secretary for Foreign Affairs. Congress adopted the proposal and delineated the duties for the new office. Three days later Congress heard the report of the committee on the other civil departments.

On February 7, Congress adopted a resolution for the creation of three new executive officers: the Superintendent of Finance, the Secretary at War, and the Secretary of Marine. The office of Attorney General was created on February 16 to prosecute all suits on behalf of the United States and to advise Congress on all legal matters submitted to him. This separation of power—the result of a painfully slow evolution of executive departments—stands as a victory not for abstract doctrine but for *force majeure*. In a striking phrase, Francis Wharton said that the Constitution "did not make this distribution of power. It would be more proper to say that this distribution of power made the Constitution of the United States."

Having taken five years to establish executive departments, Congress let several months go by before choosing their Secretaries. Robert Morris, unanimously elected Superintendent of Finance on February 20, refused to take the post unless Congress strengthened it according to his instructions. The chairman of the committee formed to study these demands confessed anxiety at this increase in executive power, but no alternative seemed possible: "Those Powers, or similar ones, must be vested in some one Person, in Order to extricate our Affairs from the Confusion in which they are at present involved. The Board of Treasury only make bad, worse. To go in the present Train is *absolutely impossible. A total Stagnation* must soon take Place, and Ruin cannot be far off. Were our Affairs in a State of *Beginning*, Powers so extensive would not be necessary; but perplexed, deranged and clogged with Abuses and Mismanagements as they are at present, it really appears to me that less Powers would be altogether unavailing." The committee agreed to Morris' terms and he accepted the position.

Alexander McDougall was elected Secretary of Marine on February 27, only to decline the offer. The position was left permanently vacant, with naval matters transferred to the new Superintendent of Finance. Rivalries within Congress postponed the selection of the Secretary for Foreign Affairs for over six months; Robert Livingston was eventually chosen. Election of the Secretary of War took over eight months, until the reluctance of members of the Board of War to surrender their influence was finally overcome, and the open opposition of Samuel Adams and those who preferred administration by committees was defeated.

Ironically, just at the point when Congress had finally consented to appoint single executives, changing events undermined their positions of responsibility. The surrender of Cornwallis in the fall of 1781, and the subsequent initiation of negotiations for peace, removed the chief incentive for stronger national powers and more vigorous executives. Since no external enemy existed to push power to the center, the centrifugal pull of state sovereignty reasserted itself.

The single executives appointed in 1781 became progressively disenchanted with their offices. Livingston complained that his correspondence with foreign nations was restricted to what Congress had declared in a public act, although effective communication required that he be permitted to say things that it would be impolitic for Congress to publicly discuss. Moreover, some matters were important to Livingston but too trivial for legislative attention. Livingston—attracted by a more lucrative position in New York, and claiming that his expenses in office were almost double his salary—offered his resignation after serving little more than a year. He remained in office at the request of Congress until June 1783, at which point the position was filled temporarily by the Secretary of Congress and the Under-Secretary.

Robert Morris had helped bring order to the confused financial condition of the general government. To hasten the progress, Congress delegated still further authority to him. Yet when he tried to tax the states to pay off interest on foreign and domestic debts and to pay soldiers' arrears, his supporters stepped aside. Morris bitingly observed that the Articles conferred on Congress the privilege of asking for everything, while reserving to each state the prerogative of granting nothing. Without power to effect financial reform, and subjected at the same time to malicious charges, he offered his resignation in January 1783. Upon his official retirement in November 1784, the management of finances fell back to the board system.

Benjamin Lincoln had accepted the position of Secretary at War. Faced as he was with insufficient funds for the army and for his own department, and harassed by actual and potential mutinies, it was an achievement on his part to keep the department intact. The army was in process of being disbanded after Cornwallis' surrender, while the evacuation of British troops from New York City, during the final months of 1783, removed the last trace of British authority from the continent—or so it was assumed at the time. Lincoln offered his resignation on October 29, 1783, whereupon the Department of War nearly passed out of existence, with only the chief clerk left in charge.

Transition to the Presidency

The illusion of national security was gradually dispelled by the presence of Indians in the Ohio Valley, British forces in the Northwest, and the Spanish in Florida and the lower Mississippi. The domestic depression that set in after 1785 provided yet another impetus for centralization. In the three years from 1784 to 1786, America purchased large quantities of British goods. An unfavorable balance of trade drew gold and silver toward Britain, and restrictive trade practices by Britain frustrated American efforts to increase her exports. Congress could not enact retaliatory tariffs, embargoes, or navigation laws, for it lacked the power to exclude or tax commerce coming into state ports.

Disputes over the Potomac River led to negotiations between Virginia and Maryland. A conference was held in March 1785 at the home of George Washington. Commissioners from the two states decided that an interstate pact would be of less value than an agreement that would include Pennsylvania, since this would open the way for water communication between the Chesapeake and Ohio Rivers. Moreover, if the commercial complex took in the region around the Chesapeake, invitations should also be sent to New York, New Jersey, and Delaware.

Under Madison's leadership, the Virginia legislature passed a resolution in January 1786, inviting all states to discuss commercial problems at a conference to be held in Annapolis, Maryland. Only five states sent commissioners. The incomplete representative, the complexity of the issues and their implications for aspects other than commerce, persuaded the delegates to adjourn in favor of a convention to be held at Philadelphia the following May, to devise "such further provisions as shall appear to them necessary to render the constitution of the Federal Government adequate to the exigencies of the Union."

The period from 1774 to 1787 demonstrates the degree to which the idea of a separation of powers was based on the search for administrative efficiency. Nothing illuminates the practical evolution of separated powers so well as the experiences of John Jay and Henry Knox as single executives; the continuity in administrative departments from the confederation to the federal government; and the manner in which the Supreme Court evolved out of its predecessor, the Courts of Admiralty.

In taking over as Secretary for Foreign Affairs in September 1784, Jay strengthened the powers of the office. Congress passed a resolution in 1785, directing that all communications relating to foreign affairs be channeled through the Secretary rather than to the committees vying for control. The treaty power of the President was anticipated in another legislative authorization in 1785, giving Jay full power to negotiate a treaty with Spain. A French minister reported that the "political importance of Mr. Jay increases daily. Congress seems to me to be guided only by his directions." Jay then served throughout the remaining years of the Continental Congress, and even continued in that same capacity as Acting Secretary of State under Washington's first administration, until Jefferson assumed the duties of Secretary of State in March 1790.

The need to administer and protect the Western Territories led to the rejuvenation of the War Department. General Henry Knox was elected Secretary at War on March 8, 1785, and remained in that post until the final days of 1794. Knox, even more than Jay, exemplifies the continuity of executive structures between the old government and the new. Still another example of administrative continuity is the service of Joseph Nourse as Register of the Treasury from 1779 to 1829.

The Supreme Court also has part of its roots in the pre-1787 period. The Continental Congress set up Courts of Admiralty to decide all controversies over captures and the distribution of prizes. Provisions were made in January 1777 for appeal to a standing committee. This committee handled 56 cases over a three-year period. In January 1780 a separate and permanent court was establishing to try all appeals: the Court of Appeals in Cases of Capture. Pending cases were transferred from Congress to this new court. Following the conclusion of the war with England and the signing of the peace treaty, the business of the Court declined, and in February 1786 Congress resolved that the salaries of the judges be terminated. Financed on a per diem basis, the Court continued to function until its last session on May 16, 1787, at the State House in Philadelphia, across the hall from the room in which delegates were assembling for the Constitutional Convention.

CONVENTION AND RATIFICATION

When George Mason reached Philadelphia in May 1787, he had a fairly accurate impression of the changes to be considered. The most prevalent idea, he told his son, appeared to be a total alteration of the federal system. In addition to a national legislature composed of two houses, with full legislative powers over the subjects of the Union, there would be a national executive and a separate judiciary system. As a statement of general principles that would do; but the extent of the separation and the relationship among the three branches were issues that would prove much harder to resolve.

The framers had had the good fortune to watch state governments function over a ten-year period. They saw that paper barriers in the state constitutions were not sufficient to prevent legislatures from usurping executive and judicial powers. They also came to appreciate the administrative bottlenecks in the Continental Congress. Faced with the extremes of an artificial and unreliable separation of powers at the state level, and no separation at all at the national level, the framers offered a subtle formulation: there had to be an overlapping of powers so as to guarantee the continued separation of the departments.

That is not to say that Madison and the other leading figures possessed a clear conception of the separation doctrine. On the contrary, no other principle gave them such trouble. The concept seemed to defy definition, since the problems for which the framers were seeking structural remedies were constantly changing. In the sections that follow, we shall examine more closely the conception of executive and legislative power; the various proposals to shield the

President from legislative encroachments; and the unsuccessful attempt to include a formulation of the separation doctrine in the Constitution itself and later in the Bill of Rights.

Attitude toward Executive Power

According to textbooks, speeches on the floor of Congress, and even Supreme Court decisions, the framers held executive power in distrust. Justice Black, for instance, in striking down President Truman's seizure of the steel mills in 1952, declared that "The Founders of this Nation entrusted the lawmaking power to the Congress alone in both good and bad times. It would do no good to recall the historical events, the fears of power and the hopes for freedom that lay behind their choice."

This suggests an antagonistic relationship between executive power and individual liberties, yet one does not find such attitudes in the writings of John Adams, Madison, Jefferson, Jay, and others, at least not before 1789. True, the attitude did prevail during the colonial period, when it was automatically assumed that the public interest was enhanced whenever the legislature gained new power from the royal governor, and such distrust of the executive persisted for a few years after independence. But an accumulation of legislative abuses on the state level, combined with a demonstration of legislative incompetence on the national, had created by this time a new outlook toward executive power.

Some of the early precedents for judicial review were in response to legislative encroachments. In 1780, the supreme court of New Jersey refused to carry out an act of the state legislature that limited the jury to six for certain offenses; the court held that the state constitution had intended the common law jury of twelve. In 1782, the Virginia supreme court of appeals reviewed a state act that withdrew from the governor his constitutional right to grant pardons. Without deciding the case in question, the court warned the legislature to stay within its bounds. Judge George Wythe maintained that it was his duty to protect one branch against usurpations by another. If the legislature should attempt "to overleap the boundaries prescribed to them by the people, I, in administering the justice of the country, will meet the united powers at my seat in this tribunal, and, pointing to the constitution, will say to them, here is the limit of your authority; hither shall you go, but no further."

A 1784 study of the Pennsylvania government disclosed numerous examples of legislative violations of the state constitution and bill of rights. The assembly had made unconstitutional invasions of the rights of property, entered homes in the daytime without warrants, deprived persons of trial by jury, and restrained the full operation of the writ of habeas corpus. The legislature intruded upon the judicial branch by dissolving marriages, and infringed upon the executive by granting pardons, making appointments, and transferring executive powers to commissioners selected by the house.

In 1785, when Madison was asked for his ideas on a constitution for Kentucky, he said that while it would be impractical to spell out all the legislative powers, the legislature should be told what it could *not* do. He then ticked off those areas in which legislatures were noted for intruding. The state constitution should expressly prohibit the legislature from "medling with religion—from abolishing Juries—from taking away the Habeas corpus—from controuling the press—from enacting retrospective laws at least in criminal cases, from abridging the right of suffrage, from taking private property for public use without paying its full Value [,] from licensing the importation of Slaves, from infringing the confederation, &c &c." The Virginia executive, he said, was the "worst part of a bad Constitution. The Members of it are dependent on the Legislature not only for their wages but for their reputation and therefore not likely to withstand usurpations of that branch."

At the Virginia ratifying convention in 1788, Edmund Randolph told how the legislature of his state had sentenced to death one of its citizens on the basis of vague reports submitted by a member of the House of Delegates. The citizen

—who did not have the opportunity to confront his accusers or to call for evidence—was put to death. Patrick Henry, that great champion of liberty known to every schoolboy, brushed aside the suggestion that there had been arbitrary taking of life: "That man was not executed by a tyrannical stroke of power. Nor was he a Socrates. He was a fugitive murderer and an outlaw. . . . He was an enemy to the human name. Those who declare war against the human race may be struck out of existence as soon as they are apprehended." And there you have a standard of civil liberty promoted on the state level!

The historical record of legislatures convinced John Adams that a strong executive was needed to protect human liberties. "If there is one certain truth," he wrote, "to be collected from the history of all ages, it is this; that the people's rights and liberties, and the democratical mixture in a constitution, can never be preserved without a strong executive, or, in other words, without separating the executive from the legislative power." Executive power in the hands of an assembly of men would "corrupt the legislature as necessarily as rust corrupts iron, or as arsenic poisons the human body." He deplored the "thoughtless simplicity" that characterized executive power as an enemy of the people.

Shielding the President

In the months prior to the Philadelphia Convention, Madison itemized for Jefferson the essential elements of the new national government, including a reorganization to provide for separate branches. Madison's interest in three branches was drawn more from administrative necessities than from the writings of Montesquieu. Congress had mismanaged its power under the confederation, he told Jefferson, while administrative responsibilities under the new government would be even more demanding. Madison confided to Edmund Randolph his uncertainty as to the details of separated powers, admitting that he had not decided on either the manner in which the executive should be constituted or "of the authorities with which it ought to be clothed." Writing to George Washington shortly before the Convention began, he still had not resolved these questions about executive power.

The Virginia Plan, presented to the Convention on May 29, 1787, provided for three branches but made no reference to "separate and distinct" or to any other formulation of the separation doctrine. In fact, the executive was to be chosen by the legislature and joined with the judiciary so as to form a council of revision. Late in July, the Convention adopted a resolution explicitly affirming the separation doctrine, stating that the three national departments were to be kept distinct and independent, except in specified cases. However, the version presented to the Convention on August 6 by the Committee of Detail omitted the separation clause, and the Constitution was adopted in September without reference to it.

On the relationship between Congress and the President, Madison reminded the delegates that experience had proved "a tendency in our governments to throw all power into the Legislative vortex. The Executives of the States are in general little more than Cyphers; the legislatures omnipotent." The separation set up in the state constitutions had turned out to be a matter of mere parchment barriers, which were incapable of preventing legislatures from drawing other branches into their orbit. The principal anxiety in 1787 was not over executive power, the threat of a dictator, or the emergence of a George III at home, even if some delegates did warn that a single executive would be the "foetus of monarchy." The people of America, James Wilson said in rebuttal, did not oppose the British King "but the parliament —the opposition was not agt. an Unity but a corrupt multitude."

The chief and overriding fear for Wilson was that the "natural operation of the Legislature will be to swallow up the Executive." Gouverneur Morris maintained that the "Legislature will continually seek to aggrandize & perpetuate themselves," while John Mercer of Maryland took it as an axiom that careful construction of the Constitution could obviate "legislative usurpation and oppression."

The veto represented one means of self-defense for the federal executive. Some of the Antifederalists, taking the doctrine of separated powers in its most rigid form, considered the executive veto an encroachment of legislative powers. One critic of the Constitution called it "a political error of the greatest magnitude, to allow the executive power a negative, or in fact any kind of control over the proceedings of the legislature."

Delegates at Philadelphia did more than accept the executive veto as a necessary check on legislative ambitions; they also proposed that it be shared with the judiciary. To those delegates who denounced this as a patent violation of the separation doctrine, Wilson replied that the executive and judiciary should share the negative, for "they cannot otherwise preserve their importance against the legislature." Madison agreed, urging that the judiciary be introduced in "the business of Legislation—they will protect their Department, and uniting wh. the Executive render their Check or negative more respectable."

Later, when the proposal for joint revisionary power was still under consideration, Madison argued that a blending of the two departments would operate as an "auxiliary precaution" in preserving a lasting and durable separation. That line of reasoning must have baffled those who adhered to strict separation, but Madison preferred to assure separation in practice by deviating from it in theory whenever necessary. Merely to declare a separation of powers, he said, was not sufficient, since experience demonstrated the need for introducing "a balance of powers and interests, as will guarantee the provisions on paper."

Ratification

After the convention had adjourned, Madison confided to Jefferson that the boundaries between the executive, legislative, and judicial powers, "though in general so strongly marked in themselves, consist in many instances of mere shades of difference." He set out in the *Federalist Papers* to contrast the overlapping of powers in the Constitution with the abstract and impracticable partitioning of powers advocated by some of the Antifederalists. Few men can compete with Madison in lucidity and precision of expression, yet he reflected in Federalist 37 on the inherent shortcomings of our language. Just as naturalists had difficulty in defining the exact line between vegetable life and the animal world, so was it an even greater task to draw the boundary between the departments of government, or "even the privileges and powers of the different legislative branches. Questions daily occur in the course of practice, which prove the obscurity which reigns in these subjects, and which puzzle the greatest adepts in political science."

The bulk of Madison's analysis of the separation doctrine appears in Federalist 47. He upheld the basic principle of the maxim that tyranny resulted whenever three branches were concentrated in the same hands, but he charged that the maxim had been "totally misconceived and misapplied." Montesquieu, he said, could not possibly have meant that the three powers of the British government were actually separate. The executive magistrate formed a part of the legislative power by making treaties with foreign sovereigns, and he had a share in the judicial power by appointing the members of the judiciary, as well as having power to remove them. Moreover, one house of the legislature formed a constitutional council for the executive, had judicial power in the impeachment process, and was invested with the supreme appellate jurisdiction in all other cases. The judges could not vote in legislative actions, but were permitted to participate in the deliberations.

Madison then turned to the state constitutions for further support, pointing out that in no instance were the several departments of power kept absolutely separate and distinct. The intent of Montesquieu, Madison concluded, could be no more than this: "that where the *whole* power of one department is exercised by the same hands which possess the *whole* power of another department, the fundamental principles of a free constitution are subverted." As we shall see, the broadness of that definition did not satisfy Madison for long.

By the late 1780s, the concept of checks and balances had gained dominance over the doctrine of separated powers, which one contemporary pamphleteer called a "hackneyed principle" and a "trite maxim." Yet several delegates at the state ratifying conventions expressed shock at the degree to which the Constitution had mingled the departments.

"How is the executive?" cried one delegate at the Virginia ratifying convention. "Contrary to the opinion of all the best writers, blended with the legislative. We have asked for bread, and they have given us a stone." The Constitution was attacked at the North Carolina ratifying convention for violating the maxim whereby the three branches "ought to be forever separate and distinct from each other." Overlapping of departments also provoked criticism in Pennsylvania. Opponents of the Constitution maintained that the Senate's judicial power in impeachment, as well as the executive's legislative power in making treaties, constituted an "undue and dangerous mixture of the powers of government." A lengthy quotation from Montesquieu was introduced to demonstrate the dependence of freedom and liberty on a separation of powers.

These three states insisted that a separation clause be added to the national bill of rights. Virginia's recommendations in June 1788 included the clause: "legislative, executive, and judiciary powers of Government should be separate and distinct," while Pennsylvania and North Carolina offered their own versions of a separation clause. Congress compiled a tentative list of restrictions on the national government, among which was the following: "The powers delegated by this constitution are appropriated to the departments to which they are respectively distributed: so that the legislative department shall never exercise the powers vested in the executive or judicial [,] nor the executive exercise the powers vested in the legislative or judicial, nor the judicial exercise the powers vested in the legislative or executive departments."

Surprisingly, Madison supported that clause, but this does not mean that he had suddenly embraced the notion of pure separation. What he feared was that additional blending, resulting from encroachment, would benefit the legislature and weaken the executive. In the House debates in 1789, he opposed Senate participation in the removal power because that might reduce Presidential power to a "mere vapor." The unity and responsibility of the executive, he said, were intended to secure liberty and the public welfare. Join the President with the Senate in the removal power, and the executive becomes a "two-headed monster," deprived of responsibility.

So concerned was Madison about the independence of the executive branch that he began to use the kind of abstract phrases he had earlier rejected. For now he was to say, "if there is a principle in our constitution, indeed in any free constitution, more sacred than another, it is that which separates the legislative, executive, and judicial powers." However, from the context of this remark, we know that Madison was presenting separation of powers not in its rigid form, but was using it rather for the explicit purpose of opposing legislative participation in the designation of officers. Once again he expresses his concern for the independence of the executive branch: "The Legislature creates the office, defines the powers, limits its duration, and annexes a compensation. This done, the legislative power ceases. They ought to have nothing to do with designating the man to fill the office. That I conceive to be of an executive nature."

These debates in the House help explain Madison's support for the separation clause in the bill of rights. The Senate journal, unfortunately, tells us very little about the discussion on that clause. It was among seventeen constitutional amendments sent to the Senate. The members struck it from the list of proposed amendments on September 7, 1789. A substitute amendment (to make the three departments "separate and distinct," and to assure that the legislative and executive departments would be restrained from oppression by "feeling and participating the public burthens" through regular elections) was also voted down. Three members of the House, Madison among them, met with the Senate in conference to reconcile their different lists of amendments. In the days that followed, the list of seventeen was cut to twelve. Among the deleted amendments was the separation clause.

It is widely argued that the separation doctrine, while not explicitly stated in the Constitution, is nevertheless implied. Perhaps so, but that does not take us a step closer to understanding exactly what is implied or to what degree the departments must remain separate. Similar questions are raised when one states that the framers believed in a separation of power. No doubt they did, but for what purpose? With what objective in mind?

From the discussion here, and the material presented in the Appendix, it seems fair to say that the framers shared a desire for greater administrative efficiency and more reliable governmental machinery. Direct experience with state government and the Continental Congress convinced them of the need for a separate executive and interdepartmental checks. Chief among their concerns was the need to protect against legislative usurpations and to preserve the independence of the executive and judicial branches. Those were the dominant thoughts behind the separation of powers, not the doctrine of Montesquieu, fear of executive power, or a basic distrust of government. If the framers had wanted weak government, they could have had that with the Articles of Confederation.

Had the separation clause been accepted by Congress and ratified by the states, its primary effect would have been a warning against departmental encroachments. It would not have affected the blending of departments and powers already sanctioned by the Constitution, nor would it have prohibited the delegation of legislative powers to the President. Congress was no more capable in 1789 of administering the nation's business than it had been during the previous decade. The complexities of national growth, the need for economic regulation, and new international responsibilities all provided fresh incentives for granting new powers to the executive branch.

2

LEGISLATIVE POWERS

In the Steel Seizure Case of 1952, Justice Jackson maintained that the President, "except for recommendation and veto, has no legislative power." Perhaps technically correct in some narrow sense, depending on how legislative power is defined, Jackson's statement is nevertheless a poor description of the President's actual legislative role.

A more generous conception of executive legislation is clearly needed, but this can lead to excesses in the opposite direction, such as referring to the President as "Chief Legislator." While it is the President who signs the bill, and sometimes acts as its main sponsor, legislative histories are highly complex phenomena. Sponsorship is not the same as authorship. To credit one person or another often becomes an arbitrary task. Large numbers of public officials, staff aides, interest groups, and private individuals are responsible for originating the idea embodied in the bill, for cultivating interest, and for mobilizing the support that is necessary for final passage.

In this chapter I focus on the scope of administrative legislation. By emphasizing the large role of the President, I do not mean to suggest that the contribution of Congress is, for that reason, necessarily small. The warning put forward by Lawrence Chamberlain bears repeating: "The legislative process is not like a see-saw where as one end goes down the other must automatically go up. It is, rather, like a gasoline engine which operates most efficiently when all of its cylinders are functioning." My emphasis on administrative legislation merely fits in with the purpose of the book, which is to trace the flow of prerogatives between Congress and the President.

In this chapter I discuss three sources of Presidential power: power expressly granted by the Constitution; power implied or considered to be inherent in the office; and power exercised by means of administrative legislation. The following chapter covers delegation of power: why Congress delegates power to the President, and the existing safeguards that prevent delegation from becoming abdication.

EXPRESS POWERS

The Constitution enumerates seventeen separate powers for Congress, capping the list with an "elastic clause" that gives Congress the authority to make whatever laws are necessary and proper for carrying into effect its enumerated powers. When the Constitution turns to the President, however, the language becomes sparse and undefined. Article II begins by stating that "The executive power shall be vested in a President of the United States of America." Scholars have wondered whether this sentence merely confers a title of office—President of the United States of America—or whether it actually confers power. If the latter, is "executive power" defined and limited by the express powers that follow, or does it include additional functions historically associated with the executive office? For example, the Constitution states that the President shall be Commander in Chief of the Army and Navy. Is this an office or a function? Is the President merely Commander in Chief, or does he possess the powers implied in the *function* of commanding the armed forces?

If we restrict executive power to specific constitutional grants, and rule out the use of implied or inherent powers, then the office of the President is indeed narrow in scope. Over sixty percent of Article II is devoted to his term of office, election, qualifications, removal, compensation, and oath of office. The remainder of the Article treats Presidential power in very general terms. The President shall be Commander in Chief; he may require the opinion, in writing, of his principal executive officers; he may grant reprieves and pardons; and he shares with the Senate the power to make treaties and appoint public officers. The Constitution directs the President to give Congress information on the state of the Union, to recommend measures, convene both Houses on extraordinary occasions and adjourn them in certain situations, receive ambassadors and other public ministers, commission all public officers, and take care that the laws be "faithfully executed." The President's veto power is described in Article I.

Presidents also wield powers that are not expressly stated in the Constitution. These extraconstitutional powers have a variety of names: implied, inherent, inferable, incident, residual, moral, aggregate, and emergency. Some writers construct a spectrum of powers, ranging from the strict notion of express powers, to a middle position of implied powers, and finally to the sweeping assertion that the President is limited only by his judgment as to what is in the national interest. While implied powers are often considered to be more restricted in scope than that of inherent or emergency powers, such distinctions are hard to establish. For instance, the President has the power to remove executive officials. Is that an implied power or an inherent power? It is possible to argue the case either way. When the President intervenes in Cambodia and Laos, for the announced purpose of protecting American lives, is that an inherent power or is it implied in the constitutional role of Commander in Chief? When the Constitution was threatened by the secession of the South, Lincoln justified his wartime initiatives partly on his oath to preserve, protect, and defend the Constitution. In this case the exercise of emergency power was based on a broadly conceived implied power.

When I speak of "inherent powers" in the following section, I have in mind no particular position in the spectrum of extraconstitutional power. I refer simply to a general class of powers which are neither expressly stated in the Constitution nor specifically delegated by Congress.

INHERENT POWERS

Pacificus-Helvidius Debate

On April 22, 1793, upon the outbreak of war in Europe, President Washington issued what has come to be known as the Neutrality Proclamation. By declaring that it was the policy of America to remain impartial toward the warring European nations, he triggered a debate on the issue of express versus inherent powers. Critics charged that the President had acted without constitutional or statutory authority. Alexander Hamilton, writing under the pseudonym "Pacificus," defended the proclamation by noting the difference between the legislative and executive grants of power in the Constitution. The article defining the powers of Congress begins with "All legislative powers" *herein granted,* which is then followed by an enumeration of powers. Article II, on the other hand, begins: "The executive power shall be vested in a President of the United States."

Hamilton concluded that the enumeration of functions for the President's office was not meant to be exhaustive but merely indicative of his principal responsibilities. Consequently, the President possessed inherent as well as express powers, subject only to the limitations and qualifications contained in the Constitution. As examples of Presidential powers that were not expressly stated, but nevertheless implied, Hamilton cited the removal power, the power to recognize new governments, and the power to judge our obligations under our treaties. The latter permitted the President to proclaim our neutrality on the basis of his interpretation of treaties.

This expansive treatment of executive power was immediately challenged by James Madison. Writing as "Helvidius," he argued that the idea of inherent executive powers was alien to the Constitution, based not on American practices but rather borrowed from the royal prerogatives of the British government. Whatever may have been the source of Hamilton's theory, it has weathered history more successfully than Madison's view of Presidential power.

Roosevelt-Taft Models

The Pacificus-Helvidius exchange has been supplanted by a more contemporary debate on inherent executive powers. Two rival models are set against one another: the "strong" executive model of Theodore Roosevelt, versus the "weak" executive model of William Howard Taft. In his autobiography, Roosevelt maintained that it was the President's right and duty to do "anything that the needs of the Nation demanded, unless such action was forbidden by the Constitution or by the laws." In sharp contrast, Taft's lectures at Columbia University in 1915 argued that the President "can exercise no power which cannot be fairly and reasonably traced to some specific grant of power or justly implied and included within such express grant as proper and necessary to its exercise. Such specific grant must be either in the Federal Constitution or in an act of Congress passed in pursuance thereof."

On the basis of those passages we have two antithetical models: Roosevelt asserting that the President can do anything unless explicitly forbidden by the Constitution or by law; Taft holding that the President can do nothing at all unless specifically authorized by the Constitution or by law. Yet this dramatic clash of polar opposites is largely a contrivance, made possible by ignoring some timid aspects of Roosevelt's record as President, and by ignoring the more assertive actions and statements of Taft.

Behind the bold posturing of Teddy Roosevelt lay a great deal of moral bluster, theatrics, and harmless harangues against the "malefactors of great wealth." His trust-busting activities were in reality so modest that Thurman Arnold later referred to the "big stick that never hit anybody." Roosevelt's "victory" in the Northern Securities case, which applied the Sherman Anti-Trust Act to the Morgan-Hill railroad combination, represented a publicity triumph that was singularly ineffective in reducing the power of the combination. While the executive decree prohibited the use of stock by the railroad combination, it returned the stock to the individuals who had originally entered into the conspiracy.

For all Roosevelt's talk of acting as "steward" of the people, intervening on their behalf whenever possible, he failed to act on pure food legislation and meat inspection until the rising tide of public protest left him no choice. According to Representative Mann, leader of the final fight for pure food legislation in the House, Roosevelt was indifferent to the pure food law, considering it the work of impractical cranks.

When journalists exposed corporate and governmental corruption, revealing the techniques by which the public was being fleeced by insurance companies and victimized by fraudulent and adulterated foods, it was Roosevelt who coined the term "muckrakers," comparing the journalists to the man who could look no place but down, content to rake the filth on the floor. When consumers were losing hundreds of millions of dollars a year because of high tariffs, not once did Roosevelt appeal to Congress and recommend a downward revision. Harold Laski pierced the Rooseveltian rhetoric by noting his "immense verbal emphasis and actual timidity."

If Roosevelt's reputation as a strong President is inflated, Taft's view of the office is underestimated. A careful look at the latter's 1915 lectures, later published as *Our Chief Magistrate and His Powers,* shows that he left considerable room for implied and emergency powers. Although

Taft spoke of specific grants of power, he said that Presidential power includes whatever can be "fairly and reasonably traced" to some specific grant or "justly implied . . . as proper and necessary to its exercise." In effect, this adds to the Constitution a "necessary-and-proper" clause for Presidential powers.

Taft's observations on the Presidency are partly in response to what Roosevelt had written about the office. The enmity between the two men caused Taft to occupy a position more extreme than he would normally choose, simply to dissociate himself from Roosevelt. It was Roosevelt who had divided Presidents into two classes and designated them "Lincoln Presidents" and "Buchanan Presidents." He placed himself in the Lincoln class and relegated Taft to the Buchanan class. Taft, with his delicate and puckish sense of humor, remarked that the "identification of Mr. Roosevelt with Mr. Lincoln might otherwise have escaped notice, because there are many differences between the two, presumably superficial, which would give the impartial student of history a different impression."

In his effort to draw a sharp distinction between his views and those of Roosevelt, Taft placed too much emphasis on a literalist interpretation of the Constitution. And yet elsewhere in *Our Chief Magistrate,* he defines Presidential power in more generous terms. For instance, even in cases where the Senate's advice and consent were necessary for appointing an office, Taft believed that the President possessed an "absolute power" to remove the individual without consulting the Senate. Removal power is not mentioned in the Constitution, but Taft maintained that it was "incident to the Executive power and must be untrammeled." Later, as Chief Justice of the Supreme Court, he propounded the same theory in *Myers* v. *United States* (1926).

Taft spoke also of "inferable" powers of the President, such as the responsibility to use armed force in protecting the lives and property of American citizens living abroad. He cited McKinley's use of land and naval forces in China, during the Boxer Rebellion, as a legitimate use of Presidential power, and referred to his own use of the life-and-property prerogative when he sent troops into Nicaragua. Nothing in the Constitution or in the statutes expressly authorized that expedition. Taft interpreted the commander-in-chief clause broadly, to mean that the President can order the army and navy "anywhere he will." Although Congress retains the constitutional power to declare war, the President could deploy armed force "such as to involve the country in war and to leave Congress no option but to declare it or to recognize its existence."

From the President's express responsibility to receive foreign ambassadors, Taft derived another power: that of recognizing foreign governments. Moreover, he spoke approvingly of the use of an executive agreement in 1899 to establish the "Open Door" policy in China. That policy had been set forth in a note by Secretary of State Hay, issued without the advice and consent of the Senate.

In addition to incidental and inferable powers, Taft recognized that executive power could be created by custom, and "so strong is the influence of custom that it seems almost to amend the Constitution." A good example of that took place during Taft's own Administration. After Congress had opened public lands in the West to encourage oil exploration, settlers extracted oil at maximum speeds, fearing that explorers on adjacent lots might be tapping from the same source. Because of the limited supply of coal on the Pacific Coast for the navy, it appeared that the Government might have to repurchase from the private sector the very oil it had given away.

To guard against that, Taft issued a proclamation withdrawing the affected lands from private exploration. The proclamation was violated and the case came before the Supreme Court, where it was argued that the President could not suspend a statute or withdraw land which Congress had thrown open to acquisition. The Court, in the Midwest Oil case, declined to approach this matter from the standpoint of abstract constitutional rights. The President's action, it said, was based upon and supported by years of precedents. Prior to 1910, there had been 99 executive orders establishing or enlarging Indian reservations; 109 executive orders establishing or enlarging military reservations; and 44 executive orders establishing bird reserves. While it was true that the President had acted without statutory authority, the Court held that "nothing was more natural than to retain what the Government already owned. And in making such orders, which were thus useful to the public, no private interest was injured. . . . The President was in a position to know when the public interest required particular portions of the people's lands to be withdrawn from entry or location."

There are other examples to show that Taft's conception of Presidential power went beyond the exercise of statutory and constitutional grants of authority. He supported Lincoln's suspension of the writ of habeas corpus during the Civil War, an act often cited as a bold usurpation of congressional authority. Taft wrote that executive power was limited, "so far as it is possible to limit such a power consistent with that discretion and promptness of action that are essential to preserve the interests of the public in times of emergency, or legislative neglect or inaction." To sum up, while he is popularly identified with the "express power" theory, Taft turns out to support implied powers, inferable powers, emergency powers, powers created by custom, and powers incident to specific constitutional authority.

Tenth Amendment

A report by the Senate Foreign Relations Committee in 1969 argued that the claim for inherent or emergency executive powers had no foundation in the Constitution or in constitutional law: "The 10th amendment states that powers not delegated to the federal government are reserved to the States or the people, leaving no residue of 'inherent' Presidential powers."

While we might sympathize with the Committee's effort to curb Presidential war powers, this particular argument is much too shallow. The idea that the 10th Amendment limits the Federal Government or the President to express powers finds no support in Supreme Court decisions or in the debates on the amendment in the First Congress. Madison fought successfully on the issue of *retaining* implied powers for the Federal Government. The Articles of Confederation, under which each state retained its sovereignty and independence, had reserved to the states all powers not "expressly delegated" to the Continental Congress. When the same phrase was proposed for the 10th Amendment, Madison objected to "expressly" on the ground that the functions and responsibilities of the Federal Government could not be delineated with such precision. It was impossible, he said, to confine a government to the exercise of express powers, for there "must necessarily be admitted powers by implication, unless the Constitution descended to recount every minutiae." Madison won his point. "Expressly" was eliminated and the 10th Amendment came to read: "The powers not delegated to the United States by the Constitution, nor prohibited by it to the States, are reserved to the States respectively, or to the people."

The Constitution was subsequently interpreted to contain implied powers for each of the three branches. When Congress established a national bank, it was objected that the Constitution did not include that authority for Congress among its enumerated powers. In upholding the bank, in *McCulloch* v. *Maryland,* Chief Justice Marshall reviewed the history of the 10th Amendment to point out that "expressly" had been omitted from it: "The men who drew and adopted this amendment had experienced the embarrassments resulting from the insertion of this word in the articles of confederation, and probably omitted it to avoid those embarrassments." Marshall concluded that the power of creating a national bank, while not expressly conferred on Congress, was an appropriate means for carrying into execution its enumerated powers.

The Court relied upon the concept of implied powers in *Marbury* v. *Madison,* where it claimed for itself the right to exercise judicial review over acts of Congress. If an act of the legislature was repugnant to the Constitution, then surely that act must be declared void. But who was to decide? Chief Justice Marshall maintained that "It is emphatically the province and duty of the judicial department to say what the law is." The reasoning in his decision need not concern us; what is important is the fact that the Court once again called upon implied powers.

The idea that the 10th Amendment contains substantive powers for the states has been deflated by several decisions. In 1920, in *Missouri* v. *Holland,* Justice Holmes denied that the treaty power was restricted in any way "by some invisible radiation from the general terms of the Tenth Amendment." A decade later, in *Sprague,* the Court held that the 10th Amendment added nothing to the Constitution as originally ratified. And in the 1941 *Darby* decision, Justice Stone laid bare the empty content of the 10th Amendment by dismissing it as a "truism" and rephrasing it to read "that all is retained which has not been surrendered."

Steel Seizure Case

In another attempt to deny the existence of inherent powers for the President, the Senate Foreign Relations Committee declared that the doctrine of inherent or emergency powers was "explicitly rejected by the Supreme Court when it ruled illegal President Truman's seizure of the steel mills during the Korean war." A Senate subcommittee on separation of powers stated in 1969 that, in the Steel Seizure Case, the Supreme Court "expressly rejected the 'inherent powers' doctrine." Articles in law journals often reach the same conclusion. Thus, the holding in the Steel Seizure Case, says one such article, "is seemingly conclusive upon the question of inherent powers. Although there was no majority opinion of the Court, two groups of three Justices each arriving at the same result by different reasoning, there was no disagreement among the six as to the lack of inherent Presidential powers."

I think that overstates the significance of the decision. In the first place, what the Court rejected was not so much the concept of inherent executive powers, but rather the claim to unlimited executive powers. When the case was argued before the District Court, Assistant Attorney General Baldridge maintained that during time of emergency, the President had the duty to take whatever steps were necessary to protect the national security and the national interest. In such situations the Court could not interfere with or restrain the President, for his power was subject to only two limitations: the ballot box and impeachment.

The White House had not claimed such vast power for the President, however, and it took steps to counteract the effects of Baldridge's statement. A letter was released in which President Truman explained that his powers were "derived from the Constitution, and they are limited, of course, by the provisions of the Constitution, particularly those that protect the rights of citizens." In a memorandum submitted to the District Court, the Justice Department also disclaimed unlimited powers for the President. But it was too late to undo the damage or correct the initial impression. Judge Pine of the District Court felt compelled to reject most vigorously the theory on which the seizure had been defended, noting the injury that would otherwise flow from "a timorous judicial recognition that there is some basis for this claim to unlimited and unrestrained executive power. . . ." Had the Truman Administration justified its action solely as an emergency measure, based upon the need to obtain steel to prosecute the Korean War, and had it acknowledged from the start the constitutional limitations that operate on the President, the verdict of the court might have been quite different.

Second, while it is true that the Supreme Court did uphold the Pine decision, the Court was badly splintered on the issue of inherent and emergency powers. Only Justices Black and Douglas insisted on specific constitutional or statutory authority for Presidential seizure of private property. The prerogative could not be used to widen executive power in time of emergency, Justice Black wrote, for the "Founders of this Nation entrusted the lawmaking power to the Congress alone in both good and bad times." This use of the separation doctrine, Professor Edward S. Corwin observed, was "a purely arbitrary construct created out of hand for the purpose of disposing of this particular case, and is altogether devoid of historical verification."

The other four concurring Justices, and the three who dissented, were careful to avoid generalizations on the boundaries of executive action. Thus, Justice Frankfurter concurred in the result of the decision, but considered it imprudent to inquire into the more general areas of Presidential powers and their relationship to those of Congress. To underline the difficulty of discovering hard and fast rules to cover the constitutionality of Presidential seizures of industrial property, he cited earlier instances in which plants and facilities had been seized by the President without statutory authority.

Justice Jackson, also concurring, cautioned that the decision to strike down the steel seizure should not become the occasion "to circumscribe, much less to contract, the lawful role of the President as Commander in Chief," especially when "turned against the outside world for the security of our society." In another concurring opinion, Justice Burton distinguished the steel seizure from a situation in which emergency powers might legitimately be invoked, as in the case of "an imminent invasion or threatened attack," or of "a mobilized nation waging, or imminently threatened with, total war." In the last of the concurring opinions, Justice Clark maintained that the Constitution "does grant to the President extensive authority in times of grave and imperative national emergency," and it mattered not to Justice Clark whether one called that residual, inherent, moral, implied, aggregate, or emergency authority.

The dissenting opinion by Chief Justice Vinson, joined by Justices Reed and Minton, reviewed Presidential responsibilities in Korea, the Truman Plan in Greece and Turkey, the Marshall Plan in Western Europe, the Mutual Security

Act of 1951, and other international obligations. It was the President's duty to execute those legislative programs and "successful execution depends upon continued production of steel and stabilized prices for steel." From these concurring and dissenting opinions, we see that seven out of nine Justices accepted a view of executive power that went beyond the mere exercise of duties specifically granted by the Constitution or by statute.

ADMINISTRATIVE LEGISLATION

The Constitution expressly grants to the President a legislative role. He has a qualified veto power and is responsible for recommending to Congress such measures as he shall judge "necessary and expedient." Through his power of appointment and through the distribution of patronage he can attempt to influence a legislator's vote. Presidential distribution of favors and executive decisions on where to locate various Federal installations can be used for the same purpose. The President's liaison men work closely with Congress to maximize support for Administration bills. Radio, television, and the President's news conferences are effective instruments for advancing the Administration's legislative program. The following sections discuss still other forms of legislative power available to the President.

Treaties

Article VI of the Constitution defines treaties as "laws." The Constitution, statutes, and all treaties are considered "the supreme law of the land." Critics of the Constitution opposed Presidential participation in the treaty process by arguing that laws should be made "only by men invested with legislative authority." To this John Jay answered, in Federalist 64, that decisions by the courts and the executive were as binding on the people as laws passed by Congress.

The Constitution empowers the President, "by and with the advice of the Senate, to make treaties, provided two-thirds of the Senators present concur. . . ." It was assumed that the President and the Senate would work jointly on both stages of treaty-making, on negotiation as well as ratification. When Washington met with Senators in August 1789 to secure their advice and consent on an Indian treaty, they refused to commit the Senate to any agreement in his presence. Moreover, they disliked having to rely solely on information supplied by his Secretary of War. Although Washington agreed to return two days later, and the Senate gave its advice and consent to the treaty, the experience convinced him that personal consultation with the Senate on treaties was ill-advised.

The lesson to be drawn from this episode is not that the President, from that time forward, regarded the negotiation of treaties as a purely executive matter, or that the role of the Senate was henceforth limited to voting up or down a treaty which the Administration had formulated and drafted. And yet this impression has been promoted and perpetuated by Professor Corwin ("it is today established that the President alone has the power to negotiate treaties with foreign governments"), by Justice Sutherland in the *Curtiss-Wright* decision ("He alone negotiates. Into the field of negotiation the Senate cannot intrude"), and by the standard annotated version of the Constitution (which calls the negotiation of treaties "a Presidential Monopoly"). Washington's experience merely ended the possibility of *personal consultation* with the Senate on treaties. Joint negotiations continued, not by personal consultation but rather by written communication. A number of Senators are currently trying to reverse the Corwin view of the treaty-making power by recapturing the Senate's constitutional responsibility to participate *prior* to treaty ratification. A resolution introduced by Senator Hartke in July 1971 stipulates that "no treaty may be constitutionally negotiated by the President without the prior advice of the Senate. . . ."

Presidential power in the treaty-making process often bypasses the Senate. In one case in which a treaty with Panama failed to specify the precise boundaries of the Canal

Zone, Taft, in his capacity as Secretary of War, issued an order clarifying the boundaries. While his action was criticized as a usurpation of the treaty-making power, the order stood. In another exercise of power with regard to treaties, Taft (this time as President) annulled a treaty with Russia before the Senate had a chance to act. He explained that he was able, in this way, to handle the matter in more diplomatic fashion.

In cases where the Senate has refused to support a treaty by the necessary two-thirds majority, Presidents have presented an international agreement to both houses. Adoption of a joint resolution favoring the agreement requires only a simple majority of each house. Annexation of Texas in 1845 and of Hawaii in 1898 were accomplished by that procedure. The St. Lawrence Seaway plan, rejected by the Senate in 1934 in treaty form, was passed by Congress in 1954 as a regular bill. Thus, the treaty-making power of the Senate has been eroded by congressional as well as by Presidential actions.

Executive Agreements

Presidents also enter into "executive agreements" with foreign nations. At first this was done with statutory support. As an example, an act in 1792 authorized the Postmaster General to make arrangements with foreign postmasters for the reciprocal receipt and delivery of letters and packets. Congress has authorized the President to enter into reciprocal trade agreements. Although such agreements lack what the Supreme Court in the *Altman* decision called the "dignity" of a treaty—since they do not require ratification by the Senate—they have been upheld as valid international compacts.

Executive officers, from an early date, entered into international agreements without any statutory authority. An exchange of notes between Acting Secretary of State Rush and the British Minister Bagot in 1817 effected a limitation of naval vessels on the Great Lakes. Not until a year later did the Administration present the matter in treaty form, which the Senate promptly ratified. As another example, in 1905 the Senate withheld its support of a financial arrangement which President Roosevelt wanted to make with the Dominican Republic. By executive agreement, he ordered American agents to take charge of Dominican customs until the Senate acted. Two years later a treaty was ratified. Other examples of executive agreements, entered into without legislative authority, include the Destroyers-Bases deal in 1940 and the Yalta and Potsdam Agreements in 1945. Table 1 shows the extent to which treaties have been replaced by executive agreements.

Table 1 Treaties and Executive Agreements (1789–1970)

Period	Treaties	Executive Agreements	Totals
1789–1839	60	27	87
1839–1889	215	238	453
1889–1939	524	917	1,441
1940–1970	310	5,653	5,963
	1,109	6,835	7,944

These figures should not be used as an index of Presidential dominance or of arbitrary executive action. Many of the agreements were based on statutory directives. Still others were entered into pursuant to a treaty provision. And in cases where executive agreements are based neither on statutory nor on treaty authority, they have been nonetheless upheld. *United States* v. *Belmont* (1937) involved a property claim resulting from President Roosevelt's recognition of the Soviet Union in 1933. The Supreme Court upheld the agreement as a valid international compact.

That does not mean that the President is free to enter into any kind of agreement. The executive agreement in the Belmont case represented the exercise of an implied Presidential power: recognition of foreign governments. Executive agreements for other purposes have been handled differently by the courts. In the 1953 *Capps* decision, for instance, the U.S. Court of Appeals declared invalid an executive agreement because it contravened an existing statute on commerce with Canada. Imports from a foreign country represented foreign commerce "subject to regulation, so far as this country is concerned, by Congress alone. The executive may not by-pass congressional limitations regulating such commerce by entering into an agreement with the foreign country. . . ."

In *Seery* v. *United States* (1955), a naturalized citizen brought action to recover damages to her property in Austria. Her home had been used as a U.S. officers' club in 1945. Despite the existence of an executive agreement, by which the United States agreed to pay Austria a flat sum of money in full settlement of all obligations incurred by American armed forces, the U.S. Court of Claims held that the woman was entitled to compensation: "we think that there can be no doubt that an executive agreement, not being a transaction which is even mentioned in the Constitution, cannot impair Constitutional rights."

A similar issue arose in *Reid* v. *Covert* (1957). The Supreme Court struck down an executive agreement which permitted U.S. military courts to exercise exclusive jurisdiction over offenses committed in Great Britain by American servicemen or by their dependents. The Court stated that executive agreements could not confer power "free from the restraints of the Constitution." Specifically at issue was trial by court martial instead of the constitutional right of trial by jury.

In addition to legal restraints, political factors limit the use of executive agreements. In programs requiring appropriations, such as with the Marshall Plan, the President has had to seek the cooperation and support of Congress. Other agreements, such as the 1963 Limited Test Ban Treaty, require public understanding and support. President Kennedy could have entered into an executive agreement with Soviet Russia, without seeking the Senate's support for a treaty, but only at the risk of public and legislative condemnation. In 1970, when the State Department preferred to enter into an executive agreement with Spain, instead of submitting a treaty to the Senate, the Senate passed a resolution expressing its view that nothing in the agreement "shall be deemed to be a national commitment by the United States."

The disturbing fact about executive agreements is not so much their wide usage, for that partly reflects the growing interdependence among nations and the heightened international responsibilities of the United States. Of much greater concern is the failure to report executive agreements to Congress. During hearings in 1969, Congress learned of a secret U.S.-Thailand contingency plan—negotiated in 1964–65—that promised the commitment of American troops to Thailand in case of external attack. Congress was not consulted in the formulation and signing of the agreement, and could look forward only to a possible advisory role in the event the agreement were placed in operation.

In 1970, Senator Clifford Case introduced a bill to require that all international agreements, other than treaties, be transmitted to Congress within 60 days of their execution. If an executive agreement was one whose immediate disclosure would prejudice national security, it would be transmitted to the Senate Foreign Relations Committee and to the House Foreign Affairs Committee, under an injunction of secrecy removable only by the President.

Rules and Regulations

Another form of administrative legislation results from the need for statutory construction. The President is to take care that laws are "faithfully executed," but it is not always clear what a statute means, or the extent to which it is to be carried out. By having to interpret the statute's purpose and intent, the President and executive officials necessarily possess substantial discretionary authority over the laws. President Taft once remarked: "Let any one make the laws of the country, if I can construe them."

To supply concrete meaning to a statute, and to set forth efficient procedures for internal administrative matters, executive authorities formulate rules and regulations. In the first fifteen months following March 4, 1933, President Roosevelt alone issued 674 Executive Orders. During the first year of the National Recovery Administration, 2,998 administrative orders were issued. Other departments and officials also issued rules and regulations, and yet nowhere were these administrative pronouncements collected and published in one place. As a result, even executive officials frequently did not know the applicable regulations.

A case arose in 1934 where an indictment was brought and an appeal taken by the Administration to the Supreme Court before it was discovered that the regulation on which the proceeding was based did not exist. Since 1936, administrative rules and regulations have been published first in the *Federal Register* and then compiled each year to form the *Code of Federal Regulations*. The latter contains departmental rules and regulations that remain in force and effect. As of January 1, 1970, the *Code* consisted of more than a hundred volumes.

The legality of administrative law-making has been upheld on various occasions by the Supreme Court. Under authority of the President, the Secretary of War issued Army regulations to govern the armed forces. The *Eliason* decision in 1842 declared that these rules and regulations "must be received as the acts of the executive, and as such, be binding upon all within the sphere of his legal and constitutional authority." Regulations issued by the Treasury Department for the collection of revenue were also upheld, in *Boske* v. *Comingore* (1900), as being legally prescribed.

The impact of executive decisions on tax rules and regulations can be appreciated by some recent examples. In March 1970, the Treasury Department reversed itself on a shipping ruling that would have meant a million-dollar windfall for a tanker company. Also in 1970, the Internal Revenue Commissioner issued a new procedure to permit certain businesses, which receive advance payments for future services, to defer taxes for one year. Not only did his decision mean a substantial revenue loss to the Treasury, but business and professional groups were able to gain through his action what they had been previously denied by Congress, by the Federal courts, and by former commissioners of Internal Revenue.

In January 1971, President Nixon approved three changes to liberalize the depreciation provisions of the tax laws. The effect: business tax payments were expected to drop by $3 billion during fiscal 1972. This exercise of executive discretion was made possible by the very general language of the tax law, which merely requires that depreciation deductions be "reasonable."

Proclamations

Proclamations by the President are generally issued to affect the activities of private individuals. Sometimes they are merely declaratory, such as the annual Thanksgiving Proclamation, or proclamations to observe Loyalty Day or Save Your Vision Week. Other types of proclamations are issued to announce Presidential actions and decisions in public policy. This category includes statements by the President when he sets import quotas, adjusts duties on certain products, or provides relief to industries that have been injured by foreign competition. These areas require the exercise of Presidential discretion within general statutory guidelines established by Congress.

Still other proclamations find their basis in Presidential prerogatives: Washington's Neutrality Proclamation; and Lincoln's proclamations in April 1861, in which he called forth the state militia, authorized the suspension of the writ of habeas corpus, and placed a blockade against the rebellious states.

In 1907, Theodore Roosevelt issued proclamations that increased the size of the national forest land by more than 43 million acres—an area comparable in size to New York, New Jersey, Connecticut, and Massachusetts. He described other tactics he used to preserve the public lands. In one case, when an agricultural appropriations bill was winding its way through the Senate, Senator Fulton of Oregon added an amendment to prohibit the President from setting aside additional land for national forests in six northwestern states. That would have affected 16 million acres. Instead of vetoing the entire bill, and losing the funds he wanted, Roosevelt used the ten-day grace period to issue proclamations. By the time he had signed the bill, the 16 million acres had passed into the public sector, secured as national forest land.

Executive Orders

Still another instrument for the exercise of legislative power is the issuance of Executive Orders. In June 1941, President Roosevelt seized North American Aviation's plant in Inglewood, California, basing his action not on specific statutory authority but rather on the general powers vested in him "by the Constitution and laws of the United States, as President of the United States of America and Commander in Chief of the Army and Navy of the United States. . . ." The same general powers were cited again when he seized a shipbuilding company and an aircraft plant in 1941, a cable company and a shell plant in 1942, and almost 4,000 soft and hard coal companies in 1943. The War Labor Disputes Act of June 25, 1943, finally provided statutory authority for seizing plants, mines, and other facilities.

On the basis of other Executive Orders, the Federal Government has threatened to withhold contracts from employers who fail to meet equal employment provisions in Federal contracts. This policy dates back to 1941, when President Roosevelt declared in an Executive Order that "there shall be no discrimination in the employment of workers in defense industries or government because of race, creed, color, or national origin. . . ." His policy was reaffirmed by Presidents Truman and Eisenhower. President Kennedy added the threat of contract cancellation to force compliance with Federal equal employment standards. Shortly after Kennedy issued his Executive Order, a decision by the Comptroller General stated that "So far as we are aware the propriety of [nondiscrimination] clauses . . . has never been seriously questioned by any responsible administrative or judicial tribunal; nor has the Congress seen fit to proscribe the use of such clauses by appropriate legislation." In still another Executive Order, issued by President Johnson, the administrative structure for executing the nondiscrimination clause was established.

Under President Nixon, Federal nondiscrimination policies evolved into what was called the "Philadelphia Plan." In order to work on Federally assisted projects, contractors had to set specific goals for hiring members of minority groups. On August 5, 1969, the Comptroller General issued a decision in which he held that the Plan conflicted with the 1964 Civil Rights Act, which prohibited the setting up of any kind of preferential treatment on the basis of race, color, on national origin. The Comptroller General said it did not matter whether one designated the hiring commitment as a "goal" or a "quota."

The Secretary of Labor promptly announced that the Administration would continue to press ahead with the Philadelphia Plan. He said that interpretation of the Civil Rights Act had been vested by Congress in the Department of Justice, and that the Department had approved the Plan as consistent with the Act. Moreover, the Secretary of Labor said that the Comptroller General had ignored the Executive Order "as an independent source of law."

A Senate subcommittee report charged in April 1971 that the Philadelphia Plan was a "blatant case of usurpation of the legislative function by the executive branch. . . ." However, the U.S. Court of Appeals for the Third Circuit upheld the legality of the Philadelphia Plan as well as the Executive Order under which the Plan was promulgated. The court justified this use of Presidential power partly on the Chief Executive's implied power—as it relates to economical procurement policy—to assure that "the largest possible pool of qualified manpower be available for the accomplishment" of Federal projects.

It should be added that Executive Orders are a source of law only when founded upon the constitutional powers given to the President or upon statutory authority. In such cases the courts have held that Executive Orders have the same effect as if they had been incorporated in an act of Congress. On the other hand, there are cases where Executive Orders have exceeded the bounds of Presidential authority. On a number of occasions the Supreme Court has struck down this type of Order, the most prominent example being the Steel Seizure Case of 1952.

Executive Orders were not numbered in the early years. Beginning in 1907, the Orders on file in the State Department were arranged chronologically and given a number. As of August 15, 1971, the numbered series had reached 11,615. Estimates of the *unnumbered* Executive Orders range from 15,000 to as high as 50,000.

Bill-drafting and Central Clearance

Executive bill-drafting began in the first Administration. Congress directed Alexander Hamilton, as Secretary of the Treasury, to prepare recommendations for a national bank, state debts, and the promotion of manufactures. Although the Jeffersonians were highly critical of executive participation in the legislative process, they changed their tune once they gained control of the Presidency. Jefferson's Secretary of the Treasury, Albert Gallatin, offered recommendations on debt retirement, abolition of excise taxes, and retrenchment in military spending. His proposals were accepted by the Cabinet and adopted by Congress. As a former member of the House of Representatives, it was second nature for Gallatin to confer with committee chairmen and even draft some of the necessary legislation.

As for Jefferson himself, not only did he as Secretary of State draft a bill "to promote the progress of the useful arts," but he also drafted the Giles Resolution, a legislative broadside directed against Hamilton's use of Federal funds. As President, he drafted bills for a number of purposes, including a government for Louisiana, harbor protection, establishment of a naval militia, creation of a national university, tariff changes, and embargo enforcement, and then saw to it that his party followers in Congress pushed his measures through to enactment. In a proposed draft for embargo enforcement, he instructed Gallatin: "If you will prepare something on these or any other ideas you like better. . . . Mr. Newton. . . . will push them through the House."

Executive bill-drafting was not the only departure from the formal model of separated powers; the judiciary also drafted legislation. Justice Story prepared a bill for reorganization of the courts in 1816, first circulating his draft among the members of the Supreme Court so as to obtain their comments. Chief Justice Taft and several members of the Court drafted the "Judges' Bill" of 1925, which was also directed toward court reorganization and more efficient judicial proceedings. Taft testified on behalf of the bill before the Senate and House Judiciary Committees, and he lobbied intensively for its passage.

Executive participation in the legislative process had fallen into disfavor after the Federalist and Jeffersonian precedents. President Taft received a cold reception in 1912 when he suggested that Cabinet officers "be given access to the floor of each House to introduce measures, to advocate their passage, to answer questions, and to enter into the debate as if they were members, without of course the right to vote." Denied access to the floor, Cabinet members and other executive officials came to enjoy essentially the same privileges when they testified before legislative committees.

After the creation of the Bureau of the Budget in 1921, new procedures were established to control the flow of agency proposals that were sent to Congress, and to control the flow of enrolled enactments being returned from Congress for Presidential action. These operations, referred to as "central clearance," gradually became more exacting, so that by 1939 the Budget Bureau was serving as the President's sole agent for clearing departmental drafts for proposed legislation, obtaining agency advice on enrolled bills, and advising the President on measures passed by Congress. By the 1960s the function of central clearance for important legislation had passed from the Budget Bureau to the policy staffs in the White House.

By the time of the postwar period, Presidents from either party were expected to prepare the major legislation and submit its program to Congress. In 1953, a senior Republican chairman of a major House committee reportedly told an Administration witness: "Don't expect us to start from scratch on what you people want. That's not the way we do things here—*you* draft the bills and *we* work them over."

It has been estimated that anywhere from fifty to eighty percent of the bills enacted into law originate in the executive branch. Such figures give the executive branch undue credit. "Originate" may simply mean that an executive agency has put into motion an idea already proposed and developed by a legislator or private group. After the President's proposal reaches Congress, it can be reworked considerably in committee and on the floor. And even in cases where the President's proposal emerges relatively unscathed, that may reflect not so much the President's power to legislate but rather his anticipation of what Congress would pass. In such cases, who is "Chief Legislator"?

3

DELEGATION OF POWER

Explanations for the growth of executive power have generally emphasized two factors: the resourcefulness of "strong" Presidents and the opportunities that history offers for enlarging their powers. The enchanting quality of this account lies in its combination of personal actions and impersonal forces, of individual determination and historical determinism. Yet this largely begs the question, for it is not much more than a tautology to attribute the growth of Presidential power to strong Presidents. And if historical forces are responsible, why has history favored the growth of the executive branch over Congress? The missing piece must be found in the admittedly imprecise and unmeasurable "qualities" that characterize the executive office.

By qualities, I do not mean those referred to in textbooks, such as energy, competence, or beneficence. Instead, I concentrate on some of the traditional properties and responsibilities that have been associated with the executive. These include continuity in office, flexibility of timing, acting as channel of communication with other nations, serving as national representative, and executive duties during domestic emergencies or during time of war. Other responsibilities, such as fact-finding and coordination of economic policy, evolved for the most part during this century.

Delegation of legislative power has had to contend, from time to time, with critics who argue that the separation doctrine requires that powers vested in Congress must be exercised only by Congress. An early court case involved the Judiciary Act of 1789, which had authorized the courts to make and establish rules for the conduct of their business. It was objected that the rulemaking power, vested exclusively in Congress, could not be delegated. In *Wayman* v. *Southard*, Chief Justice Marshall answered that while certain legislative powers had to be exercised solely by Congress, there were other powers "of less interest" that could be delegated either to the judicial or the executive branch. Although the departments of government were different in that "the legislature makes, the executive executes, and the judiciary construes the law . . . the maker of the law may commit something to the discretion of the other department, and the precise boundary of this power is a subject of delicate and difficult inquiry, into which a court will not enter unnecessarily." It was permissible for Congress to supply guidelines for national policy while leaving to other departments the responsibility to "fill up the details."

In its decisions on the delegation of legislative powers to the President, the Court characteristically offers high-sounding tributes to the genius of the separation doctrine, and then proceeds to adopt a practical and workable definition of the concept. This pattern is evident in two decisions on Presidential tariff power. In *Field* v. *Clark* (1891), the Court declared it "a principle universally recognized" that Congress could not delegate legislative power to the President. Having made the proper gesture, the Court then upheld the delegation. In 1928, in the *Hampton* decision, the Court said it would be "a breach of the National fundamental law" if Congress were to transfer its legislative power to the President. Once again the delegation was upheld.

The permissibility of delegation thus becomes a matter of definition, with strong pragmatic overtones. In reconciling the abstract merits of the separation doctrine with the practical needs of government, the Supreme Court inspired one author to compose an ingenious syllogism, laying bare the rationale:

MAJOR PREMISE: Legislative power cannot be constitutionally delegated by Congress.

MINOR PREMISE: It is essential that certain powers be delegated to administrative officers and regulatory commissions.

CONCLUSION: Therefore the powers thus delegated are not legislative powers.

REASONS FOR DELEGATING POWER

Why is it "essential" that Congress delegate a portion of its powers to the President and to executive officials? Subsequent chapters on the spending power, tax power, and the war power will explore this question in greater detail, but at this point we can identify some of the basic factors that account for delegation.

Continuity in Office

Congress has become accustomed to nearly year-round sessions in recent decades, sometimes remaining in session from January to December, relieved in part by short recesses. In the early days of the Republic, however, when sessions often lasted but a few months, Congress found it necessary to delegate to the executive branch certain programs and policies that required continuous administration.

The need for independent executive action had been stressed by John Locke. The legislature could not always be in sitting, nor could it provide laws to cover every conceivable contingency: "It is not necessary—no, nor so much as convenient—that the legislative should be always in being; but absolutely necessary that the executive power should, because there is not always need of new laws to be made, but always need of execution of the laws that are made." At the

Philadelphia Convention, it was recommended that the executive carry out such powers "as may from time to time be delegated by the national Legislature." However, since the legislative capacity to delegate was considered to be included in the power to carry all laws into effect, the clause seemed superfluous and was omitted.

Some of the early enactments by Congress on embargo policy depended on the President's continuity in office. A resolution in March 1794 proposed that the President be vested with general embargo powers when Congress adjourned. Action on the resolution was avoided by laying a 30-day embargo in March and renewing it again in April. But with the spring term about to end, Congress had to provide for embargo policy during the summer recess. Instead of eliminating the embargo altogether, or having it remain in operation until Congress returned later in the year, Congress delegated the policy to the President. He was authorized to lay an embargo during the summer, and even revoke his own order, whenever he felt the public safety so required.

An act in 1798, suspending commercial intercourse with France and her dependencies, authorized the President to remove the suspension—during the period between congressional sessions—whenever he was "well ascertained" that French hostilities against America had ceased. In the debates the following year on renewing the restrictions, one delegate described the commercial advantages to be derived from vesting suspension powers in the President: "During the long recess of Congress great changes may take place—changes which may make it beneficial to the people of the United States to have the intercourse opened . . . without waiting for an extraordinary call of Congress." Legislative adjournment during 1806 provided yet another occasion to delegate functions to the President. Congress suspended a prohibition on the importation of certain goods until July 1, leaving it to the President to continue the suspension if he felt the public interest required it.

Jefferson's proposal for an embargo after December

1807 also depended upon the President's continuity in office. With Congress about to recess the following spring, the members debated whether to empower the President to suspend the embargo during the summer. Some members contended that the power to suspend or repeal a law was exclusively a legislative function and could not be delegated. Others replied that Congress retained legislative power by stating its suspension policy in a statute, as had been done in previous years. Commercial arguments were again presented to support Presidential discretion. It was to the nation's advantage, said one legislator, to have the embargo lifted as soon as possible: "All the business of the nation is deranged. All its active hopes are frustrated. All its industry stagnant. Its numerous products hastening to their market, are stopped in their course. A dam is thrown across the current, and every hour the strength and the tendency towards resistance is accumulating." Widespread evasion, smuggling, emigration of unemployed seamen, and a sharp increase in coastal trade had combined to frustrate Jefferson's embargo.

Congress had three choices: repeal the embargo, continue it, or give the President power to suspend it. Congress was not ready to repeal it. How could it continue it? A delegate asked: "Shall we stay by and watch? This has been recommended. Watch! What? 'Why, the crisis!' And do gentlemen seriously believe that any crisis which events in Europe are likely to produce will be either prevented or meliorated, by such a body as this, remaining, during the whole summer, perched upon this hill? To the tempest which is abroad we can give no direction; over it we have no control. . . . The only course that remains is to leave with the Executive the power to suspend the embargo." Congress took that step on April 22, 1808.

When Congress convened in the autumn, the constitutionality of delegated powers was again debated. Senator Giles found it a stale and tiresome subject, leading to endless discussion. Although he could accept the general principle of separated powers in the abstract, it was more difficult to apply it to specific situations. "This is not possible," he said.

"You might attempt the search for the philosopher's stone, or the discovery of the perpetual motion, with as much prospect of success."

Flexibility of Timing

Presidential discretion came to be exercised not only during the summer recess, while Congress was adjourned, but was used also to implement and retract policies while Congress was in session. Flexibility of timing by the executive was discussed in the eighteenth century by Blackstone. Although he confined the making of laws to the legislature, he added that "the manner, time, and circumstances of putting these laws in execution must frequently be left to the discretion of the executive magistrates."

Congress recognized this need for executive discretion in many of its early statutes. For example, it renewed commercial restrictions against France and her dependencies in 1799, leaving it to the President to discontinue the restrictions "if he shall deem it expedient and consistent with the interest of the United States. . . ." He could not only order the policy discontinued, but could also later revoke his own order. The act remained in force for slightly over a year, covering the fall and spring sessions of Congress as well as the summer recess. In 1806 the President was authorized to discontinue commercial restrictions against certain ports of the islands of St. Domingo when he felt it consistent with the interests of the United States. This act also permitted Presidential discretion while Congress was in session.

Presidental discretion on the timing of legislative policy resulted in a legal controversy during Madison's administration. The nonintercourse act against Britain took effect March 1, 1809. When its provisions lapsed the following March, Congress left it to the President to renew the restrictions at his discretion. A proclamation by Madison in November 1810 led to the seizure of cargo that had been shipped from Liverpool to New Orleans. The claimant of the goods objected to the revival of the nonintercourse act by Presidential proclamation, arguing that the proclamation had the force of law and was thus legislative in nature. The Supreme Court dismissed that argument in the *Brig Aurora* case, stating that Congress could legislate conditionally and leave to others the decision as to when legislative policy becomes operable. There was "no sufficient reason, why the legislature should not exercise its discretion in reviving the act of March 1st, 1809, either expressly or conditionally, as their judgment should direct."

When faced with contingent or conditional legislation, the Supreme Court frequently relies on the language of a decision by a Pennsylvania court, which declared in 1873 that it was essential to phrase statutes in general terms when events were "future and impossible to be fully known." Although the legislature could not delegate its power to make a law, it could allow some other agency to determine the fact or state of things upon which the law was to be applied. To prohibit this, the court said, "would be to stop the wheels of government. There are many things upon which wise and useful legislation must depend, which cannot be known to the law-making power, and must, therefore, be a subject of inquiry and determination outside of the halls of legislation."

The 1922 flexible tariff provision, empowering the President to adjust tariff rates, was attacked as an unconstitutional delegation of power. The Supreme Court once again rejected a doctrinaire reading of the separation of powers: "Congress may feel itself unable conveniently to determine exactly when its exercise of the legislative power should become effective, because dependent on future conditions, and it may leave the determination of such time to the discretion of an Executive. . . ."

Congressional inability to anticipate future needs also results in considerable discretionary spending power for the President. This gives rise to transfer authority, contingency funds, "no-year money," and other forms of executive spending power, to be discussed in the next chapter.

Channel for Foreign Communication

The executive, by long tradition, has acted as the channel for communication with foreign nations. Locke's federative power, which he combined with the executive power, included "all the transactions with all persons and communities without the commonwealth. . . ." Blackstone also discussed the executive prerogative in communicating with other nations. In foreign affairs the King was the sole representative of his people. Individuals of a state could not possibly "transact the affairs of that state with another community equally as numerous as themselves. Unanimity must be wanting to their measures, and strength to the execution of their counsels."

Several efforts were made at the Philadelphia Convention to define the President's role in foreign affairs. The Committee of Detail recommended that the President be authorized to receive ambassadors and to correspond with supreme executives from other countries. It was later proposed that the Secretary of Foreign Affairs serve at the pleasure of the President and assume responsibility for all correspondence with foreign ministers, and "generally to attend to the interests of the United States, in their connections with foreign Powers." Neither proposal was accepted. As a result, the Constitution does not contain an explicit statement on the President's duty to communicate with other nations, except for his reception of ambassadors and other public officials. The full scope of executive responsibilities in foreign affairs had to evolve as an implied power.

In 1793, following a French request addressed to Congress, Secretary of State Jefferson notified the French minister that the President was the only channel of communication between the United States and foreign nations: "it is from him alone that foreign nations or their agents are to learn what is or has been the will of the nation. . . ." Jefferson felt no obligation to offer evidence that the Constitution did in fact ascribe such responsibilities exclusively to the President: "I inform you of the fact by authority from the President."

In 1798, after negotiations with France had failed to resolve a dispute, a Dr. George Logan set sail for France to try his hand at diplomacy. His trip provoked a resolution which was directed against private citizens who "usurp the Executive authority of this Government, by commencing or carrying on any correspondence with the Governments of any foreign Prince or State. . . ." Congress subsequently passed what became known as the Logan Act, providing for fines and imprisonment to punish U.S. citizens who carry on unauthorized correspondence or intercourse with foreign governments in an effort to influence American policy. No individual has ever been fined or imprisoned for violating the Logan Act, although private citizens quite obviously have carried on unauthorized correspondence with foreign governments. In recent years, for instance, pacifist groups have been in contact with North Vietnam and with the peace delegation at Paris.

The significance of the Logan Act is not so much its prohibition against private diplomacy, but rather that it recognized as an *executive* function the responsibility for commencing and carrying on any correspondence with foreign governments. As the President became the accepted channel for the flow of information between the United States and foreign governments, new responsibilities moved in his direction. An 1822 statute prohibited ports in the British West Indies from shipping goods to America unless the President received satisfactory evidence that our vessels could enter those same ports. An act in 1845, governing trade between America and French islands of Miquelon and St. Pierre, allowed a reduction of tonnage duty on French vessels whenever the President received evidence that American ships sent to those colonies enjoyed the same advantage.

Commercial disputes with other nations often put the United States at the brink of war. Responsibilities for foreign commerce, in such situations, became intertwined with questions of foreign policy and national defense. In the

1880s, for example, American seamen complained of harassment and unreasonable restrictions by Canadian officials. Congress responded by authorizing the President to protect American fishing and trading vessels. It was within his discretion, whenever he considered the rights of Americans to be either denied or abridged by Canada, to forbid their vessels or goods from entering the United States. A few years later, in response to commercial barriers placed by Canada on the St. Lawrence River, the President received authority to suspend, at such time and for such duration as he saw fit, the right of free passage by Canadian vessels through the Saint Marys Falls Canal. The use of this economic weapon by the President was characterized by one Senator in these words: "So it is, whipping back and forth, that this power in the hands of the President of the United States is a necessary power to preserve the balance of commercial differences between countries, and that we cannot abandon that as a part of our statutory system without crippling our own Government."

Joint resolutions in 1912 and 1922 authorized the President to prohibit the shipment of arms or munitions to any country in South America whenever he decided that the materials would promote domestic violence. On the basis of still another joint resolution in 1934, President Roosevelt proclaimed that the shipment of machine guns to Bolivia was in conflict with American policy to reestablish peace in the Chaco region. The company charged with conspiring to sell this material argued that the joint resolution constituted uncontrolled discretion for the President, allowing him to substitute his will for that of Congress. The Supreme Court sustained the delegation in *United States* v. *Curtiss-Wright*. Speaking for the Court, Justice Sutherland stated that in external affairs "the President alone has the power to speak or listen as a representative of the nation," and that legislation over the international field must often accord to the President "a degree of discretion and freedom from statutory restriction which would not be admissible were domestic affairs alone involved."

All that was necessary, in this particular case, was for Sutherland to uphold the right of Congress to delegate embargo powers to the President. Instead, he added pages of *obiter dicta* on the far-reaching dimensions of executive power in international affairs. He referred to "this vast external realm, with its important, complicated, delicate and manifold problems," and stated that the President, not Congress, had "the better opportunity of knowing the conditions which prevail in foreign countries, and especially is this true in time of war."

These gratuitous remarks have since been used to justify the expansion of Presidential war powers, based not on new powers delegated by Congress but rather on inherent powers residing in the President's office. The sweeping declarations of Sutherland should be taken as *dicta,* and nothing more. Their source is not in the Constitution but in his political point of view. He had earlier served on the Senate Foreign Relations Committee and was a forceful exponent of the use of American power abroad. His biographer, Joel Francis Paschal, writes that Sutherland had "long been the advocate of a vigorous diplomacy which strongly, even belligerently, called always for an assertion of American rights." Many of the arguments in Sutherland's *Curtiss-Wright* decision had appeared earlier in his *Constitutional Power and World Affairs* (1919).

If we ignore his sweeping assertions about Presidential power in external affairs, and limit our discussion to what Congress will and will not delegate, the external-internal distinction can be helpful. Congress would not look kindly upon a request by a President who wanted discretionary authority over domestic taxes. But when the request involves international matters, Congress is less likely to object. In 1967, President Johnson asked Congress for discretionary authority to vary the rate of the interest equalization tax, which had been imposed in 1963 to reduce the outflow of investment capital and to improve the balance of payments. Congress delegated the power, authorizing the President to vary the tax so that the effective annual interest cost to foreign borrowers would range between zero and 1.5 percent. President Johnson reduced the interest equalization tax from 1.50 percent to 1.25 percent, and President Nixon later reduced it still further to 0.75 percent. This Presidential authority was renewed in 1971.

National Representative

Important tariff and spending powers have been delegated to the President because legislators found themselves too vulnerable to pressures from special interests and the voting public, and concluded that the retention of certain powers involved too great a political cost. Delegates at the Philadelphia Convention had anticipated part of this development. Gouverneur Morris argued that it was necessary to make the President capable of resisting the wealthy classes and of providing protection for "the Mass of the people." Madison looked upon the President as a national officer, "acting for and equally sympathising with" every part of the nation.

The concept of the President as a direct representative of the people, having been popularized and dramatized by Jackson, was stated explicitly by Polk: "If it be said that the Representatives in the popular branch of Congress are chosen directly by the people, it is answered, the people elect the President. If both Houses represent the States and the people, so does the President. The President represents in the executive department the whole people of the United States, as each member of the legislative department represents portions of them."

It is a crude generalization, of course, to depict Congress as the servant of selfish interests, while idealizing the President as one who acts for the nation as a whole. The President and his party followers face similar problems of reelection, and in soliciting campaign contributions it is not always possible to effect reforms for the general welfare without simultaneously antagonizing your financial backers. Moreover, the President is also besieged by pressure groups.

When Congress delegates new authority to the President or to a regulatory commission, interest groups simply shift their attention from Congress to the administrative body placed in charge of the program. Thus, the hope of taking "politics out of the tariff" in the 1920s, by investing the Tariff Commission with new powers, was sorely disappointed. One study, by Philip Wright, concluded that it was impossible to follow the development of the Tariff Commission without realizing that once it had received authority to adjust rates, "the same business interests that had gone into politics to get a tariff to their liking through Congress continued in politics to get a tariff to their liking through the Tariff Commission."

Despite these disappointments, the delegation of tariff powers to the executive branch continued. The Smoot-Hawley Act of 1930, which raised tariff rates to record levels, was widely condemned as a monstrosity of legislative tariff-making. Senator Walsh remarked that if logrolling, or vote-trading, had not been practiced, then "some other invisible influence has brought about a shifting of votes and reversals of judgment that is unparalleled in the history of legislation." Senator La Follette spoke of lobbyists testifying under oath that they had proposed deals to various legislators: "Votes were changed overnight, not by arguments nor by new evidence but as consideration for the conferring of new privileges upon favored interests and sections."

After that experience, Congress never again attempted general tariff-making. A study on the politics of foreign trade offered this explanation for Congress' willingness to delegate tariff-making powers to the executive branch: "every favor which can be conferred is also a danger, because it must sometimes be refused. Responsibility involves blame. And, if the demands exceed what the congressman can effectively handle, then he may happily yield up a significant portion of his power. That is what happened with the tariff."

Large portions of the spending power have been delegated to the President because of fragmentation in the legislative committee system, and because of Congress' inability —toward the end of the 19th century—to resist demands for greater spending. As a result, it was the President, not Congress, who assumed the role "protector of the purse." Professor Edward S. Corwin dismissed as childish the theory that, in the area of spending, Congress was the most representative and responsible branch: "the truth is that in no other field is it less representative and less responsible, being constantly exposed when left to itself to be overridden by corrupt amalgamations of thievish interests."

Budget-making powers were transferred to the President in 1921; within a few years Congress delegated substantial budget-cutting powers to him as well, having first demonstrated that it was poorly equipped to do the job. In 1931, when deficits appeared for the first time in a decade, President Hoover asked for authority to effect savings by reorganizing the executive departments. Prior efforts by Congress to reduce spending had been effectively thwarted by influential lobbyists. Senator Reed told his colleagues that economies could be expected only by placing greater power in the hands of the President: "Leave it to Congress and we will fiddle around here all summer trying to satisfy every lobbyist, and we will get nowhere."

During debates in 1933 on whether to delegate broad authority to President Roosevelt to effect spending reductions, Representative Griffin said that there were thousands of individuals on the rolls of the Veterans Bureau drawing compensation they were not entitled to: "Why not be frank enough to admit it?" Since the Veterans' Committee had failed to suggest how those names might be dropped from the rolls, there appeared to be no other alternative than to shift an unpopular task to the President. Roosevelt subsequently received authority to reduce veterans' benefits and Federal salaries, prompting some legislators to complain that he had asked for dictatorial powers. Senator Tydings countered: "Of course he did. Why? Because Congress itself refused to do its duty, to protect the integrity of the national credit."

A more recent delegation of spending power is included in the Postal Revenue and Federal Salary Act of 1967. Congress established a commission to recommend pay levels for Members of Congress, members of the Federal judiciary, and top-level officials of the executive branch. The commission was directed to report its recommendations to the President, who could accept or modify the pay rate proposals and then submit them to Congress. Unless either house disapproved the proposals within 30 days, or unless Congress enacted other pay rates, the Presidential recommendations would become law. During debate on the bill, several legislators condemned the proposal to delegate authority to the President to decide pay rates for Members of Congress and the judiciary. The separation of powers doctrine was invoked to discredit the plan, but the majority of legislators considered it a convenient way to protect themselves from angry constituents. Representative Holifield remarked: "Certainly, any time we vote for a raise in our wages we are accused of conflict of interest because we have done something for ourselves."

Fact-finding and Coordination

The increase in administrative discretion over the past century is an inevitable result of government intervention in the economy—an area in which the conditions to be regulated are complex, interrelated, and constantly undergoing change. By an act of 1891, the President was authorized to set apart and reserve lands as forest reservations. Subsequent acts, in 1897 and 1905, elaborated on the legislative policy. Following an announcement by the Secretary of Agriculture in 1906 of new regulations for the forest reserves, the Federal Government prosecuted a group for grazing sheep on national lands without a permit. The defendants claimed that the regulations represented an unconstitutional exercise of legislative power by an administrator. The Supreme Court upheld the delegation in *Grimaud,* explaining that broadness and generality in statutes were unavoidable:

"What might be harmless in one forest might be harmful to another. What might be injurious at one stage of timber growth, or at one season of the year, might not be so at another. In the nature of things it was impracticable for Congress to provide general regulations for these various and varying details of management."

Similar decisions were handed down in other cases dealing with administrative fact-finding. Executive responsibilities for guaranteeing the importation of pure and wholesome tea were attacked as an exercise of legislative power, but the Court, in *Buttfield* v. *Stranahan* (1904), answered that Congress legislated "as far as was reasonably practicable, and from the necessities of the case was compelled to leave to executive officials the duty of bringing about the result pointed out by the statute." In cases in which an executive officer exercised discretionary power to ensure that all bridges were of such height and construction as to permit the free navigation of interstate commerce, the Court upheld the delegation, stating that it would be impractical for Congress to investigate every bridge in the country. It had only to declare a general policy and leave to an administrative officer the responsibility for applying the statute to particular cases.

Only in the two NRA cases in 1935 did the Supreme Court strike down a delegation of power to the President. The National Industrial Recovery Act was based on the principle of industrial self-regulation. In order to minimize competition, raise prices, and restrict production, codes were drawn up by industrial and trade associations and presented to the President for his approval. If acceptable codes were not received, the President was empowered to prescribe codes and enforce them by law.

In the "Hot Oil" case in January 1935, the Court ruled that Section 9(c) of the NIRA was unconstitutional. That section, governing the petroleum code, had authorized the President to prohibit the interstate transportation of oil produced in excess of state allowances. The Court, voting 8 to 1, struck down the section because it lacked adequate guidelines and standards for executive action. The Chief Justice was careful to point out that the unconstitutionality lay in the lack of guidelines, not in delegation per se. The Court did not insist on extensive statutory details: "The Constitution has never been regarded as denying to the Congress the necessary resources of flexibility and practicality. . . ."

The petroleum code suffered from procedural defects as well. The administrator was not required to make public his findings or to announce the reasons for his decisions. By raising this point, the Court relied more on standards of due process than on the doctrine of separated powers. Careless drafting was also evident. The paragraph in the code making violations a criminal offense had been inadvertently eliminated when the code was revised. The Administration was thus placed in the embarrassing position of having prosecuted citizens for violating a law that did not exist.

Of the three liberals on the Court—Justices Stone, Brandeis, and Cardozo—only the latter defended the petroleum code. "Discretion is not unconfined and vagrant," said Justice Cardozo. "It is canalized within banks that keep it from overflowing." Yet in the *Schechter Poultry* decision announced a few months later, striking down the remainder of the NIRA, Cardozo abandoned his defense of the code system and joined his brethren in a unanimous decision. He found the Act too loosely phrased, exclaiming: "This is delegation running riot."

Much has been made of the supposed intransigence of a conservative Court toward New Deal measures, frustrating each attempt by the Administration to lead the country out of depression. After the Schechter decision, one cartoon depicted a figure representing the American public trying to climb aboard a lifeboat. Roosevelt was pushing the poor wretch back into the sea, saying "I'm sorry, but the Supreme Court says I must chuck you back again." By 1935, however, few analysts of the economy looked upon the NIRA as a lifeboat. An editorial by *The New York Times* doubted that the Schechter decision would stir up much resentment against the Court: "The judges simply pronounce to be dead a statute which the great mass of the people had already decided to be dead."

Production statistics rose sharply in 1933 when the code system was announced, but the appearance of recovery was an illusion. Businessmen, anticipating higher wages and more costly materials, were simply producing at a faster clip before the codes could take effect. Afterwards, it became obvious that purchasing power was inadequate to support this inventory boom. Production, employment, and payrolls began to slide downward. As Marriner Eccles explained it: "Labor could get high wages and no jobs; businessmen could get higher prices and no markets." The codes were also criticized because the largest corporations, which dominated the trade associations, had formulated the codes for their own advantage and protection. By the time the Court invalidated the NIRA, the Roosevelt Administration had concluded that the "fair trade" provisions in the codes were in fact favoring monopoly and big business. The Second New Deal now turned toward greater competition and antitrust action to promote recovery.

After 1935, delegation of legislative powers to executive officials encountered little resistance from the Court. Bills were drafted with more specific rules to govern administrators, the composition of the Court changed, and Federal regulatory efforts were no longer hampered by artificial formulas that tried to distinguish between "interstate" and "intrastate" commerce. In one case after another, the Supreme Court upheld the delegation of various powers to the Administration. "Delegation by Congress," said the Court in its 1940 *Sunshine Anthracite* decision, "has long been recognized as necessary in order that the exertion of legislative power does not become a futility . . . the burdens of minutiae would be apt to clog the administration of the law and deprive the agency of that flexibility and dispatch which are its salient virtues."

These decisions culminated in a unanimous decision by the Court in *Opp Cotton Mills,* in 1941. Petitioners had urged that the minimum wage boundaries set by Congress at

30 to 40 cents an hour were too indefinite to keep the administrator within constitutional channels. Selection of the wage depended upon the administrator's judgment that, among other factors, competitive advantages would not accrue to any group in the industry and that the wage would not substantially curtail employment. Wages were to be based upon transportation costs, living and production costs, as well as the wage scale for comparable work in industries with collective bargaining rights. It was up to the administrator to collect data from across the country and then compute comparable minimum wages for each region.

Administrative fact-finding, petitioners said, represented a step in the legislative process and therefore violated the separation doctrine. Justice Stone conceded the link between fact-finding and legislation, but ruled that insufficient ground for turning aside the act. Speaking for a unanimous Court, he emphasized the unusual administrative demands created by the modern economy: "In an increasingly complex society Congress obviously could not perform its functions if it were obliged to find all the facts subsidiary to the basic conclusions which support the defined legislative policy in fixing, for example, a tariff rate, a railroad rate or the rate of wages to be applied in particular industries by a minimum wage law. The Constitution, viewed as a continuously operative charter of government, is not to be interpreted as demanding the impossible or the impracticable."

The Federal Pay Comparability Act of 1970 is one of many recent examples where delegation by Congress depends on the fact-finding and coordinating apparatus of the executive branch. The principle of pay comparability was adopted in 1962 to keep Federal pay levels comparable to wage scales in private industry. Based on surveys conducted by the Bureau of Labor Statistics, the Civil Service Commission evaluated the data and advised the President on what rates should be paid Federal employees. The President then recommended pay adjustments to Congress.

Delays by Congress were responsible for considerable time lags between the BLS surveys and the effective dates of new salary rates. Because of inflation in the late 1960s, delays had a particularly adverse effect. Senator McGee pointed out that legislative action had been "sporadic and in accordance with the ups and downs of election dates. To this extent it has not been even and often lagged in some categories where the realities would have recommended otherwise."

The Federal Salary Act of 1967 authorized the President to make pay adjustments to close the gap between Federal and private pay rates. In 1970, Congress finally adopted a permanent solution. The Federal Pay Comparability Act of 1970 directs the President to have a report prepared each year to compare the Federal and private rates of pay. After considering this report, along with the findings and recommendations of an Advisory Committee on Federal Pay, the President adjusts Federal pay rates in order to carry out the policy of comparability. If, because of "national emergency or economic conditions affecting the general welfare," the President considers full pay adjustment inappropriate, he shall submit an alternative plan to Congress. If Congress does not act, the alternative plan becomes effective. If either house, before the end of 30 days, adopts a resolution disapproving the President's alternative plan, the original plan goes into effect.

National Emergencies

John Locke argued that the executive had to be free, at times, to act in the absence of law and sometimes even against it, for the legislature was not always capable of acting in an emergency situation. The framers of the American constitution also recognized this special quality of the executive. Instead of having Congress "make war"—and possibly react to an emergency with such slowness as to endanger national security—Congress was granted power to "declare war." Because of this change in language, the President was expected to repel sudden attacks without waiting for legislative authorization.

In anticipation of an emergency, Congress has delegated

substantial powers to the President. During the emergency, delegation of additional functions expands Presidential power still further. And even after the emergency is over, the President retains power during the demobilization phase, until the economy is considered to be back to "normal." That phase can last for a number of years. Chapter 6 will explore this area more thoroughly.

Why have legislators acquiesced in the transfer of greater war powers to the executive branch? A very intriguing explanation appears in a committee report issued by the Senate Foreign Relations Committee in 1969. The report contends that Congress, being unprepared for America's new role as a world power, and lacking experience for the extraordinary demands made on the Constitution, chose to acquiesce and allow the executive branch to make use of expedients and extraconstitutional measures. An atmosphere of "real or contrived" urgency in recent years encouraged this legislative passivity. Congress may also have been "overawed by the cult of executive expertise." Still another factor offered was a sense of guilt remaining in the Senate because of its rejection of the Covenant of the League of Nations in 1919. That led to a kind of legislative penance for its prewar isolationism—a penance that has "sometimes taken the form of overly hasty acquiescence in proposals for the acceptance of one form or another of international responsibility."

Another frequent explanation for legislative acquiescence is based on the superior information and technical knowledge which, presumably, reside in the executive branch. As one Member of Congress said: "How the hell do we know what should be considered anyway? We mostly reflect what the military men tell us." Yet Members do not hesitate to push their views in other areas that require special expertise, such as tax policy, housing, and foreign trade. The "How do we know?" answer probably conceals another factor, namely, an unwillingness to be held politically accountable for questions of national security and military preparedness. Delegation and acquiescence are natural by-products of the better-safe-than-sorry approach.

Congress delegates power not only in time of war or threatened invasion, but also in the midst of domestic emergencies. Agencies set up during the 1930s to deal with the Depression were modeled after World War I agencies, with similar organizational structures and procedures and even some of the same personnel. When President Hoover asked Congress in 1931 for a Reconstruction Finance Corporation, there was a marked similarity between it and the War Finance Corporation. William E. Leuchtenburg has pointed out that when the RFC began operations, "it employed many of the WFC's old staff, followed its pattern and that of the wartime Treasury in financing, and even took over, with slight modifications, the old WFC forms for loan applications."

In his 1933 inaugural address, Franklin D. Roosevelt compared the Great Depression to a time of war: "we must move as a trained and loyal army willing to sacrifice for the good of a common discipline. . . ." If Congress failed to face up to the emergency, he said that he would ask for "the one remaining instrument to meet the crisis—broad Executive power to wage war against the emergency, as great as the power that would be given to me if we were in fact invaded by a foreign foe." In his first official action—proclaiming a national bank holiday—he relied on a provision of the Trading with the Enemy Act of 1917.

An atmosphere of crisis was maintained throughout the "Hundred Days," during which Congress delegated to the President broad powers over banking and currency, government economies, agriculture, home mortgages, and public works. When legislators paused to think about what they were doing, shouts of "Vote! Vote!" urged them forward. One legislator pressed for action by saying that "The house is burning down and the President of the United States says this is the way to put out the fire."

Other Presidents have also employed the metaphor of war to gain greater powers from Congress for domestic programs. One of President Johnson's first legislative actions in taking office was to state, in January 1964, that "This administration today, here and now, declares unconditional war on poverty in America. . . . It will not be a short or easy struggle, no single weapon or strategy will suffice, but we shall not rest until that war is won." Shortly thereafter he presented a legislative program on poverty, reminding Congress that on "many historic occasions the President has requested from Congress the authority to move against forces which were endangering the well-being of our country. This is such an occasion." Within a few years a new kind of war on domestic problems was announced. In his remarks at the swearing in of Ramsay Clark as Attorney General, on March 10, 1967, President Johnson declared that "America can win this war against crime and the fear that crime inspires—if America is determined to win that war. . . . I have sought, and I think I have found, a man who, as our Attorney General, will be our commander, our leader, and our general in this war on two fronts against fear."

CHECKS ON ARBITRARY EXECUTIVE ACTIONS

The nondelegation doctrine was established to guarantee accountability, yet it is clear that Congress is able to delegate almost any of its powers that the Court does not choose to call "legislative." A further loss in accountability has resulted from the President's need to subdelegate responsibilities to his departmental heads. The latter find it necessary, in turn, to subdelegate powers still further to their subordinates.

The Supreme Court has been as lenient toward subdelegation as it has been toward delegation. The Army Reorganization Act of 1920, to take but one example, provided for a classification of officers to accomplish a reduction in numbers while retaining those with the greatest competence. An officer who had been placed in a class that was not to be retained contended that the act imposed upon the President a personal, nondelegable duty to review the record of the Board of Final Classification. That task was actually being carried out by the Secretary of War. The Supreme Court, in

French v. *Weeks,* decided that such a construction would place "a burdensome, if not impossible, personal duty upon the President," and could not be so construed as the legislative intent unless Congress so stated.

Congress took steps after World War II to explicitly recognize the President's need to subdelegate some of the functions invested in him by law. Representative McCormack recalled that, during a visit to the White House, President Truman pointed to a pile of papers on his desk and said: "I have got to take that over to Blair House every night and I have to spend 3 hours going over these things and signing my name. I have to know what I am signing when I sign. Many of the duties imposed upon me I could delegate to others." A survey taken to determine the President's workload uncovered at least 1,100 statutes under which he had to act, either expressly or by inference. On the basis of this knowledge, Congress authorized the President in 1950 to subdelegate functions to his department heads, on the condition that this did not relieve him of his responsibilities. It seems apparent, however, that responsibility is lost in practice if not in law. If the President has no time personally to discharge the functions assigned him, surely he has no time to monitor all the functions that he has delegated to others. How, then, is accountability to be retained?

Statutory Guidelines

The traditional answer to the problem of accountability has been to have Congress establish clear guidelines for administrative action. Theodore J. Lowi, in *The End of Liberalism* (1969), calls for a return to the Schechter rule as the first step in replacing liberalism with what he calls Juridical Democracy. Lowi argues that the Court must once again declare invalid and unconstitutional "any delegation of power to an administrative agency that is not accompanied by clear standards of implementation."

On the other hand, Kenneth Culp Davis, an outstanding authority on administrative law, offers several reasons why clear guidelines are not always feasible or even desirable. First, legislators and their staff lack the time and the expertise to draft bills for highly specialized areas; that invites vague formulations of objectives. Second, even the experts find it difficult to develop standards that will be both specific and workable, and they prefer, for that reason, general formulations in order to give agency heads some flexibility in applying the statute to concrete problems. Third, if the statement of objectives becomes too specific, the consensus needed for legislative and Presidential support is likely to melt away. Previous supporters begin to say, "Oh, is *that* what you meant!" Furthermore, a too precise statement of objectives might make implementation troublesome:

When the society is sharply divided, when the problems are new and opinions have had insufficient time to crystallize, when biting off one concrete problem at a time is clearly preferable to trying to legislate in gross, or when sustained staffwork may contribute significantly to policy choices, a legislative body may wisely keep the policy objectives largely open. Vague or meaningless standards may then be preferable to precise and meaningful ones.

Davis suggests that the opportunity for arbitrary executive can be narrowed not necessarily by more stringent legislative standards, but rather by guides furnished by the administrators themselves. Since they have to apply statutes to specific cases on a day-to-day basis, they are often in a better position than Congress to use their rulemaking power as a means of clarifying standards and of justifying their decisions. In cases where Congress has failed to provide adequate standards, the administrative agency should be given a reasonable amount of time to do so.

Procedures for Administrative Action

Standards of due process offer a second safeguard against arbitrary executive action. Where an administrative agency provides notice and hearing prior to its ruling, supplies findings of fact in the record, and where procedures exist for appeal, the Supreme Court has permitted delegation on such general guidelines as "in the public interest," "excessive profits," "reasonable rates," and "unjust discrimination." The Administrative Procedure Act of 1946 established procedures and uniform standards for rulemaking and adjudication by Government agencies, in an effort to guarantee fairness and due process in administrative actions. Some of the major features of the Act include adequate notice to parties concerned, separation of prosecution and decision functions, and standards for judicial review.

Steps were taken within a few years to further improve administrative procedures. President Eisenhower set up an Administrative Conference in 1954, and a second temporary Conference was established in 1961 by President Kennedy. In 1964, Congress established a permanent body called the Administrative Conference of the United States to study and make recommendations on the "efficiency, adequacy, and fairness of the administrative procedure used by administrative agencies in carrying out administrative programs. . . ." The Conference did not begin its organizational work until January 1968. Since that time, it has offered a number of recommendations to improve the fairness, efficiency, and effectiveness of administrative proceedings. Among the more controversial suggestions is a proposal to provide representation of the poor in agency rulemaking which has a direct effect on them. Federal agencies are urged to engage "more extensively in affirmative, self-initiated efforts to ascertain directly from the poor their views with respect to rulemaking that may affect them substantially. For this purpose, agencies should make strong efforts, by use of existing as well as newly devised procedures, to obtain information and opinion from those whose circumstances may not permit conventional participation in rulemaking proceedings."

The extent to which administrative discretion is reviewable in the courts has been the topic of extended discussion in the law journals. The fact is, however, that the Supreme

Court has challenged a number of administrative actions in the postwar period on procedural grounds. In cases involving exclusion of aliens, dismissal of so-called security risks from Governmental service, and denial of passport privileges, the Court has played an activist role in upholding procedural safeguards. These cases will be discussed at the end of Chapter 6.

Congressional Oversight

Congress has at its disposal a number of methods for overseeing the operations of administrative agencies. It first of all exercises a "pre-oversight" role in having the Senate offer advice and consent on appointments. In statutes that create agencies, Congress can set forth qualifications for appointees, including such factors as professional attainments, occupational experience, and industrial or regional affiliations. In delegating power, statutes can provide for a waiting period to give Congress an opportunity to study administrative decisions and perhaps take adverse action through the regular legislative process. The waiting-period requirement is sometimes referred to as a "laying on the table" device.

Congress can also direct that the agency submit reports on a regular basis, consult with specified committees, and even include committees in the decision-making process. For example, an agency may be allowed to act only after it "comes into agreement" with certain committees. In other cases, Members of Congress work directly with the executive branch. The Trade Expansion Act of 1962 directed that there be two members from the House Ways and Means Committee, and two members from the Senate Finance Committee, to participate as delegates in tariff bargaining sessions.

Legislative requests for information can, at times, be denied by the Administration. Denial may be based on the need for secrecy, which was the reason offered by President Washington when he refused to give the House of Representatives certain papers regarding the Jay Treaty. Presidents have also justified the withholding of papers on the ground that it would violate the confidence and trust that must exist between the President and his assistants.

Efforts are underway to increase the amount of reporting to Congress. We have already mentioned the bill introduced by Senator Case in 1970, to provide for regular reporting of executive agreements. Senator Sam J. Ervin, Jr., recommended in 1971 that the Office of Management and Budget report instances of impounded funds on a regular basis. Also in 1971, Senator Chiles proposed that the Administration report information on the revenue that is lost because of various tax provisions. If these revenue losses were translated into positive terms, into what is called "tax expenditures," the amounts would be more visible and therefore more susceptible to congressional oversight. Another restriction in delegatory statutes would be to provide for a time limit, so that powers automatically terminate after a fixed period of time. For instance, in resolutions which involve the use of armed forces, the Senate Foreign Relations Committee recommended in 1969 that a time limit be placed on the resolution, "thereby assuring Congress the opportunity to review its decision and extend or terminate the President's authority to use military force."

The customary procedure for enacting legislation is to have Congress pass a law and allow the President to sign it or veto it. In recent decades this procedure has occasionally been reversed by the "legislative veto," which allows the President to put forth a proposal, subject to the approval or disapproval of Congress. That reverses the customary procedure for enacting legislation, and also reverses the roles of the President and Congress. The executive branch bears a larger burden of the legislative power, while Congress expands its administrative role.

The legislative veto has become increasingly immune to Presidential control, first by denying him the opportunity to override congressional action, and later by delegating the legislative veto from Congress to a single house and finally to a single committee. The first development is evident in the trend in reorganization authority for the President. In 1938, President Roosevelt asked for authority to reorganize the executive branch, subject to disapproval by a joint resolution of Congress. The latter requires the President's signature, and in the event that a joint resolution encountered a veto, legislators were pessimistic that they could muster the necessary two-thirds majority to override the President.

The following year, it was proposed that disapproval of reorganization plans take the form of a concurrent resolution. This type of action does not require the President's signature, and since he therefore had no opportunity to exercise his veto power, the question was raised as to whether a concurrent resolution would be "legislative in effect." Representative Cox argued that it would: "to say that the Congress cannot attach the condition that it is within the power of either house to vacate whatever is done under the grant is clearly unsound. The condition is part of legislation." The Reorganization Act of 1939 subsequently authorized the President to submit plans for executive reorganization. The plans would become effective after 60 days, unless within that time they were disapproved by a concurrent resolution passed by both houses of Congress.

Congress has used the concurrent resolution (passed by both houses) or the simple resolution (passed by one house) to accomplish a variety of objectives: (1) it has reserved power to terminate a statute or program by concurrent resolution; (2) it has asserted power to enable or require executive action by concurrent resolution; and (3) it has made administrative exercise of delegated power contingent upon congressional approval or disapproval by concurrent or simple resolution.

The legislative veto has gradually become more specialized: at first requiring a vote of both houses; later permitting action by a single house; and finally permitting a "veto" by a single committee. The "committee veto" obligates an executive agency to submit its program to designated committees before placing the program in operation. Both Presidents Eisenhower and Johnson expressed their opposition to the committee-veto procedure, contending that it was an invasion of administrative responsibilities. On one occasion President Johnson withheld funds from a program because an act included the committee-veto provision.

The Legislative Reorganization Act of 1946 directed each standing committee of the House and the Senate to exercise "continuous watchfulness" over the execution of laws by administrative agencies. The Act also directed the Comptroller General to make an expenditure analysis of each executive agency to enable Congress to determine whether public funds had been economically and efficiently administered. That provision was never implemented, however, since Congress failed to appropriate funds to carry it out. The Legislative Reorganization Act of 1970 reissues the same type of mandate. The Comptroller General is directed to review and analyze the results of Government programs and activities, "including the making of cost benefit studies, when ordered by either House of Congress, or upon his own initiative," or when requested by any committee having jurisdiction over such programs and activities.

The 1970 Act also provides for an increase in professional staff members for each standing committee. Cost-effectiveness analysts will be made available from the General Accounting Office. They will evaluate cost-benefit studies furnished by executive agencies and will conduct cost-benefit studies of programs under the jurisdiction of the committee. The Congressional Research Service (formerly the Legislative Reference Service) is scheduled to undergo a major expansion, both in terms of staff size and in scope of responsibilities. It will be the duty of CRS to advise committees in the analysis, appraisal, and evaluation of legislative proposals; assist in determining the advisability of enacting a proposal; estimate its probable results; and evaluate alternative methods of accomplishing the same results.

Subsequent chapters on the spending power, the taxing power, and the war power will discuss additional efforts by Congress to oversee the work of the executive branch.

4

SPENDING POWERS

Previous chapters have traced the shift of legislative power to executive officials in three steps: (1) the period from 1774 to 1787, when functions were transferred from committees to boards and finally to single executives; (2) the creation of the Presidency in 1787 as a separate branch with its own prerogatives; and (3) subsequent decades during which Federal regulation required the delegation of new authority to the executive branch.

Even if it be granted that the President has a legitimate and far-reaching role in the legislative process, a more sensitive question involves his participation in the spending and taxing powers. Were these domains marked out exclusively as a congressional preserve? To what extent have they been shifted to the Presidency? Why have these shifts occurred? This chapter, and the following, will attempt to provide some of the answers.

DEVELOPMENT OF EXECUTIVE BUDGET

The period prior to the Philadelphia Convention demonstrates the important role played by Robert Morris as Superintendent of Finance. Upon his retirement in 1784, however, the management of finances fell back to the Board of Treasury. The relative responsibilities of legislators and administrative officials in the spending power were thus in a state of flux when the new national government was being organized.

Establishing the Treasury Department

In 1789, members of the first Congress had to create the executive departments and determine their relationship to Congress. The Departments of Foreign Affairs and War were recognized as purely executive and therefore assigned directly to the President; departmental heads were under no obligation to come before Congress and present reports. Both departments had clearly retained their identity as administrative agencies during the transition from the Articles of Confederation to the Constitution. Robert Livingston and John Jay held the post of Secretary for Foreign Affairs from 1781 to 1790, while Henry Knox served as Secretary of War from 1785 to 1794.

The Treasury Department occupied a more ambiguous position. A proposal on June 25, 1789, to permit the Secretary of the Treasury to "digest and report" plans for the improvement and management of the revenue, prompted several legislators to object on the grounds that this would intrude upon the power of Congress and would abridge the privilege of the House to originate all bills for raising revenue. The attitude here was paradoxical. Congress did not recognize Treasury as a purely executive department, as was true of Foreign Affairs and War, and yet legislators were already reacting to Treasury as part of the executive branch. Representative Goodhue told his colleagues: "We certainly carry our dignity to the extreme, when we refuse to receive information from any but ourselves. It must be admitted, that the Secretary of the Treasury will, from the nature of his office, be better acquainted with the subject of improving the revenue or curtailing expense, than any other person." Congress subsequently directed the Secretary to digest and *prepare* plans for improving and managing the public revenue, and yet at the same time directed him to "prepare and report" estimates of revenue and expenditure. The Secretary was to report to either branch of Congress, in person or in writing, as required.

During debate on this bill, the House Ways and Means Committee was set up to advise Congress on fiscal matters. Within a few months the committee passed out of existence, its duties absorbed by the new Secretary of the Treasury, Alexander Hamilton. He was directed to prepare recommendations for a national bank, state debts, and the promotion of manufactures. Hamilton thus found himself in an office that he himself had anticipated earlier, in Federalist 36: "Nations in general, even under governments of the more popular kind, usually commit the administration of their finances to single men or to boards composed of a few individuals, who digest and prepare, in the first instance, the plans of taxation, which are afterwards passed into law by the authority of the sovereign or legislature."

Although Congress originally anticipated a close working relationship with the new Secretary, some members found the contact too close for comfort. Hamilton asked to come before Congress in 1792 to answer questions concerning the public debt, but legislators protested against the practice of mixing the two branches. Members objected to having the heads of departments originate legislation or even voice an opinion that might influence Congress. The legislative attack on Hamilton was unrelenting. A House resolution in 1793 charged him with violating appropriations laws, ignoring Presidential instructions, failing to discharge essential duties, and committing an indecorum against the House. Hamilton was exonerated on every count, but the criticism continued. A new charge in 1794, regarding a pension claim, was later dismissed by Congress as "wholly illiberal and groundless." Investigation of the Treasury Department persisted until Hamilton, in December 1794, satisfied his critics by announcing his intention to resign.

The assault on Hamilton was but one part of a general revolt against executive influence. Fisher Ames, a Federalist legislator, remarked that within a few years the heads of departments had been reduced to the status of chief clerks: "Instead of being the ministry, the organs of the executive power, and imparting a kind of momentum to the operation of the laws, they are precluded even from communicating with the House by reports." In place of an open system, permitting executive officials to come before Congress and explain and defend their proposals, subsequent Presidents and departmental heads worked privately with party followers in Congress.

Following Hamilton's resignation, the House revived its Ways and Means Committee to handle recommendations for taxes and appropriations. In 1802 it became a standing committee. In 1815, the Senate established a "Select Committee on Finance and an Uniform National Currency." The following year the Senate Committee on Finance became a standing committee, and within a few years it firmly established its jurisdiction over tariffs and appropriations.

During the early 1800s, Congress was able to handle the nation's finances with little difficulty. An abundance of customs revenue easily covered the modest expenses of the national government. By possessing responsibility over both revenue and appropriations, the House Ways and Means Committee, together with the Senate Finance Committee, could maintain a coherent picture of national financial needs. The small number of legislators—186 Representatives and 34 Senators in 1810—allowed discussion on the floor as well as close attention to committee work.

Annual estimates of expenditures originated in the various bureaus and agencies of the executive branch. Sometimes the Secretary of the department reviewed the estimates; often he did not, merely forwarding them to the Treasury Department. At that point they were assembled to form a "Book of Estimates" and sent on to Congress. Estimates were not compiled in a consistent manner, expenditures were not related to revenues, and there was no accompanying budget message to marshal national resources toward national goals.

An exception to this record was Jefferson's Secretary of the Treasury, Albert Gallatin. His financial policy depended on a systematic budget and close scrutiny of bureau estimates. Since his principal goals included reduction of the national debt and elimination of excise taxes, he first had to estimate the revenue from customs, postage, and public lands. From this he subtracted the annual payment on the debt to arrive at a sum of $2,650,000 to run the government. That required stringent reductions in expenditures for the naval and military establishments. His recommendations were accepted by the Cabinet and later by Congress, where he had previously served on the Ways and Means Committee. His financial reports in future years, particularly during 1807–08 and in 1811, demonstrate a continuing effort to relate estimated expenditures to anticipated revenue, and to present financial options for the questions of foreign policy facing the Administration.

Executive Control, 1812–1861

Although Gallatin had consulted with Jefferson on departmental estimates, Madison was kept less informed on financial matters, and Monroe complained that Treasury reports were being sent to Congress without first being communicated to him. Matters between Monroe and his Secretary of the Treasury, William H. Crawford, became so strained that personal communication between them ceased altogether.

John Quincy Adams was told of the dreadful confrontation that had led to the break. Crawford had visited Monroe concerning the nomination of certain customs officers. When Monroe expressed several objections, Crawford "at last rose in much irritation, gathered the papers together, and said petulantly, 'Well, if you will not appoint the persons well qualified for the places, tell me whom you will appoint, that I may get rid of their importunities.' Mr. Monroe replied with great warmth, saying that he considered Crawford's language as extremely improper and unsuitable to the relations between them; when Crawford, turning to him raised his cane, as in the attitude to strike, and said, 'You damned old scoundrel!' Mr. Monroe seized the tongs at the fireplace for self-defense, applied a retaliatory epithet to Crawford, and told him he would immediately ring for servants himself and turn him out of the house; upon which Crawford, beginning to recover himself, said he did not intend, and had not intended, to insult him, and left the house. They never met afterwards."

During his own Presidency, John Quincy Adams was kept much better informed on estimates of receipts and expenditures. At one point, when his Secretary of the Treasury pressed for reduction of departmental estimates to the lowest possible level, Adams suggested that it was advisable to include a little padding. Congressional committees felt an obligation to "retrench something from the estimates presented to them; and if some superfluity be not given them to lop off, they will cut into the very flesh of the public necessities."

The struggle between Andrew Jackson and the Second United States Bank opened a new chapter on the relative spending powers of Congress and the President. The Secretary of the Treasury was frequently treated by Congress as its agent. For instance, Congress delegated to him, rather than to the President, the responsibility for placing Government money either in the national bank or in state banks. Jackson wanted the funds deposited in state banks, but he had to remove two Secretaries of the Treasury before he could find a man who was willing to execute his plan. A Senate resolution censured Jackson for acting in what the legislators felt to be derogation of the Constitution and the laws. In defense, he contended that the Secretary of the Treasury was "wholly an executive officer" and could be removed whenever the President was no longer willing to be responsible for the Secretary's actions. Jackson regarded the safekeeping of public funds as an executive, not a legislative, responsibility.

After the Whigs gained control of the White House in 1841, William Henry Harrison warned of the "unhallowed union of the Treasury with the executive department," declaring that the essential difference between monarchy and the American Presidency was the former's control over public finances. It was a great error, he said, for the founding fathers not to have made the Secretary of the Treasury entirely independent of the President. John Tyler, on succeeding Harrison, reiterated the Whig philosophy in his inaugural address: "I deem it of the most essential importance that a complete separation should take place between the sword and the purse. No matter where or how the public moneys shall be deposited, so long as the President can exert the power of appointing and removing at his pleasure the agents selected for their custody the Commander in Chief of the Army and Navy is in fact the treasurer."

Matters changed in 1844 with the election of James K. Polk. Drawing upon his legislative experience as chairman of the Ways and Means Committee, he became an active participant in controlling departmental estimates and determining the level of Federal expenditures. In his first year in office he directed his Cabinet to pay close attention to the estimates submitted by bureau chiefs, who were, he said, "favourable to large expenditures, and in some instances included objects which were unconstitutional, especially in regard to internal improvements."

Polk's interest in budgetary matters was fully aroused two years later when he learned that his plan to call up volunteers for the Mexican crisis might have to be postponed because of insufficient funds. After an investigation pointed to the Quartermaster Department, the President said he was "astounded" by its expenditures and equally appalled by the condition of the department's books. The situation became worse when Quartermaster General Jesup returned to Washington to offer an explanation. He finally admitted to having requisitioned $2 million to be transferred to New Orleans, allowing two bankers to act as the transfer agents. They had deposited $400,000 with the quartermaster in New Orleans and retained the balance for stock speculation. Polk said the disclosure nearly made him sick.

After this experience, he redoubled his scrutiny of departmental estimates. In his last year in office, he lowered as best he could the level of Federal spending. He reviewed estimates first with Cabinet members and even with bureau chiefs in the War Department. In directing his Cabinet to eliminate padding from bureau estimates, he called attention to requests from the military departments: "These Heads of Bureau are [in] the habit of estimating for very large and sometimes extravagant sums. They do this for two reasons, first, because they suppose their own consequences depends somewhat on the sums they may [have] to disburse in their respective branches of the service during the year; and secondly, because they say their estimates may be cut down by Congress." When cutbacks by Cabinet members seemed too timid, Polk intervened to reduce items and sometimes to eliminate them altogether.

His active involvement in formulating the budget was not duplicated by his immediate successors. Of course, they extolled the virtues of frugality and economy in their annual messages, but the level and allocation of Federal spending was considered to be a legislative prerogative. And so it remained until the Civil War.

Splintering of Committee Structure

The magnitude of war finances after 1861 proved to be too great a strain on the legislative committee structure. The Senate Finance Committee's responsibility over appropriation measures was handed over to a new Committee on Appropriations in 1867. The jurisdiction of the House Ways and Means Committee had been reduced to revenue bills in 1865, with its former responsibilities assigned to two new committees: the House Appropriations Committee, and the

House Banking and Currency Committee. Proponents of this division of labor in the House credited the Ways and Means Committee with faithful and diligent service, but said that "no set of men, however enduring their patience, studious their habits, or gigantic their mental grasp, when overburdened with the labor incident to the existing monetary condition of the country growing out of this unparalleled civil strife, can do this labor as well as the people have a right to expect of their Representatives." The newly-created House Appropriations Committee was reminded that the "tendency of the time is to extravagance in private and in public," and that their full labors would be required to restrain excessive and illegal appropriations.

The House Appropriations Committee was subjected to heavy criticism over the next two decades for acquiring too much control over the programs of other committees. In addition to exercising stringent economies, the Committee was accused of introducing new legislation at the appropriation stage. Step by step its powers were reduced. For all practical purposes, the Committee on Commerce gained jurisdiction over the rivers and harbors bills in the 1870s. An effort in 1880 to restore those bills to the Appropriations Committee was rejected by the House; it gave the Committee on Commerce "the same privileges in reporting bills making appropriations for the improvement of rivers and harbors as is accorded to the Committee on Appropriations in reporting general appropriation bills." A separate Committee on Rivers and Harbors was authorized in 1883 as a standing committee. The Committee on Agriculture and Forestry gained the right, in 1880, to receive estimates and report appropriations in its area.

Splintering of the committee system continued. In 1885, the House Appropriations Committee was stripped of six additional areas: consular and diplomatic affairs, army, military academy, navy, post office, and Indian affairs. This fragmentation has been explained as an act of political retaliation against the chairman of the House Appropriations Committee, Samuel J. Randall, who had opposed his party's tariff policy. Whatever the motive, the result was greater legislative extravagance in the use of public funds. The separation of revenues and appropriations in 1865, followed by the scattering of appropriations bills among various committees, destroyed the prospects for a responsible and coherent management of public finances by Congress.

The performance of legislators throughout the 19th century, particularly during the latter half, did not strengthen the reputation of Congress as "protector of the purse." The strings were seldom tied, as land speculators, railroad men, and other business interests amassed private fortunes at the expense of public lands and public moneys. The historian Francis Wharton reported in 1858 that politicians were publicly bought and sold at the Washington brokers' board "like fancy railroad stock or copper-mine shares. . . ." Congress was especially vulnerable to criticism in its handling of rivers and harbors bills and pension bills. Significantly, in both areas it was the President who emerged as the more trusted guardian of public funds.

"Protector of the Purse"

Rivers and harbors bills constitute one reason for the growth of Presidential vetoes. Polk vetoed one in 1846, claiming that it exceeded the powers of the Federal Government and represented a "disreputable scramble for the public money. . . ." In 1847 he vetoed another rivers and harbors bill, which had begun its legislative course with a modest grant of $6,000 for Wisconsin and ended up, by the time it reached his desk, with 38 additional items at a total cost of more than a half million dollars. Polk called attention to the abuse involved in using public funds to create harbors where there were neither towns or commerce, thus enabling individuals "to build up a town or city on its margin upon speculation and for their own private advantage." While preparing his last budget, he discovered that some rivers and harbors projects had been smuggled into the Treasury estimates, and he directed that they be struck out.

In vetoing a rivers and harbors bill in 1882, President Arthur put his finger on the perverse mechanism that nourished such legislation. Citizens from one state, after learning that public revenues were being used for projects elsewhere, demanded projects for themselves. "Thus," Arthur noted, "as the bill becomes more objectionable it secures more support." Congress promptly passed the bill over his veto, but Arthur received publicity for his effort. A cartoon by Thomas Nast shows the President armed with a rifle, watching an oversized vulture, sitting atop the Capitol, consume his veto message. At the bottom of the cartoon were these words of encouragement: "President Arthur, hit him again! Don't let the vulture become our national bird."

Another heavy drain on the Treasury was the pension system, sanctified by an aura of patriotism and self-sacrifice. Both the Revolutionary War and the War of 1812 had been followed by widespread pension frauds. A House committee in 1835 reported that men "in the highest walks of life" were ready to draw money from the Treasury by means of outlandish acts of forgery and perjury. An agent dispatched from Washington in 1853 found that, out of a total of some ninety men on the pension rolls in Illinois, seventy were able-bodied.

The full measure of chicanery by pension claimants and their agents was not felt until after the Civil War. A member of the House in 1886 said that there were not enough minutes in the day to consider intelligently the thousands of private pension bills introduced each year. If only ten minutes were set aside to debate the merits of a pension claim, and if the President took ten or fifteen minutes to examine every bill that was sent him by Congress, then neither he nor the legislators would have time for anything else. Of course pension bills rarely received such scrutiny, sometimes sailing through the House at rates of two to three per minute.

Charles Francis Adams ridiculed the patriotic motives attributed to veterans of the Civil War. Far from enlisting at the call of duty, ready to sacrifice life and fortune for the good of their country, many of the men had been attracted by enlistment bounties, and many deserted the moment they were paid, departing at once for a new camp in search of additional bonuses. The number of deserters during the Civil War was officially estimated at over a half million. Adams called the soldiers "far more battle-scared than battle-scarred," and marveled at the amount of "cant and fustian—nauseating twaddle, perhaps, would not be too extreme a term," that had been used by legislators in praise of veterans.

Federal outlays for military pensions reached record heights from one decade to the next: $29 million in 1870, $57 million in 1880, $106 million in 1890, and $139 million by the turn of the century. The last veteran's benefit for the Revolutionary War was not paid out until 1906—123 years after the war had ended. Veterans met slight resistance from Congress, while Cleveland stands as the only determined counterforce among the Presidents. In his first term he vetoed 304 bills, which was almost three times as many as all the Presidential vetoes before him. A full 241 of the Cleveland vetoes were leveled at private and general pension bills.

Even these statistics do not measure the poor quality of pension legislation. Forty-two pension bills were killed by his pocket vetoes. Other bills became law without his signature simply because he lacked time to study them. On a single day in 1886 he was handed nearly 240 private bills granting new pensions, increasing their benefits, or restoring old names to the list. A check by the Pension Bureau disclosed that most of the claims had been there before and had been rejected. Some disabilities existed before the claimant's enlistment; others were not incurred in the line of duty; still others had their origin after discharge. Upon being denied funds by the Bureau, individuals turned to their congressmen and received pensions by means of private bills.

Cleveland's vetoes of pension bills in 1886 earned him a reputation for their sarcastic quality. One claimant, who enrolled in the army on March 25, 1865, entered a post hospital a week later with the measles. He returned to duty on May 8, and three days later was mustered out of the service. Cleveland observed that fifteen years after this "brilliant service and this terrific encounter with the measles," the claimant discovered that the measles had somehow affected his eyes and spinal column. Cleveland could find no possible merit to the claim. He bristled at another pension request from a widow whose husband had joined the service on October 26, 1861, only to desert several weeks later, without any record of ever having done a single day's service. "Those who prosecute claims for pension," said Cleveland, "have grown very bold when cases of this description are presented for consideration." Within the space of three days, in June 1886, he turned out forty-three pension vetoes. A Thomas Nast cartoon captures the President in his new role as protector of the purse. Cleveland is shown manfully blocking the door to the U.S. Treasury while unsuccessful pension agents slink from his presence.

Cleveland's steadfast position on pension abuses may well have cost him the 1888 election. The Grand Army of the Republic, as self-appointed spokesman for veterans, campaigned vigorously against him. The crucial loss of Indiana and New York, which Cleveland had carried in 1884, appears to have been the price of his numerous pension vetoes. The newly elected Benjamin Harrison promptly repaid the G.A.R. by appointing James Tanner, a former member of their Pension Committee, to the office of Commissioner of Pensions. Cleveland was reelected in 1892, however, and continued to decry the "barefaced and extensive pension frauds," the pension agents who urged "reckless pension expenditures, while nursing selfish schemes," and the "increasing latitude clearly discernible in special pension legislation."

Studies on Economy and Efficiency

Expenditures by the national government expanded sharply at the turn of the century. On top of pension bills and rivers and harbors projects, Federal outlays were further swelled by the Spanish War and by construction of the Panama Canal. After 28 straight years of surpluses, from 1866 to

1893, the nation was to encounter deficits for the next six years. Some surpluses appeared at the turn of the century, but a decline in customs revenue in 1904, coupled with a sharp rise in expenditures (reflecting a $50 million right-of-way payment for the Panama Canal), produced a sizable deficit for the Roosevelt Administration.

Year	Receipts	Expenditures	Surplus/Deficit
1900	$567,241,000	$520,861,000	$ 46,380,000
1901	587,685,000	524,617,000	63,068,000
1902	562,478,000	485,234,000	77,244,000
1903	561,881,000	517,006,000	44,875,000
1904	541,087,000	583,660,000	− 42,573,000

On his own initiative, President Roosevelt appointed the Keep Commission in 1905 to determine how the executive branch might conduct its affairs on the "most economical and effective basis in the light of the best modern business practices." Roosevelt criticized the military services for issuing paperwork that reduced the efficiency of fighting units, and rebuked civil departments for superfluous letter-writing. After the commission's work was under way, he again stressed the need to eliminate duplication of work, wasteful habits, and inordinate attention to paperwork. He recalled one naval officer who prided himself on his ability to determine, from a big case of papers, the number of bottles of violet ink assigned to each captain of a battleship.

As a result of larger receipts from customs and from internal revenue in 1906 and 1907, the budget moved back to a surplus, but only momentarily. Revenues fell the next year, while new legislation pushed pension costs from $139 million in 1907 to over $161 million in 1908. Heavy deficits consequently reappeared in 1908 and 1909, and another deficit of $73 million was forecast for fiscal 1910.

Responding to this new rash of deficits, Congress directed the Secretary of the Treasury in 1909 to estimate revenue for the coming year. If a deficit appeared likely, he was to recommend reductions in appropriations. If he considered that impracticable, it was his responsibility to recommend loans or new taxes to cover the deficiency. At the same time, President Taft announced that departmental estimates would be submitted to him and considered by the Cabinet in relationship to expected revenues. The Secretary of the Treasury told Congress that there could "scarcely be more scrutiny" of estimates than was given by the President and his Cabinet.

Year	Receipts	Expenditures	Surplus/Deficit
1905	$544,275,000	$567,279,000	$ − 23,004,000
1906	594,984,000	570,202,000	24,782,000
1907	665,860,000	579,129,000	86,732,000
1908	601,862,000	659,196,000	− 57,334,000
1909	604,320,000	693,744,000	− 89,423,000

In 1910, at the request of President Taft, Congress appropriated $100,000 for an investigation into more efficient and economical ways of conducting the public business. Taft used the money to set up a five-member Commission on Economy and Efficiency. Over the next two years the Commission prepared comprehensive reports on the management of the executive departments.

In June 1912, Taft submitted to Congress the commission's proposals for a national budget. A complete reversal of procedures was contemplated. Departmental estimates were no longer to be transmitted in a loosely organized report that failed to relate estimates either to revenue or to national objectives. Instead, the President would review departmental estimates and organize them into a coherent document, and the latter would serve as the basis for intelligent legislative action. The commission said that the budget was "the only effective means whereby *the Executive* may be made responsible for getting before the country a definite, well-considered, comprehensive program with respect to which *the legislature* must also assume responsibility for action or inaction."

The proposals for an executive budget were not adopted during Taft's Administration. Ironically, that was partly because of his own success in erasing the string of deficits. Expenditures were cut by Presidential review of departmental estimates, and revenue from the 1909 tariff bill exceeded any customs revenue in the history of the country.

Year	Receipts	Expenditures	Surplus/Deficit
1910	$675,512,000	$693,617,000	$ − 18,105,000
1911	701,883,000	691,202,000	10,631,000
1912	692,609,000	689,881,000	2,728,000

On June 10, 1912, President Taft directed departmental heads to prepare two sets of estimates: one for the customary Book of Estimates, and a second for the national budget recommended by his commission. Since the budgetary situation had improved, and legislators feared that Taft might use the new budget authority to reduce programs in their districts, Congress moved to block his plans. An act of August 23 directed administrative personnel to prepare estimates and submit them to Congress only in the form required by law.

The two branches had now locked horns on the budget issue, each contending that its prerogatives were being invaded. Congress considered the budget format to be part of its spending prerogative, while the President regarded the form in which he transmitted recommendations to Congress as a purely executive matter. Taft went ahead with his plan to submit two budgets, rejecting as unconstitutional the legislative directive to his administrative personnel. He reminded departmental heads once again of his request for two sets of estimates: *it is entirely competent for the President to submit a budget,* and Congress can not forbid or prevent it.* A model budget was transmitted to Congress for the fiscal year ending June 30, 1914, but was almost completely ignored. After leaving office, Taft remarked that dust was accumulating on the reports of his commission. It took the financial shock of another war to precipitate action on budget reform.

Budget and Accounting Act of 1921

Woodrow Wilson entered office with a keen interest in budget reform, but he appeared to seek coordination and accountability simply by way of centralization of the appropriations committees. On the other hand, John J. Fitzgerald, chairman of the House Appropriations Committee, called for more far-reaching change: Presidential formulation of estimates (to fix responsibility), and a system that would make it as difficult as possible for legislators to raise spending levels beyond those set by the President.

Although war in Europe diverted the Government's attention from budget reform, executive budgets were adopted by a number of states and municipal governments. Moreover, the platforms of the three major parties in 1916 all agreed on the need for budget reform at the national level. Republicans rebuked the Democratic administration for failing to enact the proposals of Taft's commission, and pledged the GOP to the establishment of a "businesslike budget system." The Progressive Party also endorsed a national budget, whereas the Democrats limited their recommendation to a return by the House to a single Appropriation Committee "as a practicable first step towards a budget system." The year 1916 also marked the creation of the Institute for Government Research, a private association set up to promote efficiency and economy in Government operations. This organization, the forerunner of the Brookings Institution, published a series of influential studies on budget reform, concluding that the "essence" of a budget was that "it shall be formulated by the executive and by the executive alone."

After 1916, World War I pushed Federal expenditures to an entirely new level, from about $700 million before the war to upwards of $12.7 billion and $18.5 billion by 1918 and 1919. Deficits reached unprecedented magnitudes. The total national debt—slightly over $1 billion in 1916—had passed beyond $25 billion by 1919. It was a foregone conclusion that debt management problems after the war would re-

quire modernization of the budget process and increased
financial responsibilities for the executive branch.

Year	Receipts	Expenditures	Surplus/Deficit
1913	$ 724,111,000	$ 724,512,000	$ − 401,000
1914	734,673,000	735,081,000	− 408,000
1915	697,911,000	760,587,000	− 62,676,000
1916	782,535,000	734,056,000	48,478,000
1917	1,124,325,000	1,977,682,000	− 853,357,000
1918	3,664,583,000	12,696,702,000	− 9,032,120,000
1919	5,152,257,000	18,514,880,000	− 13,363,623,000

In his annual message to Congress in December 1917,
President Wilson repeated his party's platform on budget reform by urging the House to centralize appropriations in a
single committee. In March 1918, Representative McCormick introduced a number of bills and resolutions calling
for unification of departmental estimates by the Secretary of
the Treasury, creation of a House budget committee to
replace the Committees on Ways and Means and Appropriations, establishment of an independent audit of departmental
accounts, and reorganization of the Treasury Department.

Critics of executive budget-making considered it a dimi-
nution of legislative power. "Uncle Joe" Cannon, Speaker of
the House from 1903 to 1911, warned that it would signify
the surrender of the most important element of representative government: "I think that we had better stick pretty
close to the Constitution with its division of powers well defined and the taxing power close to the people." Edward Fitzpatrick, another critic of the executive budget concept,
called it a step toward autocracy and a Prussian-style military
state. The executive budget in England, he said, could not
possibly serve as a model for the American system. In the
United States there was "a hiatus between the executive and
the legislature, and there is suspicion and distrust that
would prevent any such delegated legislative power as the
British practice and the American imitation propose."

President Wilson continued to withhold his public endorsement of an executive budget. From the Peace Confer-

ence in Paris, in February 1919, he cabled Swager Sherley, the new chairman of the House Appropriations Committee: "I hear you are again endeavoring to work out a budget system plan. I hope that you will succeed." But it was Wilson's position that reliable studies on the budget could begin only after Senate action on the peace treaty, for that would decide the level of defense spending, disposal of military surplus property, and demobilization of the economy.

In July 1919, the House passed a resolution by Rep. James W. Good to create a Select Committee on the Budget. The resulting committee report criticized the lack of internal executive checks on departmental estimates. Economy and efficiency could be secured only by making an officer responsible for receiving and scrutinizing the requests for funds by bureau and departmental chiefs: "In the National Government there can be no question but that the officer upon whom should be placed this responsibility is the President of the United States." A bill for an executive budget passed the House on October 21, 1919.

Wilson finally announced, on December 2, his support for an executive budget. The Senate, preoccupied with the peace treaty, did not act until the following spring. The bill that finally emerged from Congress was vetoed by Wilson because it excluded the President from the removal procedure as it applied to the comptroller general and his assistant. Congress had provided for removal solely by impeachment or by concurrent resolution. Wilson regarded Presidential removal power as an "essential incident" of the appointing power of the President.

Congress passed a new bill early in 1921, placing the budget bureau in the Treasury Department and authorizing the President to appoint his own budget director. Removal of the comptroller general and his assistant was to be done by joint resolution, a procedure that requires the signature of the President. On June 10, marking an end to a 130-year dispute over the meaning of the separation doctrine and the spending prerogative, Warren G. Harding signed the Budget and Accounting Act.

Centralization of Budget Controls

Both Congress and the President have centralized their controls over the budget. In 1920, the House acted to consolidate jurisdiction over all appropriations in a single committee. In 1922, the Senate changed its rules to give appropriations jurisdiction to a single committee. This appearance of centralization was offset by the substantial degree of autonomy enjoyed by the appropriations subcommittees. Partly because of the intense specialization required in each subcommittee, there exists a norm of reciprocity according to which the full committee is expected to defer to subcommittee recommendations.

Centralization of budget controls in the executive branch has involved a number of steps. The first budget director, Charles G. Dawes, issued a circular in 1921 setting forth procedures for establishing reserves and for effecting savings. Appropriations from Congress were to be treated as mere ceilings on expenditures, rather than as directives to spend the full amount.

Economic collapse in 1929 led to broader Presidential authority over expenditures. The Economy Act of 1933 authorized the President to reduce veterans' benefits and salaries of Federal employees. Acting under authority of that act, President Roosevelt issued Executive Order 6166 to reorganize, transfer, and abolish certain executive agencies and functions. Roosevelt's order transferred the functions of "making, waiving, and modifying apportionments of appropriations" from departmental heads and bureau chiefs to the budget director. Instead of having individual bureau chiefs adjust apportionment schedules to satisfy their constituencies, such decisions were centered in the budget director and the President.

A reorganization bill passed in 1939 directed the President to effect savings by consolidating or abolishing agencies for more efficient operation. Reorganization would take effect after 60 days unless voted down by concurrent resolution. Roosevelt strengthened his control over the budget by using the reorganization authority to transfer the Budget Bureau from the Treasury to the newly formed Executive Office of the President.

The final step toward centralization of control under the President began in March 1970, when President Nixon proposed that the Bureau of the Budget be replaced by an Office of Management and Budget (OMB). The President explained that the dominant concern of the new agency would not be preparation of the budget but rather "assessing the extent to which programs are actually achieving their intended results, and delivering the intended services to the intended recipients."

Congress was not upset by the change in name of the new agency or by the greater emphasis on program evaluation. The disturbing factor in the reorganization plan was this: the functions previously vested by law in the Bureau of the Budget, or in its director, were to be transferred to the President. He could then re-delegate those functions to someone who was not subject to the Senate's appointment responsibilities. That marked a significant departure from the McCormack Subdelegation Act of 1950, which authorized the President to delegate his statutory functions only to agency heads and to officers who were appointed with the Senate's consent.

The House Committee on Government Operations, to which President Nixon's reorganization plan was referred, recommended that it be rejected. The Committee pointed out that there were at least 58 statutory provisions whereby Congress placed specific functions in the Bureau of the Budget. Since Congress created the Bureau, and had prescribed certain powers and duties for it, Congress could reasonably expect the Bureau to report and give an account of its performance. In contrast, the degree of legislative oversight over the new Office of Management and Budget would be less. The Committee observed that Congress "cannot expect quite the same response when the self-same statutory functions are vested in the President, for the President represents the head of a separate branch of Government. . . ."

Although the House Committee on Government Operations voted 20 to 9 to reject the reorganization plan, the House upheld the President on May 13, 1970, by a vote of 193 to 164.

Spending Ceilings

Federal responsibility for economic stability—tacitly admitted during the 1930s and during World War II—received official acknowledgment with the Employment Act of 1946. Explicit objectives of the Act included the promotion of maximum employment, production, and purchasing power. Although control of inflation was not mentioned specifically (a postwar depression seemed more likely), price stability could be inferred from the goal of maximum purchasing power and the development of policies to "avoid economic fluctuation." The fact is that all postwar Presidents have interpreted the Act to include Federal responsibility for combating inflation. The question was whether that responsibility would be discharged by Congress or by the President.

Prior to 1950, the President's authority to spend less than Congress appropriated had been drawn initially from the Budget Bureau's interpretation of the Budget and Accounting Act. That interpretation was later fortified by Executive Order 6166 issued in 1933 by President Roosevelt. The 1950 omnibus appropriations act elaborated further on the Budget Bureau's authority to set aside funds: "In apportioning any appropriation, reserves may be established to provide for contingencies, or to effect savings whenever savings are made possible by or through changes in requirements, greater efficiency of operations, or other developments subsequent to the date on which such appropriation was made available."

The meaning of "changes in requirements" and "other developments" has been interpreted broadly to include inflationary pressures. Representative Mahon told the House in

1967 that President Johnson had impounded funds the previous year when "we had inflationary problems, and a changing condition following the time the appropriations were
made, and I assume the President relied upon the portion of
the law [the 1950 omnibus appropriations act] to which I
have referred."

In the fall of 1967, Congress considered a proposal to direct the President to cut spending by $5 billion. Central to
the debate was the issue of who should be held responsible
for cutting the budget: Congress or the President. Ironically,
it was the Republicans—traditional critics of executive
power—who chose to delegate that responsibility to the
President. Democrats in the House voted against the proposal 155 to 67, while Republicans lined up 171 in favor and
only 9 opposed.

The Senate refused to go along with the $5 billion man-
datory reduction. Between late October and December 6,
House and Senate conferees met six times in search of a compromise solution, but to no avail. The conference report attributed the deadlock to the "extremely complex and controversial nature of broad reduction propositions" and to the
Administration's pending tax surcharge request. On the
basis of an acceptable budget-cutting formula put forth by
the Administration, Congress directed a spending cut of $4.3
billion. Congress reduced spending by $1.8 billion, leaving
the President with the responsibility for trimming off an additional $2.5 billion.

The Revenue and Expenditure Control Act of June
1968 combined a surtax with a spending ceiling of $180.1
billion. The ceiling required a $6 billion reduction in the
Administration's budget for fiscal 1969. Congress accepted
responsibility for making about half of the mandatory cut,
while additional cutbacks by the Johnson and Nixon Administrations brought total reductions to $8.4 billion. How-
ever, that was largely offset by increases elsewhere in the
budget. Areas exempted from the expenditure control (Vietnam operations, interest on the debt, veterans services and
benefit payments, and payments from social security trust

funds) increased by $5.4 billion. Still other exceptions to the expenditure control were added later by Congress: price support payments, public assistance grants to states, and school assistance to impacted areas. The total increase in exempted and excepted areas came to $6.9 billion. As a result, the *net* reduction represented only $1.5 billion, and budget outlays totaled $184.6 billion instead of the "ceiling" of $180.1 billion.

Congress adopted a more stringent method of control in July 1969, setting the spending ceiling for fiscal 1970 at $191.9 billion (a billion below President Nixon's request), but this time allowing no exemptions. As a substitute, Congress permitted the President some flexibility by authorizing him to raise the ceiling by as much as $2 billion to cover certain "uncontrollable" items: interest on the public debt, farm price supports, Medicare, and other social insurance trust funds not subject to administrative control. The ceiling could thus range from $191.9 billion to $193.9 billion.

Two factors combined to frustrate the spending ceiling. In the first place, Congress retained for itself the freedom to add funds to the President's budget, producing what President Nixon called a "rubber ceiling." In the second place, "uncontrollables" increased beyond the $2 billion that were allowed. Actual outlays for fiscal 1970 came to $196.6 billion, compared to the initial $193.9 billion ceiling.

Congress adopted another spending ceiling the next year for the fiscal 1971 budget. The "ceiling" of $200.8 billion was subject to two adjustments: increases voted on by Congress, and a cushion of $4.5 billion to cover certain uncontrollables. When the Nixon Administration first submitted its budget, it predicted a small surplus of $1.3 billion. Actually, a "surplus" was possible only because of a change in the budget format. The "unified budget"—first used in fiscal 1969—now takes into account all Federal activities, including trust funds. These are funds held in trust for such programs as social security, unemployment compensation, railroad retirement, and highways. The amount of funds held in trust regularly exceeds the amounts that must go out.

In recent years, the surplus for trust funds has been in the neighborhood of $8 to $10 billion.

Even with a trust fund surplus of that magnitude, the fiscal 1971 budget faced a deficit. Expenditures continued to climb; revenues fell short of expectations. Instead of the modest surplus of $1.3 billion, it was widely predicted by congressmen and private economists that the budget would be in the red by more than $10 billion. That was confirmed in January 1971, when President Nixon presented the new budget. The estimated deficit was now placed at $18.6 billion. By the time the fiscal year had ended, however, receipts declined still further to produce a deficit of *$23.2 billion*. Omitting the borrowed trust fund surplus of $7 billion, the deficit on a Federal funds basis actually came to $30.2 billion. Budget outlays exceeded the spending ceiling by $6.3 billion (*Table 2*).

Table 2 Results of Spending Ceilings
for 1969–1971
(in billions)

Fiscal Year	Initial Ceiling	Budget Outlays
1969	$180.1	$184.6
1970	$193.9	$196.6
1971	$205.3	$211.6

Just as deficits in previous years had been offset and partially hidden by the trust fund surpluses, a new change in the budget format promised similar results. The new format was the "full employment budget," which is the budget that would exist if the economy operated at full employment and therefore produced larger revenues. The concept had been debated by earlier Administration officials as a technique for placing greater emphasis on a balanced economy rather than on a balanced budget. President Nixon's first budget to Congress, in February 1970, advocated the latter: "I have pledged to the American people that I would submit a balanced budget for 1971. . . . The budget I send to you today —the first for which I bear full responsibility as President

—fulfills that pledge." A year later, facing a deficit of impressive proportions, and after heavy unemployment had contributed to the discouraging 1970 election results, he became the first President to use the full employment budget concept in a budget presentation. The occasion was propitious. In full employment budget terms, a deficit of $23.2 billion was transformed into a "surplus" of $2.5 billion (the Administration estimated that a full employment economy would have generated $214.1 billion in revenues).

EXECUTIVE SPENDING DISCRETION

On the basis of the Constitution and traditional legislative prerogatives, Congress lays claim to exclusive control over the purse. Nevertheless, while it is up to Congress to appropriate funds, it is also true that the President and executive officials enjoy considerable discretion as to how those funds are spent. It is a mistake to regard executive spending discretion as essentially a 20th century phenomenon, originating with the Budget and Accounting Act. Administrative discretion over the expenditure of public funds has been a fact of life since the first Administration, as will be evident from the following examples.

Lump-sum Appropriations

It is commonly believed that the Federalists and the Jeffersonian Republicans divided sharply on the question of lump-sum appropriations. We are told that the Jeffersonians advocated specific appropriations as a means of maintaining legislative control, while the Federalists wanted lump-sum appropriations to permit executive discretion. This belief is not borne out by the facts.

The first appropriation act of 1789 provided lump sums for four general classes of expenditures: $216,000 for the civil list; $137,000 for the Department of War; $190,000 to discharge warrants issued by the previous Board of Treasury; and $96,000 for pensions to disabled veterans. The appropriation acts for 1790 and 1791 also provided lump sums, but the funds were to be spent in accordance with estimates given Congress by the Secretary of the Treasury. His estimates, of course, had been broken down into specific items.

Beginning with the appropriation act of December 23, 1791, Congress narrowed executive discretion still further by using a "that is to say" clause. For instance, a little over a half million was appropriated for the military establishment —"that is to say," $102,686 for pay of troops, $48,000 for clothing, $4,152 for forage, and so forth. By 1793, appropriation acts were descending to such minutiae as an item of $450 for firewood, stationery, printing, and other contingencies in the Treasurer's office. Thus, long before the Jeffersonians had gained control of the Presidency, the practice of granting lump sums had been abandoned.

The dispute between the Federalists and the Jeffersonians is grounded more in party rhetoric than in administrative reality. After Jefferson's election as President in 1801, he told Congress that it would be prudent to appropriate "specific sums to every specific purpose susceptible of definition." Hamilton promptly denounced that recommendation as "preposterous," insisting that nothing was "more wild or of more inconvenient tendency. . . ." The biting quality of Hamilton's attack no doubt reflected his assumption that Jefferson's message to Congress was an indirect criticism of Federalist financial policies. Understandably, Hamilton was quick to take offense. Moreover, Jefferson was in error on two counts: first for implying that lump-sum appropriations had been the practice in the past, and second for suggesting that sums should be appropriated for every purpose susceptible of definition.

Jefferson's Secretary of the Treasury, Albert Gallatin, knew that it was impossible for Congress to foresee, "in all its details, the necessary application of moneys, and a reasonable discretion should be allowed to the proper executive department." Instead of $1,857,242 being appropriated for the War Department, Gallatin had simply wanted such a sum broken down into smaller categories—$488,076 for officers' pay and subsistence, $400,000 for ammunition and arms, $141,530 for clothing, and so forth. There was nothing at all novel about that suggestion; appropriation acts had been passed with that level of detail since December 23, 1791. Jefferson himself, as President, recognized that "too minute a specification has its evil as well as a too general one," and thought it better for Congress to appropriate in gross while trusting in executive discretion.

Lump-sum appropriations become particularly noticeable during emergency periods of war or national depression. During the Civil War, Congress appropriated $50 million to pay two- and three-year volunteers; $26 million for subsistence; another $14 million for transportation and supplies; and $76 million to cover an assortment of items, to be divided among them "as the exigencies of the service may require. . . ." During World War I, Wilson received $100 million for "national security and defense"—to be spent at his discretion—and $250 million to be applied to construction costs under the Emergency Shipping Fund.

Emergency relief programs during the Great Depression set aside billions to be spent at the President's discretion. Congress appropriated $950 million in 1934 for emergency relief programs and the Civil Works Program, making the money available "for such projects and/or purposes and under such rules and regulations as the President in his discretion may prescribe. . . ." The Emergency Relief Appropriation Act of 1935 appropriated $4 billion for eight general classes of projects, the money to be used "in the discretion and under the direction" of the President. Appropriations for World War II included such lump sums as $6.3 billion for the increase and replacement of naval vessels, and $23.6 billion for the Army Air Corps. A general description accompanied these appropriations, but the figures were not broken down.

The atomic bomb project was financed for several years from funds for "Engineer Service, Army" and "Expediting Production." When larger sums for manufacturing the bomb could no longer be concealed by this method, a few legislative leaders were told of the project and asked to provide funds without letting other legislators know how the money would be spent. Accordingly, the money was tucked away unnoticed in an appropriation bill. Total appropriations for the Manhattan Project came to over $2 billion. Members of the House Appropriations Committee told one writer that about $800 million had been spent on the project before they knew about it.

The public works appropriation act of 1970 makes available a lump sum of $1.9 billion to the Atomic Energy Commission. Instead of breaking down the figure into individual line items, there exists a moral understanding between the Commission and the appropriations subcommittees involved. The money is expected to be spent fairly much in accordance with the Commission's budget estimates, as amended by congressional actions and directives included in committee reports. This kind of nonstatutory control depends on a "keep the faith" attitude among agency officials, as well as a trust by the subcommittees in the integrity of administrators. If the AEC were to violate that trust and abuse its discretionary power, it would face the prospect the next year of budget cutbacks and line-item appropriations.

Contingency Funds. Congress realizes that future events cannot be anticipated—or anticipated with great precision —and that it must therefore provide special funds to cover contingencies and emergencies. Emergency funds were particularly large during World War II. In statutes from June 13, 1940, to October 26, 1942, Congress appropriated a total of $425 million in funds for "emergencies affecting the national security and defense," plus another $320 million in funds for temporary shelters in areas suffering from housing shortage because of the war.

Contingency funds have been used for purposes not even contemplated by Congress when it appropriated the money. For instance, on March 1, 1961, President Kennedy issued an executive order establishing the Peace Corps. Not until seven months later did Congress appropriate funds for the agency. In the meantime, the President financed the agency by using contingency funds from the Mutual Security Act. Also in 1961, the Foreign Assistance Act provided a contingency fund of $275 million, to be used by the President "when he determines such use to be important to the national interest." The contingency fund for foreign aid the next year was set at $250 million.

The Department of Defense Appropriations Act of 1965 made available $1.7 billion for an Emergency Fund for Southeast Asia. The executive branch enjoyed complete discretion. Upon determination by the President that such action was necessary in connection with military activities, the Secretary of Defense could transfer the money to any appropriation available to the Defense Department for military functions.

Other sources of emergency funds are found in statutes providing for disaster relief. The Federal Disaster Act of 1950 and subsequent statutes offer financial assistance to state and local governments whenever the President declares a major disaster. From 1951 through 1970, the President issued 338 declarations and allocated $857 million from the disaster relief fund.

Free World Forces. The financing of the Vietnam war illustrates how billions can be spent for purposes known to relatively few legislators. In September 1966, President Johnson expressed his "deep admiration as well as that of the American people for the action recently taken by the Philippines to send a civic action group of 2,000 men to assist the Vietnamese in resisting aggression and rebuilding their country." Other announcements from the White House created the impression that not only had the Philippines volunteered troops, but so had Thailand, South Korea, and other members of the "Free World Forces."

Hearings held by the Symington Subcommittee in 1969 and 1970 revealed that the United States had offered sizable subsidies to these countries. It was learned that the Philippines had received river patrol craft, engineer equipment, a special overseas allowance for their soldiers sent to Vietnam, and additional equipment to strengthen Philippine forces at home. The total cost to the United States for the sending of one Philippine construction battalion to Vietnam came to $38.8 million. Senator Fulbright remarked that it was his own feeling that "all we did was go over and hire their soldiers in order to support our then administration's view that so many people were in sympathy with our war in Vietnam."

The Philippine Government denied that U.S. contributions represented a subsidy or a fee in return for sending the construction battalion, but an investigation by the General Accounting Office (GAO) confirmed the fact that "quid pro quo assistance" had indeed been given to the Philippines. Moreover, there was evidence that the Johnson Administration had increased other forms of military and economic aid to the Philippines in return for the battalion.

The Symington Subcommittee also uncovered an agreement that the Johnson Administration had made with the Royal Thai Government, in 1967, to cover any additional costs connected with the sending of Thai soldiers to Vietnam. An interim GAO report estimated that the U.S. Government had invested "probably more than $260 million in equipment, allowances, subsistence, construction, military sales concessions, and other support to the Thais for their contribution under the Free World Military Assistance program to Vietnam."

U.S. subsidies were used once again to support the sending of South Korean forces to Vietnam. American assistance included equipment to modernize Korean forces at home; equipment and all additional costs to cover the deployment of Korean forces in Vietnam (including the payment of overseas allowances); additional loans from the Agency of International Development; and increased ammunition and communications facilities in Korea. For the period from fiscal 1965 to fiscal 1970, U.S. costs resulting from the dispatch of Korean forces to Vietnam were estimated at $927.5 million. Until the Symington Subcommittee hearings, few Members of Congress were aware of this financial arrangement.

Transfers between Classes

Transfer authority permits the President to take funds that have been appropriated for one class of appropriations and apply them to another. In 1793, Representative Giles offered a number of resolutions charging Hamilton with improper use of national funds. The first resolution stated that "laws making specific appropriations of money should be strictly observed by the administrator of the finances thereof." Representative Smith of South Carolina proceeded to refute Giles point by point, arguing that the Administration ought to be free to depart from congressional appropriations whenever the public safety or credit would thereby be improved. When exercised for the public good, executive spending discretion would "always meet the approbation of the National Legislature." All the Giles resolutions were subsequently voted down by the House.

This appears to be a typical collision between the legislative and executive branches, but the dispute was not so much constitutional as it was partisan and personal. It was Hamilton's colleague in the Cabinet, Thomas Jefferson, who had drafted the resolutions for Giles. The author of Smith's effective rebuttal? Why, none other than Hamilton himself.

Jefferson's strictures against transfers were excessively narrow and failed to curb the practice. During his own Administration, Representative Bayard explained that it was sometimes necessary to allow expenditures to deviate from appropriations, by transferring funds from one account to another. Such transfers were technically illegal, but "its being the custom palliates it." Proposals to abolish transfers altogether were countered by two arguments. Secretary of the Treasury Crawford told Congress in 1817 that in receiving reports of transfers, legislators automatically learned where appropriations had been redundant and where deficient, thereby providing a convenient guide for future appropriation bills. Second, removal of transfer authority would compel executive departments to submit inflated estimates as a cushion against unexpected expenses. Crawford warned Congress: "The idea that economy will be enforced by repealing the provision will, I am confident, be found to be wholly illusory. Withdraw the power of transfer, and the Departments will increase their estimates."

Statutes over the next few decades permitted transfers under various circumstances. Beginning in 1860, departmental heads were prohibited from using surplus funds to cover deficiencies in other accounts, but that restriction had little impact after the outbreak of the Civil War. General lump-sum appropriations during the war gave departmental heads adequate flexibility. In 1868, Congress repealed all previous acts authorizing transfers, and stipulated that "no money appropriated for one purpose shall hereafter be used for any other purpose than that for which it is appropriated."

Nevertheless, Congress has found it necessary at times to delegate broad transfer authority to the Administration. The 1932 Economy Act cut Federal spending so hastily and in such indiscriminate fashion that Congress permitted the executive branch to transfer funds from one agency to another to repair the damage. The Lend Lease Act of 1941 appropriated $7 billion for ordnance, aircraft, tanks, and for other categories of defense articles. The President could transfer as much as 20 percent of the appropriations from one category to another, provided that no appropriation would be increased by more than 30 percent. In 1943, the Budget Director was authorized to transfer 10 percent of military appropriations made available for fiscal 1944, subject to certain conditions. Appropriations in that particular act came to about $59 billion.

Aid to Cambodia. Current law provides that "Except as otherwise provided by law, sums appropriated for the various branches of expenditures in the public service shall be applied solely to the objects for which they are respectively made, and for no others." Exceptions to this general rule are fairly common. Appropriations for the Defense Department and for foreign assistance are especially generous in permitting the transfer of funds. It was on the basis of transfer authority that President Nixon was able to extend financial assistance to Cambodia after his intervention there in the spring of 1970. At the end of the year, he appealed to Congress for $255 million in military and economic assistance for Cambodia. Of that amount, $100 million was to restore funds which the President had *already* diverted to Cambodia from other programs.

He was able to do that because under Section 610 of the Foreign Assistance Act, the President may transfer up to 10 percent of the funds of one foreign aid program to another, provided that the second program is not increased by more than 20 percent. Operating under that authority, the Nixon Administration borrowed $40 million from aid programs originally scheduled for Greece, Turkey, and Taiwan; took another $50 million from funds that had been assigned largely to Vietnam; and diverted still other funds, until a total of $108.9 million in military assistance had been given —or committed—to Cambodia.

Reprograming. Reprograming is a term used to describe the shifting of funds *within* an appropriation item. Reprograming differs from transfers in two respects. Unlike transfers, funds are not shifted from one account to another. The total amount available in an account remains constant under reprograming, while the purpose to which funds are applied can be changed. Second, reprograming, while it must conform to the general appropriation language, does not require specific statutory authority, as is the case with transfers. Instead, an informal clearance procedure takes place between executive agencies and legislative committees, as a means of providing required flexibility, and of meeting contingencies, emergencies, new requirements, and other urgent developments.

The reprograming technique recognizes that during the interval between an agency's justification of a program and its actual expenditure of funds, new and better applications of the money might come to light. Especially is that true of the Defense Department, where various factors can often dictate that funds be used in a different manner than called for in an appropriations bill. In recent years, military reprograming generally runs over a billion dollars a year. When a new Administration takes office, the figure can be considerably higher. For instance, several budget revisions by the Kennedy Administration brought the fiscal 1961 reprograming figure for the Defense Department to $3.8 billion. That includes reprograming actions only on major procurement and for research, development, test, and evaluation.

In the past decade and a half, Congress has gradually tightened its control over the reprograming of funds. In 1955 the House Committee on Appropriations insisted that the Defense Department submit semi-annual reports on all reprograming actions. A 1959 report by House Appropriations observed that semi-annual tabulations had been helpful but not sufficiently timely. The Committee directed the Defense Department to report periodically—but in no case less than 30 days after departmental approval—the approved reprograming actions involving $1,000,000 or more in the case of operation and maintenance; $1,000,000 or more for research, development, test, and evaluation; and $5,000,-000 or more in the case of procurement.

In 1963, in response to the Committee's request for an immediate revision of reprograming procedures, the Defense Department called for prior approval by committees, not only by the appropriations committees but by authorizing committees as well. Prior approval of selected items and programs was required of the House and Senate Committees on Armed Services and of the House and Senate Committees on Appropriations. In an effort to bring reprograming under broader legislative review, Senator Chiles introduced a bill in 1971 to require the Comptroller General to compile information on reprograming and to furnish such information to all committees and to all Members of Congress.

Transfers in Time

In addition to being transferred from one class to another, funds may be transferred from one year to the next. Congress enacted a law in 1795 to restrict this practice. With certain exceptions, any unexpended funds remaining in the Treasury for more than two years were to be transferred to a surplus fund, at which point the appropriation would lapse. Administrative actions quickly nullified the law's intent. For instance, Congress passed legislation in 1819 to suppress the slave trade and to punish crimes of piracy. In so doing, it neglected to appropriate funds to finance these new responsibilities. President Monroe supplied the necessary vessels by using old balances remaining on the books of the Navy Department. When legislators objected that this violated the two-year limit on appropriations, they were told that the balances were exempt from the law because they had been in the hands of the *Treasurer* (who acted as agent for the military departments), rather than being in the Treasury itself.

An 1820 statute directed the Secretary of the Treasury to place funds that had been left unexpended by the Departments of War and Navy into a surplus fund. Implementation of that statute, however, depended on a statement by the Secretary of the department that "the object for which the appropriation was made has been effected." Failure to make that declaration meant that the money still remained available for future use.

A more stringent provision appeared in 1852. Congress directed that any moneys unexpended after two years should be carried immediately to a surplus fund and the appropriation regarded as having ceased. Decisions by the Attorney General diluted the force of the statute. In cases of contracted items, personal service, or other claims on the Government, appropriations would remain available from year to year until the obligation was fully discharged. In such situations "unexpended" came to mean "unobligated," and the appropriation would not lapse into the surplus fund. In a second decision, the Attorney General held that a department could spend any balance on hand from the previous year. According to that rule of construction, it would be impossible for a balance of two or more years to exist "unless the balance of a previous year exceed in amount the whole expenditure of the present year. . . ."

New statutes appeared in 1870 and 1874 to restrict the use of unexpended balances. Specifically excluded from those restrictions were appropriations for projects that usually take more than two years to complete. Current law, for instance, permits appropriations to "remain available until expended" for public works under the Bureau of Yards and Docks and for public buildings. Such appropriations are referred to as no-year money.

No-year money permits the President to release funds when he determines that they can be spent in the most effective manner, depending on the availability of labor, of materials, and on the state of technical developments. In the Department of Defense, appropriations for procurement and for research, development, test, and evaluation (R.D.T.&E.) have generally been made available on a no-year basis. For fiscal 1970, the amount of no-year funds for those categories came to $25.5 billion. The fiscal 1971 appropriation bill for the Defense Department brought carryover balances under closer control. Appropriations for major procurement became available for only three fiscal years (except for shipbuilding, which requires a five-year term), while appropriations for R.D.T.&E. were made available only for a two-year period. In order to "dry up" the large amounts of no-year funds available from prior years, this kind of restriction would have to be enacted for about three straight years.

Despite legislative concern about carryover balances, and the existence of statutory restrictions, a huge volume of funds continues to flow from one year to the next. For fiscal 1972, an estimated $259.5 billion in unspent authority remained available from prior years. Of that amount, only $87.4 billion was expected to be spent in fiscal 1972. The remainder will be carried forward to later years.

Speeding up Expenditures. In addition to stretching out the period for making expenditures, Presidents can also speed up expenditures. Accelerated spending was employed in 1958 as an anti-recession measure by the Eisenhower Administration. Public works were accelerated, Housing and Home Finance programs speeded up, and Government supply levels raised—all in an effort to pump more money into the economy and stimulate recovery. Advance procurement adds to the cost of storage space and inventory checks, however, and also creates administrative complications by forcing agencies to depart from prior schedules and long-term contractual commitments. Moreover, with a fixed amount appropriated for programs, acceleration must at some point be offset by deceleration, unless new funds are provided. Thus, at the very moment when the recovery phase needs reinforcement, the depletion of allotted funds has a retarding effect. That is especially serious, since the automatic stabilizers, in the recovery phase, reverse direction and have a retarding effect of their own.

In 1961, President Kennedy also relied on accelerated programs to combat recession. He directed the Veterans Administration to speed up the payment of $258 million in life insurance dividends, making the money available in the first quarter instead of over the entire year. A special dividend payment of $218 million was made later, thereby reinforcing the speed-up with new funds and contributing a permanent boost to the economy. Kennedy also directed the heads of each department to accelerate procurement and construction wherever possible; he hastened payments to farmers under the price support program; increased the annual rate of free food distribution to needy families (from about $60 million to more than $200 million); and made immediately available to the states the balance of Federal-aid highway funds ($724 million) that had been scheduled for the entire fiscal year.

Impoundment

Impoundment of funds is a "transfer in time" that deserves separate treatment. During the past three decades, Presidents have withheld funds from such programs as the B-70 bomber, Air Force groups, antimissile systems, flood control projects, highways, supercarriers, urban renewal, and Model Cities. By refusing to spend appropriated funds, the President provokes the charge that he is obligated under the

Constitution to execute the laws, not hold them in defiance —obligated to interpret appropriation bills not as mere permission to spend but rather as a mandate to spend as Congress directs. Otherwise, the argument runs, he encroaches upon the spending prerogatives of Congress, violates the doctrine of separated powers, and assumes unto himself a power of item veto neither sanctioned by the Constitution nor granted by Congress.

A number of law journal articles, in advancing this line of argument, invoke phrases from Supreme Court decisions to bolster their case. I have examined these decisions and find that they have only the most tenuous relationship to the issue of impoundment. The decisive appeal over the years has not been to legal principles and Court decisions. As one writer has put it, the President "can and may withhold expenditure of funds to the extent that the political milieu in which he operates permits him to do so."

Political leverage is maximized, naturally, by claims of constitutional support, and both sides therefore invoke the separation doctrine and "intent of the framers" to their own advantage. Thus, when Congress appropriates and the President refuses to spend, legislators chastise him for encroaching upon their spending prerogatives. And yet if Congress tried to compel the President to spend the funds, he could charge usurpation of executive responsibilities.

Instead of introducing into this discussion pieces of evidence from prior Court decisions, I think it is more instructive to understand the larger political and legal framework within which impoundment takes place. Certain statutes require that funds be withheld under conditions and circumstances spelled out by Congress. Title VI of the 1964 Civil Rights Act empowers the President to withhold funds from Federally financed programs in which there is discrimination by race, color, or national origin. Special desegregation grants may be terminated when school districts violate civil rights requirements. A 1968 act requires states to update their welfare payment standards to reflect cost-of-living increases; failure to comply with the act can lead to a cutoff of

Federal welfare aid. The Revenue and Expenditure Control Act of 1968 required expenditure reductions, most of which were achieved by administrative action. Spending ceilings and debt limit requirements provide other opportunities to withhold funds.

By law, the President is expected to set aside funds for contingencies, or to effect savings whenever they are made possible, "by or through changes in requirements, greater efficiency of operations, or other developments" that take place after funds have been appropriated. The Department of Housing and Urban Development suspended a mortgage-subsidy program in January 1971 after the discovery of widespread abuses. President Eisenhower impounded funds for the production of antiballistic missiles, insisting that funds should not be released until developmental tests were satisfactorily completed.

When the President impounds funds to prevent deficiencies or to effect savings, few legislators are likely to challenge him. George H. Mahon, chairman of the House Appropriations Committee, has said that "the weight of experience and practice bears out the general proposition that an appropriation does not constitute a mandate to spend every dollar appropriated. . . . I believe it is fundamentally desirable that the Executive have limited powers of impoundment in the interests of good management and constructive economy in public expenditures."

Cases have arisen in the past, and will arise in the future, where the President withholds funds on the basis of what he considers to be "good management and constructive economy," whereas Congress looks at the issue in an entirely different manner. In 1961, Congress added $180 million to the $200 million requested by the Kennedy Administration for the development of the B-70 bomber. Defense Secretary McNamara, stressing the U.S. advantage over the Soviets in bombers and the deterrent capability of American missile strength, refused to release the unwanted funds. The following year the House Armed Services Committee threatened to "direct" the Administration to spend money toward production, but later removed the language at the urging of President Kennedy. Even if Congress had gone through with its threat to mandate expenditures, the President could well have argued that there were too many developmental unknowns, too many technical questions unsolved, and therefore no justification for proceeding beyond the prototype stage.

In such situations it is contended that the President thwarts the will of Congress. It is not always easy, however, to know what that will is. President Truman's impoundment of Air Force funds in 1949 would appear to be a clear denial of legislative intent, and yet the situation was not at all that simple. The House had voted to increase Air Force funds, while the Senate sided with the President in opposing the increase. The matter lay deadlocked in conference committee, with adjournment close at hand and the military services in need of funds to meet their payrolls. A Senate motion to vote continuing appropriations was rejected by the House. To break the impasse, the Senate reluctantly accepted the extra Air Force funds, but with the understanding, as Senator Thomas said, that "if the money is appropriated it may not be used" by the President. In light of that legislative history, it is clearly an exaggeration to claim that impoundment in this case was a denial of "the will of Congress."

In the cases cited thus far, funds have been withheld either in response to specific statutory directives or on grounds of prudent use of funds in weapons procurement. An entirely different situation has developed under the Nixon Administration, where funds have been withheld from domestic programs because the President considers those programs incompatible with his own set of budget priorities. In the spring of 1971, the Nixon Administration announced that it was withholding more than $12 billion, most of which consisted of highway money and funds for various urban programs. When Secretary Romney appeared before a Senate committee in March, he explained that funds were being held back from various urban programs because there was no point in accelerating programs that were "scheduled for termination." He was referring to the fact that Congress had added funds to grant-in-aid programs which the Administration wanted to consolidate and convert into its revenue-sharing proposal. To impound funds in this prospective sense—holding on to money in anticipation that Congress will enact an Administration bill—is a new departure for the impoundment technique. Impoundment is not being used to avoid deficiencies, or to effect savings, or even to fight inflation, but rather to shift the scale of priorities from one Administration to the next, prior to congressional action.

Political pressures have sometimes been enough to pry loose impounded funds. After the November 1966 elections, President Johnson announced a $5.3 billion reduction in Federal programs. Economic and legal justifications presented by the Administration failed to placate the localities affected by the cutbacks. Sensitive to criticism from the states, President Johnson released some of the money in February 1967, and on the eve of a conference the next month with governors he released additional amounts.

In the fall of 1970 it was learned that the Nixon Administration planned to withhold some education funds. Criticism began to build up in Congress and in the school districts. Two weeks before the November elections, the Administration announced that the money would be released. When the Secretary of Health, Education, and Welfare was asked whether the pending elections had prompted the Administration to reverse its position and release the funds, he replied, smiling, that there was "no connection whatsoever." Another example: early in 1971 the Nixon Administration decided to impound some Model Cities funds to help finance its revenue sharing proposal. Letters explaining the cutoff of funds were ready to be mailed to the mayors. They learned of the plan, however, issued a strong protest, and the letters were never sent out.

These pressure tactics and confrontations, even when successful, are not satisfactory to the mayors. In the midst of their busy schedules they must come to Congress first to support an authorization bill. They testify a second time in behalf of the appropriation bill. Now they must come to Congress and the Administration a third time to see that the money, having already been authorized and appropriated, is actually spent.

In March 1971, the Senate Subcommittee on the Separation of Powers held hearings for the purpose of establishing better legislative control over impounded funds. Senator Sam J. Ervin, Jr., subcommittee chairman, introduced a bill several months later to require the President to notify Congress within 10 days whenever he impounds funds appropriated for a specific purpose or project. The President's message would include the amount of funds impounded, the specific projects or functions affected, and the reasons for impounding the funds. Congress would then have 60 days to pass a joint resolution disapproving the impoundment.

In effect, the Ervin bill gives the President a form of item-veto authority without having to amend the Constitution. It also assumes, in the case of a resolution of disapproval, that Congress has the power to compel expenditures. While it is true that a legal memorandum issued by an official in the Nixon Administration affirms the power of Congress to mandate expenditures in the area of formula grants for the impacted areas program, the President could exert his prerogatives elsewhere. In the area of defense procurement, in particular, the President could deny that Congress has the power to deprive him of his judgment and discretion in the administration of programs and in the management of funds.

Unauthorized Commitments

The Constitution provides that "No money shall be drawn from the Treasury but in consequence of appropriations made by law." Presidents have nevertheless found it expedient at times to enter into financial obligations not authorized by Congress. For instance, Jefferson agreed to accept France's offer to sell the whole of Louisiana for $11,250,000—plus an additional $3,750,000 to cover private claims against France—even though the offer exceeded instructions set forth by Congress. Another example of an unauthorized commitment occurred in 1807. After Congress had recessed, a British vessel fired on the American ship *Chesapeake*. Without statutory authority, Jefferson ordered military purchases for the emergency, disclosing to Congress his action when it convened. "To have awaited a previous and special sanction by law," he said, "would have lost occasions which might not be retrieved."

In 1861, after the firing on Fort Sumter, and while Congress was adjourned, Lincoln directed his Secretary of the Treasury to advance $2 million to three private citizens, to be used by them for "military and naval measures necessary for the defense and support of the Government. . . ." Lincoln acted without statutory authority, but the regular channels could not be trusted, since many Treasury officials were Southern sympathizers.

Theodore Roosevelt was determined to send an American fleet around the world as a show of force, despite the insistence of the chairman of the Senate Committee on Naval Affairs that the fleet could not go because Congress would refuse to appropriate the funds. Roosevelt answered that he had enough money to take the fleet halfway around the world, and that "if Congress did not choose to appropriate enough money to get the fleet back, why, it could stay in the Pacific. There was no further difficulty about the money."

Presidential actions in creating unauthorized commitments did not reach the courts, but the Supreme Court reviewed financial initiatives taken by other executive officials. One case involved an agreement made between a Government contractor and Buchanan's Secretary of War, John B. Floyd. The contractor, lacking sufficient funds to complete the order, was allowed to draw time-drafts and have them purchased by his suppliers to provide interim assistance. The Government subsequently accepted drafts of $5 million, but over a million dollars remained unpaid. Holders of unpaid drafts contended that Secretary Floyd's acceptances were binding on the Government. The Court dismissed their claim, denying that Floyd possessed either constitutional or statutory authority to enter into his agreements.

In trying to prevent unauthorized commitments, Congress has had to soften the language of statutes at times in order to allow army and navy supply agencies to sign contracts in advance of appropriations. Otherwise, material would not have been available in time. When Congress prohibited unauthorized commitments in 1820, an exception was allowed for contracts for subsistence and clothing for the army and navy, as well as for contracts by the Quartermaster's Department. Legislative delays in passing appropriation bills (enacted after one-fourth to a third of the year had elapsed) forced departments to make expenditures not legally authorized. Legislative instructions for the new appropriations were also delayed. The Secretary of the Navy reported to Congress in 1825 that his department, for nearly half the year, acted in "perfect ignorance of the law under which it is bound to act." As a result, "The law is, necessarily, not complied with, because it is passed after the act is performed."

Administrative discretion in the handling of funds regularly provoked the ire of Congress. The Gilmer Committee reported in 1842: "Under color of what are termed *regulations,* large amounts of money are often applied to purposes never contemplated by the appropriating power, and numerous offices are sometimes actually created in the same way. . . . It is hoped that in future this code of Executive legislation may cease to be known in our history."

Cambodia and the C-5A. Contemporary regulations on unauthorized commitments are far more explicit than the Constitution. The U.S. Code contains the following admonition: "No officer or employee of the United States shall make or authorize an expenditure from or create or authorize an obligation under any appropriation or fund in excess of the amount available therein; nor shall any such officer or employee involve the Government in any contract or other obligation, for the payment of money for any purpose, in advance of appropriations made for such purpose, unless such contract or obligation is authorized by law."

President Nixon's intervention in Cambodia, followed by his request for $255 million in assistance for Cambodia, was made entirely at his own initiative. Here is a clear case where the executive branch involved the Government in an obligation—at least a moral obligation—in advance of appropriations. Not only did the intervention lead to a financial obligation in this case, but future requests in addition to the $255 million are expected. As Secretary of State Rogers explained on December 10, 1970: "I think it is true that when we ask for military assistance and economic assistance for Cambodia we do certainly take on some obligation for some continuity."

The cost overrun problem with the C-5A cargo plane is another example where the Administration can, in effect, commit Congress to hundreds of millions in additional expenditures. The Air Force selected the Lockheed Aircraft Corporation as the airframe prime contractor in 1965. During hearings in November 1968, the Joint Economic Committee learned that the original estimate of $3.4 billion had climbed to $5.3 billion—that is, a cost overrun of almost $2 billion. Problems with other Lockheed contracts, including the Cheyenne helicopter, put the company near bankruptcy. The Pentagon presented a plan to rescue the company with Federal funds, at a cost of several hundred million dollars. Critics called this "bailout money," while the Pentagon contended that the collapse of Lockheed would trigger a chain of events injurious to the national defense effort. As was the case with the Cambodian intervention, and the expenditures which that entailed, Congress faced the prospect of funding an executive *fait accompli*.

If a 1958 statute is interpreted broadly enough, the Pentagon has sufficient authority to cover any of its cost overruns. That statute authorized the President to modify any defense contract "whenever he deems that such action would facilitate the national defense." The sole restriction is that the act remains in effect during a national emergency declared by Congress or by the President. The United States is currently in a state of national emergency, not because of Vietnam, but because of a proclamation issued by President Truman on December 16, 1950, after China had intervened in Korea. Two decades later that proclamation has yet to be terminated.

Existing studies tell us how the President formulates the budget and how Congress acts on his budget requests. Surprisingly, we know relatively little about how the money, once appropriated, is actually spent.

For a number of good reasons, expenditures must deviate from appropriations. Appropriations are made many months, and sometimes years, in advance of expenditures. Congress acts with imperfect knowledge in trying to legislate in fields which are themselves highly technical and undergoing constant change. New circumstances will develop to make obsolete and mistaken the decisions reached by Congress at the appropriation stage. It is not practicable for Congress to adjust to these new developments by passing large numbers of supplemental appropriation bills. Were Congress to control expenditures by confining administrators to narrow statutory details, it would perhaps protect its power of the purse but it would not protect the purse itself. Discretion is needed for the sound management of public funds.

While there no doubt exists a need for executive flexibility, that is an abstract term capable of hiding much mischief. It is evident that in a number of areas, including covert financing, impoundment, and unauthorized commitments, Congress has yet to discover a satisfactory means for controlling expenditures. Public policy is then decided by administrators rather than by the elected officials and the budgets they adopt. The results are often incongruous. Congress goes through the motions of authorizing and appropriating funds but the money is never spent. On the other hand, Congress can find itself locked in to paying for administrative commitments it never authorized. New statutory and nonstatutory controls are needed. The objective must be an expenditure process in which administrators enjoy substantial discretion in exercising judgment and taking responsibility for their actions, but those actions will have to be directed toward executing congressional, not administrative, policy.

5

TAXING POWERS

Article I, section 8 of the Constitution reserves to Congress the power "to lay and collect Taxes, Duties, Imposts, and Excises. . . ." That reservation of power has not prevented Congress from delegating to the President a substantial portion of its responsibilities for the collection of duties and the adjustment of tariff schedules. In recent years the President has also gained discretionary powers over the interest equalization tax, as a means of alleviating balance-of-payment problems. With respect to domestic taxes, administrative rulemaking confers additional discretionary tax power upon the President. It was up to President Nixon in 1971, for instance, to decide what would be a "reasonable allowance" for the depreciation of machinery and equipment.

This chapter discusses two areas in which delegation of the taxing power has been most debated: Presidential discretion over tariff rates, and the request by President Kennedy in 1962 for discretionary power to adjust domestic taxes.

TARIFF POWERS

Domestic taxes and foreign duties have essentially the same properties: both are revenue-producing measures; both impose financial burdens on members of the community. During the 1912 Presidential campaign, Woodrow Wilson told the voters that when they bought an imported article, part of the price included the customs duty added by the Federal Government. Higher duties on imported goods thus had an effect similar to new taxes on domestic products. Because of this, Wilson was attracted by the idea of putting two price tags on an article: one showing the price as it is, the second showing the price as it would be without the tariff.

As an exercise of the taxing power, it is perhaps tempting to dismiss Presidential actions in international trade as insignificant. Out of $193.7 billion in Federal revenue collected in fiscal 1970, customs receipts amounted to only $2.4 billion. But in the early years of the Republic, and indeed well into the twentieth century, customs revenues were the mainstay of our financial system. They accounted for about nine-tenths of total Federal revenue from 1837 to 1861, and for almost half from 1891 to 1916. In addition to the President's discretionary authority over tariffs, he also wields considerable power over such nontariff barriers as the import quotas placed on foreign oil, sugar, meat, and dairy products.

Development of Protective Tariff

Tariff bills have had two separate purposes: to raise revenue, and to protect domestic industries from foreign competition. George Washington's first annual address to Congress declared that the safety and interest of the people require that they should "promote such manufactures as tend to render them independent of others for essential, particularly military, supplies." The first tariff act of 1789 justified the laying of duties as necessary for revenue and "the encouragement and protection of manufactures." Alexander Hamilton's *Report on Manufactures,* submitted to the House of Representatives on December 5, 1791, recommended protective tariffs to encourage domestic manufactures. For the first few decades, however, American tariffs were imposed primarily as a source of revenue. Not until the tariff act of 1816 did protectionism become a conspicuous feature.

During those early decades, the President obtained a number of powers to remove trade restrictions. I have already mentioned executive powers over embargoes in 1794, over commercial restrictions in 1798, over embargoes again in 1808, and other early responsibilities of the President in international trade (pp. 58–61). In addition, an act passed in 1815 authorized the President to repeal discriminating duties whenever he was satisfied that countervailing duties placed on American vessels and goods had been removed. An act in 1823 required him to collect information on duties of tonnage or impost levied on American vessels by certain British colonial ports. When those rates were lower than the American rates, the President could order reductions. An act in 1824 extended that policy to include a number of European countries, thus permitting the suspension of discriminating duties by the President whenever the foreign nation had made reciprocal exemptions. Presidents who issued proclamations under the authority of that act, or of amendments to it, include John Quincy Adams, Jackson, Polk, Fillmore, Buchanan, Lincoln, Andrew Johnson, Grant, and Hayes.

The McKinley Tariff Act of 1890 empowered the President to suspend duty-free arrangements (in effect *adding* a tax) on certain articles, whenever he discovered inequalities in reciprocal trade provisions. In taking their case to the Supreme Court, appellants charged that Congress had surrendered the one power it should most scrupulously retain: the power to tax. Although the taxing power was central to legislative integrity, "here we have a law which delegates to the President of the United States the power, by a mere stroke of his pen to impose an onerous and burdensome tax on articles. . . ." The Supreme Court reviewed for appellants in *Field* v. *Clark* (1892) the many occasions in the past when Congress—in time of war as well as peace—had found it necessary to delegate economic functions to the President. To the Court, those prior enactments constituted tangible proof that Congress often found it desirable and essential "to invest the President with large discretion in matters arising out of the execution of statutes relating to trade and commerce with other nations."

Presidential responsibility in international trade was recognized again by the Dingley Tariff Act of 1897. Section 3 authorized the President to enter into negotiations with foreign countries for the purpose of securing reciprocal and equivalent concessions on certain articles. After securing concessions, through a commercial agreement, the President was empowered to suspend the imposition and collection of duties on those articles without further congressional action. Section 4 permitted the President to negotiate treaties for the reduction of tariffs by as much as 20 percent, in return for concessions on American exports. Such treaties required ratification by the Senate and approval by Congress. Eleven treaties were negotiated under Section 4 authority, but not one was ever ratified.

As the President became increasingly active in matters of international trade, efforts were made to devise a more scientific formula for tariff-making. The Republican platform of 1908 declared that "the true principle of protection is best maintained by the imposition of such duties as will equal the difference between the cost of production at home and abroad, together with a reasonable profit to American industries." The platform also recommended the establishment of "maximum and minimum rates to be administered by the President under limitations fixed in the law. . . ." The latter concept was incorporated in the Payne-Aldrich Tariff Act of 1909. The rates of duty prescribed in the act were taken as the "minimum tariff." Whenever the President discovered that a foreign country had imposed trade restrictions on American products, he could increase the minimum tariff by 25 percent ad valorem—a level defined as the "maximum tariff."

To assist in the administration of the maximum and minimum clause, Congress authorized the President to appoint experts. Taft set up a tariff board of three members and expressed the hope that "the question of the rate of a duty imposed shall become more of a business question and less of a political question, to be ascertained by experts of long training and accurate knowledge." He recommended that the tariff board be transformed into a permanent commission. During the short session of Congress, following the congressional elections of 1910, a bill for a bipartisan tariff board passed both houses, but failed of adoption on the last day of the session because of a filibuster. Taft proceeded on the assumption that Congress wanted a tariff board, and added two Democrats to the three Republicans already selected. The board quickly passed out of existence. One writer observed that the Democrats, having gained control of the House in the 1910 elections, regarded the tariff board as "an impudent attempt of a defunct Congress to perpetuate a tariff policy that had been discredited at the polls."

Flexible Tariffs

In subsequent messages to Congress, Taft urged greater flexibility in the tariff schedules. Instead of a fixed choice between maximum and minimum rates, he wanted a "graduated means" of meeting varying degrees of discriminatory treatment. As a step in that direction, he asked that the President be authorized to apply a graduated scale of duties up to the 25 percent rate on restrictive trade practices. "Flat tariffs," he said, "are out of date."

Woodrow Wilson did not pursue Taft's goal of a flexible tariff. Instead, Wilson directed his energies toward a general lowering of duties. The Underwood tariff bill of 1913 passed the House handily by a vote of 281 to 139, and generated hope that the tariff structure would indeed be reduced. When the Senate threatened to tack on protectionist amendments, Wilson publicly denounced the "industrious and insidious" lobbyists at work in Washington.

Some members of the Senate felt that his remark impugned the honor and integrity of their institution. For the purpose of embarrassing the President, a resolution was introduced to have a special committee investigate the accuracy of the charge. That tactic backfired, however, when Senator James A. Reed amended the resolution to direct that the committee determine whether any Senator had a financial interest in any articles mentioned in the tariff bill, and whether any Senator was connected directly or indirectly with any firm producing those articles. Each Senator came before the committee. In the words of Professor Arthur Link, they "dutifully told how many shares of coal or steel stock, or how many acres of sugar or grazing land he owned. For the first time in American history the economic interests of the members of the Senate were laid bare for the whole country to see." The result of public disclosure was astounding. Not only did the Senate contain its protectionist impulse; it even cut tariffs below the House version. The Underwood Tariff Act of 1913 constituted the first comprehensive reduction of tariff rates since 1846.

The act was in operation less than a year before war had broken out in Europe. Under the heavy demand from European countries for war goods, American industry enjoyed a rapid growth in output and in rates of profit. After the Armistice, Wilson warned that a revival of protectionist legislation would prevent imports from coming in and exports from going out, thus leading to industrial stagnation and unemployment. "If we want to sell," he said, "we must be prepared to buy." But along with the war-induced prosperity in America came higher wages and prices. New industries ("war babies") were created during this period. A strong demand arose after the war for higher tariffs to shelter the domestic producer from foreign competition. Wilson vetoed a protectionist bill early in 1921, but the Republican victory the previous year had already signaled a new era of high tariffs. The Fordney-McCumber Tariff Act of 1922 brought tariff rates back up to record levels.

The Republican platform in 1920 had pledged the party "to end executive autocracy and restore to the people their constitutional government." Oddly enough, in this moment of congressional reassertion, with a Republican as President and both houses dominated by his party, the 1922 tariff act empowered the President to adjust duty rates by as much as 50 percent in order to equalize production costs between the U.S. and competing countries. Why did the flexible tariff provision make its appearance at a time of "free enterprise normalcy," when Congress was in process of recapturing powers that it felt Wilson and other Presidents had usurped?

In part, the flexible tariff feature was a sop to opponents of the higher tariff structure. It was also a product of the war. Conditions of world trade were so unsettled that Congress could not fix duties with confidence as to their adequacy either for revenue or for protection. Senator McCumber, chairman of the Senate Finance Committee, told his colleagues that "of all times in our history this is the very worst time to formulate and put into effect a new tariff measure. . . ." As long as costs and prices were moving erratically, it was felt that the President should have some limited powers to adjust selected duties without having to convene Congress for a general revision of the tariff schedule.

Delegation of tariff-adjustment powers to the President was defended as a temporary expedient, made necessary because of the extraordinary condition of the world market. In response to legislative objections to this increase in executive authority, McCumber announced that he had no intention of converting the Tariff Commission into a tariff-making body. He said that Congress could never lay down a general rule under which it could safely delegate tariff power. Instead, McCumber argued that "the exigencies of the chaotic condition that now confronts us in the commercial world are the only justification for the added power that is to be given the President, and I want it taken away just as soon as those exigencies no longer exist."

An increase in the duty rate on barium dioxide by President Coolidge brought the constitutionality of the flexible tariff provision before the Supreme Court. Petitioners claimed that executive tariff discretion amounted to a delegation of legislative and taxing powers: "The President cannot be delegated the authority to levy taxes for the regulation of commerce any more than he can be delegated authority to levy taxes for the raising of revenue." Government counsel insisted that Congress had merely delegated a fact-finding power. In the 1928 *Hampton* decision, the Court unanimously upheld the flexible tariff. There is considerable irony in the fact that the Chief Justice, and author of the opinion, was the former advocate of flexible tariffs: William Howard Taft. Chief Justice Taft explained that Congress, having to contend with the ever-changing conditions of the world market, decided that it was necessary to delegate tariff-adjustment powers to the President. Unable to determine when legislative power should be exercised, because dependent on future conditions, it was constitutionally permissible for Congress to leave the determination of the time to the President.

"Scientific" Tariff-making

The concept of flexible tariffs promised to "take the tariff out of politics." Presidential action would be based upon investigation by the Tariff Commission. In place of the log-rolling and special-interest legislation that had previously characterized congressional efforts, there emerged the reassuring picture of experts at work, gathering facts, subjecting them to rational analysis, and then inserting the facts into a cost-of-production formula. This new technique appeared to possess all the virtues: it would be nonpartisan, nonpolitical, flexible, and scientific.

Appearances can deceive, of course, and the Tariff Commission was no exception. Nonpartisan tariff-making was supposed to be secured by structuring the six-man Commission so that no more than three could be from the same party. That restriction could be circumvented without difficulty. Even though Democrats were identified nationally as advocates of lower tariffs, and Republicans were labeled as protectionists, the President could easily pick a protectionist Democrat or a Republican free-trader in order to fashion the Commission in his own image.

A study by Philip Wright reveals the influence of party pressures under Wilson, Harding, and Coolidge. For chairman of the Tariff Commission, Wilson picked Professor Frank W. Taussig, who was registered in Massachusetts as a Republican and yet favored free trade. The second Republican, William Kent, was also classed as a free-trader. The third Republican member, William S. Culbertson, was protectionist, although more moderate in his tariff position than his party. Two of the Democrats picked by Wilson—Daniel C. Roper and David J. Lewis—leaned toward free trade. The illusion of party labels was particularly evident in the case of the sixth member of the Commission, Edward P. Costigan, who stated that he had once defined himself as "a Progressive with Republican antecedents and Democratic consequences." A believer in moderate protection, Costigan followed La Follette and Teddy Roosevelt in the Progressive Movement and he supported Wilson in 1916. Thus, regardless of nominal party status, the political complexion of the first Tariff Commission was clearly Wilsonian.

Wright shows that the next two Presidents also shaped the Commission to their own ends. Harding appointed as Republican members Thomas O. Marvin and William Burgess, both of whom were strongly protectionist. For a Democratic vacancy, he chose Henry H. Glassie, who voted with Marvin and Burgess on the important cases. Coolidge then tried to force Lewis (a Wilson appointee) off the Commission in order to make room for a protectionist Democrat; he got rid of Culbertson (another Wilson appointee) by dispatching him to Rumania as Minister. He then appointed a Republican who was more faithful to party tariff principles. The dream of nonpartisan, nonpolitical tariff-making was obviously slow in materializing. A Senate investigation of the Tariff Commission simply reinforced what was already common knowledge: that the flexible tariff was being manipulated for political purposes.

Subject as it was to partisan and political pressures, the "flexible" tariff was bent in one direction more than another. It was expected, at the time of the 1922 tariff act, that

Presidents would generally use their adjustment powers to lower duty rates. The tariff structure had been set unusually high as a hedge against unforeseen postwar developments. Senator Smoot had predicted that "if the President is given this power I think there will be many, many more occasions when he will exercise it in lowering rates than in increasing them. . . ."

His remark was scarcely prophetic. Most of the rate adjustments by Presidents Harding, Coolidge, and Hoover were in the upward direction. By 1930, only 38 reports by the Tariff Commission had been acted upon by the President. Considering that the tariff list included thousands of schedules, and that these Presidential actions occurred over an eight-year period, not much can be said here for flexibility. Moreover, of the 38 tariff changes, all but five were *increases*. The nature of the changes made the burden even worse. Increases were ordered on such essentials as butter, eggs, cheese, wheat, pig-iron, and milk and cheese, while decreases applied to such esoteric items as mill feed, bobwhite quail, paintbrush handles, cresylic acid, and phenol.

It should come as no surprise that the hope for "scientific" tariff-making was severely disappointed. The idea of equalizing costs of production between the United States and competing countries—though it may have had about it a sense of fair play—contradicted a basic tenet of world trade. If nations are to benefit by exchanging the products of their specialization, efficiency, and natural advantages, trade between them obviously depends on *differences* in costs of production. "Equalization of costs," if taken literally, would come close to a virtual embargo on foreign goods. Senators who objected to the flexible-tariff formula said that it was "nothing short of a legislative guaranty for the maintenance of existing prices and profits and an implied assurance to the industries thus protected that they may further advance these prices without incurring the risk of foreign competition, and to the latter end the President is given power to increase rates to the extent deemed necessary in that event to safeguard them against such outside competition. . . ."

Besides discouraging trade, the cost-of-production formula represented a vague standard for executive action. What costs should the Tariff Commission select—those from the most efficient manufacturers or those from industry as a whole? Taking an average, as was done, removed the incentive for efficiency. The disincentives applied also to rate adjustments. If an industry improved its process and cut costs, the Commission would theoretically reduce the tariff, leaving the industry not much better off than it had been before in competing against foreign goods. On the other hand, if costs increased because of poor management and obsolete equipment, such inefficiency would be rewarded by higher tariffs.

From what years should production costs be taken? The most recent year might be unrepresentative; but if costs were to be taken from an average of several years, from what period of time? How could reliable comparisons be made between the U.S. and foreign countries, when foreign manufacturers were under no obligation to supply information to the Tariff Commission, and often refused to do so? There was not even agreement on what factors to include as "costs." In its investigation on butter, the Commission estimated money values for the farmers' labor, for work done by their families, and for such articles as feed and roughage produced on the farm, even though no money was actually paid out. Through such computations, the Commission was able to reach the absurd conclusion that 74 percent of domestic butter was being produced at a loss.

Herbert Hoover carried on the Republican policy of basing tariff rates on comparative-cost studies. In April 1929, he urged a limited revision of the tariff structure for the purpose of relieving agriculture and protecting those industries in which there had been "a substantial slackening of activity" in recent years and "a consequent decrease of employment due to insurmountable competition in the products of that industry." Congress seized upon the opportunity to produce the Smoot-Hawley Tariff Act of 1930, which was even more protectionist than the 1922 act. Senator La Follette said that the 1930 act eclipsed the "tariff of abominations" of 1828 in its imposition on the public. Other Senators spoke of vote-trading and secret conferences held with lobbyists. In his study of Smoot-Hawley, E. E. Schattschneider observed that policies inevitably change when reduced to statute form, but that in tariff-making, "perhaps more than in any other kind of legislation, Congress writes bills which no one intended." So discredited was this legislative attempt at general tariff-making that Congress, within a few years, delegated to the President the power to bargain with other countries for the reciprocal reduction of duties.

Reciprocal Trade Agreements

The economic nationalism of the 1920s continued during President Roosevelt's first year in office. In his Inaugural Address on March 4, 1933, he subordinated international trade to his program for domestic recovery: "I favor as a practical policy the putting of first things first. I shall spare no effort to restore world trade by international economic readjustment, but the emergency at home cannot wait on that accomplishment." In an effort to raise commodity prices and restore prosperity, and faced with inadequate gold reserves, Roosevelt took the country off the gold standard and instituted production controls under the National Industrial Recovery Act and the Agricultural Adjustment Act. Trade barriers were erected as part of the effort to revive American industry. Section 3(e) of the NIRA empowered the President to restrict imports, either by prescribing quotas or by imposing financial penalties whenever imports threatened code agreements. Section 15(e) of the AAA levied a tax on imports to offset a processing tax that had been applied to domestic commodities.

In the midst of these legislative and administrative actions, Roosevelt agreed to send a delegation to London in 1933 to seek international agreements on problems of world trade and currency stabilization. In April of that year he had expressed an interest in an immediate cut in tariffs by all countries, and he appeared to be ready to seek authority to negotiate further reduction in trade barriers. His "Fireside Chat" of May 7 emphasized that the domestic situation was "inevitably and deeply tied in" with conditions elsewhere in the world, and on May 16 he appealed to all nations to seek stabilization of currency, expansion of world trade, and international action to raise price levels.

Secretary of State Cordell Hull, an ardent supporter of free trade, was chosen to head the delegation to the London Conference. Hull expected Roosevelt to sponsor a reciprocal trade agreement bill; but, midway across the Atlantic, he learned that the President had decided not to ask Congress for tariff-negotiating power. When the Conference foundered because of ambivalence in the objectives of the United States, Roosevelt dispatched Raymond Moley to London to act as his liaison officer. He subsequently rejected Moley's proposal for temporary stabilization of currencies, and sent a tart message to the Conference to say that currency matters could be discussed only when the majority of nations learned to balance their budgets and live within their means. That message wrecked the London Conference. In 1933, Roosevelt was seeking recovery by way of domestic actions, and he was unwilling to jeopardize that prospect by tying the dollar to foreign currencies.

By the end of 1933, American prices declined to the point where American producers could more easily compete with foreign producers. In early 1934, Roosevelt turned toward greater world trade. The Export-Import Bank was created by an Executive Order in February to provide financial aid for international trade. As for tariff reduction, the flexible-tariff approach was considered to be hopelessly inadequate. Representative Hill said that the average time it took the Tariff Commission to complete an investigation and make a finding was about 11 months, and "in many cases it is 14 or 18 months, and in some cases over 2 years." As an alternative to flexible-tariff power, Roosevelt asked Congress for authority to make reciprocal trade agreements, calling this "an essential step" in his program for national economic recovery. The Reciprocal Trade Agreements Act of 1934 gave the President authority to adjust duties by up to 50 percent by entering into reciprocal agreements with other nations. For the first time, the President possessed advance authority to enter into trade agreements without the advice and consent of the Senate. From June 1934 to June 1940, the United States entered into 22 agreements for reciprocal trade.

Supplements to the Lend-Lease Act of 1941 included agreements by which the United States and recipients of lend-lease assistance agreed to take measures conducive to "the elimination of all forms of discriminatory treatment in international commerce, and to the reduction of tariffs and other trade barriers." This language, adopted under the stresses of wartime needs for cooperation, and embodying Secretary Hull's well-known aspiration, proved to have mainly rhetorical force. Because of unwillingness on the part of the countries involved to abandon preferential trade relationships with their territories and possessions, the agreements did not result in tariff reduction.

Deterioration of economic and political systems during World War II stimulated the search for new forms of international cooperation. At the Bretton Woods conference in 1944, the United States took the lead in encouraging new international institutions that would promote monetary stability and assist in the recovery of war-shattered economies. Out of this conference came the International Monetary Fund and the International Bank for Reconstruction and Development (the World Bank).

This shift from economic nationalism to international cooperation has been explained by several factors. Tariff policy had always been double-edged with regard to business. Protection was sought for finished goods from abroad; for the raw materials they needed, the goal was free trade. From the 1920s onward, the United States became increasingly dependent on foreign sources for many raw materials. In 1954, the President's Commission on Foreign Economic Policy reported that "from the standpoint of our long-term economic growth and the viewpoint of our national defense, the shift of the United States from the position of a net exporter of metals and minerals to that of a net importer is of overshadowing significance in shaping our foreign economic policies." The study could cite only five mineral substances— coal, sulfur, potash, molybdenum, and magnesium—in which the United States was fully self-sufficient.

Moreover, as American firms developed investments abroad and established subsidiaries overseas, they cast their support for tariff reduction as a means of broadening their markets. The United States also emerged from World War II as the only country that was capable of exporting in substantial quantity. An expansion of world trade was thus in our national interest. Such postwar developments as the Cold War, Western military alliances, and the Marshall Plan gave added impetus to an international outlook.

This reorientation of American policy shows up in the voting record of the Republican Party, which moved from its traditional position of protectionism to one of greater support for world trade. From 1934 to 1940, no more than five Republicans in either house had voted for a reciprocal trade bill. From 1943 through 1958, Republicans supported 13 of 16 rollcalls (*Table 3*). Some of this support was cast for such restrictive devices as "peril points" and "escape clause," to be discussed later. Thus, while these votes fall short of an advocacy for free trade, they at least represent an acceptance of executive tariff-making.

Democrats, on the other hand, began to experience defections within their ranks on the issue of world trade. The migration of the textile industry from New England to the South stimulated protectionist sentiments in the once free-trade South. Additional Democratic votes against a low-tariff policy came from the coal regions of Pennsylvania and from various industrial districts of Massachusetts that had encountered economic hardship.

Table 3 Republican Support for Reciprocal Trade Legislation (1934–1958)

	Senate		House	
	For	Against	For	Against
1934	5	28	2	99
1937	0	14	3	81
1940	0	20	5	146
1943	16	14	145	52
1945	15	16	33	140
1948	47	1	218	5
1949	15	18	84	63
1951	34	2	(voice vote)	
1953	(voice vote)		179	25
1954	37	2	126	39
1955	38	7	109	75
1958	36	10	133	59

Multilateral Bargaining

The 1930s approach to reciprocal trade agreements was replaced, beginning in the 1940s, by multilateral (or general) agreements on tariffs. An International Trade Organization (ITO) was proposed to head off a threatened tariff war in the postwar period. Instead of waiting for the charter of that organization to be adopted, the United States called for an immediate effort to reach tariff agreements. Representatives from 23 nations, meeting in Geneva in 1947, produced the General Agreements on Tariffs and Trade (GATT). This marked the first time that the United States had conducted tariff negotiations on a multilateral, instead of a bilateral, basis. When Congress refused to ratify the ITO charter, GATT became the main vehicle for tariff bargaining.

On the basis of their authority under the Trade Agreements Act, Presidents participated in additional GATT conferences to secure lower tariffs. Various methods exist for measuring the "height" of a country's tariff. If we compare the duties collected with the value of dutiable imports, the downward trend in American tariffs is striking. From a ratio of 59.1 percent in 1932, following the Smoot-Hawley tariff act, the ratios decline sharply. This is partly because of tariff reduction, and partly because of the general upward direction of world prices (*Table 4*).

Table 4 Ratio of Duties Collected to Values of Dutiable Imports (1932–1960)

Year	Percent	Year	Percent
1932	59.1	1946	25.3
1933	53.6	1947	19.3
1934	46.7	1948	13.9
1935	42.9	1949	13.5
		1950	13.1
1936	39.3	1951	12.3
1937	37.8	1952	12.7
1938	39.3	1953	12.0
1939	37.3	1954	11.6
1940	35.6	1955	12.0
1941	36.8	1956	11.3
1942	32.0	1957	10.8
1943	32.8	1958	11.1
1944	31.4	1959	11.5
1945	28.2	1960	12.2

A new GATT conference began in 1960, but by that time the President's authority to negotiate tariff reductions had been successively narrowed by Congress. Extension of the Trade Agreements Act in 1948 included the "peril point" provision, which directed the Tariff Commission to make an investigation of anticipated tariff adjustments for the purpose of determining at which point reductions might cause serious injury to a domestic industry. That provision put pressure on the President not to cut duties below the rate fixed by the Commission. The peril-point provision was repealed in 1949 but restored in 1951. Also in 1951, Congress added the "escape clause," which prohibited any reduction in the rate of duty when an imported product caused or threatened serious injury to a domestic industry. Further legislation in 1955 directed the President to restrict imports whenever they "threaten to impair the national security." The latter provision was greatly elaborated by Congress in 1958 when it extended the Trade Agreements Act.

The U.S. balance of payments deteriorated sharply during the late 1950s. Exports had not kept pace with American investments abroad. The need to stimulate exports was made difficult by the success of the European Economic Community (the Common Market), which had thrown an outer wall of protective barriers around the European nations in order to promote free trade within. Trade discrimination on American exports was expected to intensify as new countries joined the Market, particularly Great Britain and other members of the European Free Trade Association (EFTA). Japan also emerged as a formidable competitor in industrial exports. Beyond the immediate problem of the balance of payments lay the larger risk of dividing the Western nations into two competitive trading blocs, thereby undermining the concept of the Atlantic Community.

The Kennedy Round

The Reciprocal Trade Agreements Act was scheduled to expire in mid-1962. In January of that year, President Kennedy asked for new authority to reduce tariffs. It was hoped that a lowering of tariff barriers would promote American exports and reduce the incentive for American firms to build new plants behind the Common Market tariff wall. An expansion of world trade was also linked to the need to accelerate economic growth at home, to control prices, and to stimulate modernization and managerial efficiency. A heavy stress was placed on national security. By negotiating a general lowering of tariff barriers between the United States and the Common Market, Kennedy predicted that "Communist hopes for a trade war between these two great economic giants would be frustrated and Communist efforts to split the West would be doomed to failure."

Trade problems of the developing nations were also discussed in terms of American foreign policy. Kennedy stated that recent trade on the part of the Soviet bloc with 41 non-communist countries in the less-developed areas had more than tripled. In his address before the Conference on Trade Policy in May 1962, he spoke of "a new chapter in American trade policy—a chapter that symbolizes our new great aspirations: for greater growth at home, greater progress around the world, and above all, the emergence of a greater Atlantic partnership." His July 4 address at Independence Hall, Philadelphia, also focused on the need to strengthen the Atlantic partnership.

The Trade Expansion Act of 1962 received top priority at the hands of the Administration. The subject of the year's first special legislative message, it was adopted by Congress in October. The identity between economic objectives and national security is evident in the Act's statement of purpose: "To promote the general welfare, foreign policy, and security" of the United States. The Act gave the President authority until June 30, 1967, to cut tariffs by as much as 50 percent. In a major departure from past procedures, the President was authorized to negotiate tariff reductions by broad categories of goods instead of by individual articles. Moreover, on commodities for which the United States and the Common Market accounted for 80 percent of world trade, the President could eliminate tariffs altogether. The latter authority evaporated in January 1962 when De Gaulle vetoed Britain's bid for membership in the Common Market.

Instead of relying on the escape clause and other devices, as a means of restricting imports and protecting domestic industry, the Trade Expansion Act provided for economic adjustments. Two members of the President's Cabinet obtained new authority to act whenever tariff reduction injured American firms or caused unemployment. The Secretary of Commerce could protect management by providing technical assistance, loans, loan guarantees, and special tax assistance. In cases where new trade agreements produced unemployment, the Secretary of Labor could provide special forms of unemployment payments and could channel Federal funds into counseling, training, and relocation allowances.

After more than four years of negotiations, the Kennedy Round concluded the most ambitious effort ever made to liberalize international trade. Agreements in May 1967 granted concessions on trade valued at close to $40 billion. Forty-six countries, accounting for about 80 percent of world trade, agreed to an average one-third cut in their duties on industrial products. Two-thirds of the items were cut 50 percent or more.

Nontariff Barriers

With the successful conclusion of the Kennedy Round, attention shifted to other means of fostering protectionism. Included among the nontariff barriers are the "Buy American" Act (giving preference to domestic suppliers in the awarding of public contracts), technical and health regulations, and restrictions on trade with Communist nations of Eastern Europe. A committee of GATT has identified as many as 276 nontariff barriers.

One example is the American Selling Price (ASP) system. Under this system, which governs certain benzenoid chemicals and a few other goods, tariffs are based on the price of the domestic product rather than on the price of the imported item. Because of the generally higher U.S. price, there are instances where this system has produced tariff protection of more than 100 percent of a product's import cost. Presidents Johnson and Nixon have both urged the repeal of the ASP system. A trade bill passed by the House in November 1970 included a procedure to eliminate the American Selling Price, but the Senate did not act on the bill.

At the conclusion of the Kennedy Round in 1967, pressure began to mount for import quotas (quantitative restrictions) to limit the influx of foreign textiles, steel, footware, and other products. Organized labor became more protectionist in response to the investment of U.S. companies in foreign subsidiaries and the growth of U.S.-based multinational corporations. To the AFL-CIO, this meant the loss of American jobs to subsidiary plants of American companies in foreign companies. Quite obviously, workers are less mobile than capital or top management officials.

During the 1968 campaign, President Nixon encouraged the trend toward import quotas by pledging to protect the textile industry from foreign competition. Intended initially as a means of attracting the Southern vote, support for textile quotas whet the appetite of other industries. The House trade bill of 1970 included import quotas not only for textiles but also for footware articles. Dozens of other industries sought protection. Wilbur Mills, chairman of the House Ways and Means Committee, expressed concern that a trade bill in 1971 would become the vehicle for numerous import quotas.

For more than two years, the Nixon Administration had tried, unsuccessfully, to negotiate a voluntary textile quota with Japan. In March 1971, the Japan Textile Federation announced a voluntary, unilateral program to limit exports of textile products to the United States. The remarkable fact about the announcement is that it followed discussions, not between the Japanese Government and President Nixon, but rather between a Japanese trade group and Chairman Mills. President Nixon denounced this "unorthodox action" and the "maneuver" of the Japanese trade group. He said that the agreement was unacceptable and that he would strongly support textile quota legislation. An editorial column in the Washington *Sunday Star* declared that it was "incredible that a member of the Congress should thus arrogate to himself the responsibilities of the executive branch." Of course the "arrogation" was made possible, if not necessary, by the Administration's inability to work out a voluntary agreement with Japan; by the pending 1971 trade bill; and by the depressed condition of the economy which threatened to add import quotas and protectionist provisions to the bill. A few months later Wilbur Mills was again instrumental in establishing a voluntary quota, this time involving shoes from Italy. In August 1971, in another move to discourage the flow of incoming goods, President Nixon announced a 10 percent surcharge on all imports except those already subject to quotas.

A number of items are already covered by quota legislation and administrative agreements. Under a voluntary restraint agreement entered into in 1962, both Japan and the European community limited their steel exports to the United States. In January 1971, after Bethlehem Steel had announced a 12.5 percent increase in its price of heavy construction steel, President Nixon warned that the Administration might allow more foreign steel into the country. Shortly thereafter Bethlehem rescinded its original price rise and announced a smaller increase.

The Agricultural Adjustment Act, as amended, authorizes the President to impose quotas on such commodities as wheat, cotton, and certain dairy products. Presidential proclamations for dairy quotas are made fairly often. The International Coffee Agreement, which became effective in 1963, established a system of export quotas as a means of smoothing out price fluctuations. Meat import quotas were enacted by Congress in 1964. President Nixon invoked authority under that act to increase the quota for meat imports during the latter half of 1970.

Sugar quotas are used to divide the annual sugar requirements among specified domestic and foreign producing areas. By setting an artificially high price for sugar, the Sugar Act guarantees a large share of the market to domestic growers—at substantial cost to the American consumer. After Fidel Castro had gained power in Cuba, and had confiscated U.S. property, Congress passed an act in 1960 which permitted the President to reduce Cuba's quota "as he shall find from time to time to be in the national interest." President Eisenhower used that authority to sharply reduce the Cuban sugar quota. Legislation in 1963 prohibited ("Except as may be deemed necessary by the President in the interest of the United States") any importation of Cuban sugar into the United States until the President determined that the Cuban government had taken steps to compensate U.S. citizens and firms for property that it had seized. Amendments to the Sugar Act in 1965 permitted the President, in the national interest, to withhold or suspend all or any part of a quota for a foreign country. In 1966, President Johnson withheld Southern Rhodesia's quota and prorated it to countries in the Western Hemisphere.

President Eisenhower, acting under authority of previous amendments to the Trade Agreements Act, established quotas for oil imports in 1959, on the basis of national security needs. By keeping out low-cost foreign oil, the quotas acted as a price support for the domestic oil industry. In December 1969, a majority of President Nixon's Cabinet Task Force on Oil Imports recommended that the quota system on oil be abandoned in favor of a tariff structure. In part, this was to end "the danger of favoritism and corruption" in the present system, where quotas were often imposed for purposes unrelated to the national security. It was suggested that oil quotas cost American consumers an estimated $5 billion a year in higher prices, and that the cost would climb to $8.4 billion by 1980. Nixon deferred action on the report and established another study committee. The House Ways and Means Committee voted in 1970 to prevent the adoption of a tariff on oil, as a substitute for quotas, but the provision was never enacted.

STANDBY TAX CONTROLS

In December 1960, several weeks before taking office, John F. Kennedy expressed his determination to return to "the spirit as well as the letter of the Employment Act of 1946." Years of high-level unemployment and economic stagnation prompted him a year later to ask Congress for two types of anti-recession controls: Presidential discretion to cut taxes by as much as 5 percent, and authority to release up to $2 billion for Federal spending. Congress denied Kennedy both requests, regarding them as brash and unprecedented attempts to expand executive power at the cost of legislative prerogatives. Yet in many respects the request for standby controls was a logical and natural development of Federal and Presidential responsibilities for full employment.

Employment Act of 1946

The prospect of an allied victory in 1945 had given rise to new concerns. How could the economy absorb the millions of veterans who would be returning home? What would happen to the economy when the war machine was dismantled? The great industrial complexes that supported the defense effort were looked upon as mere artificial props underneath an otherwise unstable structure.

In contrast to earlier periods, the specter of another depression was not met with complacency and resignation. The experience of mass unemployment throughout the 1930s, combined with the more recent years of war-induced prosperity, had helped foster a new attitude toward government. No longer could public officials sit back and remain passive about widespread suffering and idle factories. Nor was it satisfactory to revive the sporadic and unsuccessful relief programs of the New Deal.

The development of a different kind of full employment policy owes much to the work of two Englishmen: John Maynard Keynes and William H. Beveridge. Lord Keynes rejected the traditional assumption that the capitalist system was self-adjusting. In fact, he considered unemployment and economic instability as inevitable byproducts of modern capitalism, unless the government was prepared to step in and assist with public spending. Classical theorists had spoken of "voluntary unemployment" produced by workers who refused to accept the going rate. To Keynes, it was a little farfetched to believe that the unemployment of millions of Americans in the 1930s could be explained as the result of labor obstinately rejecting the available wage structure. It was the system itself that was fundamentally defective. He therefore promoted government intervention as the only possible remedy for a crumbling capitalist system, the sole means left for preventing the total destruction of existing economic forms and individual initiative.

Sir William Beveridge published his *Full Employment in a Free Society* in 1945. Much more than with Keynes, his work was infused with a deep passion for social justice and human needs. Unemployment was not merely wasteful or a threat to the capitalist order; it corrupted the spirit and demoralized the soul. "The greatest evil of unemployment," he wrote, "is not physical but moral, not the want which it may bring but the hatred and fear which it breeds." To look to individual employers for full employment was pointless; only the government possessed the requisite powers to discharge that responsibility. Beveridge also stressed that the goal was not simply employment and adequate demand, as Keynes had written. It was essential that public spending be directed toward social priorities and the satisfaction of human needs. Man needed the feeling that he was rendering useful service. For Beveridge, employment that was merely "time-wasting, equivalent to digging holes and filling them again, or merely destructive, like war and preparing for war, will not serve that purpose. Nor will it be felt worth while. It must be productive and progressive."

As a result of the experiences during the Great Depression and World War II, access to a job had evolved as a basic human right. In his annual message to Congress in January 1944, President Roosevelt spoke of a new Economic Bill of Rights, including the "right to a useful and remunerative job in the industries or shops or farms or mines of the Nation." The Full Employment Bill of 1945 reiterated that principle, by declaring that all Americans "able to work and seeking work have the right to useful, remunerative, regular, and full-time employment." The bill centered major powers and responsibilities in the Presidency. In cases where the private sector failed to provide full employment, Section 3(c) of the bill directed the President to prepare a program of Federal investment and expenditures that would close the gap. He was further directed, in Section 6, to review Federal programs on a quarterly basis and to alter their rate as he considered necessary for assuring full employment. The Senate passed this landmark bill in September 1945 by an overwhelming vote of 71 to 10.

Conservative groups emasculated the bill, however, as it journeyed through the House. Opponents charged that the bill contained within it the seeds of paternalism, socialism, and even communism. The existence of free enterprise, individual initiative, and business confidence were all said to be threatened with extinction. According to critics, passage of the Full Employment Bill would lead to wild government spending, a dangerous concentration of executive power, and ruinous inflation.

Substantive and forceful passages in the Senate version were either diluted or deleted. The crucial commitment to employment as a basic human right was taken out. The two sections on Presidential discretionary powers were removed. The original goal of full employment was whittled down to "maximum employment," and instead of the Federal Government *assuring* employment it would only "promote" it. The specific reliance on public works and Federal loans, as instruments for economic recovery, was replaced by the noncommittal phrase "all practicable means."

The resulting declaration of policy in the Employment Act of 1946 was a monument of compromise and ambivalence. It stated that the Federal Government, assisted by industry, agriculture, labor, and state and local governments, was responsible for coordinating "all its plans, functions, and resources for the purpose of creating and maintaining, in a manner calculated to foster and promote free competitive enterprise and the general welfare, conditions under which there will be afforded useful employment opportunities, including self-employment, for those able, willing, and seeking to work, and to promote maximum employment, production, and purchasing power." The ambiguity of the Act—mixing positive declarations of government responsibility with the promotion of the free enterprise system—meant that it could be implemented by Presidents in entirely different ways.

For President Truman, the Employment Act showed that America no longer accepted recurrent depressions as natural events, to be borne with patience and fortitude. The business cycle was no more natural than floods, and no less exempt from human control. The nation had come to expect the Federal Government to take prompt and positive action to prevent economic instability. The Government, Truman said, had to be ever ready to perform "its complementary role in sustaining and strengthening the economy." After the 1948–49 recession, he said that the early reversal was accomplished by a composite of private and public policies.

President Eisenhower, in contrast, sought to minimize the economic role of the Federal Government. He thus placed the accent of the Employment Act on the need to promote free enterprise. To Eisenhower, the Act "made it explicit that Government, in seeking to achieve maximum production, employment, and purchasing power, should do so 'in a manner calculated to foster and promote free competitive enterprise.' Accordingly, . . . we place reliance on measures that involve a minimum of direct intervention in the affairs of individuals and private groups." In recalling the recovery from the 1953–54 recession, he said that one fact about the subsequent economic expansion had to be emphasized: "the federal government did not create it. But another fact is equally certain: by unwise policies the federal government might well have wrecked it." Federal action could be exercised, but it should be in support of the free enterprise system. The Federal Government should instill a mood of confidence, protect the incentive to work, save, and invest, and provide a climate to encourage initiative by individuals and by state and local governments.

The two Presidents also differed in their use of Federal controls. Truman put the primary emphasis on a balanced economy, rather than on a balanced budget. Economic and social deficits were worse than a temporary deficit in the budget. It was "well-nigh axiomatic" to Truman that the Federal budget should have a surplus in years of prosperity and a deficit in periods of recession. He also advocated the use of tax adjustments as one means of stimulating or restraining the economy.

While the Eisenhower Administration supported such anti-recession controls as Federal credit programs, accelerated spending, and a temporary extension of unemployment payments, manipulation of the budget or of tax rates was to be avoided. Eisenhower did not adhere rigidly to the concept of a balanced budget. In general, however, Government could best discharge its responsibilities by "the prudent conduct of its own financial affairs"—namely, by operating under a balanced budget. Eisenhower also disapproved of using tax adjustments to control the economy. He looked upon proposals for tax reductions in the 1957–58 recession as a "hasty and disproportionate" solution. In leaving office in 1961, he discouraged the use of a "hasty improvisation" of tax rates for anti-recession purposes. Tax policy could be used to stimulate the economy—not by affecting the level of aggregate demand, as in Keynesian economics, but by promoting incentives and maintaining the vigor of the free enterprise system.

Countercyclical Record, 1945–1960

Compared to the 1930s, or the convulsive depressions and financial panics of earlier periods, the years from 1945 to the Kennedy Administration seemed relatively smooth and prosperous. Economic growth was interrupted now and then by recessions, but they were not as deep as before, nor were the human consequences quite so harsh. Unemployment benefits, social security, and the progressive income tax helped provide partial relief to the unemployed and contributed an automatic stabilizing influence over economic fluctuations.

Yet the economic loss over the postwar period was of considerable magnitude. The recession that began in November 1948 was followed by 11 months of contraction. Recessions occurred again in 1953 and 1957. From one recession to the next, the drop in production grew more severe. During the 1948–49 recession, real GNP dropped by 2.3 percent. During the next two recessions, real GNP dropped by 3.7 percent and 4.3 percent. Moreover, the length of the recovery period grew shorter from one recession to the next: there were 45 months of expansion after the first recession; 35 months after the second; and 25 months after the third. By May 1960, after a short period of growth, the economy had slipped into its fourth postwar recession. Estimates of the cost of these four recessions range from $109 billion (just counting the dips in the economy) to over $200 billion (taking into account the fact that the entire economy was operating below its full employment potential).

The postwar record would have been far worse had it not been for a number of fortuitous events. Each recovery was assisted by a fiscal *deus ex machina*. Consider the recession of 1948–49. Congress proposed a revenue act in 1948 that included reductions in individual tax rates, increases in standard exemptions, and other changes that would have strengthened private consumption. President Truman opposed the tax cut, insisting that the economy was already overheated and subject to dangerous inflationary pressures. The bill had to be passed over his veto.

By early 1949 it was recognized that the economy had slipped into a recession. The subsequent recovery was helped along nicely by the tax cut of the previous year. As H. A. Holmans has noted: "If there was ever a case of broadly sound economic measures being taken in very good time through good luck rather than good judgment, this was it." Of comparable good fortune was the special $2 billion dividend paid out of the National Service Life Insurance Trust Fund. It helped reinforce purchasing power and support the recovery, but was well under way long before the Federal Government was aware of the recession.

Fortune smiled again during the next recession. Personal tax rates were scheduled for reduction in 1953, to bring them back to their level before the Korean war. Another war measure, the excess profits tax, was also scheduled to expire. Through exceptional luck, both tax reductions were on the verge of taking effect at the time of the 1953–54 recession. This boost to consumption and private investment was timed with a precision that contemporary fiscal analysts find enviable, yet neither tax reduction had been taken with countercyclical intent. Once the downturn was conceded, the Eisenhower Administration announced that it would let the tax reductions take place as scheduled. Paul A. Samuelson remarked that this was "a little like deciding to let the sun set at eventide."

The recovery from the 1957–58 recession was also dominated as much by the force of events as by deliberate public policy. The Eisenhower budget of January 1957 had been criticized by Secretary of the Treasury Humphrey, who predicted that a failure to reduce Federal spending would produce a depression "that will curl your hair." Eisenhower ordered his Budget Director to seek additional ways to reduce expenditures; members of Congress and the private sector joined in the cry for budget cutbacks. While this retrenchment was under way, the summer brought disturbing evidence of a possible business downturn. Critics now charged that cutbacks had been *too* severe. In October 1957, an astonished world learned of Russia's launching of Sputnik I, followed the next month by a second satellite weighing over a thousand pounds.

The Administration could no longer ignore the defense and security implications of this development. Eisenhower now moved the nation toward heavier defense spending and pushed for Federal expenditures to aid science education. These steps were more important to the recovery than deliberate anti-recession actions. Farm price supports and a reduction in transportation excises, which also helped in the recovery, were not part of countercyclical policy either.

Although another recession began in May 1960, it did not become a feature of the Presidential campaign. The Eisenhower Administration was not eager to speculate on such an event—three recessions in eight years of Republican rule —and the evidence was too inconclusive for Kennedy to make it a centerpiece of his attack on the Eisenhower economic record. Instead, he hammered away at the sluggish growth rate and promised to get the country moving again.

Kennedy Standby Proposals

After his victory in the November election, Kennedy appointed Walter Heller to be chairman of the Council of Economic Advisers. Heller lost no time revealing his preference for a system of flexible tax rates as an economic control. The problem of gold outflow, which had restricted the use of monetary policy, placed a greater burden on fiscal means for stimulating the economy.

The details of Kennedy's anti-recession policy were not known until the 1962 legislative program, after the recent recession had passed. Believing that the "time to repair the roof is when the sun is shining," Kennedy asked for discretionary power over tax cuts and public spending. He recommended these procedures:

1. Before invoking the tax authority, the President would have to make a finding that economic conditions required a tax adjustment as a means of achieving the objectives of the Employment Act. He could then submit to Congress a proposal for temporary uniform reduction in all individual income tax rates by as much as 5 percent. Unless this was rejected by a joint resolution of Congress within 30 days, the reduction would take effect for a six-month period. Renewal would be by the same process, or by joint resolution. If Congress was not in session, the President's proposal would go into effect automatically, and terminate 30 days after Congress reconvened.

2. For the standby spending proposal, Kennedy suggested a statistical "trigger." The President would have discretion to accelerate and initiate up to $2 billion in capital improvements whenever the unemployment rate increased by at least one percentage point during a specified number

of months. The President could then act within two months in disbursing the money: up to $750 million for accelerating Federal programs previously authorized by Congress; up to $750 million for grants-in-aid to state and local governments; up to $250 million in loans to states and localities that were unable to meet their share of project costs; and up to $250 million distributed among these three categories as the President considered best.

To President Kennedy, these two standby proposals represented the greatest steps forward in stabilization policy since the Employment Act itself. A number of congressmen agreed. Representative Henry Reuss praised the 1962 Economic Report for recognizing congressional intent in conferring upon the executive branch broad responsibility for economic policy: "In doing so, the President and the council have restored to the Employment Act a usefulness which has long been lacking." This was not a mere echo of support from a congressional liberal. The idea of Presidential tax and spending discretion, far from being the brainchild of the Administration, had originated in Congress itself and in the private sector. Moreover, it enjoyed support from liberals and conservatives alike. Paul McCracken, former member of the Council of Economic Advisers under Eisenhower, and later the chairman of the CEA under Nixon, offered this view in 1962: "I'd give the President power to vary tax rates somewhat during business ups and downs. This may sound radical, but it's actually conservative. It would reduce pressures to spend our way out of a recession."

The idea of adjusting Federal spending and tax rates, to control the economy, had taken several decades to develop. The use of public works to stabilize the economy was part of the Employment Stabilization Act of 1931, which was signed by President Hoover. Lump-sum appropriations for public works and relief programs during the 1930s gave President Roosevelt considerable discretion in distributing the funds. In the Full Employment Bill of 1945, one section allowed for Presidential adjustments in the rate of Federal investments and expenditures, but that provision was deleted by the House.

During the postwar period, a number of congressmen introduced legislation to give the President greater responsibility and flexibility in initiating public works. Senator Paul Douglas and Representative Richard Bolling introduced companion bills in 1954 to focus responsibility for public works planning in the Presidency. Under their proposal, the executive branch would have been responsible for determining when acceleration of public construction would do the following: use manpower and productive capacity most effectively, create needed public facilities for the public welfare, and offset declines in private investment. In May 1960, six Senators introduced the "Stand-by Anti-Recession Act of 1960," which proposed that the President be authorized to initiate a $3 billion public works and housing program when national unemployment rose for six months and was above 5 percent. Whenever unemployment indicators revealed the onset of a recession, the President was to declare the existence of an emergency period and to authorize the acceleration of Federal programs: up to $1 billion for community facility loans; up to $1 billion in additional commitments and purchases of mortgages; and up to $1 billion for accelerating Federal or Federally assisted projects.

In August 1961, President Kennedy notified one of the co-sponsors of this bill, Senator Joseph Clark, that he intended to embody the principle of standby spending authority in his 1962 legislative program, along with such other measures as might be needed to protect the economy from high levels of unemployment. Kennedy repeated that promise at the AFL-CIO Convention in December 1961.

The idea of Presidential tax discretion goes back to the 1940s. Alvin Hansen, an early advocate of Keynesian economics, recommended in 1947 that the President be empowered to raise and lower income tax rates as part of stabilization policy. At about the same time another economist, Albert Hart, combined Presidential tax discretion with a "gong-and-whistle" system. The "gong" would go off when unemployment exceeded a certain minimum; the "whistle" would sound when prices rose above a predetermined level. The gong signaled the need for tax reduction, while the whistle called for tax increases and tightening of bank credit. If neither indicator sounded, then control would be left to the automatic stabilizers. Both Hansen and Hart proposed that the President be authorized to adjust the tax rates, subject to legislative veto.

As for legislative proposals, Representative Wright Patman introduced a bill in May 1960 that called for tax adjustments whenever the President determined that economic conditions warranted them. Within the range of a maximum adjustment of 10 percent, the President could decrease income taxes to prevent or counteract a recession, and increase them either to balance the budget, to reduce the public debt, or to avoid high interest rates. Representative Morris Udall introduced two bills in 1962 for Presidential tax discretion, for the purpose of assuring reduction of the Federal debt. The Joint Economic Committee endorsed the principle of tax discretion in 1960, but without specifying whether Congress or the President should make the adjustment. In January 1961, the Samuelson Task Force (which Kennedy had established) recommended discretionary tax powers for the President.

The most significant endorsement of Presidential tax discretion came in a study issued in 1961 by the Commission on Money and Credit (CMC). This private commission—composed of members of the banking, business, government, labor, and academic communities—devoted three years to a study of the nation's monetary and credit policies. Yet its most controversial recommendation was fiscal: Presidential tax discretion. Henry Wallich and Bela Balassa, writing in the *Harvard Business Review,* suggested that if the Commission's proposals were transcribed onto an agenda, "the #1 item probably would have to be the proposal for administrative variability of income tax rates."

The Commission realized that its proposal ran counter

to long-established traditions, but it considered tax discretion by the President to be a necessary adjunct to the Employment Act. At congressional hearings on the CMC report, Frazar B. Wilde, chairman of the Commission, stressed that throughout the study the members were aware of the "towering role which the President must play in our democratic form of government." Robert Nathan, a member of the Commission, told Congress he considered Presidential tax discretion "perhaps the Commission's most important single tax proposal." Paul A. Samuelson applauded the proposal, insisting that it was not quixotic. Proposals like these "are bound to come, and they will come in our lifetime, and the sooner the better." Other prominent economists, who testified before Congress and expressed their support for Presidential tax discretion, include John Gurley, Richard Musgrave, Alvin Hansen, Paul McCracken, and Joseph Pechman.

Congressional Response

Part of the resistance to the Kennedy proposals came from those who still questioned the propriety of Federal controls on the business cycle. Actions taken in recent years to avoid recession and restrain inflation have accustomed us to positive governmental action, but 1962 still carried with it attitudes from earlier decades. Rep. Thomas B. Curtis, member of the Joint Economic Committee, argued that the business cycle was a natural force, not to be tampered with. It was a question of whether the economy does or does not move forward through business cycles. "Do we agree it does," asked Curtis, "that that is normal, to go forward in periods of expansion and then contractions like the peristaltic action, if I can be a little earthy? Is that a natural thing? If it is a natural thing what are we trying to do—interfere with a natural process?" In addition to threatening what some considered to be the delicate balance of natural forces, Kennedy challenged fundamental notions about the Constitution. To critics, Presidential standby tax and spending powers represented a flagrant assault on the structure of the governmental system, especially the separation doctrine and congressional prerogatives.

The Kennedy tax proposal was referred to the Ways and Means Committee on May 8, 1962. Wilbur Mills, committee chairman, considered executive tax-cutting to be at least a debatable issue, but he regarded discretion to raise taxes as out of the question. The Administration's draft had been limited to tax-cutting powers. which Walter Heller said was "more consistent with the congressional powers and prerogatives in the field of fiscal matters, specifically in the field of taxation." President Kennedy also insisted that the tax-cutting proposal was not a request to Congress that it delegate its power to levy taxes. Along with this deference to legislative sensitivities, it was of course true that the major threat to the economy at that time was sluggishness and recession, which required tax reduction.

The sole action by the Committee on Ways and Means was this entry in its calendar: "A communication from the President of the United States, transmitting a draft of proposed legislation entitled 'A bill to amend the Internal Revenue Code of 1954 to provide standby authority for temporary reduction in the individual income tax when needed to meet the objectives of the Employment Act of 1946.'" The draft was never introduced in bill form. Congressional criticism was intense. To Senator Harry Byrd, chairman of the Finance Committee, the delegation of tax-reduction powers to the President would be "in fundamental violation of the Constitution." Senator Kenneth Keating viewed the standby tax proposal as part of an over-all pattern in the usurpation of congressional authority. Minority views in the 1962 Joint Economic Report declared that the Kennedy proposals gave the President "dangerously unprecedented powers at the expense of the traditional powers of Congress to lay taxes and to appropriate." Tax discretion of this type was called a direct violation of the Constitution.

During the 1962 campaign, Eisenhower spoke out against the request for standby tax and spending powers, cit-ing it as an example of "the apparent thirst for more and more power centered in the Federal Government—and particularly in the executive branch." To grant such powers would demonstrate the willingness of Americans to have "one-man government" and to satisfy the "unconscionable grab of power" by the President. Eisenhower felt that Congress was "degraded when they have to consider whether they are going to pass the regulation of the taxing power to the President. What is Congress for?"

After 1962, the executive branch gradually retreated from the subject of Presidential tax discretion. The 1963 Economic Report asked Congress to reconsider the Kennedy proposals when the calendar of fiscal legislation was lighter. When Walter Heller appeared before the Senate Finance Committee in 1963, to argue the case for a tax cut, Senator George Smathers recalled the standby tax idea and asked: "Dr. Heller, the last post at which you taught, did you teach constitutional law or a course in economics?" Heller gave the anticipated reply and was thereupon treated to a lecture on congressional prerogatives and the separation doctrine.

The 1964 Economic Report made no mention of tax discretion, except to say in the accompanying CEA report that the standby tax proposal was one way to add flexibility to fiscal policy. Subsequent Economic Reports concentrated on changes in legislative procedures that might facilitate prompt fiscal action.

In a 1964–65 congressional study on fiscal policy, George Bach, Robert Eisner, Richard Goode, and James Tobin—all extremely well-known economists—advocated Presidential standby tax powers. Henry Wallich, member of the CEA under Eisenhower, told a congressional committee in 1966 that the "pragmatic advantages" were in favor of delegating limited tax power to the President, along the lines of the CMC and Kennedy proposals.

On the other hand, the Republican Party, in a 1966 resolution, cited the "clear language of article I, section 8" of the Constitution as the reason for being "unalterably opposed" to granting to the President any authority to raise or lower taxes. The resolution was subsequently endorsed by the Joint Senate-House Republican Leadership. Edwin Nourse, who had been CEA chairman under President Truman, issued a caveat in 1966 on the economic power of the executive branch: "Did passage of the Employment Act of 1946 mark a subconscious or intentional departure, or revision of, the traditional American principle of 'checks and balances' and toward monolithic central government?" Nourse envisioned a modern version of the separation doctrine: an "economic troika" consisting of Government fiscal actions, monetary management by the Federal Reserve, and autonomous operations of the private market.

Prospect for Standby Tax Powers

As a substitute for Presidential adjustment of tax rates, three other proposals have been put forward. First, there can be "formula flexibility." A certain combination of economic indicators—unemployment rate, consumer price index, layoff rate, etc.—are selected to represent the barometer of the national economy. As the barometer moves up and down, it automatically triggers the appropriate fiscal response. Yet economic indicators, unless interpreted in the light of overall economic developments and anticipated actions by the Federal Government, can be deceptive and produce miscalls. Advocacy of formula flexibility, Professor Carl Shoup has said, "can too easily become just a way of seeking to escape from assuming responsibility, making decisions, and learning from mistakes." And in the words of a Joint Economic Committee report, formula flexibility amounts to "Presidential discretion without any discretion and this inflexibility is the principal argument against it."

If human judgment is needed to interpret economic indicators, a "Fiscal Authority" could be established and made independent of the President. That would supposedly insulate the experts from political influence, but past experience with regulatory agencies has not been reassuring in that respect. Moreover, the overriding need of stabilization policy in the postwar period has been to coordinate the actions of the fiscal, credit, and monetary authorities—not to fragment them still further. Government would be made less accountable by shunting tax-adjustment powers to an independent board. There are already too many instances in which the Federal Reserve has moved in one direction and executive agencies in another.

If proposals for formula flexibility and a Fiscal Authority have their drawbacks, can Congress modernize its procedures to permit prompt and knowledgeable fiscal action? Congress acted rapidly in 1965 in reducing excise taxes, but that is not compelling evidence that legislators would act as decisively with personal or corporate tax adjustments, particularly if the movement was in the upward direction. Business had lobbied for years in trying to reduce or abolish the excise tax. When the reduction did come, it could not be counted as a pure exercise in countercyclical policy.

The Tax Adjustment Act of 1966, which placed large corporations on a current payments basis for income taxes, and introduced a graduated withholding of individual income taxes, was enacted into law only two months after the proposal appeared in the State of the Union Message. This, too, was cited as evidence that Congress can move swiftly with tax legislation, and that there is no need to delegate new powers to the President. Yet Congress' reputation for responsible action on tax legislation was not enhanced later in 1966 when an Administration bill, designed to alleviate the balance-of-payments problem, became the vehicle for so many extraneous amendments for special-interest groups that it became known as the "Christmas Tree Bill." When President Johnson asked for a surcharge in 1967 on personal and corporate income taxes, it took Congress almost a year to complete action.

This legislative record stimulated new interest in Presidential tax discretion. In 1966, Senator Eugene McCarthy recommended that the Administration ask Congress for limited discretionary power to adjust or modify individual and corporate income taxes, and to modify the investment tax credit in the event of inflationary pressures. Also in 1966, Representative Moorhead introduced a bill to authorize the President, during congressional adjournments, to increase temporarily certain income tax and withholding rates.

Less than a month before his assassination in Los Angeles, Senator Robert Kennedy urged Congress to adopt the standby tax proposal that had been requested by his brother. President Johnson took the issue to the Business Council on December 4, 1968, stating that it would be "highly desirable" to grant the President some limited tax authority. A month later, in his final Economic Report, he asked Congress to give the President discretionary tax authority, subject to congressional veto. In a statement released in January 1969, the Committee for Economic Development supported Presidential authority to raise or lower the personal and corporate income taxes by up to 10 percent, subject to statutory guidelines.

With President Nixon in office, Republicans managed to find the standby tax power concept a little less offensive. In the 1969 Joint Economic Report, three Republican Senators and four Republican Representatives joined in this statement: "To increase the ability of fiscal policy to deal with an unforeseen economic downturn, we recommend that along with the extension of the 10-percent surtax, the President be given the authority to reduce its size or eliminate it completely. The Congress could grant the Executive the power to implement its decision after 60 days, unless either House of Congress passes a contrary resolution during that period." In April 1970, Senator Edward Brooke charged that anti-inflation efforts in the past had been fought with "primitive and inadequate weapons." He introduced a "Flexible Fiscal Policy Act" to give the President authority to raise or lower tax rates by up to 10 percent after determining that inflationary or deflationary trends threatened the economy. The plan would take effect if neither house passed a resolution disapproving it within 60 days.

Disappointment in monetary policy during the first two years of the Nixon Administration also helped revive interest in fiscal policy. Previously, the "monetarist" school had argued that short-run fiscal changes were ineffective, if not actually injurious, and that changes in the money supply represented the most reliable macroeconomic tool available to the Government. However, a restrictive monetary policy in 1969–70 failed to bring inflationary pressures under control, and when monetary policy shifted in 1970, to stimulate the economy, business activity remained sluggish. More money and credit were made available, but consumers and businessmen were reluctant to spend and invest. A high-ranking Administration official remarked, "I'm less of a monetarist now than when I came here."

When the question of Presidential tax discretion is again debated by Congress, a more reasonable and mature concept of the Constitution will hopefully enter the discussion. Administrative efficiency and the theory of separated powers are not antagonistic concepts, nor is there anything sacrosanct about legislative prerogatives over the taxing and spending powers. Once it has been decided that short-run tax changes are necessary for economic stability, the relevant issue at that point is simply whether Congress is able, in terms of its procedures and organization, to discharge such a task. If not, there is nothing constitutionally objectionable to delegating that responsibility to the President.

6

PRESIDENTIAL WAR POWERS

While the Constitution divides the war power between Congress and the President, it has been left to history to determine which branch would have the predominant voice. With few exceptions, the power to initiate and wage war has shifted to the executive branch. The President's power as Commander in Chief has grown in response to three major developments.

First, the President acquired the responsibility to protect American life and property abroad. He has invoked that vague prerogative on numerous occasions to satisfy much larger objectives of the executive branch. Second, the time boundaries of the "war period" have become increasingly elastic. The President may initiate military operations before congressional action, and he retains wartime powers long after hostilities have ceased. Third, the postwar period, which has been marked by nuclear weapons, the Cold War, intercontinental missiles, military alliances, and greater U.S. world responsibilities, has accelerated the growth of Presidential power. Postwar developments have all taken place in a twilight zone that is neither war nor peace. Because of this uncertainty, the President has had extra latitude to dispatch troops abroad to discharge what he considers to be U.S. obligations and to satisfy rather generous definitions of "defensive war."

PROTECTING LIFE AND PROPERTY

Although the Constitution does not expressly direct the President to protect American life and property in foreign countries, Presidents have sent U.S. forces abroad for that purpose on many occasions. In so doing, they have based their actions not on legislative authority but rather on inherent executive responsibilities.

The constitutionality of such actions was examined by a circuit court in 1860. An American ship had been ordered to Greytown (now San Juan del Norte), Nicaragua, in 1854, to compel local authorities to make amends for an affront to an American diplomat and for property losses sustained by an American firm. The authorities failed to offer reparations that were satisfactory to the commander of the American vessel, and he proceeded to bombard the town from nine in the morning to mid-afternoon, stopping periodically to see whether town officials would yield. American forces subsequently went ashore to destroy by fire most of what remained of the town. A resident sued for damages to his property, but the court, in *Durand* v. *Hollins,* upheld the commander's actions: "as it respects the interposition of the Executive abroad, for the protection of the lives or property of the citizen, the duty must, of necessity, rest in the discretion of the President. Acts of lawless violence, or of threatened violence to the citizen or his property, cannot be anticipated and provided for; and the protection, to be effectual or of any avail, may, not unfrequently, require the most prompt and decided action." The court did not attempt to explore the extent to which the President could destroy foreign property or commit acts of violence while protecting American interests.

The number of instances in which American forces have been sent abroad to protect U.S. citizens is subject to various counts. In a 1928 study, Milton Offutt compiled a list of 76 instances between 1813 and 1927. His list omits such well-known cases as Pershing's expedition into Mexico in 1916 and our intervention in Russia in 1918. In a 1945 study, James Grafton Rogers collected 148 examples of U.S. military operations abroad. His list, however, includes our declared wars, as well as many actions taken by President Roosevelt prior to Pearl Harbor: the Destroyers-Bases agreement with Great Britain, our occupation of Greenland, and the armed convoy ordered by the President. A 1970 compilation by the Library of Congress cites 165 instances in which the United States has used armed force abroad. Only five cases involved declared wars. Most of the other actions were taken in the name of protecting life and property.

The traditional justification for using American forces to protect life and property expanded in 1904 when President Theodore Roosevelt defined America's policy toward other nations in the Western Hemisphere. Those nations need not, he said, fear interference in their internal affairs, provided that they acted with "reasonable efficiency and decency in social and political matters," and kept order and paid their obligations. Yet if mismanagement created a situation where they could not meet their foreign obligations, and thereby invited European nations to intervene in South America and the Caribbean to protect their interests, the United States would have to act first. "Chronic wrongdoing," Roosevelt said, "or an impotence which results in a general loosening of the ties of civilized society," might require American intervention.

Known as the Roosevelt Corollary to the Monroe Doctrine, this Presidential announcement signaled a new departure in American policy. Instead of serving as a restriction on European intervention in the Western Hemisphere, it was a justification for U.S. intervention there. Troops would be sent abroad not to protect American lives and property but to protect American foreign policy.

Roosevelt had already given his new doctrine a trial run in 1903, after Colombia had refused to ratify a treaty giving the United States a canal right-of-way in Panama. In a draft message to Congress, he considered taking possession of the isthmus "without any further parley with Colombia," but events made it unnecessary to deliver the message. Roosevelt encouraged a "revolt" by Panamanians, and then sent in U.S. warships to prevent Colombia from suppressing the insurrection. He promptly recognized Panama as an independent republic and gained control of the canal zone.

To justify his action, he pointed to past revolutions, rebellions, insurrections, riots, and other outbreaks that had occurred in Panama: "In short, the experience of over half a century has shown Colombia to be utterly incapable of keeping order on the Isthmus." Partial restitution was later offered by the United States when it signed the Thompson-Urrutia Treaty. The treaty gave Colombia special canal rights and a cash grant of $25 million to compensate, in effect, for Roosevelt's venture.

Self-determination and nonintervention ranked high among the guiding principles of Woodrow Wilson, at least in theory; yet they were often made subordinate to his crusading determination to export constitutionalism to other lands. Thus, taking the Greytown bombardment of 1854 as an acceptable precedent, he ordered American forces to occupy Veracruz in 1914. The episode began with a trivial incident involving U.S. seamen in Tampico, and ended with U.S. bombardment of Veracruz, occupation of the town for seven months, and the downfall of the Mexican president, Victoriano Huerto.

In 1915, Wilson intervened in Haiti in an effort to secure a government that would be more acceptable to the Administration, although he confided to his Secretary of State that "we have not the legal authority to do what we apparently ought to do. . . ." American troops did not leave Haiti until 1934. Wilson's intervention in the Dominican Republic in 1916 resulted in a military occupation that lasted eight years. Also in 1916, in a variation of the life-and-property prerogative, he ordered General Pershing on a "hot pursuit" after Pancho Villa. The expedition penetrated several hundred miles into Mexico, lasted almost a year, and came close to outright war. Wilson sent marines into Cuba in 1917 to put down an insurgent force, and he intervened in Russia from 1918 to 1920 to work with anti-Bolshevik forces.

On four occasions during the post-1945 period, Presidents have invoked their prerogative to use armed force abroad for the protection of American lives and property. Protection of life provided a semblance of constitutionality for our military intervention in Lebanon in 1958. Although President Eisenhower could have justified his action on the basis of the Middle East Resolution passed the previous year, he announced that U.S. forces were being sent to Lebanon "to protect American lives and by their presence there to encourage the Lebanese government in defense of Lebanese sovereignty and integrity." When President Johnson ordered troops into the Dominican Republic in 1965, he was able to claim later, despite all the fears of a Communist takeover, that "99 percent of our reason for going in there was to try to provide protection for these American lives and for the lives of other nationals." On April 30, 1970, President Nixon explained that he was sending American troops into Cambodia, after concluding that enemy actions "clearly endanger the lives of Americans who are in Vietnam now and would constitute an unacceptable risk to those who will be there after withdrawal of another 150,000." On February 8, 1971, after the Nixon Administration had provided support for the South Vietnamese invasion of Laos, the State Department justified the action, in part, on the grounds that it would "protect American lives."

TIME BOUNDARIES OF "WAR PERIOD" (1789–1945)

In addition to life-and-property actions, Presidents have dispatched U.S. troops to fight in a number of undeclared wars, including the "quasi-war" with France from 1798 to 1800, the Barbary War from 1801 to 1805, and the Second Barbary War in 1815. The existence of limited, partial, or imperfect wars—conducted without a congressional declaration of war—was recognized by the Supreme Court in *Bas* v. *Tingy* (1800). The Court decided that the hostilities with France were "sufficiently described, without declaring war, or declaring that we were at war. Such a declaration by congress, might have constituted a perfect state of war, which was not intended by the government." The following year, in *Talbot* v. *Seeman,* the Court again held that Congress could either declare a general war or authorize and finance a partial war.

Presidents also invoke the full scope of their war powers during declared wars: the War of 1812, the Mexican War (1846–48), the Spanish-American War of 1898, and the two world wars. In all those conflicts, only once—in the War of 1812—did Congress actually debate the merits of entering war. The vote on that occasion was quite close: the Senate voted 19 to 13, and the House 79 to 49, in favor of a declaration of war. In all other cases, Congress simply recognized that war did in fact exist.

Presidential war-making power is discussed here in its three phases: executive prerogative before legislative action; the President's waging of war after Congress has declared or recognized that war exists; and the demobilization powers that are retained by the executive branch after hostilities have ceased.

Executive Prerogative

According to the Lockean prerogative, the executive has to be free, in cases where a strict and rigid observance of law would do harm, to act in the absence of law and sometimes even against it. The law-making power was not always in session and was too numerous and slow to act in the face of an emergency. Locke said that it was impossible "to foresee and so by laws to provide for all accidents and necessities that may concern the public. . . ."

Delegates to the Philadelphia Convention appreciated the need for executive action without specific legislative authority. They realized that the President might have to begin military operations for defensive wars before receiving legislative sanction, for otherwise a dangerous time gap could exist between the outbreak of hostilities and formal action by Congress. When one of the delegates proposed that the legislature be empowered to "make war," it was objected that congressional proceedings could be too slow for the safety of the country. Madison and Gerry were successful in substituting "declare" for "make"—thus empowering Congress to declare war while giving the President discretionary authority to repel sudden attacks. In subsequent years this produced a continuing constitutional dilemma: how to reconcile the war-making powers of the President with the war-declaring powers of Congress.

The authority of Congress to set limits on the war power was recognized by both the President and the Supreme Court during the first few decades of our history. When the John Adams Administration exercised emergency powers contrary to an act of Congress, the Supreme Court upheld the statutory position. The case arose when the Secretary of the Navy ordered the seizure of vessels bound to or from a French port; Congress had merely authorized seizure of vessels bound *to* a French port. The Court ruled in *Little* v. *Barreme* that the executive order exceeded the bounds of the statute and was consequently invalid. The authority of Congress in this case was particularly strong, for the Constitution specifically empowers Congress to "make Rules concerning Captures on Land and Water" (Article I, Section 8).

Jefferson respected the distinction between defensive and offensive wars in 1801, when he sent a naval squadron to the Mediterranean to protect American commerce against threatened piracy. He told Congress that he was not authorized by the Constitution, without legislative sanction, to go beyond "the line of defence," and asked whether the legislators intended to place U.S. forces "on an equal footing with that of its adversaries." In other situations Jefferson operated on the basis of pure prerogative. He was later to write that the observance of the written law was one of the high duties of a public official, but it was not the highest: the laws of self-preservation and national security enjoyed a higher priority. "To lose our country by a scrupulous adherence to written law," wrote Jefferson, "would be to lose the law itself, with life, liberty and all those who are enjoying them with us; thus absurdly sacrificing the end to the means." Having acted outside the law, the executive would come before the legislature, disclose the action taken, and ask for acquittance.

Statutes in 1792 and 1795, enacted to safeguard the country against insurrection and invasion, authorized the President to call forth the militia of the states "as he may judge necessary," to repel an invasion or a threatened invasion. When President Madison invoked that authority during the War of 1812, several New England states refused to place their militia at his disposal, contending that this exercise of executive power was unconstitutional. A unanimous decision in *Martin* v. *Mott* (1827) held that the decision as to whether an exigency had actually arisen belonged exclusively to the President.

President Polk relied on the war prerogative, in 1846, in ordering General Zachary Taylor to occupy disputed territory on the Texas-Mexican border. He thereby precipitated a clash on April 25 between American and Mexican soldiers. Unaware that hostilities had actually begun, Polk met with his Cabinet on the afternoon of May 9. He decided to recommend "definitive measures" to Congress and ask that it declare war on Mexico. All but one member of the Cabinet agreed, and steps were taken to prepare the necessary documents. About six that evening, Polk learned of the April 25 clash. General Taylor reported that hostilities "may now be considered as commenced"; he had already called upon Texas and Louisiana for volunteers. Polk notified Congress on May 11 that "war exists" and urged Congress to recognize that fact. Two days later Congress did so. Polk's initiative was subsequently censured by the House in 1848 by an 85 to 81 vote; it declared that the war had been "unnecessarily and unconstitutionally begun by the President of the United States."

One of Polk's critics at the time was Congressman Abraham Lincoln, who wrote to a friend: "Allow the President to invade a neighboring nation whenever he shall deem it necessary to repel an invasion, and you allow him to do so whenever he may choose to say he deems it necessary for such purpose, and you allow him to make war at pleasure." During his own years as President, however, Lincoln did not hesitate to invoke executive power without legislative approval or even advice. In April 1861, after Congress had adjourned, he issued proclamations calling forth the state militia; he authorized the suspension of the writ of habeas corpus; and he placed a blockade on the rebellious states. Vessels violating the blockade were to be seized and their cargo taken as prize. A 5-4 decision by the Supreme Court in *The Prize Cases* turned aside the argument that the absence of enabling legislation had cast a shadow of illegality over Lincoln's actions. Either with or without legislation, the President remained responsible for using the necessary force to protect the Union. The decision as to the existence of war was his alone. It was his duty to counter force with force, and resist war "in the shape it presented itself, without waiting for Congress to baptize it with a name; and no name given to it by him or them could change the fact."

After Congress convened, it empowered the President to declare when and where a state of insurrection existed. On the question of the beginning date of the Civil War, the Court held unanimously in *The Protector* that it was necessary to refer to some public act of the political departments, and that "for obvious reasons, those of the executive department, which may be, and, in fact, was, at the commencement of hostilities, obliged to act during the recess of Congress, must be taken."

In the Spanish-American War of 1898, executive prerogatives were intermixed with statutory authority. Congress and the press had clamored for forceful intervention to take Cuba from Spain. In an address to Congress on April 11,

1898, President McKinley defended intervention as a means of ending a conflict "right at our door." Intervention would also, the President said, protect American lives and property in Cuba and avert serious injury to American business interests there. He requested authority to use military and naval force in order to put an end to hostilities between Spain and the people of Cuba.

Congress responded on April 20 by authorizing the President to use whatever force was necessary to compel Spain to withdraw from Cuba, disclaiming, at the same time, any American interest in exercising control over the island. McKinley issued proclamations blockading Cuban ports and calling up volunteers. On April 24, the Secretary of the Navy cabled Commodore George Dewey at Hong Kong: "War has commenced between the United States and Spain. Proceed at once to the Philippine Island. Commence operations at once, particularly against Spanish fleet." On the following day, Congress declared the existence of war between the United States and Spain, advancing the date so that war existed as of the 21st. The fact that war had come into existence, several days before Congress actually acknowledged it, was later affirmed by the Supreme Court in *The Pedro*.

Upon the outbreak of the European war in 1914, President Wilson closed the Marconi Wireless Station at Siasconset, Massachusetts, because it had refused to comply with naval censorship regulations. His Attorney General justified the action by stating that it was the President's right and duty, in the absence of any statutory restriction, to close down or seize any plant, "should he deem it necessary in securing obedience to his proclamation of neutrality." Wilson asked for legislation in 1917 to allow him to arm American merchant ships and to protect them from German submarine attacks. The House passed the bill, but a number of Senators joined in a filibuster to block action on the proposal. Wilson denounced them as a "little group of willful men" and proceeded to arm the vessels after Congress had adjourned. It was Wilson who made the basic decisions in moving from neutrality to armed neutrality, and finally to a state of belligerency, with Germany.

Even more than Wilson, Franklin Roosevelt led the country from a state of neutrality to one of war. On September 8, 1939, after Germany had invaded Poland, Roosevelt proclaimed a state of limited emergency. In response to a Senate resolution, the Attorney General collected a list of statutes that became active upon the proclamation of a state of emergency or war. The Attorney General did not claim to be presenting a complete list, but nevertheless referred to about fifty statutes granting powers that could be exercised by the President in time of national emergency or during a war in which the United States was neutral.

An unprecedented use of the executive prerogative took place on September 3, 1940, when the President announced an agreement to exchange fifty "over-aged" destroyers with Britain, in return for the right to use bases on British islands in the Atlantic and Caribbean. The Destroyers-Bases deal was made solely by executive agreement, thereby circumventing the Senate and the treaty process. Attorney General Jackson defended the constitutionality of the agreement by claiming that the President's function as Commander in Chief placed upon him a responsibility "to use all constitutional authority which he may possess to provide adequate bases and stations for the utilization of the naval and air weapons of the United States at their highest efficiency in our defense." The phrase "to use all constitutional authority" obviously begged the question as to the legality of the President's action.

In April 1941, Roosevelt signed an agreement with Denmark, pledging America's defense of Greenland (a Danish possession) in return for the right to construct and operate defense installations on the island. Also in April, he announced his decision to extend American naval patrols halfway across the Atlantic. The Navy would search for German submarines and report their presence to British convoys.

On May 27, 1941, Roosevelt proclaimed the existence of an unlimited national emergency. Within two weeks he had signed another agreement, with Iceland, to permit U.S. forces to land there so as to prevent Germany from occupying it and using it as a naval or air base against the Western Hemisphere. Still operating on the basis of the executive prerogative, Roosevelt seized the North American Aviation plant in Inglewood, California, on June 7, 1941, and followed this with the seizure of several other defense facilities. On June 14, 1941, Roosevelt ordered the freezing of all remaining assets of Germany, Italy, and Axis-controlled countries. Three months before Pearl Harbor, he issued his "shoot-on-sight" order to U.S. forces in defense waters, warning that German and Italian vessels would enter those areas at their own risk.

Waging War

Once Congress has declared war and voted the necessary funds to prosecute it, Presidents have through their own actions enlarged the scope of the conflict and acquired new territory. The Mexican War, which started as a border dispute, became the occasion for extending American control across the continent. Prior to the outbreak of hostilities, President Polk tried unsuccessfully to acquire some of the Northern Provinces from Mexico. Immediately after Congress declared a state of war with Mexico on May 13, 1846, Polk gave orders to Colonel Kearney to move his regiment to Santa Fe "to protect our traders." By May 30, Polk was ready to reveal to his Cabinet his determination to acquire California, New Mexico, and "perhaps some others of the Northern Provinces of Mexico whenever a peace was made." He proposed that Kearney leave a portion of his force at Santa Fe and take the remainder of his men on to California, a plan to which the Cabinet assented.

When the expeditions proved successful, Polk recommended to Congress that Mexico cede the area to the United States. He asserted that Mexico was too "feeble a power" to govern its territories and that they might, as a result, fall to foreign powers and violate the Monroe Doctrine. Polk spoke frankly of the benefits that would accrue to America from annexation: a vast expanse of land contiguous with existing U.S. territory; new resources to develop; and important harbors along the California coast that would shelter the U.S. navy and provide a base for profitable commerce with Asia. The President's justification even went so far as to argue that the Province of New Mexico was populated by bands of "fierce and warlike savages," who constituted a threat to the northern states of Mexico. It thus appeared to Polk to be "a blessing to all those northern States to have their citizens protected against them by the power of the United States."

The peace treaty with Mexico in 1848 ceded New Mexico and California to the United States, a huge grant of territory that includes the present states of California, Nevada, and Utah, practically all of Arizona (filled out in 1853 with the Gadsden Purchase), and parts of New Mexico, Colorado, and Wyoming.

During the Civil War, Congress delegated vast power to Lincoln to enable him to prosecute the war. Several months after he issued his proclamations calling up the state militias and ordering the blockade, Congress passed an act "approving, legalizing, and making valid all the acts, proclamations, and orders of the President, etc., *as if they had been issued and done under the previous express authority and direction of the Congress of the United States.*" Lincoln was later authorized to take possession of railroad and telegraph lines whenever in his judgment the public safety so required. His power over the draft was almost unlimited, for he could call for "such number of men for the military service of the United States as the public exigencies may require."

In the Spanish-American War, President McKinley followed up Admiral Dewey's victory at Manila by sending an army of occupation to the Philippines; he also acquired Wake Island and occupied Puerto Rico. In the midst of this expansionist fervor, Congress passed a joint resolution to annex Hawaii. The peace treaty with Spain extended American territory still further by ceding Guam to the United States. All this occurred despite Congress' previous disclaimer of any intention to exercise control over Cuba, much less over other territories. But U.S. aims in Cuba could most likely have been secured by diplomatic rather than by military means. A few days after war was declared, Senator Spooner wrote to a friend: "I think . . . possibly the President could have worked out the business without a war, but the current was too strong, the demagogues too numerous, and the fall elections too near."

By the time of World War I, when the Government was more active in regulating the economy, the powers delegated to President Wilson were extensive and far-reaching. He was authorized to take possession of American vessels and declare embargoes; fix prices and sell war material; operate the railroads and take control of communication systems; provide for war housing, license commerce and manufacture, and store and distribute the necessaries of life.

The powers exercised by President Roosevelt during World War II were far more vast. After Roosevelt's Destroyers-Bases agreement with Great Britain in September 1940, Congress acted the following March by passing the Lend-Lease Act, which authorized the President to manufacture any defense article and to "sell, transfer title to, exchange, lease, lend or otherwise dispose of" the defense articles to any country whose defense he deemed vital to the defense of the United States. The Priorities Act of May 31, 1941—passed six months before Pearl Harbor—authorized the President to allocate any material he deemed necessary for the public interest or to promote the national defense. The power to mobilize the resources of the business community was upheld by the Supreme Court in *United States* v. *Bethlehem Steel.* If the power of the Government was great enough to draft men for battle, "its power to draft business organizations to support the fighting men who risk their lives can be no less."

After Pearl Harbor and Congress' declaration of war,

mobilization authority was extended to the control of facilities and the operation of plants closed by strikes. Under the Emergency Price Control Act of 1942, the President appointed a Price Administrator who was authorized to designate areas in the country in which defense activities had caused an increase in housing rents. In April 1942, the Price Administrator designated 28 such areas, set maximum rents, and gave the Rent Director discretion to order decreases on his own initiative. Judicial machinery was supplied to handle appeals. This administrative apparatus was attacked as an unconstitutional delegation of power. In *Bowles* v. *Willingham*, the Court rejected the assertion that administrative discretion was unbridled. Congress did not abdicate its responsibility by describing the job to be done, who must do it, and the scope of the authority: "In our complex economy that indeed is frequently the only way in which the legislative process can go forward."

In the autumn of 1942, President Roosevelt notified Congress that it had failed to enact two of his recommendations for inflation control. Now that four months had passed, the President told Congress that if it did not pass such legislation in the next month, authorizing him to stabilize the cost of living, he would be left with "an inescapable responsibility to the people of this country to see to it that the war effort is no longer imperiled by threat of economic chaos. In the event that the Congress should fail to act, and act adequately, I shall accept the responsibility, and I will act."

Congress provided the additional inflation controls only one day after his deadline. The President was authorized to adjust prices, wages, and salaries "to the extent that he finds necessary to aid in the effective prosecution of the war or to correct gross inequities." The scope of this new price-setting authority was challenged in the courts. Petitioners charged that the vague statutory boundaries had transferred the legislative power to the executive branch. The Court held, in *Yakus* v. *United States,* that the theory of separated powers did not deny Congress the power to give "ample latitude" to an administrative officer. It was for Congress to say whether the data for fixing prices were to be confined within a broad or narrow range.

In another case contesting the broadness of delegated powers, the Administration filed claim for a sum of money that a construction company had realized from war contracts. Under the Renegotiation Act, the Under Secretary of War was to decide when war demand and Government orders created "excessive profits." The Supreme Court upheld the delegation in the *Lichter* case. It was not necessary for Congress to supply administrative officials with a specific formula in a field where "flexibility and the adaptation of the congressional policy to infinitely variable conditions constitute the essence of the program."

Demobilization Powers

President Roosevelt announced in 1942 that, when the war was over, "the powers under which I act automatically revert to the people—to whom they belong." Yet when are wars actually over? The change-over from emergency war powers to normal executive responsibilities is by no means a rapid process. Long after hostilities have ended, many economic controls remain in force.

The Civil War had already presented the first major problem in defining the end of a war. Rebellious districts were brought under control on different dates: Generals Lee and Johnson surrendered in April 1865; General Taylor on May 4; and General Kirby Smith on May 26. Executive decrees for the date of suppression were released on June 13, 1865, for the rebellion in Tennessee; the following April for nine other states; and on August 20, 1866, for Texas and throughout the United States.

Congress had passed an act in 1863 restricting the return of abandoned or captured property to a period within two years after the suppression of the rebellion. The Supreme Court, in *United States* v. *Anderson,* was confronted with this question: when was the rebellion to be considered suppressed, with regard to the rights secured by this statute? Handling this as a political question, the Court accepted the last date issued by the President and subsequently adopted by Congress. In *Stewart* v. *Kahn* (1870), the Court explained that the war power was not "limited to victories in the field and the dispersion of the insurgent forces. It carried with it inherently the power to guard against the immediate renewal of the conflict, and to remedy the evils which have arisen from its rise and progress." At the end of the Spanish-American War the Court emphasized anew, in the *Hijo* decision, that a state of war does not cease with the end of hostilities.

After the Armistice ending World War I had been signed on November 11, 1918, and hostilities had come to an end, President Wilson reported to Congress that wartime controls over foodstuffs and shipping could not be removed immediately: "the world has still to be fed from our granaries and the ships are still needed to send supplies to our men overseas and to bring the men back as fast as the disturbed conditions on the other side of the water permit. . . ."

On the question of when war actually ceased, the Supreme Court once again deferred to the political branches. A 1918 act prohibited liquor traffic until the termination of demobilization, as determined and proclaimed by the President. Contestants before the Supreme Court claimed that by October 1919 it was evident that hostilities would not be resumed, that demobilization had been accomplished, and that the statute was therefore void. Public statements by the President were introduced as evidence to show that war was over and peace had come. Yet despite those statements by the President, the Court noted that he still controlled the fuel supply, still operated the railroads, still exercised control over the supply of grain and wheat, and still regulated the price of sugar. Moreover, he had not yet issued the proclamation for the end of demobilization. In this *Hamilton* v. *Kentucky Distilleries* decision, the Court emphasized that the war power was not to be construed narrowly to cover only military engagements. It carried with it the power to prevent a renewal of war and to remedy the immediate postwar effects.

On July 2, 1921, President Harding signed a joint resolution stating that the war with Germany "is hereby declared at an end." That did not, however, automatically end all wartime controls. In *Commercial Trust* v. *Miller* (1923), the Court refused to accept the contention that an emergency statute had ceased with the joint resolution and the President's proclamation. The Court could not "estimate the effects of a great war and pronounce their termination at a particular moment of time." Such decisions were legislative, not judicial. The extension of rent controls to May 1924 strained the patience of the Court, however. It warned in *Chastleton Corp.* v. *Sinclair* that laws must square with the facts, and that a law depending on "the existence of an emergency or other certain state of facts to uphold it may cease to operate if the emergency ceases or the facts change even though valid when passed."

On May 8, 1945, President Truman announced the end of the war in Europe. On August 14 he announced the surrender of Japan. The following May, Truman seized certain bituminous coal mines under authority of the War Labor Disputes Act, which empowered the President to take possession of any plant, mine, or facility as may be required for the "war effort." Such authority remained in force until the President proclaimed the "termination of hostilities," a step Truman did not take until December 31, 1946—more than 16 months after Japan's surrender. By proclaiming that hostilities had terminated, Truman relinquished certain wartime powers, but retained others that remained in force during "a state of war" or "a state of emergency." Truman stressed that "a state of war still exists."

The Housing and Rent Act of 1947 provided for an extension of wartime rent controls. The Court conceded, in *Woods* v. *Miller,* that war in modern times left an impact on the economy for years after, and created a dangerous situation in which the war power "may not only swallow up all other powers of Congress, but largely obliterate the Ninth and Tenth Amendments." Yet the Court held that continuation of rent controls in this case did not contain such implications. A housing deficit still existed in 1947 because of the return of veterans and the slowdown in wartime residential construction. The concurring opinion by Justice Jackson expressed uneasiness about this "vague, undefined and undefinable 'war power'," but agreed that Federal rent controls in 1947 had been validly retained.

On July 25, 1947, Congress terminated certain temporary emergency and war powers. About 175 statutory provisions were involved, many dating back to the First World War. Even after taking that action, 103 war or emergency statutes remained in effect. Not until April 28, 1952, did President Truman sign a statement terminating the state of war with Japan, as well as the national emergencies proclaimed by President Roosevelt in 1939 and 1941. Thus, even though actual hostilities between U.S. and enemy forces lasted for less than four years, Presidents Roosevelt and Truman together exercised emergency and war powers for more than twelve years.

WAR POWERS, 1945-1971

The President's warmaking powers were drawn originally from (1) his responsibilities as Commander in Chief, (2) his oath to preserve, protect, and defend the Constitution, (3) his duty to protect the nation from sudden attack, and (4) the inherent powers derived from the general heading "executive power."

In recent decades, the definition of inherent and implied powers has become increasingly generous because of treaty commitments, vaguely worded congressional resolutions, and an accumulation of emergency statutes. Moreover, the President's constitutional responsibility for repelling sudden attacks and waging defensive war has expanded in scope until it is now used to justify involvement in full-scale wars without legislative approval.

"Defensive War"

However well-defined defensive war may have been in 1787, it knows few limits today. An attack on the United States can include our bombers in constant flight, ships in the Mediterranean and the Pacific (as well as in Tonkin Gulf and Wonsan Bay), our troops overseas, and other elements of our far-flung defensive system. The President's power to send arms to foreign countries can lead to substantially larger commitments, so that, after a chain of events, the United States finds itself engaged in war. Since weapons are complicated, the President must send advisers along to instruct the countries on how to use them. "The next step," Senator John Williams has noted, "is sending a few troops to protect the advisers. And then more troops will be sent in to protect those troops. The next thing we know we are involved in a war. To be frank, that is how we got involved in Vietnam in the first place."

Provisions in the United Nations Charter have also been invoked to justify the use of troops by the President without legislative approval. A legal memorandum by the State Department, in 1950, defended Truman's sending of troops to Korea on these grounds: "Both traditional international law and article 39 of the United Nations Charter and the resolution pursuant thereto authorize the United States to repel the armed aggression against the Republic of Korea."

The State Department equivocated by referring to "the" resolution. There were two resolutions, and only in the second did the Security Council call for armed force. The first resolution, adopted June 25, 1950, merely called for a cessation of hostilities and for the withdrawal of North Korean forces to the 38th parallel. Not until two days later, in the second resolution, did the Security Council recommend armed force to repel the armed attack. But by that time President Truman had already, on June 25, directed General MacArthur to evacuate Americans. To accomplish that task, MacArthur was authorized to take whatever air and naval actions were necessary to prevent the Inchon-Kimpo-Seoul area from falling into enemy hands. Furthermore, on June 26, MacArthur was informed that all military targets south of the 38th parallel could be attacked by the Air Force, and that the Navy could operate against forces engaged in aggression against South Korea.

After Secretary of State Dean Acheson had reviewed the situation for congressmen at noon on June 27, explaining why military action was necessary, the President exclaimed: "But Dean, you didn't even mention the U.N.!" Twelve hours later, at 11:45 P.M., the Security Council passed the second resolution, calling upon UN members to furnish military assistance. Acheson was later to write: "Thus some American action, said to be in support of the resolution of June 27, was in fact ordered, and possibly taken, prior to the resolution."

Was President Truman obligated under domestic law to seek congressional approval before sending U.S. troops to Korea? The United Nations Participation Act of 1945 stipulated that the armed forces made available by the United States to the Security Council, under Article 43 agreements, would be subject to the approval of Congress. Those agreements never materialized. The question remains whether the 1945 Act required congressional approval for any *other* type of arrangement for a UN force. It would seem as though it did. The Act provided that "nothing herein contained shall be construed as an authorization to the President by the Congress to make available to the Security Council for such purpose armed forces, facilities, or assistance," in addition to Article 43 assistance.

In short, whatever the political merits of Truman's initiative, legally it was on weak ground. First, it used armed force before the Security Council authorized it. The purpose of the first resolution was to bring about a cessation of hostilities and to avoid open military conflict. Second, Truman's action was inconsistent with domestic law by failing to obtain congressional approval before using military force in Korea.

As a result of bilateral and multilateral defense treaties, an outbreak of hostilities in another country can automatically involve the United States in another form of "defensive war." The North Atlantic Treaty provides that an armed attack against one or more of the Parties in Europe or North America "shall be considered an attack against them all." The Rio Treaty, signed by the United States and nations from Central and South America, contains the same type of understanding. Under defense treaties with countries in Southeast Asia and the Southwest Pacific (SEATO), with Australia and New Zealand (ANZUS), and with the Philippines, South Korea, Nationalist China, and Japan, the United States recognizes that an armed attack on those countries would be "dangerous to its own peace and safety" and it would therefore act to meet the common danger in accordance with its "constitutional processes." The executive branch has made it clear that constitutional processes do not necessarily involve the express approval of Congress. A legal memorandum by the State Department on Vietnam made this claim: "The Constitution leaves to the President the judgment to determine whether the circumstances of a particular armed attack are so urgent and the potential consequences so threatening to the security of the United States that he should act without formally consulting the Congress."

Executive policy statements and communiqués are other instruments for deepening U.S. commitments. In a note to the Philippine Foreign Secretary in 1954, Secretary of State Dulles said that our air and naval installations in that country were such that "an armed attack on the Philippines could not but be also an attack upon the military forces of the United States. As between our nations, it is no legal fiction to say that an attack on one is an attack on both. It is a reality that an attack on the Philippines is an attack on the United States." In a 1964 communiqué, President Johnson maintained that "any armed attack against the Philippines would be regarded as an attack against United States forces stationed there and against the United States and would instantly be repelled."

The decision of the Johnson Administration in 1964 to transfer B-57 bombers from the Philippines to Bien Hoa in South Vietnam was followed by Viet Cong mortar attacks on the air base. The result: substantial damage to U.S. troops and aircraft and a further upward twist in the escalation of the Vietnam war. Some of our bases agreements elsewhere, the Senate Foreign Relations Committee has warned, form "a kind of quasi-commitment, unspecified as to their exact import but, like buds in springtime, ready, under the right climatic conditions, to burst into full bloom."

The geographic sweep of modern-day defensive wars was dramatized by several crises of the 1960s. In 1962, when President Kennedy announced the sending of additional U.S. forces to Thailand, he asserted that a threat to Thailand was of "grave concern to the United States," and emphasized that the sending of U.S. military forces was "a defensive act." After the discovery of missile sites in Cuba, President Kennedy declared that the Western Hemisphere ("as far north as Hudson Bay, Canada, and as far south as Lima, Peru") was in danger. He gave notice that the launching of any nuclear missile from Cuba, against any nation in the Western Hemisphere, would be regarded as "an attack by the Soviet Union on the United States, requiring a full retaliatory response upon the Soviet Union."

When President Johnson requested the Tonkin Resolution two years later, he maintained that a threat in Southeast Asia "is a threat to all, and a threat to us." A number of congressmen elaborated on that theme. Senator Frank Lausche called Southeast Asia "our first line of defense; when an enemy attacks us there, he is, in principle, attacking us on our native land." Under such generous definitions, the President's power to wage defensive war is clearly of vast proportions.

Another open-ended prerogative—the right to use armed force for the protection of American lives and property—has been invoked by the President four times in the past dozen years: in Lebanon (1958), in the Dominican Republic (1965), in Cambodia (1970), and in Laos (1971). The doctrine of "hot pursuit" offers yet another opportunity for the President and his military commanders to initiate war or expand hostilities without congressional approval. The original objective of the United States in Korea, as defined by the Security Council resolution of June 25, 1950, was to have the North Korean forces cease hostilities and withdraw to the 38th parallel. Yet once the North Koreans had been pushed back, and the *status quo* restored, the objective was enlarged to seek the establishment of "a free, independent and unified" Korea. General MacArthur's push into North Korea was followed by massive Chinese intervention and the start of a full-scale war. For the past several years, U.S. troops have been crossing the Laotian border from South Vietnam in hot pursuit of the enemy—what the Pentagon calls "protective reaction" missions.

The formal approach to Senate ratification of defense treaties, or congressional approval of resolutions (as with the Tonkin incident), has been replaced in recent years by purely administrative action. The extension of the Vietnam war into Thailand, Laos, and Cambodia was carried out by the executive branch without congressional approval. In fact, it was carried out at times by the Defense Department with the State Department appearing to play a subordinate role.

In 1969, for instance, it was learned that the military had played a large role in a secret U.S. Thailand contingency plan negotiated in 1964–65. The plan promised the commitment of American troops to Thailand in case of external attack. During a July 1969 public session with the Senate Foreign Relations Committee, Secretary of State Rogers said that he would obtain the plan for the committee. When the plan failed to arrive, Senator Fulbright wrote to the State Department to ask that it be delivered to the committee for examination. He was informed, August 4, that the *Defense* Department was "extremely reluctant to allow the full text to get out of its own hands." Fulbright was able to learn, however, that the agreement with Thailand was signed on behalf of the United States by the commander of the U.S. Military Assistance Advisory Group and subsequently approved by the Joint Chiefs of Staff. Moreover, Fulbright said he had reason to believe that even the State Department was not allowed to have a copy of the plan. Congress was not consulted in the formulation and signing of the agreement. It was further advised by the State Department that it could look forward only to a possible advisory role, in the event the agreement were to be placed in operation by the Administration.

Apprehension about military influence was heightened by a news story in the *Washington Post,* February 25, 1969. An American military team had entered into negotiations with Spain concerning the two air bases and the submarine base we have there, nearly involving the United States in a NATO-type commitment to defend Spain against various alleged threats. These threats included such unlikely developments as Algerian aggression or a proxy war (backed by Russia) in the Spanish colonies. The military team kept the papers locked in a safe. The U.S. embassy in Madrid was given no word on the conduct of the talks, nor did it have access to the papers. The signed agreement was not initially shown to the State Department. After a hectic struggle to regain control, the State Department finally succeeded in turning back this military venture in diplomacy.

When hearings that had been held by the Symington Subcommittee were released in April 1970, the record showed that previous State Department testimony—during a secret session with the Senate Foreign Relations Committee —had failed to disclose the extent of U.S. military operations in Laos. Even Senator Symington, who was a member of both the Foreign Relations and the Armed Services committees, admitted that he was unaware that American pilots had been spotting bombing targets in northern Laos for the Royal Lao Air Force. A State Department official, when asked under what authority American personnel were operating in Laos, replied simply: "They are there under the executive authority of the President."

Legal Limits

Because of the vastness of delegated war powers and the wide channels through which the President and his assistants move, it is often claimed that the Constitution is virtually suspended in time of war or national emergency. This view finds expression in the maxim *inter arma silent leges* ("in the midst of arms, the laws are silent"), yet the Supreme Court has not been entirely silent and insensitive to constitutional rights during such times.

No doubt much of foreign affairs and the war power is poorly suited for judicial review. Information, on which a decision must be based, can be withheld from the Court for reasons of secrecy. In *C. & S. Airlines* v. *Waterman Corp.* (1948), Justice Jackson said it would be "intolerable that courts, without the relevant information, should review and perhaps nullify actions of the Executive taken on information properly held secret. . . . But even if courts could require full disclosure, the very nature of executive decisions as to foreign policy is political, not judicial." Denied relevant information, the Supreme Court has refrained from deciding questions respecting boundaries of nations, recognition of foreign governments, diplomatic status of envoys, or whether a foreign government is empowered to make agreements with the United States. Moreover, it is evident from the preceding section that the Court has been unwilling to intrude its judgment as to when war begins and ends.

While there are severe limits to the exercise of judicial authority, collisions often occur between actions taken in the name of "national security" and individual freedoms protected by the Constitution, and in such situations the Court has invoked its power of judicial review. As the Court noted in *Baker* v. *Carr* (1962), "it is error to suppose that every case or controversy which touches foreign relations lies beyond judicial cognizance." The Court has been active in striking down repressive actions by Congress, particularly legislative controls over subversive activities. In the case of Eugene Frank Robel, in 1967, Chief Justice Warren remarked that the phrase "war power" could not be invoked as a "talismanic incantation to support any exercise of congressional power which can be brought within its ambit."

While the Court has rebuffed Congress on several occasions, it has stepped more cautiously in its confrontations with the executive branch. The Steel Seizure Case of 1952 stands as the most significant challenge to Presidential war powers, but the Court, in striking down Truman's seizure of the steel mills, was deeply divided on the issue of emergency powers. As pointed out earlier, in Chapter 2, seven out of nine Justices accepted a view of executive power that went beyond the mere exercise of duties specifically granted by the Constitution and by statutes. Had the Truman Administration justified its action solely as an emergency measure, based upon the need to obtain steel to prosecute the Korean war, and had it acknowledged from the outset that Presidential powers are limited by the Constitution, the verdict might have been quite different.

Less well known are some other postwar cases contesting executive actions. In *Ludecke* v. *Watkins* (1948), a 5-4 decision held that Presidential power to remove alien enemies in a "declared war" continued even after the cessation of hostilities. "War does not cease," wrote Justice Frankfurter, "with a cease-fire order. . . ." The four dissenters responded by saying that the idea that America was still at war with Germany was a "pure fiction," and insisted that due process required a fair hearing reviewable by the courts.

Two years later, in a 4-3 decision, the Court again upheld the power of the executive branch to exclude an alien without a hearing. Dissenters on the Court condemned the "abrupt and brutal exclusion" of Ellen Knauff, a German-born wife of an American citizen. The Administration had argued that the evidence which justified the exclusion was withheld from the courts for reasons of national security. Justice Jackson countered by saying that security was like liberty "in that many are the crimes committed in its name." Members of Congress pressed the Attorney General to provide justification for his action. When the information was finally released, "it shrank to insignificance." The Board of Immigration Appeals decided that the evidence for exclusion was insubstantial, and Mrs. Knauff was allowed to enter the country.

In 1953, the Court divided sharply on the question of excluding Ignatz Mezei, an alien resident, without a hearing. He had lived in the United States for 25 years before traveling to Eastern Europe to visit his ailing mother. Upon his return to the United States, he was excluded by the Attorney General on the grounds that his entry would be prejudicial to the public interest. For two years he was held virtual prisoner on Ellis Island, denied entry to the United States and unable to find another country that would take him. The Government was upheld in a 5-4 decision. In one of the dissents, Justice Jackson insisted that Mezei was entitled to a fair hearing with fair notice of the charges. "It is inconceivable to me," he wrote, "that this measure of simple justice and fair dealing would menace the security of this country. No one can make me believe that we are that far gone." Mezei was eventually allowed to remain in the country.

In several cases during the 1950s, the Supreme Court restricted the power of the Administration to dismiss alleged loyalty risks. In a 1955 case, the Civil Service Commission's Loyalty Board had determined that there was reasonable doubt as to the loyalty of Dr. John P. Peters, a consultant who had twice before been cleared of charges. His work had not been of a confidential or sensitive nature, nor did it require access to classified material. He had no opportunity to confront and cross-examine his secret accusers. The Court rejected the Board's action as being in excess of the authority delegated to it. The next year, in a case regarding the suspension of Kendrick Cole from his position with HEW, the Court insisted that "in view of the stigma attached to persons dismissed on loyalty grounds, the need for procedural safeguards seems even greater than in other cases." The Court decided that Cole's discharge was unauthorized.

In 1959 the Court reviewed the case of William Greene, an aeronautical engineer who had been discharged from his company after the Government revoked his security clearance. In hearings before the administrative boards handling his appeal, he denied ever having been a Communist and spoke at length in opposition to doctrines that advocated the common ownership of property. Yet, on the basis of confidential reports that were never made available to him, the Government offered damaging information on the political activities of his wife and her friends, and concluded that the decision to deny him access to classified security data was justified. He had no opportunity to confront and question the persons whose statements reflected adversely on him, nor could he confront the Government investigators who collected those statements. The Court held that these administrative procedures were unauthorized, and that executive departments were not empowered to rely on "faceless informers" to deprive an individual of his job in a proceeding that lacked the safeguards of confrontation and cross-examination.

The Court has progressively circumscribed the power of the State Department to revoke passport privileges for reasons of national security. The policy of refusing an applicant a passport because of his political views was adopted by the State Department for the first time in 1947. In 1958, the Court reviewed a decision by Secretary of State Dulles to refuse a passport to Rockwell Kent on the grounds that he was a Communist and had "a consistent and prolonged adherence to the Communist Party line." The Court ruled that the State Department had no authority to deny a passport to an individual because of his beliefs and associations. In 1964, the Court examined a legislative provision which denied passport privileges to members of Communist organizations. On the basis of that provision, the State Department had revoked the passports of Herbert Aptheker and Elizabeth Gurley Flynn. The Court declared that the legislative provision was too broad and that it indiscriminately restricted the right to travel, as well as the closely related rights of free speech and association.

In 1967, the Court decided that the Government lacked authority to punish Lee Levi Laub criminally for traveling to Cuba, which had been designated "off limits" by the State Department. And in that same year, in a case involving Staughton Lynd's trip to North Vietnam, the U.S. Court of Appeals held that the Secretary of State could not revoke or withhold a passport because of a citizen's refusal to promise that he would not travel to restricted areas without a passport.

On the legality of the Vietnam war, the Supreme Court has consistently handled that issue as a "political question" to be resolved by Congress and the President. On each occasion the Court has refused to hear the case. Justice Douglas, who regularly dissented in these cases, insisted that there should not be the "slightest doubt that whenever the Chief Executive of the country takes any citizen by the neck and either puts him in prison or subjects him to some ordeal or sends him overseas to fight in a war, the question is a justiciable one." In the 1971 *New York Times* case the Nixon Administration tried to prevent publication of the Pentagon Papers, a classified study on the U.S. decision-making process on Vietnam policy. The right of the President to classify material therefore collided directly with the constitutional right to a free press. Justice Black joined with five members of the Court to reject the Administration's request. "The word 'security,' " he wrote, "is a broad, vague generality whose contours should not be invoked to abrogate the fundamental law embodied in the First Amendment. The guarding of military and diplomatic secrets at the expense of informed representative government provides no real security for our Republic."

7

CONGRESS AND THE WAR POWER

By 1970, congressional scrutiny of defense spending and foreign policy had attracted a surprisingly broad base of support. Allies could be found among liberals and conservatives, Democrats and Republicans. That was in striking contrast to earlier decades, when legislative activity in international affairs was often criticized as mischievous and ill-advised. The area was said to be so complex and fluid that only the executive branch—possessing unity, expertise, secrecy, and speed—could manage it with the necessary competence.

The rationale for broad Presidential discretion was undermined by the war in Vietnam and has been further discredited since by a number of other Administration actions. As a result, it is no longer sufficient to borrow a few sonorous passages from the 1936 *Curtiss-Wright* decision, which gave the President a preeminent position in foreign affairs. Nor is it adequate to cite the hundred or so instances in the past when Presidents sent troops abroad without consulting Congress. The "high-flying prerogative men" (Professor Corwin's phrase to describe those who defended Truman's dispatch of troops to Korea without prior congressional approval) have now become the most vociferous critics of Presidential war powers.

Arthur Schlesinger, Jr., for instance, counseled in 1966 that "something must be done to assure the Congress a more authoritative and continuing voice in fundamental decisions in foreign policy." Henry Steele Commager, a supporter of Presidential prerogatives in 1951, told the Senate in 1967 that there should be "a reconsideration of the relationship of the executive and the legislative branches, particularly the executive and the Senate in the conduct of foreign relations. . . ." In March 1969, at the Congressional Conference on the Military Budget and National Priorities, scholars and scientists from both parties called upon Congress to reassert its control over defense spending and the course of international commitments. Senator J. W. Fulbright, who had written in 1961 that "for the existing requirements of American foreign policy we have hobbled the President by too niggardly a grant of power," later found himself in the forefront of those who tried to place limits on the President.

EXECUTIVE QUALITIES REEXAMINED

The time is long overdue for reassessing Congress' role in the war power and in foreign policy generally. Holbert Carroll, in his study on Congress and foreign affairs, estimated that the proportion of bills concerning international matters in 1925 was not more than 1 in 25. The situation since World War II has been radically different. About half the standing committees now play some role in international affairs. If the President chooses to ignore Congress while acting in external affairs, his domestic and foreign programs become targets for reprisal. The feeling among legislators that President Johnson overreached himself in Southeast Asia, and failed to treat Congress as a coequal branch, produced a voting record marked by negativism and defiance. Unable to control the President's policy in Vietnam, legislators turned against other Administration programs.

Deep slashes in foreign aid, for example, were interpreted by Senator Joseph Clark in 1967 as a method of "getting back at the President for the conduct of the war in Vietnam." When President Nixon delivered a broad-brush attack on critics of the military in a June 1969 address, his foreign aid program was immediately placed in jeopardy by legislators who found the speech offensive.

The Senate's rejection of Clement F. Haynsworth, Jr., and G. Harrold Carswell for the Supreme Court also reflects a reassertion of legislative prerogatives. President Nixon, in a letter to Senator William Saxbe, contended that Senate opposition to his choice of nominees was somehow a usurpation of his constitutional responsibilities. Two rejections in a row may have convinced the President that the Senate also has responsibilities and is willing to discharge them. Senator Frank Church remarked that the Senate had "pulled off the shelf its all-but-atrophied confirmation power" as one step in restoring a better balance between Congress and the President. After the Senate confirmed Judge Harry A. Blackmun, who was Nixon's third choice for the Supreme Court vacancy, Senator Marlow Cook declared that Senatorial assertion against "an all-powerful Executive, whoever he may be, whether it is in foreign affairs or in Supreme Court appointments, is good for the country."

By tradition, foreign policy has been set aside as a Presidential preserve, with separate domains marked out for external and internal affairs. This neat arrangement owes much to the *Curtiss-Wright* decision, in which Justice Sutherland argued that legislation for the international field must often accord to the President "a degree of discretion and freedom from statutory restriction which would not be admissible were domestic affairs alone involved." Earlier in the book (pp. 64–65) I examined the decision in terms of the *dicta* that Sutherland had added while expounding his own personal conception of foreign policy. His ironclad distinction between foreign and domestic problems seems increasingly artificial to most observers today, and the same can be said of the many qualities we attribute to the executive branch.

"Unity"

The properties of the executive anticipated by the Founding Fathers are not always to be found in our sprawling bureaucracy today. Instead of "unity," we find the apparatus for foreign policy-making splintered within the State Department, as well as between it and other agencies competing for control. The interservice rivalries of the postwar period were supposedly remedied by "unification" of the military services and by the coordinating apparatus of the National Security Council, but scholars pointed to the type of logrolling and vote-trading that persisted within the executive branch. Samuel P. Huntington observed that "Just as Congress often wrote tariff legislation by giving each industry the protection it wanted, the N.S.C. and the Joint Chiefs make decisions on weapons by giving each service what it desires."

Before joining the Nixon Administration, Henry Kissinger spoke of a "sort of blindness in which bureaucracies run a competition with their own programs and measure success by the degree to which they fulfill their own norms, without being in a position to judge whether the norms made any sense to begin with." A vivid example of that came to light in 1969 when former Budget Director Charles Schultze appeared before the Joint Economic Committee. He described the effort of the Budget Bureau to select an optimum continental air defense system. Various alternatives were studied before selecting the system that was "more effective at slightly lower cost than most." An impressive exercise in program budgeting, and yet what the Budget Bureau had failed to ask, Schultze said, was whether we needed an air defense system of that magnitude at all. Other basic questions, such as the need to spend $5 billion a year on the Chinese contingency, also received far too little attention. While it has been customary to regard the Budget Bureau as the unifying, coordinating element in the executive branch, it is evident that military spending has received less scrutiny than domestic spending.

"National Interest"

The foreign-policy bureaucracies, in the view of many congressmen and Federal officials, have often become juggernauts, each operating on its own momentum, sustained by its own special-interest constituency, and propelled toward narrow objectives. Decisions on defense spending offer the most graphic illustration of this. An Air Force colonel testified in 1969 that evidence of cost-overrun problems on the C-5A cargo plane had been withheld from Congress. For what reason? Because disclosure might have jeopardized the contractor's position in the financial market. In another instance of public operations acquiring a quasi-private character, five Air Force officers who had worked on the Minuteman missile contract for the Government later retired and went to work for the contracting company.

Instead of an "adversary relationship" between the Defense Department and private contractors, with the buyer seeking the lowest cost and the seller the highest profit, officers and contractor personnel have been operating under the "team concept"—apparently a euphemism for collusion. A top-ranking naval procurement official put the matter bluntly to Congress: "We play games. We know that if we tell the DOD [Department of Defense] across the river how much something is really going to cost, they may scrub it. And they know that if they tell the Congress how much it is really going to cost the Congress may scrub it. So you start in with both sides knowing that it is going to cost more. And that is not an overrun, because we know."

How easy it is now to appreciate the prescient and ironic warning of Hubert Humphrey in 1959. Congress could not, he said, submit to the Executive will even if it wanted to, because "there is not one Executive will, but a number of conflicting wills which have not yet surrendered to the authority of an overriding national purpose."

"Expertise"

A close look at the administrative record in defense procurement and military operations justifies the skepticism of the Senate Foreign Relations Committee when it speaks of the "cult of executive expertise." Although the executive branch has access to vast quantities of information, it may resort to "selective declassification" or outright doctoring of information in an effort to sustain its position. A series of deceptive announcements and maneuvers helped discredit the Johnson Administration: conflicting and contradictory explanations of the Tonkin incident and the Dominican intervention; a host of unreliable estimates on Vietnam spending, civilian casualties, and the number of refugees; a dreary succession of various "turning points" in the war and "lights at the end of the tunnel." Executive expertise did not prevent blunders in the production of Cheyenne helicopters and Main Battle Tanks, nor did it eliminate mismanagement in the Minuteman and C-5A programs.

Executive officials may be "expert" and at the same time deceptive, but it is the strong and often justified suspicion of many congressmen that the deceptions are used to conceal incompetence. Testimony by executive officials before congressional committees betrays a lack of that professional objectivity which is the hallmark of true expertise.

Representative Jonathan Bingham offered a revealing story of how the Pentagon juggled figures in trying to exaggerate the Soviet threat. In a presentation comparing Soviet and U.S. strengths in submarines, the Navy deducted a certain percentage from the U.S. figure to allow for vessels confined at home port at any given time. When a civilian systems analyst asked what percentage had been deducted from the Soviet figure for the same reason, "the answer was that no deduction had been made; the incredible excuse was that 'we don't know what their lay-up percentage is.'" Senator Proxmire disclosed how the Air Force shifted figures in an effort to conceal the magnitude of cost overruns on the

C-5A. Sophisticated cost-benefit studies can be manipulated simply by underestimating the cost of a weapons system and overstating its benefits.

During the past few years, Congress has unearthed some remarkable practices in military procurement. A study by the General Accounting Office in 1967 disclosed that billions of dollars of Government plant and equipment had been used by private industry for commercial purposes, instead of for work on defense contracts. To take but one example, the Defense Department supplied a $1.4 million forge press to a contractor to turn out jet-engine parts for the military. Over a three-year period, the company ran the press 78 percent of the time for its own commercial production.

The Government is regularly fleeced in its procurement of small parts, often paying 5 to 10 times more than the catalog price. On a precision shafting part catalogued at 50 cents each, the Defense Supply Agency managed to buy twenty at $25.55 each. Among many other examples of this type, the Navy Department estimated the cost of a fuel oil tube at $2.00 each. The supplier sold twenty to the Government at $120 each, having bought them first from another supplier for $12 each.

When expertise is actually applied in the interest of economy, it is sometimes discouraged. Several individuals in the Defense Department were harassed by their superiors, and in one case fired, for telling Congress about fuel pilferage and cost overruns. John M. McGee angered the Navy by reporting that lax inspection procedures by his superiors had resulted in thefts amounting to millions of gallons of gasoline and jet fuel in Thailand. As a reward for his conscientious discharge of public duty, he was reprimanded by the Navy and denied an in-grade salary increase. Senator Proxmire said that the moral of the story was self-incident: "to get along, go along. Don't report any wrongdoing. . . . If you do, you may well be reprimanded. Instead of investigating the problem, we will investigate you. Your life for the past decade will be gone into. Your old forms will be examined for any minor error. You can expect no automatic in-grade promotions. In fact, we will try to fire you."

Precisely that kind of situation arose in the case of A. E. Fitzgerald, former Deputy for Management Systems in the Department of the Air Force. In testimony on the C-5A, after Senator Proxmire had asked whether the program was running $2 billion above initial cost estimates, Fitzgerald replied that the figure was "approximately right." The Pentagon, which had yet to acknowledge the overrun, proceeded to punish Fitzgerald by taking away his Civil Service protection, by assigning him menial tasks, searching into his private life for incriminating evidence, and finally dismissing him from his job.

SAFEGUARD ABM SYSTEM

One of the most dramatic examples of legislative assertion in national security matters is Congress' challenge to the Nixon Administration on the deployment of an antiballistic missile system. The principal challenge was not over the technical merits of the Safeguard ABM system, or even over the larger strategic considerations. Few congressmen were in a position to know how many SS-9 missiles Russia would have by the mid-1970s, or whether they would be fitted with MIRVs, or carry 25-megaton warheads, or hit within a quarter-mile of their target. Nor could congressmen talk confidently about the failure rate of the SS-9 or its capability of being retargeted after failure. And since most of the American ABM components were still in the research and development phase, or had been tested under carefully controlled conditions, it was mere conjecture to claim that the system would or would not "work."

What Congress *could* do, however, was to judge the Safeguard ABM system in terms of the consistency and coherence of Administration statements. The ABM controversy therefore provides a good opportunity to examine more closely executive competence in questions of national defense.

From 1958 to 1967, the Eisenhower, Kennedy, and Johnson Administrations had consistently opposed the construction of an ABM system. Administration officials contended that production on the Nike-Zeus (later the Nike-X) system should not begin until technological problems were first overcome. In September 1967, however, Defense Secretary McNamara announced that there were "marginal grounds" for deploying a light ABM system to protect American cities from a possible Chinese attack in the 1970s. The proposed "Sentinel" system relied on long-range Spartan missiles and shorter-range, rapid-accelerating Sprint missiles.

McNamara's announcement was met by considerable skepticism. Jerome Wiesner, former science adviser to President Kennedy, said, "We ought to regard the Sentinel as a bad joke perpetrated on us by Mr. McNamara and Mr. Johnson in an election year. It seems to me that their very rationalization—that it was to defend us against the Chinese, but we would stop building it if the Russians agreed not to build one—demonstrates this well enough." Critics charged that Sentinel was designed not so much to defend the United States from Chinese attack, but to protect Democrats from Republican charges that the country had been left vulnerable to Communist attack.

After the Republican victory in 1968, President Nixon instructed his Secretary of Defense to initiate a thorough review of the Sentinel system. On March 14, 1969, Nixon announced his decision to proceed with a modified ABM system, which would be designed to protect Minuteman missile sites instead of cities. He explained that his new system would be "a safeguard against any attack by the Chinese Communists that we can foresee over the next 10 years. It is a safeguard of our deterrent system, which is increasingly vulnerable due to the advances that have been made by the Soviet Union since the year 1967 when the Sentinel program was first laid out. It is a safeguard also against any irrational or accidental attack that might occur of less than massive magnitude which might be launched from the Soviet Union."

Within the space of a few weeks, this carefully constructed rationale began to collapse. Secretary of State Rogers, in an appearance before the Senate Foreign Relations Committee, said that, in the event of successful arms control talks with the Russians, the United States would be "delighted" to halt construction of the Safeguard ABM system. Heartening news, but what had happened to the threat of Chinese attacks, irrational attacks, and accidental launchings? Those props in the Safeguard rationale had somehow disappeared.

First-strike Capability

The central prop—the Soviet threat—moved in and out of focus. Senator Fulbright wryly observed that the Russians, in terms of military capacity, are depicted by the Administration as 10 feet tall, capable of doing "all sorts of things; their skill and talents are almost unbelievable. Yet when we discuss them as a society, they are inadequate in practically every respect." The perennial warning by the Pentagon that the Russians are about to overwhelm the United States, Fulbright said, was "a kind of fear technique," used to obtain legislative support for defense programs.

Defense Secretary Laird warned the Senate on March 21 that, in view of the large tonnage of Soviet SS-9 missiles, the Russians were going "for our missiles and they are going for a first strike capability. There is no question about that." Yet in a news conference April 7, Secretary Rogers said that he had "difficulty in believing that the Soviet Union would initiate a first strike." Moreover, in hearings held May 14, Senators Gore and Fulbright disclosed that predictions of a Russian first-strike capability did not square with estimates given them by the intelligence community.

It became clear that Secretary Laird, in warning of a Russian first-strike capability by the mid-1970s, had relied on his own speculation rather than on solid information. As he himself admitted when testifying in May 1969 before the

House Appropriations Committee, intelligence projections over a 2- or 3-year period are "reasonably firm," whereas projections over a 5- or 6-year period are made in an area of "considerable uncertainty, particularly insofar as actual deployments are concerned . . . national intelligence projections for the mid-1970's involve a large measure of judgment rather than hard evidence."

To clear up the dispute, Secretary Laird was invited back to the Senate Foreign Relations Committee on June 23. The hearings show that the U.S. Intelligence Board had *not* concluded that Russia was striving for a first-strike capability. Laird now abandoned his confident there's-no-question-about-it attitude and assumed a more modest position. It was simply his "belief" that the Soviet Union was developing a first-strike capability. After four hours of testimony, the Committee finally learned what Secretary Laird meant by first-strike capability: not the ability of an aggressor to destroy simultaneously all elements of the American retaliatory force—including Minuteman missiles, overseas bases, bomber fleet, and Polaris submarines—but merely a weapon's potential to "be used against hardened missile sites."

Thick or Thin System?

Considerable confusion surrounded the question of whether Safeguard could grow into a thicker, city-oriented system and thereby provoke a new arms race. President Nixon claimed that Safeguard was not provocative since it did not provide defense for the cities: "there is no way, even if we were to expand the limited Sentinel system which was planned for some of our cities to a so-called heavy or thick system—there is no way that we can adequately defend our cities without an unacceptable loss of life." A massive city defense was ruled out for two reasons: it was not "feasible," and it tended to be more provocative to an arms race.

Since Safeguard protected Minuteman sites, rather than cities, the President said that this made it "so clearly defensive in character that the Soviet Union cannot interpret this as escalating the arms race." To reinforce his argument, Nixon referred to a statement by Premier Kosygin in 1967 that ABMs placed around Moscow would not escalate the arms race because they were solely defensive in character. It is indeed peculiar for a President to recommend an ABM system primarily to protect the United States from a Soviet attack, while ostensibly accepting at face value public comments by Soviet leaders on their weapons systems. Why not accept their statements about peaceful coexistence?

It is evident that the Nixon Administration did not, in fact, believe Kosygin's statement. Secretary Laird cited Russian ABMs as one factor for the arms buildup. He told the House Appropriations Committee in May 1969 that the United States had "already begun to provide a hedge (i.e., Poseidon and Minuteman III, both equipped with MIRV's) against the possibility that the Soviet Union might deploy an extensive and effective ABM defense." Dr. John S. Foster, Jr., the Pentagon's research director, stressed the need for new offensive weapons to offset the Russian ABM system: "One simple way is to exhaust it simply by sending more warheads than the system can intercept. That is a primary reason why the Administration and the Congress decided to provide MIRV's—multiple, independently targeted re-entry vehicles—for the U.S. missile force. MIRV should enable us to saturate the Russian defenses."

Further provocation would result if Safeguard developed into a thick, city-oriented system. The Administration regularly denied that this could happen, and yet the area defense system provided by long-range Spartan missiles already included a certain level of city protection. President Nixon said that the U.S. position in the Pacific would not be credible "unless we could protect our country against a Chinese attack aimed at our cities. The ABM system will do that, and the ABM safeguard system, therefore, has been adopted for that reason."

Additional city protection could be included at a later date. Deputy Secretary of Defense Packard told newsmen that a thick anti-Soviet defense of American cities had been looked into carefully, but was rejected "as not being a desirable thing to do at this time." With "present day technology," he explained, "it is not possible to provide a complete defense of our cities." Secretary Laird told a Senate committee that defense of U.S. cities against a Soviet attack was rejected, not because of a lack of interest in complete protection, but simply because "it is not now in our power to do so."

During this same period, the Senate Armed Services Committee listened to Acting Assistant Secretary of the Army Charles L. Poor, accompanied by General A. W. Betts, describe research efforts on the ABM:

SENATOR MCINTYRE. You said that Secretary McNamara had set up this advanced ballistic missile system study. Do I understand it correctly, this is an ongoing continuous program probing for new ideas?

GENERAL BETTS. That is right.

SENATOR MCINTYRE. And trying to reach the zenith, I suppose, of perfection in a thick system some day, if God help us, we ever come to it?

GENERAL BETTS. Or a thin, either one.

SENATOR MCINTYRE. Thick or thin. It is ongoing.

MR. POOR. Yes, sir.

Donald F. Hornig, former adviser to the Pentagon, warned the Senate that ABM deployment plans were "patently the first phase of a 'thick' system, including missile sites close to cities. It was so regarded in the Pentagon and this is presumably what made it palatable; it was a foot in the door."

Independent Analysis

The Gore Subcommittee on disarmament exposed a number of contradictions and misrepresentations in the Safeguard program. Senator Fulbright asked Mr. Packard this question: "did you go outside and employ any independent people to analyze the feasibility and advisability, the wisdom of this program?" Packard replied: "One of the men that I talked to, I have a high regard for, is Professor Panofsky."

The following morning, Professor Panofsky appeared before the Gore Subcommittee to tell Fulbright that he had not participated in any advisory capacity in the decision to deploy the Safeguard system. The "meeting" with Packard was nothing more than a chance encounter at the San Francisco airport, lasting about a half hour. Matters were doubly embarrassing for the Administration when Panofsky expressed his own opinion that Safeguard was unsound technically, economically, and politically. Packard tried to recoup this setback by submitting a lengthy list of scientists from outside the Defense Department who had been consulted on Safeguard. That too backfired when the Subcommittee learned that the scientists had been consulted on March 17, three days *after* the President's decision to proceed with Safeguard.

Deputy Secretary Packard told Senator Fulbright that he did not consider it important in scientific matters whether experts were recruited from outside the Pentagon. Scientists, Packard said, are "objective about such matters." That must have raised a few eyebrows; committee members had already received testimony from three former Presidential science advisers—Herbert York, George Kistiakowsky, and James Killian—and all three of them had expressed opposition to an ABM system. In fact, Senator Gore said he could not locate a single Presidential science adviser from past Administrations who favored the system.

Mr. Packard backtracked a little on his thesis that scientists are always objective about such matters. As for York's opposition, Packard said that while he held him in high regard, "I think if you will look at the record as I recall, he is the one who did not think the Polaris would work. All this merely says that the scientists have different views on things. . . ." Even that nicely balanced statement failed to end the controversy. Dr. York got off a telegram to Senators Cooper and Gore to say that he had always, during his tenure with the Defense Department, "recommended positively to the Secretary of Defense concerning the development and deployment of the Polaris system."

Command and Control

Another area of ambiguity was whether Safeguard would permit the President to retain control over the firing of nuclear weapons. Dr. York emphasized the inherent contradiction in trying to design an ABM that would have both a "hair trigger" (to prevent a surprise attack) and a "stiff trigger" (to prevent accidental firings). There was great concern that the warning time would be so short that the decision to release a Spartan or Sprint missile would have to be delegated to a computer or to some junior officer.

The Administration firmly denied that this would happen. Mr. Packard told the Gore Subcommittee that the range of radar for Safeguard was in excess of 1,000 miles and that missiles would arrive at speeds of about 18,000 miles an hour. He assured the Senators that the time remaining after radar contact would be "about 15 to 20 minutes, something in that order of magnitude, depending upon the point of interception." However, based on Packard's figures, two members of the Subcommittee reached the conclusion that the time would be closer to *four* minutes. Packard then corrected himself and put the time at "Something less than 10 minutes."

When Packard later explained the timing dilemma to the House Armed Services Committee, committee members were clearly shaken by the scenario. Though the testimony is heavily shrouded with deletions, the uneasiness and discomfort of the legislators could not be concealed. Representative Bray protested that if "you have to go to the President of the United States and all the redtape of getting it through in [deleted] minutes, in view of what Mr. Pike said, I think we are on a waterhole . . . if they are coming over and you wait [deleted] minutes, you might as well throw in the sponge. . . ." The time for Presidential action was so short that some committee members recommended that the decision to fire the missiles be delegated to Army officers. The question of command and control was raised again in 1970. When the chairman of the House Armed Services Committee suggested that the President could delegate his authority on the ABM, the chief counsel for the committee quickly noted: "I don't see how you could help but delegate it."

Cost Estimates

When President Nixon announced his decision to proceed with the Safeguard system, on March 14, 1969, he put the cost at between $6 and $7 billion. It was soon evident that the $7 billion maximum was merely one floor of a taller structure, whose final height has yet to be determined. DMS, Inc., a subsidiary of McGraw-Hill, released a special report on March 19, estimating that the various components of Safeguard would cost at least $11 billion. Two months later, in testimony before the House Appropriations Committee, Secretary Laird admitted that costs would run that high. He explained that a $6.6 billion Safeguard system covered only procurement and construction costs for the Defense Department. Research and development would run an additional $2.5 billion, and the development and testing of warheads by the Atomic Energy Commission another $1.2 billion.

Thus, Safeguard was up to at least $10.3 billion by the Administration's own reckoning; that did not include $500 million to extend the system to Alaska and Hawaii, or $350 million a year for operating costs. Other evidence suggested that substantial changes in design would be needed. The Senate Foreign Relations Committee learned that studies by the Institute of Defense Analysis, the Aerospace Corporation, the Defense Science Board, and the Advanced Research Projects Agency—all of which were either Pentagon agencies or Pentagon-funded—had stressed that technical requirements for missile base defense (Safeguard) and city defense (Sentinel) were fundamentally different. In the event that Safeguard was poorly designed for its mission, the project would have to be redesigned during deployment. Costs would then leapfrog by the billions.

The Pentagon's procedure for controlling such cost overruns is to slow down the development-production cycle, to make certain that a new weapons system is thoroughly tested during research and development before initiating the production phase. With that policy in mind, Senator Margaret Chase Smith asked Secretary Laird whether he felt it was prudent to go ahead with Safeguard before completing the testing and development phases. He replied that the only major item to be tested was the perimeter acquisition radar (PAR)—the long-range radar that is responsible for first detecting an incoming target. All the components of the PAR, he said, had been tested.

A more primitive picture emerged two months later when Laird appeared before the House Appropriations Committee. The Missile Site Radar (MSR), which is responsible for guiding the interceptor missiles, was still in the prototype stage. Work on the complex data processing system was still under development. Spartan and Sprint missiles had been tested, but only under carefully controlled conditions—that is, directed against single test missiles and where the course of the test missile and the intercept point were known in advance. Laird did not expect the first MSR-directed Spartan intercept of a single ICBM to take place before the spring or summer of 1970, or the first intercept of multiple targets until early 1971.

To protect the Safeguard system from a submarine-launched attack, additional PARs might have to be installed at the four corners of the United States. Lt. Gen. A. D. Starbird, system manager for Safeguard, estimated that the cost of extra PARs, plus some additional MSRs, would be on the order of $2.5 billion. Deputy Secretary Packard suggested other possible alterations in the Safeguard system: longer-range radars, faster missiles with greater accuracy, homing devices on intercept missiles, and non-nuclear destruction techniques.

New modifications were proposed and tested to improve

the Safeguard system. Development was under way on a smaller radar, to be deployed in the Minuteman fields as backup capability. Deployment of smaller radars with additional Sprint interceptors was also considered, while some of the Spartan missiles were being modified to provide greater range and speeds for protection against sub-launched missiles. The computer program had been redesigned to permit its expansion later if necessary. Other possible improvements included some type of terminal guidance on the interceptor missiles.

Predictably, cost estimates continued to climb. The Administration disclosed that the cost increase from 1969 to 1970 was $1.6 billion: $395 million because of inflation, $575 million due to stretchout of the deployment period, and $650 million in design changes and revised estimates. Those figures did not include the cost of smaller radars (estimated at $200 million for fiscal 1971), or additional Sprints (no estimates given), or for the improved Spartan. Estimates of the cost for warheads for the improved Spartan ranged from $200 to $500 million. Since the Pentagon has consistently underestimated the cost of the Safeguard program, it would be well to work with the larger figure.

The cost increase from 1970 to 1971 came to $3 billion: $1.9 billion because of inflation, $700 million due to stretchout, and $400 million resulting from revised estimates and costs. A partial allowance for future inflation was incorporated into the estimates, but the system manager of the Safeguard program warned that "the inflation allowances which we were permitted to use are quite conservative. . . . It may well be that the inflation predicted is less than that which will occur."

Table 5 shows the cost growth of Safeguard in four stages: March 14, 1969, when President Nixon used the figure of $6–$7 billion; May 22, 1969, when Secretary Laird admitted that expenditures for research and development, along with the development and testing of warheads by the Atomic Energy Commission, had been omitted from the first cost estimate; March 9, 1970, when the Administration announced the $1.6 billion cost increase, including other possible increases; and finally April 19, 1971, when the Pentagon announced new cost increases. The Administration originally estimated that the cost of *operating* a full 12-site Safeguard ABM system would be $350 million a year. However, on the basis of an April 1971 estimate of $135 million a year to operate three sites, the total operating cost now appears to be closer to $500 million.

Table 5 Cost Increases for Safeguard (in billions)

	March 14, 1969	May 22, 1969	March 9, 1970	April 19, 1971
Installation Costs	$6–$7	$ 6.6	—	$13.7
Research and Development	—	2.5	—	
Development and Testing of Warheads	—	1.2	—	1.1
		$10.3	$10.3	
Extending System to Hawaii and Alaska	—	0.5	0.5	0.5
Cost Growth (1969–70)			1.6	**
Smaller Radars			0.2	0.2
Additional Sprints			???	???
Improved Spartans			0.5	0.5
Future Cost Growth			???	???
ADMINISTRATION ESTIMATES *	$6–$7	$10.8	$13.1++	$16.0++

* Does not include operating costs ($350–$500 million a year).
** $3 billion, which is included in the total of $13.7 billion for installation costs and R&D.

The closest legislative challenge to Safeguard came on August 6, 1969. The Senate voted on an amendment by Senator Margaret Chase Smith which would have prohibited any funds for Safeguard, including even funds for research and development. The vote was 50 to 50, falling one vote short of adoption. Vice President Agnew cast an unnecessary vote against the amendment, making the final count 51 to 50. On the next vote, which would have blocked deployment of Safeguard while allowing funds for research and development, Mrs. Smith voted in opposition, and the final tally against Safeguard came to 49 to 51. Later, the House rejected by a 219 to 105 vote an amendment to eliminate procurement funds for Safeguard.

The issue was reopened on January 30, 1970, when President Nixon announced his intention to seek approval for additional ABM sites. He had explained in 1969 that Safeguard was a "phased" program, thus permitting the Administration to take "maximum advantage of the information gathered from the initial deployment in designing the later phases of the program." His explanation had helped overcome some legislative doubts as to the technical feasibility of an ABM system. Dr. Foster also argued that deployment of the first two sites would provide an opportunity to "shake down" the system—"to find and remove those technical and operational bugs which are not likely to show up in research and development efforts." Yet by the time of the President's announcement on January 30, 1970, asking for additional sites, deployment had yet to take place. Bids had not come in for the North Dakota site, nor had they even been sent out for the Montana site.

Congress supported the Safeguard system again in 1970, but on a less ambitious scale than the Administration had requested. The President wanted to continue deployment at the North Dakota and Montana sites, begin a new site at Whiteman Air Force Base in Missouri, and proceed with advanced preparation at Warren Air Force Base in Wyoming and at four other sites. The latter four, which would have been a start on an anti-Chinese ABM system, were eliminated from the bill passed by Congress.

LEGISLATIVE INFLUENCE IN FOREIGN POLICY

In the postwar period, Congress has made several attempts to limit the President's power to send troops abroad and wage war without legislative approval. During the "Great Debate" in early 1951, concerning Truman's authority to send ground forces to Europe, Representative Coudert introduced a resolution requiring congressional authorization for sending military forces abroad. A few days later, Senator Kenneth Wherry submitted a resolution providing that "no ground forces of the United States should be assigned to duty in the European area for the purposes of the North Atlantic Treaty pending the formulation of a policy with respect thereto by the Congress." Neither measure was adopted. Instead, the Senate passed a resolution approving the President's decision to send four additional divisions of ground forces to Western Europe, but also stated it to be the sense of the Senate that, "in the interests of sound constitutional processes, and of national unity and understanding," congressional approval should be obtained before sending additional troops to Europe.

In January 1953, Senator John W. Bricker introduced a constitutional amendment, intended primarily as a restraint on the President's power to enter into executive agreements. The Bricker Amendment was rejected the following year by a vote of 42 to 50, while a substitute amendment proposed by Senator Walter F. George fell one vote short of Senate adoption.

National Commitments Resolution

A new round of legislative reassertion began in the late 1960s. Disillusioned with the Vietnam war, and reacting to the dubious constitutionality of executive military initiatives abroad, Congress reasserted its powers in foreign affairs. In July 1967, Senator Fulbright introduced a resolution, stating it to be the sense of the Senate that a national commitment by the United States to a foreign war "necessarily and exclusively results from affirmative action" taken by Congress and the President by means of a treaty, convention, or other legislative instrumentality specifically intended to give effect to such a commitment.

By the time the resolution emerged from committee that November, it contained a number of escape clauses for the President. The resolution was limited to circumstances that might arise in the future pertaining to situations in which the United States "is not already involved." It recognized the President's duty to repel an attack on the United States and to "protect United States citizens or property properly." The resolution ended obscurely by saying that a national commitment would result from decisions made in accordance with "constitutional processes," which, in addition to "appropriate" executive action, required "affirmative action" by Congress specifically intended to give rise to such commitment. The executive branch could obviously interpret those words and phrases to satisfy its own objectives and actions.

The resolution was not put to a vote in 1967 or 1968. In February 1969, Senator Fulbright reintroduced it, and this time it was reported out of committee without cumbersome amendments. In June 1969, by an overwhelming 70 to 16 vote, it was adopted by the Senate. The resolution defined a national commitment as "the use of the armed forces of the United States on foreign territory, or a promise to assist a foreign country, government, or people by the use of the armed forces or financial resources of the United States, either immediately or upon the happening of certain events." The resolution declared it to be the sense of the Senate that a national commitment by the United States results "only from affirmative action taken by the executive and legislative branches of the United States Government by means of a treaty, statute, or concurrent resolution of both Houses of Congress specifically providing for such commitment."

As a sense-of-the-Senate resolution, it is not legally binding on the President, but is intended as a restraint on his power to dispatch troops abroad without congressional approval. More importantly, it signaled the Senate's determination to exercise more forcefully its prerogatives in foreign policy. Senator Fulbright expressed the hope that the resolution would effect a change in the attitude of the Senate toward its responsibilities, as well as a change in the attitude of the President toward the Senate.

The actual meaning and scope of the National Commitments Resolution is subject to varying interpretations. When Senator Fulbright introduced it in 1969, he explained that it was not meant to prevent the President from responding "immediately and appropriately" to an attack on the United States. Examples in the last chapter show that the meaning of "defensive war" in the postwar period has been magnified to include attacks on our bases and troops overseas, on the Western Hemisphere, and has involved military actions related to the protection of American lives and property as well as to hot pursuit.

The Senate Foreign Relations Committee also noted that the resolution would not alter "existing treaties, acts of Congress including joint resolutions, or other past actions or commitments of the Government of the United States." That would permit the use of armed forces by the President under "defensive war" provisions of defense treaties, under the general grants of power provided by postwar resolutions, and would even permit the use of troops to satisfy commitments made by Administration communiqués or policy statements.

Presidential war prerogatives were acknowledged by the House in November 1970, when it passed a war powers resolution by a vote of 288 to 39. The resolution admitted that the President "in certain extraordinary and emergency circumstances has the authority to defend the United States and its citizens without prior authorization by the Congress." The resolution did not try to define when the President could, and could not, act. Instead, it sought to introduce new procedures.

In the first place, the President should consult Congress "whenever feasible" before involving U.S. forces in armed conflict. And second, in the event that the President commits U.S. forces without prior authorization of Congress, he is to submit a report to Congress "promptly" (that is, within several days), including the circumstances necessitating his action; the constitutional, legislative, and treaty provisions authorizing his action, together with his reasons for not seeking specific prior congressional authorization; and the estimated scope of activities. The Senate did not act on the measure.

Reassertion of Legislative Authority

If Senate and House resolutions turn into mere parchment barriers because of inescapable ambiguities in our language, what concrete actions are needed to reassert legislative authority in foreign affairs? Congress must first of all take part in the early stages of foreign policy-making, when options are still open and positions have yet to harden. At the time of the Tonkin crisis in 1964, Congress could do little else but follow along in the footsteps of the Administration. The time for influence was during the prior decade, when our involvement in Vietnam was beginning to take shape and when Congress was appropriating the funds to make that involvement possible. It could, of course, have used its power of the purse to withhold funds at that time. But the long prevailing faith in executive "expertise" in the field of national security, combined with the postwar tradition of "bipartisan" foreign policy, had accustomed the legislature to accept rather uncritically most Presidential definitions of military need.

Short of slashing executive fund requests—essentially a negative reaction—Congress can and should participate more than has been its tradition in the formation of specific foreign policies. I am not suggesting that it participate in each detail of executive policy-making, yet it will have to ignore the traditional division of labor that limits itself to "broad policy" questions while delegating "day-to-day" decisions to the executive branch. Congress must monitor policies *and* operations. Day-to-day decisions, upon accumulation, have a way of forming policy—what the Senate Foreign Relations Committee has called "a process of commitment by accretion." Congress will have to organize itself to influence policy at the formative stage and maintain close review thereafter.

A few examples will suggest how Congress can begin to play a more positive and influential role. An amendment to the defense appropriations bill in December 1969, sponsored by Senator John Sherman Cooper, specified that no funds were to be used by the President to introduce ground troops into Laos or Thailand. Cooper said that "In bluntest terms, the amendment is offered with the purpose of preventing, if possible, the United States from moving step by step into war in Laos or Thailand, as it did in Vietnam."

As it turned out, however, the Nixon Administration took its first military initiative not in Laos or Thailand but rather in Cambodia. The Cooper-Church amendment, aimed at barring the retention of U.S. troops in Cambodia after July 1, 1970, recognized the close relationship between "tactical maneuvers" in the field and larger policy questions affecting the whole of Southeast Asia. The Special Foreign Assistance Act of 1971, enacted on January 5, 1971, stipulated that none of the funds authorized or appropriated pursuant to that Act, or any other, "may be used to finance the introduction of United States ground combat troops into Cambodia, or to provide United States advisers to or for Cambodian military forces in Cambodia." In its bombing operations in Cambodia, and in its subsequent "incursion" into Laos, the Administration interpreted air power in such broad terms as to circumvent some of the earlier legislative restrictions. When helicopter gunships have the capability of patrolling at tree-top level, the distinction between "air power" and "ground troops" begins to disappear.

Congress can also continue to use its traditional right to inform itself, and the public, by questioning the executive and conducting its own studies and inquiries. The most recent example of this is the continuing series of hearings held by the Symington Subcommittee on United States Security Agreements and Commitments Abroad. During 1969 and 1970, the two man staff of the Subcommittee travelled to 23 countries for on-the-scene investigations. Subsequent hearings examined U.S. policies and operations in 13 countries, plus NATO. The Subcommittee pressed the executive bureaucracies to defend and explain their policies, secured the declassification of much nonsensitive information which an overzealous officialdom labeled "secret," and was able to shed new light on some of the 2,200 U.S. overseas bases in 33 countries. A number of these bases, the hearings suggested, were products of bureaucratic inertia, anachronous relics dating back to the 1940s but unnecessary in the 1970s. In much the same spirit, Senator Mike Mansfield for the past five years has been pushing for substantial troop reductions of U.S. forces stationed in Europe, arguing that the era of occupation, Cold War, and one-sided financial preeminence of the United States are things of the past. In another effort to change outmoded policies, Senator Charles McC. Mathias, Jr., called for the repeal of resolutions granting emergency powers to the President: the 1955 Formosa Resolution, the 1957 Middle East Resolution, the 1962 Cuban Resolution, and the 1964 Tonkin Gulf Resolution. The latter was finally repealed on January 12, 1971. In March 1971, Senator Lawton Chiles introduced a bill to repeal an emergency proclamation by President Truman which has been in existence since December 16, 1950. Senator Clifford Case has introduced a bill to require regular reporting of executive agreements.

Congress is also reexamining some of our foreign policy principles. Senator Alan Cranston introduced a resolution in 1969 on our recognition policy, stipulating it to be the sense of the Senate that recognition of a foreign government does not imply that we necessarily approve of the form, ideology, or policy of that government. Cranston said that our "self-righteous and moralistic" recognition policy led to military intervention in Mexico and Nicaragua in earlier decades, while nonrecognition of Communist China contributed to miscalculations and a widening of the Korean War: "perhaps we would have marched to the Yalu River even if we had been well-informed—but the price we paid and the losses we suffered would have been far less if we had been prepared for China's violent reaction." The Senate Foreign Relations Committee adopted the Cranston Resolution unanimously and it passed the Senate on September 25, 1969, by a 77 to 3 margin.

Structural and Procedural Reforms

A little more than three decades ago, the President's Committee on Administrative Management made this terse observation: "The President needs help." The same could be said of Congress today. Much of the legislative decline in influencing foreign policy, James A. Robinson has written, "must be attributed to the profound change in the requirements of public policy-making and to the failure of Congress to alter its organization to cope with the new demands made upon it."

For instance, it is clear that the crowded schedules of Senators and Representatives do not permit effective oversight of Administration policies. Senator Everett Dirksen, at one time a member of more than a dozen committees and subcommittees, used to claim that he needed roller skates to get to all the meetings. During a 1970 debate, Senator Lee Metcalf remarked that a Senator in the previous session of Congress had 39 separate committee assignments.

Steps are being taken to ease this pressure and to streamline procedures. The Legislative Reorganization Act of 1970, by reducing the size of a number of Senate committees, promises junior Senators a greater opportunity to develop expertise and to hold leadership positions earlier in their careers. The tight schedule of Representatives may be relieved somewhat once the House installs electronic voting equipment. During 1970, the House consumed 238 hours for roll calls and quorum calls. That represents about 28 percent of the time the House was in session. Electronic voting should cut the half-hour vote to a 15-minute voting period. One result might be an increased use of record votes, thus making legislators more responsible and accountable to their constituents.

Another mechanical innovation is the new Senate amplification system. That is not without substantive importance. During the 1964 Tonkin debate, Senator Gaylord Nelson complained that he could not hear the discussion between Senator Fulbright and two other Senators, while Fulbright admitted at one point that a diversion had prevented him from hearing what Nelson had said. Other Senators must have experienced difficulty in hearing the debate, but considered it indelicate to advertise that fact in the public record. A resolution in 1969 for an amplification system prompted Senator George Murphy to remark on the anomaly of hearing astronauts a quarter million miles from earth while at the same time "we in this Chamber are denied the opportunity to hear our colleagues."

Larger, more expert staffs are also needed. Stewart Udall, former congressman and Secretary of the Interior, told the Joint Economic Committee that one of the things that struck him in moving from the legislative to the executive side was how "pathetically" understaffed the Congress was. Senator Proxmire commented on the fact that there were only two or three staff members assigned to the Senate subcommittee on defense appropriations. At those same hearings, Senator Barry Goldwater admitted that the Senate Armed Services Committee, on which he sits, lacked time to scrutinize Pentagon requests: "We need help on it."

With smaller committees aided by bigger professional staffs, Congress will be better able to conduct its own background studies and check the accuracy and consistency of executive statements. The Legislative Reorganization Act of 1970 increases the number of professional staff members for each standing committee and makes available to the committees cost-effectiveness analysts from the General Accounting Office. The Congressional Research Service (formerly the Legislative Reference Service) will help committees evaluate legislative proposals in order to determine the merits of bills, to estimate their probable results, and to evaluate alternative means of accomplishing the same results.

A number of other provisions in the Legislative Reorganization Act of 1970 have increased the visibility and accountability of legislative actions. However, staffing and better floor and committee procedures will not overcome the problem of the unrepresentative structure of committees; military types dominate the committees and subcommittees that authorize and appropriate funds for the Defense Department. Part of that ideological bias is in fact caused by liberals when they concentrate their interests on such committees as Senate Foreign Relations, Senate Labor and Public Welfare, and House Education and Labor. Surely a seat on Armed Services is important for urban constituencies—in terms of establishing a balance between military and domestic spending. Ideological biases of the committees are also a result of the conservative cast of the Senate and House committees responsible for making committee selections. New appointments to the Senate Steering Committee in 1971 helped liberalize its structure, while efforts are underway in both houses to make committee chairmen more responsive and sensitive to party caucuses. Subcommittee chairmanships and ranking minority positions are being distributed to a broader spectrum of legislative leaders. Partly as a result of the limitation on subcommittee chairmanships adopted by the House Democratic Caucus early in 1971, four subcommittee chairmanships were made available on the House Foreign Affairs Committee. The new chairmen— Representatives Fraser, Rosenthal, Culver, and Hamilton— are all distinctly of a liberal outlook.

Other techniques are available for broadening congressional participation. In hearings in 1969, the Senate Foreign Relations Committee conducted an intensive inquiry into the Safeguard ABM system, anti-submarine warfare, and MIRVs—items normally considered on the agenda of the Armed Services Committee. That form of encroachment was made possible when the Foreign Relations Committee scrutinized those weapons systems within the larger context of arms control and the Nonproliferation Treaty. From 1968 to 1970, the Joint Economic Committee held hearings on "Economics of Military Procurement," "The Military Budget and

National Economic Priorities," and "The Acquisition of Weapons Systems." Those hearings contributed important insights into deficiencies within the executive branch. Extensive hearings in the area of government procurement, held by the House Committee on Government Operations in 1969, helped uncover additional defects in the management of defense contracts.

Still another technique for broader participation is the bicameral, bipartisan group known as Members of Congress for Peace Through Law. In recent years its special subgroup on military spending has offered an independent analysis of weapons systems and force levels. The Democratic Study Group also prepares a separate analysis of the defense budget, supplying a fact sheet on the bill reported out by the House Armed Services Committee and comparing the bill to the Senate version and to the original Administration request. Private groups, such as the Brookings Institution, publish studies on the range of options that are available for strategic nuclear forces and general purpose forces.

As another means of providing independent, technically qualified evaluations of Defense Department programs, Representative Abner Mikva introduced a bill to establish an Office of Defense Review. As a permanent agency of Congress, it would be trained in systems analysis, cleared to deal with material of the highest security classification, and held responsible for dealing with such fundamental questions as strategic planning, the validity of planning assumptions, the relationship between military planning assumptions and overall U.S. foreign policy goals, and the contribution of individual weapons systems to U.S. national security. Mikva observed that those are the fundamental questions that neither congressmen nor the committees have had time to explore.

Legislative reassertion is not in itself, of course, a foolproof antidote for future Vietnams and large defense budgets. Congress' past record of partnership with the military is plain enough. But neither is there hope in legislative acquiescence to "executive expertise," especially when the latter becomes a synonym for incompetence and deceit. That is why Congress has begun to build an independent expertise to monitor and question foreign commitments, which all too often have been the personal undertakings of the President, abetted by the bureaucracy, rather than a commitment by the government and the nation as a whole.

To complement this new congressional competence there must be a new temperament and attitude among legislators: a courage to resist being stampeded into granting power simply because the President waves the flag; a resolve to defer to no one in the exercise of independent judgment; a determination to treat "reassertion" not as a temporary phenomenon—needed to restore constitutional balance—but as a permanent, nondelegable legislative responsibility. Congress has demonstrated rather impressively that it can change its attitudes and its procedures and contribute intelligently to foreign policy-making. The larger question is whether it has the will and the staying power to contribute from one year to the next, in times of crisis as well as relative calm, without reverting to its habitual acquiescence to the President.

CONCLUSION

The intended thrust of this book is neither pro-President nor pro-Congress. In earlier years I was an admirer of the Presidency. I am no longer, and can only hope that disenchantment has not made me too distrustful of the executive branch or too trusting in Congress. Developments over the past two centuries do not seem to warrant placing trust primarily in one branch or the other. Congress does well in some areas but not in others. The same holds true for the executive branch. And what is true for one period need not be so for another.

That leads to some extremely curious results. The liberals of 1970 attacked Presidential war powers in language essentially the same as that used two decades earlier by the conservatives. Each branch strives to protect its "prerogatives," but that is a term without any fixed meaning. What is a rightful exercise of prerogatives by one branch might be considered an improper transgression by the other. The President currently wields vast power in spending and taxing: traditionally a prerogative of the legislature. On the other hand, Congress now acts more boldly in the field of foreign policy and in the selection of weapons systems.

Conventional wisdoms about the Presidency have been profoundly altered. A few decades ago, in the spirit of the *Curtiss-Wright* decision, it was assumed that the President should have broad discretion in foreign affairs but very little at home. A number of scholars now advance the opposite thesis that the President needs greater discretion over domestic programs, such as having the power to make short-run tax adjustments, but that Congress should place more stringent controls on his actions abroad.

In identifying the major factors that account for the delegation of congressional power to the executive branch, I have attributed to the President certain properties and basic responsibilities. In doing so, I have steered clear of the "textbook qualities" of the President: such romantic properties as competence, omnipotence, or beneficence. Furthermore, the properties I discuss are relative. It is not so much that the President possesses them in any fixed or pure sense. The point is rather that Congress, compared to the President, lacks the properties, or decides that it is politically onerous and unrewarding to exercise them.

In studying the flow of power from Congress to the President, I would make the following observations. First, the flow is not always "to" the President, for it often passes beyond him, subdelegated to dozens of agencies and bureaus over which he can exercise only imperfect control. It frequently happens that an executive agency is allied more closely with a congressional committee than with the President and his budget advisers.

Second, it is not true that Congress, after delegating power, is placed in a weaker position than before. Few would argue that Congress would strengthen its position by taking back from the executive branch the responsibility for general tariff-making or for preparation of the budget. Congress could do so, but only at the cost of abandoning a number of other duties which it is better equipped to handle.

Third, it is easy to be misled as to the true nature of Presidential or congressional power. The President may receive credit for the enactment of a bill which, in fact, depended largely on the efforts of certain congressmen. Or the President may give credit to specific legislators, not because they deserve it, but because he wants their support for his legislative program. Or actual credit may belong with staff personnel, who remain anonymous out of deference to their committees and legislators. A Presidential action that at first glance appears to be an arbitrary exercise of power may, after closer investigation, turn out to be a reasonable exercise of administrative discretion. The opposite may also be true: what initially appears to be reasonable may actually be arbitrary. Deeper probing by the student may not always produce a clear picture, but at least it dislodges some superficial notions.

Lastly, there is nothing preordained or irreversible about the shift of power to the President. So much is expected of the executive branch, and so much has been delegated to it, that it sometimes finds itself overwhelmed and subject to the same kind of criticism that was leveled two centuries ago at the Continental Congress. And as the Legislative Reorganization Act of 1970 illustrates, Congress can change its procedures and organization to better match the resources of the executive branch.

Having reviewed the origin of a separation of powers during the 1774–1789 period, of what relevance is that today, especially when the executive and judicial branches have shown a more than adequate capability of protecting themselves against congressional encroachments? What benefit can come from invoking the intent of the framers from a period that bears so little resemblance to today?

One benefit, as I see it, is to contest a number of opinions that are still widely held and expressed: the framers' "fear" of executive power, their dependence on Montesquieu, and the alleged incompatibility between the separation of power and governmental efficiency. Issues are difficult enough today without carting along this intellectual baggage. Experience taught the framers the need for a strong executive: to overcome the administrative deficiencies of the Articles of Confederation and to avoid the encroachments of executive power that had occurred on the state level. If we must talk about the framers, that would be closer to the truth.

But we would do well to keep their thoughts on the separation doctrine where they belong—in the eighteenth century—and decide current issues on the basis of our own understanding, our own experiences, and the priorities we set for legislative and executive control. For if the framers intended anything, it was to exercise independent judgment and take responsibility for the outcome. They did that in their time and expected us to do the same in ours.

APPENDIX

HISTORICAL AND PHILOSOPHICAL BACKGROUND ON THE SEPARATION DOCTRINE

The framers drew their principles of government from a variety of sources, and continually redefined those principles in the light of changing political conditions. John Adams offered this advice in 1776: "Let us study the law of nature; search into the spirit of the British constitution; read the histories of the ancient ages; contemplate the great examples of Greece and Rome; set before us the conduct of our own British ancestors, who have defended for us the inherent rights of mankind against foreign and domestic tyrants and usurpers." Additional lessons on how to structure government came from the experiences of the American colonies and the Continental Congress.

MIXED GOVERNMENT

Although refinements have been added over the centuries, the principle of mixed government, as a technique for stabilizing government, is an old one. Plato combined monarchy and democracy in the *Laws* to form the well-governed city, while Aristotle devised an elaborate formula for mixing different types of oligarchies and democracies in order to achieve a stable state. Aristotle also took a step toward dividing government into separate departments—the deliberative, executive, and judicial—but they do not correspond to the three branches of government as we have come to know them. Moreover, the purpose of separation was to apportion different functions, not to balance one force against another.

The concept of balance was put forth explicitly by Polybius. In order to prevent the various types of constitutions from degenerating into their perverted forms, he advocated a mixture of kingship, aristocracy, and democracy: "the force of each being neutralized by that of the others, neither of them should prevail and outbalance another, but that the constitution should remain for long in a state of equilibrium like a well-trimmed boat." Machiavelli, to cite another example, also considered pure forms of government to be defective. The best government would partake of each form: "when there is combined under the same constitution a prince, a nobility, and the power of the people, then these three powers will watch and keep each other reciprocally in check."

The concept of balance is present in both the mixed government and in the separation doctrine. In the mixed state, however, stability is achieved by dividing the sovereign power among different social classes: the king, the nobility, and the people. In a system of separated powers, authority is divided into three different functions, with each function assigned to a distinct body.

This latter concept was promoted by John Locke, who looked to a balance not between classes but rather between institutions: legislative, executive, and federative. Moreover, he looked to these different institutions not merely for the discharge of different functions, but as a system of mutual checks. During the evolution of governmental forms, men learned to think of "methods of restraining any exorbitances of those to whom they had given the authority over them, and of balancing the power of government by placing several parts of it in different hands." Governmental functions could not be entrusted to any one department, for "it may be too great temptation to human frailty, apt to grasp at power, for the same persons who have the power of making laws to have also in their hands the power to execute them. . . ."

Although Locke considered a balance of power to be important, he did not advocate strict separation between the legislature and the executive. The legislature could punish the executive for maladministration of the laws, while the executive had the power to assemble and dismiss the legislature. Locke made no provision for an independent judiciary; instead, he placed judicial functions for the most part under the executive department. In 1701, a decade after the appearance of his treatise, the Act of Settlement in England contributed to judicial independence by guaranteeing tenure to judges during good behavior.

Montesquieu specifically provided for the legislative, executive, and judicial branches, relying on the British Constitution as his model for separated powers. For this, he has been heavily criticized. Maitland wrote that it was "curious that some political theorists should have seen their favourite ideal, a complete separation of administration from judicative, realised in England; in England of all places in the world, where the two have for ages been inextricably blended." Bagehot described the secret of the English system as the "close union, the nearly complete fusion, of the executive and legislative powers." It is said that Montesquieu misread the British Constitution and that the framers compounded the problem by incorporating his misconception into the American constitution. The latter is certainly an overstatement; and the operation of the British system was, as we shall now see, more complicated than Maitland and Bagehot would have had us believe.

THE BRITISH MODEL

Political conflict in 17th-century England offered two basic lessons for students of government. First, the abuses of monarchy could be matched and even exceeded by oppressive actions on the part of Parliament. Second, it was desirable to secure greater independence for the judiciary, first from the King and then later from Parliament.

On the question of judicial independence, the reign of James I (1603–1625) was marked by clashes between the King and the ecclesiastical courts, on the one side, and Parliament and the courts of common law on the other. Jurisdictional disputes thus arose between spiritual law and temporal law. In 1605, Chief Justice Coke of the Common Pleas upheld the legislative supremacy of Parliament, stating that the King was not above the law and that the "law of the realm cannot be changed but by Parliament." Two years later Coke again rejected the argument that the King may determine cases in accordance with his own judgment: "the King in his own person cannot adjudge any case, either criminal, as treason, felony, etc., or betwixt party and party, concerning his inheritance, chattels, or goods, etc., but this ought to be determined and adjudged in some court of justice according to the law and custom of England."

In the famous Dr. Bonham's Case in 1610, Coke sought to protect the court from legislative encroachments by declaring that Parliament could not issue legislation that was repugnant to the common law. Throughout his service on the bench he advocated an independent judiciary. Later, as a member of the House of Commons, he was equally vociferous in upholding the privileges of the House of Commons against the Crown and the House of Lords. As is so often the case, the question of where one stands depends on where one sits.

The danger of fusing legislative and executive power into a single branch was demonstrated repeatedly during the middle of the 17th century. The Star Chamber accused John

Lilburne in 1637 of sending "scandalous Bookes" from Holland into England; he denied the charge, but refused to submit to random interrogation. As punishment he was publicly beaten, pilloried, and placed in solitary confinement. Following his release in 1640, his continued protests against the government resulted in frequent incarceration. From prison he was to write: "to me it is one of the most unjust things in the world, that the Law-makers should be the Law executors. . . . And therefore it were a great deal better for the Common-wealth, that all the executors of the Law should be such persons as doe not in the least belong to the Parliament. . . ."

The use of separate branches as a means of balancing the government was also explored by Philip Hunton. In 1643, he wrote that the purpose of a division of responsibility between King, Lords, and Commons was that "one should counterpoise and keep even the other." John Sadler, also writing in the 1640s, looked upon the threefold separation of powers as having mystical significance; he spoke of a "sacred unity in trinity."

Clement Walker, a member of the Long Parliament during the 1640s, became a victim of legislative caprice. Having originally joined with those who opposed the King, he later came to distrust Cromwell and the Independents, and after the army's victory at Naseby, urged acceptance of the royal terms. Indicted for treason, he died in the Tower in 1651. In his writings he formulated the principle that the gathering of all power in the hands of any one department was tantamount to tyranny: "Now for any one man, or any Assembly, Court, or Corporation of men (be it the two Houses of Parliament) to usurpe these three powers: 1. The Governing power. 2. The Legislative power. 3. And the Judicative power, into themselves, is to make themselves the highest Tyrants, and the people the basest slaves in the world; for to govern supremely by a Law made, and interpreted by themselves according to their own pleasure, what can be more boundlesse and arbitrary?"

A system of mutual checks supplied by separate departments was thus part of the effort to stabilize the English government. Still another reason for separating executive from legislature was the realization that Parliament was unfit to administer the details of war. Professor Clayton Roberts, in his study on Stuart England, concludes that by the middle of the 17th century, Englishmen had come to "prize the principle of the separation of powers because they learned to their cost the disadvantages of ignoring it, of placing executive power immediately in Parliament. They learned that it bred inefficiency, that it promoted faction and self-seeking, and that it begat a terrible tyranny. They discovered its inefficiency first." Professor W. B. Gwyn identifies a number of arguments put forth during this period to justify a separation of powers between King and Parliament: a separation was necessary for efficiency, for serving the common interest and safeguarding the rule of law, for holding the government accountable to the people, and for establishing a balance of powers as a means of preventing arbitrary action.

After the second revolution of 1688, which drove James II out of London, Parliament consolidated its own strength and placed new restraints on the royal power. By the time George I, former Elector of Hanover, acceded to the throne in 1714, the English had a King who was ignorant of their language. Though he could confer with his ministers in French, he was not able to converse with his subjects, to address Parliament, or read the laws, and he often had to sign measures of whose contents he had only an imperfect knowledge. Even the sessions in French with his ministers proved unsatisfactory, for they could not always find the right expression to explain matters properly to him. Besides the King's difficulty with the language, Professor J. H. Plumb has observed that he was both ignorant and stupid: "one he did nothing to dispel, the other was incurable."

With the King absenting himself from meetings of the Cabinet Council, active formulation of policy passed into the hands of the leading ministers. Robert Walpole became chief minister in 1721. Having established a base of power within the House of Commons, and enjoying considerable patronage through his offices as Paymaster-General and First Lord of the Treasury, he dominated Parliament for the next two decades. England subsequently ushered in the system of parliamentary government, with the Cabinet acting as a disciplined unit connecting the King with Parliament—one party controlling government and the other in opposition—and the Prime Minister eventually displacing the King as chief executive.

The struggle for political power then centered on the Prime Minister, a development that did not go unnoticed in America. At the Philadelphia Convention in 1787, Gouverneur Morris voiced his concern about legislative efforts to remove the President, pointing to parallel moves by Parliament to remove the King. By the King of England, Morris explained, he meant "the real King, the Minister."

This shifting balance of power in English politics, and the intensity of partisan maneuvers, was not discussed by Montesquieu. Yet Rapin de Thoyras, a French historian who visited England shortly before Montesquieu, displayed a firm grasp of British politics and the party system. Even though the essential characteristic of the government was the "close and absolutely necessary union between the King and the Parliament," that union was not so close as to obliterate the identity of the two branches. Rapin found the British government to be unlike any system in Europe: it had a king, but was not monarchical, since the nobility and the people shared legislative power with the King. Nor was the government identical to either an aristocracy or a democracy. It was a mixed government, he said, "differing from, and yet composed of, all three. The prerogatives of the Sovereign, and the privileges of the Nobles and people, are so tempered together, that they mutually support one another. At the same time, each of the three powers, concerned in the Legislature, may insuperably obstruct the attempts of one or both the others, to render themselves independent." Included in Rapin's history of England was his *Dissertation sur les Whigs et les Tories,* published in 1717. Not only did he itemize the differences between the two major parties, he even noted factional variations within each: Moderate Tories, Rigid Tories, Church Tories, and so forth.

INFLUENCE OF MONTESQUIEU

Montesquieu's visit to London from 1729 to 1731 coincided with partisan struggles between the Tories and the Whigs and the evolving cabinet system under Walpole. The latter's policy of exercising control over Parliament, to the extent that ministerial measures were practically certain to be adopted, generated partisan arguments for and against a separation of powers. Bolingbroke, exiled in France since 1715, and kept in that status when Walpole on several occasions defeated efforts to pardon him, finally returned to England in 1725 to become one of the most vehement critics of Walpole.

Montesquieu was in London when Bolingbroke unleashed his attack. A periodical supported by Bolingbroke warned of the fusion of executive and legislative bodies: "In a constitution like ours, the safety of the whole depends on the balance of the parts, and the balance of the parts on their mutual independency on one another." The *London Journal,* an administration paper, printed a rejoinder on July 4, 1730: " 'Tis plain to common sense and the experience of all the world, that this independency is a mere imagination; there never was really any such thing, nor can business be carried on or Government subsist by several powers absolutely distinct and independent."

Elements of truth were contained in both positions, but Montesquieu chose to present a tidy, uncomplicated model of separated powers, free of partisan battles and of the developing cabinet system. It was an idealized form of government, and corresponded more to his conceptions than to the realities of English politics. Justice Holmes spoke bluntly of this contrivance: "His England—the England of the threefold division of power into legislative, executive and judicial —was a fiction invented by him, a fiction which misled Blackstone and Delolme."

In what sense did the framers borrow from Montesquieu? It must first be noted that his system resembles a *mixed form of government,* relying on a balance between distinct social classes. One branch of the legislature would be reserved for the people, and a second legislative house set aside for nobles with hereditary privileges. No such class distinction exists for the two houses of Congress. The Constitution explicitly forbids the Federal Government and the states to grant titles of nobility.

It is said that an independent judiciary, coequal with the legislative and executive branches, owes its existence to Montesquieu. Yet it is clear that the drive for an independent judiciary began long before Locke, had been written in part into English law by 1701, and, as we saw in the first chapter, evolved by a natural process in America. Moreover, the judiciary envisioned by Montesquieu was not to be a permanent branch. It was to be drawn from the body of the people at certain times of the year, as had been the practice in Athens during the time of Socrates. Compared with the other two powers of government, Montesquieu called the judiciary *en quelque façon nulle*—"in some measure next to nothing." That bears little resemblance to the Supreme Court with its permanent character, original jurisdiction, and life tenure granted its members.

Still another contribution by Montesquieu is said to be a more explicit separation between executive and legislature. While it is true that he erected a fairly strict separation between the departments, he was conscious of the danger of dividing government to such a point that it reached a state of paralysis. The course of human affairs, he said, made movement and cooperation between the executive and legislature essential to the public welfare. The safety of the people was the primary goal, and to this end the branches of government would be "forced to move, but still in concert." He favored a single executive over a multiple one, for the reason that "this branch of government, having need of despatch, is better administered by one than by many."

Montesquieu saw three situations in which the legislature would exercise judicial functions: mitigation of sentences imposed by the national judges; impeachment of public officials; and trials by the Senate of its own members. In one section he appears to advocate a system of checks more than one of separation: "To form a moderate government, it is necessary to combine the several powers; to regulate, temper, and set them in motion; to give, as it were, ballast to one, in order to enable it to counterpoise the other." This is summed up in his axiom, where power checks power: *il faut que, par la disposition des choses, le pouvoir arrête le pouvoir.*

For the most part, however, he adhered to a strict separation of powers. He maintained that the legislative body should not impeach the executive, for the "moment he is accused or tried there is an end of liberty." The framers were also concerned about the executive's independence when subject to impeachment, but Madison thought it "indispensable that some provision should be made for defending the Community against the incapacity, negligence or perfidy of the chief Magistrate." What Madison objected to were such vague grounds for removal as "maladministration," since it would be up to the Senate to define what that meant. To Madison, that was equivalent to having the executive serve at the pleasure of the Senate. He accepted the clause limiting impeachment to treason, bribery, and high crimes and misdemeanors. Still, he preferred that impeachment be handled by the Supreme Court or by a tribunal of which the Court would form a part.

Montesquieu gave his "senate" (the house of nobles) the power to reject bills relating to supplies, but no authority to amend them. Article I, Section VII of the Constitution specifically grants amending rights to the Senate on revenue bills. Montesquieu allowed the executive to reject legislation, but opposed any other participation in the legislative process. The Constitution empowers the President to make treaties with the advice and consent of the Senate (such treaties being considered the supreme law of the land), and it authorizes the President to recommend such measures as "he shall judge necessary and expedient."

Nothing would have been more out of character at the Philadelphia Convention than for one delegate to buttress his argument with a quotation from Montesquieu, only to have that quotation challenged by a passage from a rival authority. The delegates did not use Montesquieu's work as a blueprint for the Constitution; that is entirely fitting. Although Montesquieu borrowed some of his ideas from England, and presumably hoped to see them applied in France, he stressed most of all the need to structure government on the basis of local laws and customs: "It is of importance that he who is to govern has not imbibed foreign maxims; these are less agreeable than those already established."

COLONIAL DEVELOPMENTS

Colonial governments accumulated their own insights into the problem of checks and balances. Virginia was originally under the supervision of two councils—one at home, and the other in London. The governor, at first chosen by the home council, was later appointed by the Crown. With the creation of an elected assembly in 1619, there existed a definite system of legislature and executive checking one another. All except five of the colonies came to be governed by this system. Moreover, the colonies of Pennsylvania, Maryland, and Delaware, which had governors appointed by proprietors who usually lived in England, represented a similar system of balanced government.

In Massachusetts, during the 1640s, the Elders of the Church used the theory of mixed government to defend and protect magistrates and the governor from popular pressures. Governor John Winthrop was confronted by the demand of some deputies that all authority—legislative, consultative, and judicial—be exercised by the people in their body representative. The elected aristocracy resisted that demand. In 1644, the Elders described the Charter as a threefold power of government: legislative, judicative, and consultative (or directive). The legislative power was shared between the deputies and the governor and assistants, as was true of the directive power. But the judicial power was to be exercised by the magistrates alone, subject only to impeachment and appeal. In 1679 the Elders again issued a statement on constitutional principles, insisting that the Charter of the Massachusetts Bay Company had established a "distribution of differing interest of power and privilege between the magistrates and freemen, and the distinct exercise of legislative and executive power."

Charges of encroachment were leveled by colonial governors, as well as by the elected assemblies. In 1723, Governor Shute of Massachusetts complained that the House of Representatives, by exercising control over the salaries of Governor and Treasurer, possessed the "whole legislative, and in a good measure the executive power of the province." And in 1742, six years before the publication of Montesquieu's *Spirit of the Laws*, the House of Representatives in Massachusetts rejected a request by Governor Shirley for a permanent salary on the ground that it "would greatly tend to lessen the just weight of the other two branches of the government, which ought ever to be maintained and preserved; especially since the governor has so great authority and check upon them."

After achieving their independence from England, many of the states wrote into their constitutions explicit guarantees for a separation between the branches of government, but the meaning of separation varied from state to state and became a source of continual misunderstanding. Despite the strong language in the Massachusetts Constitution, forbidding one department from exercising the powers of another, the executive possessed a qualified veto over the legislature; the senate acted as a court of impeachment; members of the judiciary were appointed by the governor; and the legislature appointed the major generals of the militia, an advisory council for the governor, and appointed several officers of the administration. Other state constitutions announced separation in strict terms but departed from the maxim in practice. New Hampshire, the last of the thirteen states to form a constitution, prudently acknowledged the gap between a literal interpretation of separated powers and the dictates of sound government. The three departments were to be kept "as separate from and independent of each other, as the nature of a free government will admit, or as is consistent with that chain of connection that binds the whole fabric of the constitution in one indissoluble bond of union and amity."

"INTENT" OF THE FRAMERS

Unless one is prepared to analyze in depth the political principles of at least twenty or thirty of the Founding Fathers, any reference to the "intent of the framers" can only be an exercise in airy generalizations. A less ambitious task, but instructive nonetheless, would be to limit oneself to a few of the leading figures and then follow their thoughts on a particular principle in detail.

In this section I discuss Washington and Hamilton, Jay and Jefferson, and John Adams and Madison, presenting their ideas on the separation doctrine in the context of political developments which surrounded them, and in light of their own changing, maturing observations. My choice includes the three authors of the *Federalist Papers* and a variety of perspectives on separated powers: the military-administrative considerations of Washington and Hamilton; the requirements of diplomacy and foreign policy-making experienced by Jay and Jefferson; and the historical-philosophical scope offered by Adams and Madison. Of course prominent names are omitted (James Wilson and Gouverneur Morris, to mention two), but by restricting myself to six men I can follow in substantial detail their thoughts on the question of separated powers.

Washington's responsibility as President of the Constitutional Convention left him scarcely any opportunity to express his views during the proceedings. Nevertheless, he held strong views on the structure of government, and we must assume that he made those views known when he met informally with the delegates. He certainly made them known in his letters. As for Hamilton, it is true that he was at the Convention only for a short time, and that his views were out of sympathy with those of other delegates, but he was a commanding figure and proved to be essential for ratification. The same is true of Jay, who did not even attend the Convention. Jefferson and Adams were not delegates to the Convention either, but they remained in close correspondence with Madison and Washington, offering advice, exchanging views, and helping to clarify the general principles on which the Constitution was founded.

(1) *George Washington* was one of the first to detect the administrative deficiencies of the Continental Congress and suggest a remedy. His sensitivity is understandable. As commander-in-chief of the campaign against the British forces, he experienced on a daily basis the inability of Congress to organize itself for the war effort. It was his lot to conduct a campaign with troops who were poorly trained, underfed, and ill-clothed, as well as badly supplied with weapons and ammunition. Promotions were held up, soldiers went unpaid, mutinies broke out. In the midst of these problems we find Washington patiently sending letters to Congress and to his friends, urging administrative reforms to expedite the war effort.

Washington emphasized the need for energy and dispatch as early as 1775, recommending that responsible executives be appointed to handle many of the tasks that the committees had undertaken. On July 10, several months after the battles at Lexington and Concord, he sent a report to Congress on the shortage of military supplies. Expressing his appreciation for what the committees had tried to do, he came to the main point: "there is a vital and enherent Principle of delay incompatible with Military service in transacting Business, through such various and different channels." Ten days later he again wrote to Congress, explaining that executive officers would "not only conduce to Order, Dispatch and Discipline, but that is a Measure of Oeconomy. The Delay, the Waste, and unpunishable Neglect of Duty arising from these Offices being in commission in several Hands, evidently shew that the Public Expence must be finally enhanced."

Congress shifted some of its functions to boards in 1777, but without noticeable improvement in efficiency and dispatch. Legislative proceedings during 1778 provoked vitriolic comments. One member of Congress told Washington that procrastinations arose from "a vapid desultory habit, which if I am not mistaken, I have seen, squander Millions and endanger States." Washington found himself so poorly informed of political developments that he felt as though he was "an alien."

Writing late in 1780, Washington agreed with James Duane that Congress "should have an *efficient* power. The want of it must ruin us." Within a few months, he again wrote to Duane: "There are two things (as I have often declared) which in my opinion, are indispensably necessary to the well being and good Government of our public Affairs; these are, greater powers to Congress, and more responsibility and permanency in the executive bodies." It would be madness, he said, to think of prosecuting the war so long as individual states were at liberty to ignore the acts of Congress. He was equally harsh toward the boards, regarding it as a deception to believe that the boards, constantly fluctuating, could adequately manage the business of war. In other letters during the winter of 1780–81, he pressed for responsible executive bodies.

In the early months of 1781, Congress established departments headed by single executives. Washington hoped that able men would be chosen to introduce "system order and oeconomy," and that Congress would invest these "Ministers of State" with greater powers. However, as months passed by and the posts remained unfilled, he grew discouraged. In a letter to John Sullivan he said that the resolution to appoint ministers over war, foreign affairs, and finance gave, "as far as I was able to learn the Sentiments of men in and out of the Army, universal satisfaction. Postponing of the 1st, delaying of the 2d, and disagreeing about the 3rd, has had the direct contrary effect."

The refusal of states to vest adequate powers in Congress, and the latter's reluctance to delegate some of its powers to single executives, placed a heavy strain on the composure and self-discipline of Washington. In the summer of 1782 he wrote to Congress for a determination concerning the murder of one of his officers, a Captain Huddy. Receiving no reply for almost a month and a half, he turned to his friend Duane with rare signs of anguish: "I shall be obliged to you, or some friend in Congress, to inform me what has been, or is like to be done, with respect to my reference of the case of Captn. Huddy? I cannot forbear complaining of the cruel situation I now am, and oftentimes have been placed in, by the silence [at this point he crossed out of his draft 'to call it by the softest name'] of Congress in matters of high importance. . . ."

When Robert Morris tendered his resignation as finance minister in 1783, Washington regarded this decision as "one of the most unfortunate" that could have fallen upon the states. But within a few years the pattern of history again reversed itself and Washington's conception of government gained support as a result of new problems: commercial friction among the states; military threats by Indians in the Ohio Valley and by British forces in the Northwest; economic depression after 1785; and regional disputes between Virginia and Maryland—leading first to the conference at Annapolis and then to the convention at Philadelphia.

On the eve of the convention, Washington wrote to Henry Knox on the need for a system with greater energy than the present government, a government that was not only "slow, debilitated, and liable to be thwarted by every breath," but was also lacking in secrecy and was defective by combining legislative, executive, and judicial functions in one body. The defect in combining the three governmental functions in one body was evident from experience, not from theory. Shortly after the Constitution had adopted the three branches of the national government, Washington explained that this separation of powers was derived not from doctrine, nor was it an expression of timidity toward power. It was, rather, a search for a more reliable and effective government, an admission of "the impotence of Congress under the former confederation, and the inexpediency of trusting more ample prerogatives to a single Body. . . ."

(2) *Alexander Hamilton* shared Washington's concern for administrative efficiency. In the winter of 1779–1780, Hamilton expressed his preference for a board to handle matters of commerce, but for "most other things single men. We want a Minister of War, a Minister for foreign Affairs, a minister of Finance and a Minister of marine. There is always more decision, more dispatch, more secrecy, more responsibility where single men, than when bodies are concerned."

By the fall of 1780, Hamilton had itemized the shortcomings of the Confederation and offered suggestions for reform. The fundamental defect—the lack of power in Congress—should be rectified by calling a convention. The second defect was a "want of method and energy in the administration," the result partly of the weak national government and partly of a prejudice against executive power. As a consequence, "Congress have kept the power too much into their own hands and have meddled too much with details of every sort. Congress is properly a deliberative corps and it forgets itself when it attempts to play the executive." The boards suffered from the same difficulties as Congress: slowness, lack of attention, and diffusion of responsibility. Hamilton proposed that Congress should immediately appoint officers to run the important departments of foreign affairs, war, marine, finance, and trade. The single executives would be "of course at all times under the direction of Congress. . . ."

A few years later, in a resolution drafted in July 1783, Hamilton called the Articles of Confederation defective in "confounding legislative and executive powers in a single body. . . . contrary to the most approved and well founded maxims of free government which require that the legislative [,] executive and judicial authorities should be deposited in distinct and separate hands." Coming from a man with unabashed admiration for the British system, and the active leadership of the Prime Minister in driving Parliament, this stress on separation and maxims has a strange ring.

Hamilton's position is less perplexing, however, if we keep in mind that by 1783 it had become evident that the experiment with single executives *inside* Congress had failed. Neither Congress nor the states were willing to vest in these men the necessary power to discharge the nation's business. Robert Livingston offered his resignation as Secretary for Foreign Affairs in December 1782, leaving office the following June. Robert Morris tendered his resignation as Superintendant of Finance in January 1783. Benjamin Lincoln was on the verge of resigning as Secretary at War. The office of Secretary of Marine, after Alexander McDougall refused to take it, had been left permanently vacant. Several months prior to drafting the 1783 resolution for "distinct and separate" branches, Hamilton expressed regret at the pending resignation of Morris: "I believe no man in this country but himself could have kept the moneymachine a going during the period he has been in office. From every thing that appears his administration has been upright as well as able." Hamilton abandoned the idea of having executives operate within Congress, and came to insist on separation as the only practicable remedy for effective administration.

A pure version of separated powers was never contemplated. In defending the Constitution at the New York ratifying convention, Hamilton demonstrated more concern for mutual checks than for separation, more interest in the exercise of power than its constraint. The legislative body, he said, was lodged in "three distinct branches properly balanced: The executive authority is divided between two branches; and the judicial is still reserved for an independent body, who hold their office during good behaviour." He was adamant in opposing the efforts to curb governmental power: "when you have divided and nicely balanced the departments of government; When you have strongly connected the virtue of your rulers with their interest; when, in short, you have rendered your system as perfect as human forms can be; you must place confidence; you must give power."

A major objection directed against the Constitution was its blending of powers, an objection for which Hamilton had little patience. The impeachment process, for example, was under attack for combining legislative and judicial powers in the same department. In Federalist 66, Hamilton replied to this general charge that the true meaning of the separation maxim was "entirely compatible with a partial intermixture," and that overlapping was not only "proper, but necessary to the mutual defence of the several members of the government, against each other." A merely nominal separation, he warned in Federalist 71 and 73, was futile "if both the executive and the judiciary are so constituted as to be at the absolute devotion of the legislative."

Hamilton had also to contend with critics who disliked the treaty process because it mixed the executive with the Senate. This level of debate he found plainly annoying, dismissing it in Federalist 75 as "the trite topic of the intermixture of powers." In later years, he was to describe the separation principle as one in which the departments or powers are "essentially" distinct and independent.

(3) *John Jay*, as member of the Continental Congress, minister to Spain, and Secretary for Foreign Affairs, witnessed firsthand the administrative weaknesses of the Articles of Confederation. In a letter to Washington in 1779, he summarized the main faults of the committee system: "want of system, attention, and knowledge." The membership of the Marine Committee was constantly fluctuating, he said, and few members understood the state of American naval affairs or had the time or inclination to attend to them.

When he became America's representative to Spain in 1780, Jay found it necessary to survive on credit while waiting for funds from Congress. With his first year in Spain drawing to a close, he had received but one letter from the Committee for Foreign Affairs, and that "not worth a farthing." He concluded that "one good private correspondent would be worth twenty standing committees. . . . What with clever wives, or pleasant walks, or too tired, or too busy, or do *you* do it, very little is done, much postponed, and more neglected."

Regarding the responsibility of single executives as a leading feature of good government, Jay expressed dismay when he heard that Robert Morris planned to resign as Superintendant of Finance. After the resignation, which Jay called a "great loss to this country," he restated his preference for a single executive over finance, adding that he would rather have each department "under the direction of one able man than of twenty able ones."

He returned to America to become Secretary for Foreign Affairs, and managed to wrest from Congress a number of executive prerogatives. Though Jay exercised initiative in proposing policies, there was no assurance that Congress would act on them. He wrote to Jefferson in 1786 regarding the failure of Congress to take action on some of his reports. Regretting the delay, Jay said that his own efforts and determination could not avoid "unseasonable delays and successive obstacles in obtaining the decision and sentiments of Congress, even on points which require despatch." He concluded that the structure of the confederation was fundamentally wrong. To vest all three powers in a fluctuating body "can never be wise. In my opinion, these three great departments of sovereignty should be forever separated, and so distributed as to serve as checks on each other."

Writing to Jefferson in December 1786, Jay repeated his support for a division of government into executive, legislative, and judicial. "Congress is unequal to the first," Jay said, "very fit for the second, and but ill calculated for the third; and so much time is spent in deliberation, that the season for action often passes by before they decide on what should be done; nor is there much more secrecy than expedition in their measures. These inconveniences arise, not from personal disqualifications, but from the nature and construction of the government."

In the months prior to the Philadelphia Convention, Jay detected increasing signs of inefficiency in the national government. He told Washington that nothing much could be hoped for unless government were divided into its proper departments: "Let Congress legislate—let others execute— let others judge." The inconvenience of the present system, he told Jefferson in another letter, would operate against the public interest; the situation could be remedied only by the establishment of separate branches. To John Adams he wrote that the people had begun to perceive the inefficiency of Congress. He regarded the failure to distribute the federal sovereignty into three departments as a great mistake in policy.

The stress in these letters was always on effective government and on a more reliable administration. When critics of the Constitution argued against Presidential participation in the treaty process, on the grounds that laws "should be made only by men invested with legislative authority," Jay dismissed this narrow interpretation of the separation doctrine, declaring in Federalist 64 that the decisions of the courts and the executive are "as valid and as binding on all persons whom they concern as the laws passed by our legislature." There was nothing to prevent the people, through their constitution, from committing the treaty power to a body other than the legislature.

Though Jay's private correspondence presents administrative reasons for separate departments, in a public address to New York citizens he takes a more theoretical approach. The delegates to the Philadelphia Convention, he said, "remembering the many instances in which governments vested solely in one man, or one body of men, had degenerated into tyrannies. . . . judged it most prudent that the three great branches of power should be committed to different hands, and therefore that the executive should be separated from the legislative, and the judicial from both."

These remarks are entirely uncharacteristic of Jay. I can only suggest that he decided it would be too confusing and tedious, in a public address, to recount the many years of administrative frustration under the Continental Congress and the subsequent search for an effective executive. It was apparently more expedient to play upon emotional sentiments and popular shibboleths by drumming up the fear of tyranny. This explanation appears to be borne out by another section in his address. In justifying the omission of a bill of rights in the Constitution, Jay presents a more sanguine view of governmental institutions. Only in the days of monarchs, he explained, was it necessary for the people to draw up enumerated rights, which could not then be infringed upon by the king. That history had no bearing on the American republic, however, for "thank God we have no such disputes—we have no Monarchs to contend with, or demand admission from—the proposed Government is to be the government of the people—all its officers are to be their officers, and to exercise no rights but such as the people commit to them." If public officials were merely "agents" of the people, it was somewhat inconsistent of Jay to advance separated powers as a means of preventing tyranny.

(4) *Thomas Jefferson's* draft of the Virginia Constitution in 1776 specified that the legislative, executive, and judicial branches be kept forever separate. As Governor of Virginia from 1779 to 1781, however, he came to appreciate the porous quality of those parchment barriers between branches. The shift of power to the legislature, coming at the expense of the governor and the courts, he called "precisely the definition of despotic government. It will be no alleviation that these powers will be exercised by a plurality of hands, and not by a single one. 173 despots would surely be as oppressive as one." Instead of depending on paper barriers placed in a constitution, it would be necessary to sup-

ply adequate means of self-defense to the executive and judiciary.

This new understanding is reflected in his proposed revision of the Virginia Constitution in 1783. In addition to the restrictions he had placed on the legislature in the 1776 draft, Jefferson now wanted to prohibit it from infringing on the constitution, abridging religious liberties, passing ex post facto laws or bills of attainder, or allowing the introduction of additional slaves. He also recommended that the position of the governor be strengthened by extending his term of office from one year to five and by allowing him to veto bills as a member of a council of revision. There had been no veto power for the governor in Jefferson's 1776 draft. Other changes between the two drafts include a new provision prohibiting the legislature from reducing the governor's salary, and permission for the delegation of certain legislative powers to the governor.

On joining the Continental Congress in 1783, Jefferson found it paralyzed by lack of attendance. In numerous letters he reported on the bleak prospect of attaining a quorum to do business, "so careless are either the states or their delegates to their particular interests as well as the general good which would require that they be all constantly and fully represented in Congress." He considered it "rational and necessary" to create independent executive and judicial branches and to join them in a council of revision over legislation.

As one member of a three-man committee created to suggest how continuity in congressional business could be provided during the summer of 1784, Jefferson proposed that the functions of Congress be separated into legislative and executive, with the latter functions delegated to a special committee for the recess period. The committee was appointed with fewer powers than Jefferson had recommended, and it soon split into factions and disbanded, leaving the government without a visible head. In the words of Edmund Burnett, its "farcical ending formed a fitting climax to the increasing failure of Congress to fulfill the requirements of a union of the States, and brought ridicule not only upon itself but upon Congress . . . through the very disgust which it aroused [it] gave a powerful impetus to the agitation, already begun, for a stronger government, a more perfect union."

In 1786, while serving as minister to France, Jefferson expressed hope that the convention scheduled to meet in Philadelphia would produce a full meeting and "a broader reformation" of the confederation. Of crucial importance was a reorganization of the national government to provide for an executive and judiciary "to enable the Federal head to exercise the powers given it, to best advantage. . . ." A separate executive body would be necessary "so that Congress itself should meddle only with what should be legislative." If Congress refused to part voluntarily with some of its powers, Jefferson advised that the redistribution of power be imposed upon it.

Later, when the Philadelphia Convention was in session, he commented again on the administrative advantages to be derived from a separation of powers. Congress had shown a propensity to wait until the "last extremeties" before executing any of its powers. "Nothing is so embarrassing," Jefferson wrote, "nor so mischievous in a great assembly as the details of execution. The smallest trifle of that kind occupies as long as the most important act of legislation, and takes place of every thing else. Let any man recollect, or look over the files of Congress, he will observe the most important propositions hanging over from week to week and month to month, till the occasions have past them, and the thing never done."

Other letters illustrate his preference for an overlapping of departments as a means of checking encroachments. He agreed with John Adams that the first principle of good government was most certainly a "distribution" of powers among the three branches. Interestingly, Jefferson's first draft of this letter spoke of a *division* of powers. He may well have deleted this because it implied a static, artificial boundary between departments, whereas "distribution" left room for overlapping. This is brought out more clearly in his reaction to the Constitution. He liked the idea of giving the veto power to the President, but would have liked even more the sharing of this power with the judiciary, as was the practice in New York.

A few years later, when the Federalists were in power, Jefferson was to enunciate a stricter view of separated powers and express alarm at the degree of executive influence on legislative proceedings. But this stage of his career has less to do with political principles than with partisan maneuvers (see pages 52–53).

(5) *John Adams,* who served with the First Continental Congress from 1774 to 1776, described legislative proceedings as "slow as snails." Every delegate felt an obligation to display his oratorical abilities and political acumen. Business was consequently "drawn and spun out to an immeasurable length." Besides the "nibbling and quibbling" of debate, the turnover in membership of the Continental Congress played havoc with committee work. "I have the melancholy Prospect before me," Adams wrote, "of a Congress continually changing, untill very few Faces remain, that I saw in the first Congress."

During the winter of 1775–1776, he turned his attention to problems of government on the local level, arguing that a representative assembly was unfit to exercise the executive power because it lacked two essential properties: "secrecy and despatch." He wanted the executive to retain "a free and independent exercise of his judgment, and be made also an integral part of the legislature." This formulation produced considerable confusion over the years, and Adams made various efforts to clarify this relationship between executive and legislative bodies. He stressed the need for three branches as a counterbalance to ambition, intrigue, and incessant factionalism. Since the executive was constantly vulnerable to legislative encroachments, he would need an absolute veto, lest he be "run down like a hare before the hunters."

In his draft for the Massachusetts Constitution of 1780 he repeated this proposal for an absolute veto for the executive, that he may have "power to preserve the independence of the executive and judicial departments." The state convention rejected the absolute veto, and provided instead for a 2/3 vote of the senate and the house to override the governor's veto. The convention also insisted on a more elaborate and rigid expression of separated powers—a fact we overlook when we speak of "John Adams' constitution of Massachusetts." He had merely proposed that the "legislative, executive, and judicial power shall be placed in separate departments, to the end that it might be a government of laws, and not of men." The final version of the constitution went beyond this to declare that the "legislative departments shall never exercise the executive and judicial powers, or either of them; the executive shall never exercise the legislative and judicial powers, or either of them; the judicial shall never exercise the legislative and executive powers, or either of them, to the end it may be a government of laws and not of men." Adams was consistent throughout his life in opposing this strict compartmentalization of powers.

During his service as ambassador to the Court of St. James, Adams watched France move step by step toward a government composed of one assembly, and heard that Massachusetts was considering doing away with the governor and the senate as needless and costly branches. "In this situation," he wrote, "I was determined to wash my hands of the blood that was about to be shed in France, Europe, and America. . . ." He produced a heavily documented and much misunderstood defense of the tripartite form of government *on the state level*. The first part of his study appeared in 1787, entitled *A Defence of the Constitutions of Government of the United States of America*. Eventually running to three volumes, this sprawling treatise was put together in great haste and suffers from a lack of organization

and reflection. It is therefore not an easy task to separate the
fervent declarations from the more circumspect pronouncements. He could lose himself, and his reader, in some baf-
fling abstractions, such as calling the tripartite system "the
political trinity in unity, trinity of legislative, and unity of
executive power, which in politics is no mystery."

Adams shuttled back and forth between theoretical and
pragmatic positions. At times he proclaimed that the concept of three powers had an "unalterable foundation in nature." At other times the concept seemed to flow from experience and experimentation. His study of the modern
republics, for example, concluded that each government contained "a multitude of curious and ingenious inventions" to
control the ambitions of governmental bodies.

In one string of sentences, he posited that the legislative
and executive branches are naturally distinct and separate;
the legislative power is sovereign and supreme over the executive; the executive must be made an essential part of the
legislature; and yet the executive should have the veto
power to defend himself against legislative encroachments.
More lucid explanations could be conceived, but in the light
of his other writings it is possible to find a fairly consistent
theme: the executive should have an integral share in the
legislative process, while retaining his independence by
means of the veto power.

Adams came to regret the many misinterpretations of
his work, particularly the notion that he adhered to a strict
separation of powers. He later explained that Turgot had attacked the state constitutions for "aiming at three orders and
a balance. I defended them in this point only. Had he attacked them for not making their orders distinct and independent enough, or for not making their balances complete,
I should have been the last man in the world to have undertaken their defence."

Adams had long welcomed the creation of single executives on the national level. He learned that Congress was
about to establish a Secretary for Foreign Affairs "to remedy
many disadvantages" under which Congress labored. After

Livingston was elected Secretary in 1781, Adams said it gave him "great pleasure" to learn that a minister would be introduced into the Department of Foreign Affairs, thereby imparting "an order, a constancy, and an activity" that could never be expected from a legislative committee. He declared his willingness and desire to do anything he could for Livingston and the new department: "I would cheerfully do it, because I am a friend to both."

After the Constitution had created the three branches of government, Adams discussed the degree to which the President was joined with the legislature. The rational objection, he said, was not that the executive was blended with the legislature, but rather that "it is not enough blended; that it is not incorporated with it, and made an essential part of it." He felt that the President, located conspicuously outside the legislature, would be less inclined to exercise his veto power. Though more blending was desirable here, Adams objected to the mixture of President and Senate on appointments and treaties—not because it violated the separation doctrine but because it would lessen the responsibility of the executive.

After serving as President of the United States, Adams dismissed as a popular error the belief that executive power endangers liberty and must be restrained. "Corruption in almost all free governments," he noted, "has begun and been first introduced in the legislature. . . . The people, then, ought to consider the President's office as the indispensable guardian of their rights."

(6) *James Madison* joined the Continental Congress in March 1780, writing back to Jefferson on the dire straits facing the confederation: exhaustion of the public credit, an army in short supply, an enfeebled Congress. Madison lent his support to the shift in 1781 to single executives, expressing optimism that the selection of Robert Morris as Superintendant of Finance would afford "a more flattering prospect in this department of our affairs than has existed at any period of the war." When Morris was later subjected to malicious attacks and forced to resign, Madison came to his de-

fense. "I have heard of many charges," he said, "which were palpably erroneous. I have known others somewhat suspicious vanish on examination. Every member in Congress must be sensible of the benefit which has accrued to the public from his administration. No intelligent man out of Congress can be altogether insensible of it."

Madison also appreciated the need for greater executive discretion and responsibility in foreign affairs. When Livingston offered financial reasons for his resignation as Secretary for Foreign Affairs, Madison added that the practice of Congress was "never fixed, & frequently improper, and I always suspected that his indifference to the place resulted in part at least from the mortifications to which this unsteadiness subjected him." Jay's insistence (as the next Secretary for Foreign Affairs) that Congress submit all foreign dispatches directly to him and not to the committees, was interpreted by some members of Congress as an encroachment upon their legislative powers. Madison denied this, calling Jay's demand as natural and proper for anyone "worthy of the station which he holds."

Though Madison realized the need for an effective and reliable executive power, he had difficulty choosing the precise form it should take. Upon being asked to offer suggestions for a constitution for Kentucky, he replied in August 1785 that he had no final opinion as to whether the executive should be chosen by legislative vote or by the people at large, or whether "the power should be vested in one man assisted by a council or in a council of which the President shall be only primus inter pares." The Virginia executive, he cautioned, was the worst of a bad constitution, being too dependent on the legislature and too vulnerable to encroachments.

At the Philadelphia Convention, Madison endorsed a variety of techniques designed to protect the executive and judiciary from legislative encroachments. When it was proposed that the veto power be shared between the President and the judiciary, some delegates denounced this as an obvious violation of the separation doctrine. Madison disagreed, claiming that the judiciary should be introduced in the business of legislation. He argued that the mixing of executive and judiciary did not violate the separation doctrine: "The maxim on which the objection was founded required a separation of the Executive as well as of the Judiciary from the Legislature & from each other. There wd. in truth however be no improper mixture of these distinct powers in the present case. In England, whence the maxim itself had been drawn, the Executive had an absolute negative on the laws; and the supreme tribunal of Justice (the House of Lords) formed one of the other branches of the Legislature."

At the end of the first chapter I discussed the arguments offered by Madison at the Philadelphia Convention, in the *Federalist Papers,* and in the First Congress. His principal concern was the protection of the executive branch from legislative encroachments, and toward that objective he recommended whatever checks and balances were necessary to preserve the President's powers.

REFERENCE SECTION

This section, while extensive, does not attempt to cite every available study that has been done on the Presidency or on Congress. I limit myself to four powers—legislative, spending, taxing, and war—and more particularly to the policy issues and philosophical and constitutional questions that are raised. A number of other books, cited below, have been written with similar titles. They nevertheless cover quite different ground.

President and Congress: The Conflict of Powers, edited by Joan Coyne MacLean (New York: H.W. Wilson Co., 1955), includes a number of short selections on executive-legislative relationships. *President and Congress,* Wilfred E. Binkley (New York: Vintage Books, 1962, 3d rev. ed.), is an historical, chronological account of the period from the Constitutional Convention through the Eisenhower Presidency. *The President and Congress,* Rowland Egger and Joseph P. Harris (New York: McGraw-Hill, 1963), discusses briefly—with a pro-presidential bias—the functions and procedures of the two branches. *Congress and the Presidency,* Louis W. Koenig (Glenview, Ill.: Scott, Foresman, 1965), studies the policy-making process in general. *The Political Process: Executive Bureau-Legislative Committee Relations,* J. Leiper Freeman (New York: Random House, 1965, rev. ed.), focuses on the subsystems of the two branches and the external forces that influence policy-making.

Congress and the Presidency: Their Role in Modern Times, Arthur M. Schlesinger, Jr. and Alfred de Grazia (Washington, D.C.: American Enterprise Institute, 1967), represents a general discussion

271

on the present balance of power between the two branches and the readjustments that are needed to effect a healthier balance. *Congress and the President: Readings in Executive-Legislative Relations,* edited by Walter Earl Travis (New York: Teachers College Press, 1967), brings together a collection of studies on Cabinet Government, political party reform, and congressional reform. *Congress and the Presidency,* Nelson W. Polsby (Englewood Cliffs, N.J.: Prentice-Hall, 1971, 2d ed.), examines the institutional and personal settings for the policy-making process; it also includes separate chapters on how bills become laws and how budgets are formulated. *Congress and the President: Allies and Adversaries,* edited by Ronald C. Moe (Pacific Palisades, Calif.: Goodyear Publishing Co., 1971), offers a number of excellent studies which would complement what I cover in my book.

Several standard works are cited with such frequency that I have used these abbreviated references:

Adams, *Works*	*The Works of John Adams,* Charles Francis Adams, ed. (10 vols., Boston: Little, Brown, 1850–1856)
Burnett, *Letters*	Edmund Cody Burnett, ed., *Letters of Members of the Continental Congress, 1774–1789* (8 vols., Washington, D.C.: Carnegie Institution of Washington, 1921–1936)
Elliot, *Debates*	Jonathan Elliot, ed., *The Debates in the Several State Conventions, on the Adoption of the Federal Constitution* (5 vols., Washington, D.C.: 1836–1845)
Farrand, *Records*	Max Farrand, ed., *The Records of the Federal Convention of 1787* (4 vols., New Haven: Yale University Press, 1937)
Hamilton, *Papers*	*The Papers of Alexander Hamilton,* Harold C. Syrett, ed. (New York: Columbia University Press, 15 vols., in progress, 1961–1969)
———, *Works*	*The Works of Alexander Hamilton,* Henry Cabot Lodge, ed. (12 vols., New York: G. P. Putnam's, 1904)
Israel, *State of the Union Messages*	Fred L. Israel, ed., *The State of the Union Messages of the Presidents, 1790–1966* (3 vols., New York: Chelsea House-Hector, 1966)
Jay, *Correspondence*	*The Correspondence and Public Papers of John Jay,* Henry P. Johnston, ed. (4 vols., New York: G. P. Putnam's, 1890–1893)
Journals	*Journals of the Continental Congress, 1774–1789* (34 vols., Washington, D.C.: Government Printing Office, 1904–1937)

Jefferson, *Papers*	*The Papers of Thomas Jefferson,* Julian P. Boyd, ed. (Princeton: Princeton University Press, 17 vols., in progress, 1950–1965)
———, *Writings*	*The Writings of Thomas Jefferson,* Paul Leicester Ford, ed. (10 vols., New York: G. P. Putnam's, 1892–1899)
Madison, *Papers*	*The Papers of James Madison,* William T. Hutchison and William M. E. Rachal, eds. (Chicago: University of Chicago Press, 6 vols., in progress, 1962–1969)
———, *Writings*	*The Writings of James Madison,* Gaillard Hunt, ed. (9 vols., New York: G. P. Putnam's, 1900–1910)
Richardson, *Messages and Papers*	James D. Richardson, ed., *A Compilation of the Messages and Papers of the Presidents* (20 vols., New York: Bureau of National Literature, 1897–1925)
Roosevelt, *Public Papers*	*The Public Papers and Addresses of Franklin D. Roosevelt,* comp. by Samuel I. Rosenman (13 vols., New York, 1938–1950)
Washington, *Writings*	*The Writings of George Washington,* John C. Fitzpatrick, ed. (39 vols., Washington, D.C.: Government Printing Office, 1931–1944)
Wkly Comp. Pres. Doc.	*Weekly Compilation of Presidential Documents,* published each week by the Government Printing Office since 1965

1. PRINCIPLE OF SEPARATED POWERS

Separated Powers: Origin and Purpose

Separated Powers and Liberty. M. J. C. Vile, *Constitutionalism and the Separation of Powers* (London: Oxford University Press, 1967), p. 207. Joseph Story, *Commentaries on the Constitution of the United States,* 5th ed., (2 vols., Boston: Little, Brown, 1905), I, 396. Carl J. Friedrich warned that "Many who today belittle the separation of powers seem unaware of the fact that their clamor for efficiency and expediency easily leads to dictatorship . . ."; *Constitutional Government and Democracy* (Ginn and Co., 1946), p. 175. Professor Friedrich repeats the same point in his article on "Separation of Powers," *Encyc. Soc. Sci.* (New York: Macmillan, 1935), XIII, 664. See also Charles H. Wilson, "The Separation of Powers under Democracy and Fascism," 52 *Pol. Sci. Q.* 481 (Dec. 1937). Arthur T. Vanderbilt writes that "Individual freedom and the progress of civilization are attainable, but only if each of the three branches of government conforms to the constitutional principles of the separation of powers"; *The Doctrine of the Separation of Powers and Its Present-Day Significance* (Lincoln: University of Nebraska Press, 1953), Introduction.

Separated Powers and Efficiency. Chief Justice Warren: *United States* v. *Brown,* 381 U.S. 437, 443 (1965). Justice Brandeis: *Myers* v. *United States,* 272 U.S. 52, 293 (1926). Philip Donham and Robert J. Fahey, in *Congress Needs Help* (New York: Random House, 1966), claim that the framers "assumed that by obstructing the assumption of absolute authority over government operations by any one branch and distributing authority among branches, the possibility of tyranny would be reduced. Loss of efficiency was a small price to pay for insurance against tyranny" (p. 6).

Influence of Montesquieu. Woodrow Wilson, *Constitutional Government in the United States* (New York: Columbia University Press, 1908), p. 56. James Bryce, *The American Commonwealth,* 2d ed. rev. (2 vols., London: Macmillan, 1891), I, 20, 26. References to "the celebrated Montesquieu" and "oracle" are from Federalist Paper No. 47. William Gladstone, "Kin Beyond Sea," *North Am. Rev.,* Vol. 127, No. 264 (Sept.–Oct. 1878), p. 185. Statement by John Stuart Mill is from Paul Merrill Spurlin, *Montesquieu in America* (Baton Rouge: Louisiana State University Press, 1940), p. 27. George Washington: *Writings,* XXX, 300–301.

National Executives, 1774–1789

Jay Caesar Guggenheimer, "The Development of the Executive Departments, 1775–1789," in *Essays in the Constitutional History of the United States,* J. Franklin Jameson, ed. (Boston: Houghton Mifflin, 1889), p. 148. The evolution of administrative bodies under the Articles of Confederation has also been handled by Charles C. Thach, Jr., "The Creation of the Presidency, 1775–1789, A Study in Constitutional History," *Johns Hopkins University Studies in Historical and Political Science,* Series XL, No. 4 (1922) [reprinted as a Johns Hopkins paperback in 1969]; Lloyd Milton Short, *The Development of National Administrative Organization in the United States* (Baltimore: Johns Hopkins Press, 1923); Jennings B. Sanders, *Evolution of Executive Departments of the Continental Congress, 1774–1789* (Chapel Hill: University of North Carolina Press, 1935); and Louis Fisher, "Presidential Tax Discretion and Eighteenth Century Theory," 23 *West. Pol. Q.* 151 (March 1970).

Administration by Committee. 1774 committees cited in *Journals,* I, 26, 53, 62, 101; April 1775 appointment of committee on ways and means: *ibid.,* II, 67; Committee of Secret Correspondence: *ibid.,* III, 392; VII, 274. Other committees after outbreak of the war of independence: *ibid.,* III, 253, 428; V, 434; VII, 274. John Adams' estimate of committee work: John T. Morse, *John Adams* (Boston: Houghton Mifflin, 1898), p. 142. Special committees for factions: George C. Wood, *Congressional Control of Foreign Relations During the American Revolution, 1774–1789* (Allentown, Pa.: H. Ray Haas, 1919), pp. 42–55. Status of Foreign Affairs committee: Henry Merritt Wriston, *Executive Agents in American Foreign Relations* (Baltimore: Johns Hopkins Press, 1929), p. 26. Remark by contemporary on ability of committee members: Wood, *op. cit.*, p. 58. John Jay on Marine Committee: Jay, *Correspondence*, I, 209.

A System of Boards. March 1776 suggestion: Burnett, *Letters*, I, 398–399. For letters by Robert Morris in 1776, regarding Congress' retention of too much executive business, see *ibid.*, II, 135–136, 178, 183–184. November 1776 authorization: *Journals*, VI, 906, 929; VII, 281; XII, 1085. December 26 appointment: *Journals*, VI, 1041. Letter by William Hooper: Burnett, *Letters*, II, 232. April 1777 plan: *Journals*, VII, 241; July plan: *ibid.*, VIII, 563; action in October 1777: *ibid.*, IX, 818–820, 874, 960. New Board of War and Ordnance: *Journals*, XII, 1076, 1101. Division of financial administration was improved somewhat with a reorganization plan for treasury matters, but Congress would not relinquish its desire to take on administrative matters. A compromise act during the summer of 1779 established a new Treasury Board with five members, of whom two were members of Congress: *Journals*, XIV, 903; see XI, 843 and XII, 956ff. Report from Maryland delegate: Burnett, *Letters*, III, 181; Gouverneur Morris letter to Washington: *ibid.*, III, 260; delegate begging to be relieved: *ibid.*, III, 322n; other caustic letters: *ibid.*, III, 283, 351, 378, 391, 394–395.

"Democratical Forms, Monarchical Substance." Gouverneur Morris' explanation of his work: *Diary and Letters*, Anne Cary Morris, ed. (2 vols., New York: Charles Scribner's, 1888), I, 12. Congress authorizing new powers to Robert Morris: Burnett, *Letters*, II, 193; see also *Out-Letters of the Continental Marine Committee and Board of Admiralty*, Charles Paullin, ed. (2 vols., New York: De Vinne Press, 1914), I, 59n, 61–62. James Lovell to Arthur Lee: Burnett, *Letters*, IV, 354; see also p. 264. Powers of Benjamin Franklin: Francis Wharton, *The Revolutionary Diplomatic Correspondence of the United States* (6 vols., Washington, D.C.: Government Printing Office, 1889), I, 483. Gouverneur Morris on laborious war years: *Diary and Letters*, I, 11–12. Letter from Maryland delegate in the spring of 1779: Burnett, *Letters*, IV, 203; Joseph Jones to James Madison: *ibid.*, V, 399.

Single Executive Officers. 1779 instructions to American representatives: *Journals*, XIII, 114. James Duane proposal: *ibid.*, XVII, 428, 505; cf. XVIII, 1156; Robert Livingston motion: *ibid.*, XVII, 791. Report on January 10, 1781: *ibid.*, XIX, 43; see also page 57. Resolutions in February: *ibid.*, XIX, 126ff, 156. Francis Wharton, *The Revolutionary Diplomatic Correspondence of the United States*, I, 663. Election of Robert Morris: *Journals*, XIX, 180; chairman of the committee studying his demands: Burnett, *Letters*, VI, 39–40; committee agreeing to powers and Morris' acceptance: *Journals*, XIX, 180, 326–327, 432–433; XX, 499. Election of McDougall and transfer of naval matters: *Journals*, XIX, 203; XX, 707, 724–725, 764ff; Robert Livingston chosen: *ibid.*, XX, 637; XXI, 851–852; election of Secretary of War: *ibid.*, XXI, 1087. Those who preferred administration by committees: Lloyd Milton Short, *The Development of National Administrative Organization in the United States*, pp. 52–53, 70.

Livingston's complaint: Henry Merritt Wriston, *Executive Agents in American Foreign Relations*, p. 19; see also *Journals*, XXII, 87ff, and Milledge L. Bonham, Jr., "Robert R. Livingston," *The American Secretaries of State and Their Diplomacy*, Samuel Flagg Bemis, ed. (New York: Pageant Book, 1958), I, 181–185. Robert Morris gaining new powers: *Journals*, XX, 734 and XXI, 820, 1142; his biting observation: Edmund Cody Burnett, *The Continental Congress* (New York: Macmillan, 1941), p. 527. Also on Robert Morris, see Charles J. Bullock, "The Finances of the United States from 1775 to 1789, with Especial Reference to the Budget," *University of Wisconsin Bulletin, Economics, Political Science, and History Series*, Vol. I, No. 2 (1895), and E. James Ferguson, *The Power of the Purse: A History of American Public Finance, 1776–1790* (Chapel Hill: University of North Carolina Press, 1961). For Benjamin Lincoln, see Harry M. Ward, *The Department of War, 1781–1795* (Pittsburgh: University of Pittsburgh Press, 1962), pp. 13–40.

Transition to the Presidency. For Washington's critique, in 1783, concerning the refusal of states to entrust Congress with requisite powers, see his *Writings*, XXVI, 184–185; XXVI, 486. Regarding domestic depression after 1785, see Curtis P. Nettels, *The Emergence of a National Economy: 1775–1815* (New York: Holt, Rinehart and Winston, 1962), pp. 45–88. Madison's role in initiating the Mount Vernon Conference and the Annapolis Convention: his *Writings*, II, 60n, 233, 238, 262, 271.

New powers to Jay in 1785: *Journals*, XXVIII, 56 and XXIX, 562; French minister's report: George Bancroft, *History of the Formation of the Constitution of the United States of America*, I, 479. Tenure of Knox: Harry M. Ward, *The Department of War, 1781–1795*, pp. 50, 183–184. Tenure of Joseph Nourse: Merrill Jensen, *The New Nation: A History of the United States During the Confederation, 1781–1789* (New York: Knopf, 1958), p. 360. Discussion on Court of Appeals in Cases of Capture comes primarily from Sidney Teiser, "The Genesis of the Supreme Court," 25 *Va. L. Rev.* 398 (Feb. 1939), but see also F. Regis Noel, "Vestiges of a Supreme Court Among the Colonies and Under the Articles of Confederation," *Records Colum. Hist. Soc.*, Vol. 37–38, p. 123 (1937).

Convention and Ratification

Mason to his son: Farrand, *Records*, III, 23; see also his letter to Arthur Lee, May 21, 1789, *ibid.*, 24. The paradox of separate yet overlapping branches, as a safeguard against encroachments, eluded many of the Antifederalists. They regarded a sharing of powers as a flat contradiction of a separation of powers. For example, see Morton Borden, ed., *The Antifederalist Papers* (East Lansing: Michigan State University Press, 1965), papers 47, 48, 64, 67, 73, 75. See also F. William O'Brien, S.J., "The Executive and the Separation Principle at the Constitutional Convention," 55 *Md. Hist. Mag.* 201 (Sept. 1960).

Attitude Toward Executive Power. Justice Black: *Youngstown Sheet & Tube Co.* v. *Sawyer,* 343 U.S. 579, 589 (1952). The 1780 New Jersey decision is *Holmes* v. *Walton;* see Edward S. Corwin, "The Progress of Constitutional Theory between the Declaration of Independence and the Meeting of the Philadelphia Convention," 30 *Am. Hist. Rev.* 511, 531 (1925), and Austin Scott, "Holmes v. Walton: The New Jersey Precedent," 4 *Am. Hist. Rev.* 456 (1899). 1782 Virginia case is *Commonwealth* v. *Caton,* 4 Call. 5; on this, see William C. Rives, *Life and Times of James Madison* (3 vols., Boston: Little, Brown, 1870), II, 266. Pennsylvania study in 1784: *The Proceedings Relative to Calling the Conventions of 1776 and 1790* (Harrisburg: John S. Wiestling, 1825), pp. 87ff; also on this theme of abuses of legislative power, see Gordon S. Wood, *The Creation of the American Republic, 1776–1787* (Chapel Hill: University of North Carolina Press, 1969), pp. 403–409. Madison's views on Kentucky constitution: *Writings*, II, 168–169. Patrick Henry's defense: Elliot, *Debates,* III, 66–67, 140. John Adams on strong executives: *Works*, IV, 290, 585.

Shielding the President. Madison to Jefferson: *Writings,* II, 328; Madison to Randolph: *ibid.,* 339–340; Madison to Washington, *ibid.,* 348. Virginia Plan joining executive and judiciary: Farrand, *Records,* I, 20–22. July resolution adopted: *ibid.,* II, 138; version presented by the Committee of Detail: *ibid.,* II, 177. Madison on the "legislative vortex": *ibid.,* II, 35. Warning about "foetus of monarchy" and Wilson's rebuttal: *ibid.,* I, 66, 71. Views of Wilson, Gouverneur Morris, and John Mercer: *ibid.,* I, 107; II, 52, 298. Critic of Constitution on veto power: an anonymous "William Penn" writing in the (Philadelphia) *Independent Gazetteer,* Jan. 3, 1788; cited by Morton Borden, ed., *The Antifederalist Papers,* p. 210. Wilson and Madison on the sharing of the veto by the executive and the judiciary: Farrand, *Records,* I, 105, 108, 139; Madison again on joint revisionary power: *ibid.,* II, 77.

Ratification. Madison confiding to Jefferson: *Writings,* V, 26. Contemporary pamphleteer on separation doctrine: M. J. C. Vile, *Constitutionalism and the Separation of Powers,* p. 153. Delegate at Virginia convention: Elliot, *Debates*, III, 280; North Carolina convention: *ibid.*, IV, 116; see also Davie's rebuttal at *ibid.*, IV, 121. Pennsylvania convention: John Bach McMaster and Frederick D. Stone, eds., *Pennsylvania and the Federal Constitution, 1787–1788* (Lancaster, Pa.: Historical Society of Pennsylvania, 1888), pp. 475–477. Separation clause by Virginia, Pennsylvania, and North Carolina: Edward Dumbauld, *The Bill of Rights and What it Means Today* (Norman: University of Oklahoma Press, 1957), pp. 174–175, 183, 199. Version adopted by Congress for submittal to the states: *Annals of Congress*, I, 453 (June 8, 1789); Madison's support of clause: *ibid.*, I, 480 (June 16, 1789), and I, 514–519 (June 17, 1789). Madison speaking of separation principle as sacred: *ibid.*, I, 604 (June 22, 1789). Action by Senate: U.S. Senate, *Journals, 1789–1794* (5 vols., Washington, D.C.: Gales & Seaton, 1820), I, 64, 73–74.

2. LEGISLATIVE POWERS

Justice Jackson on legislative power: *Youngstown Co.* v. *Sawyer*, 343 U.S. 579, 655 (1952). Lawrence H. Chamberlain, *The President, Congress and Legislation* (New York: Columbia University Press, 1946), p. 14. Two recent studies credit Congress with a large role in the legislative process: Nelson W. Polsby, "Policy Analysis and Congress," 18 *Public Policy* 61 (Sept. 1969), and Ronald C. Moe and Steven C. Teel, "Congress as Policy-Maker: A Necessary Reappraisal," 85 *Pol. Sci. Q.* 443 (Sept. 1970). The latter updates the Chamberlain study.

Express Powers

The meaning of "executive power" is discussed in Edward S. Corwin, *The President: Office and Powers, 1787–1957* (New York: New York University Press, 1957), pp. 3–30. The ambiguity of the President's power as Commander in Chief is explored by Samuel P. Huntington, "Civilian Control and the Constitution," 50 *Am. Pol. Sci. Rev.* 676, 690 (Sept. 1956). A vigorous critique of executive power can be found in Alfred de Grazia, *Republic in Crisis: Congress Against the Executive Force* (New York: Federal Legal Publications, 1965). An excellent analysis of the "textbook Presidency" appears in a paper delivered by Thomas E. Cronin to the 66th annual meeting of the American Political Science Association (September 1970); the paper is reprinted in 116 Cong. Rec. S17102–17115 (daily ed., Oct. 5, 1970).

Inherent Powers

A number of other references on inherent powers are cited later, but a general work to be mentioned here is Norman J. Small, *Some*

Presidential Interpretations of the Presidency. Originally published in 1932 as Series L, No. 2 in the *Johns Hopkins University Studies in Historical and Political Science,* it was reprinted by the Da Capo Press in 1970. Small examines the opinions of Washington, Jefferson, Lincoln, Teddy Roosevelt, and Wilson as to the limits of the authority of their office. Also valuable in this respect is a study of the two Roosevelts, Wilson, Taft, Hoover, and Eisenhower by Erwin C. Hargrove, *Presidential Leadership: Personality and Political Style* (New York: Macmillan, 1966).

Pacificus-Helvidius Debate. Excerpts from the exchange between Hamilton and Madison are reprinted in a number of readers on the Presidency. For the full text of "Pacificus, No. 1," see *The Works of Alexander Hamilton* (Lodge ed.), IV, 432–444. For the complete "Helvidius," see *The Writings of James Madison* (Hunt ed.), VI, 138–188.

Roosevelt-Taft Models. Roosevelt's statement can be found in *The Works of Theodore Roosevelt,* XX, 347; Taft's position is included in his *Our Chief Magistrate and His Powers* (New York: Columbia University Press, 1916), pp. 139–140, now available in paperback under the title *The President and His Powers* (New York: Columbia University Press, 1967). Thurman Arnold, *The Folklore of Capitalism* (New Haven: Yale University Press, 1937), p. 217. In *Northern Securities* v. *United States* (1904), Justice White observed: "If the conspiracy and combination existed and was illegal, my mind fails to perceive why it should be left to produce its full force and effect in the hands of the individuals by whom it was charged the conspiracy was entered into" (193 U.S. 197, 373). With regard to pure food legislation, Dr. Harvey Wiley reported that a Senator who shared that goal received a letter from Roosevelt "begging him to cease his efforts for such an impractical measure, and aid him in passing a bill to restore to the Naval Academy three students who had been dismissed for drunkenness." Harvey W. Wiley, *The History of a Crime Against the Food Law* (Harvey W. Wiley Publisher, 1929), p. 270. Wiley was scarcely free of bias when commenting on Roosevelt, and yet I have yet to find evidence that Roosevelt took an active, vigorous interest in pure food legislation until the issue was forced upon him. Harold Laski's remark is in his *The American Presidency: An Interpretation* (New York: Harper & Bros., 1940), p. 24. For some excellent studies that look behind the rhetoric of Teddy Roosevelt, see Henry F. Pringle, *Theodore Roosevelt* (New York, 1931); chapter IX of Richard Hofstadter, *American Political Tradition* (New York, 1948); and Erwin C. Hargrove, *Presidential Leadership: Personality and Political Style* (New York, 1966), pp. 11–31.

The statements by Taft are from his *Our Chief Magistrate and His Powers.* Presidential power includes whatever can be "fairly and reasonably traced" to some specific grant or "justly implied . . . as proper and necessary to its exercise" (pp. 139–140); Roosevelt identifying himself with Lincoln (p. 144); the President's "absolute power" of removal (p. 56, but see also p. 76); "inferable" powers (p. 95); McKinley's use of force in China (pp. 114–115) and Taft's sending of troops into Nicaragua (p. 96); President's power as Commander in Chief (p. 94); power to recognize foreign governments (p. 113); support of executive agreements (p. 114); powers created by custom (p. 135); suspension of habeas corpus (p. 147); need for executive discretion and promptness of action (p. 156). The court case is *United States* v. *Midwest Oil Co.*, 236 U.S. 459, 469–471 (1915); for statement by Court on public lands held as trust for all the people, see *United States* v. *Trinidad Coal Co.*, 137 U.S. 160, 170 (1890). A recent doctoral dissertation argues that Taft's *actions* as President demonstrate a much stronger conception of Presidential power than is evident in his Columbia University lectures: Donald Francis Anderson, *William Howard Taft: A Conservative's Conception of the Presidency* (Ph.D. dissertation, Cornell University, 1968).

Tenth Amendment. Report by Senate Foreign Relations Committee: *National Commitments,* Senate Report No. 129, 91st Cong., 1st Sess., p. 31. Madison on the issue of implied powers: *Annals of Congress,* I, 761 (Aug. 18, 1789). *McCulloch* v. *Maryland,* 4 Wheat. 316, 406–407 (1819). *Marbury* v. *Madison,* 1 Cr. 137, 177 (1803). *Missouri* v. *Holland,* 252 U.S. 416, 434 (1920); *United States* v. *Sprague,* 282 U.S. 716, 733 (1931); *United States* v. *Darby,* 312 U.S. 100, 124 (1941).

Steel Seizure Case. Statement by the Senate Foreign Relations Committee is in *National Commitments, op. cit.,* p. 31; the Senate subcommittee position is from Senate Committee on the Judiciary, *Report, Separation of Powers,* Senate Report No. 549, 91st Cong., 1st Sess., p. 13. The law journal article quoted is by Robert E. Goostree, "The Power of the President to Impound Appropriate Funds: With Special Reference to Grants-in-aid to Segregated Activities," 11 *Am. U. L. Rev.* 32, 40 (1962), reprinted in Aaron Wildavsky, ed., *The Presidency* (Boston: Little, Brown, 1969), pp. 727–741. Material on Assistant Attorney General Baldridge and Judge Pine is taken from Alan Westin, *The Anatomy of a Constitutional Law Case* (New York: Macmillan, 1958), pp. 60–68, and from Grant McConnell, *The Steel Seizure of 1952* (Indianapolis: Bobbs-Merrill, 1960), pp. 40–41. Justice Black's remark on the "lawmaking power" is at page 589 of *Youngstown Co.* v. *Sawyer,* 343 U.S. 579 (1952). Professor Corwin's critique is from his "The Steel Seizure Case: A Judicial Brick Without Straw," 53 *Colum. L. Rev.* 53, 64–65 (Jan. 1953); for another trenchant critique of the Court's decision, see Glendon A. Schubert, Jr., "The Steel Case: Presidential Responsibility and Judicial Irresponsibility," 6 *West. Pol. Q.* 61 (1953). Comments from the other Justices in the *Youngstown* case appear on the following pages of that decision: Frankfurter (595, 621 ff), Jackson (645), Burton (659), Clark (662), and the dissenting opinion (672).

REFERENCES TO PAGES 42-43 · 281

Administrative Legislation

In addition to the studies referred to in this section, the reader should consult Ralph Volney Harlow, *The History of Legislative Methods in the Period Before 1825* (New Haven: Yale University Press, 1917); Henry Campbell Black, *The Relation of the Executive Power to Legislation* (Princeton: Princeton University Press, 1919); John A. Fairlie, "Administrative Legislation," 18 *Mich. L. Rev.* 181 (Jan. 1920); James Hart, "The Ordinance Making Powers of the President of the United States," *Johns Hopkins University Studies in Historical and Political Science,* Series XLIII, No. 3 (1925); John Preston Comer, *Legislative Functions of National Administrative Authorities* (New York: Columbia University Press, 1927); Frederick F. Blachly and Miriam E. Oatman, *Administrative Legislation and Adjudication* (Washington, D.C.: The Brookings Institution, 1934); Nathan A. Grundstein, "Presidential Power, Administration and Administrative Law," 18 *G.W. Law Rev.* 285 (April 1950); Wilfred E. Binkley, "The President as Chief Legislator," *The Annals* (Sept. 1956); and Abraham Holtzman, *Legislative Liaison: Executive Leadership in Congress* (Chicago: Rand McNally, 1970). A remarkable and highly controversial use of the "pocket veto" power occurred during the 5-day Christmas recess of the 91st Congress in 1970. See *Constitutionality of the President's "Pocket Veto" Power,* hearing before the Senate Committee on the Judiciary, 92d Cong., 1st Sess. (1971) and *The Pocket Veto Power,* hearing before the House Committee on the Judiciary, 92d Cong., 1st Sess. (1971).

Treaties. Washington's experience with the Indian treaty is described by William Maclay, *Sketches of Debate in the First Senate of the United States,* George W. Harris, ed. (Harrisburg: Lane S. Hart, 1880), pp. 122–126. Those who have promoted the idea that the negotiation of treaties is purely an executive prerogative include Edward S. Corwin, *The President: Office and Powers, 1787–1957* (New York: New York University Press, 1957), pp. 211–212; Justice Sutherland in *United States* v. *Curtiss-Wright Corp.,* 299 U.S. 304, 319 (1936); and *The Constitution of the United States of America: Analysis and Interpretation,* Senate Document No. 39, 88th Cong., 1st Sess., p. 463 (1964). Senator Hartke placed two articles in the *Congressional Record,* both of which argue that Senate participation in the treaty-making process should take place prior to ratification. The two articles are "The United States Senate and the Treaty Power" by Forrest R. Black, which appeared in the *Rocky Mountain Law Review* in 1931, and "Treaty Making and the President's Obligation to Seek the Advice and Consent of the Senate with Special Reference to the Vietnam Peace Negotiations" by Richard B. Webb, which appeared in the Summer 1970 issue of the *Ohio State Law Journal.* For Hartke's resolution and these articles see 117 Cong. Rec. S12059ff (daily ed., July 26, 1971).

Experiences of Taft are cited in his *Our Chief Magistrate and His Powers*, pp. 111–112, 115–117. For opinion by Acting Attorney General McGranery, Aug. 20, 1946, upholding the legality of an executive agreement made pursuant to a joint resolution (instead of a treaty) see 40 Op. A.G. 469. Two excellent studies on the role of the House in treaties: see Chalfant Robinson, "The Treaty-Making Power of the House of Representatives," 12 *Yale Rev.* 191 (Aug. 1903), and Ivan M. Stone, "The House of Representatives and the Treaty-Making Power," 17 *Ky L. J.* 217 (March 1929).

Executive Agreements. For some general studies, see David M. Levitan, "Executive Agreements: A Study of the Executive in the Control of the Foreign Relations of the United States," 35 *Ill. L. Rev.* 365 (1950); Wallace McClure, *International Executive Agreements* (New York: Columbia University Press, 1941); Myers S. McDougal and Asher Lans, "Treaties and Congressional-Executive or Presidential Agreements: Interchangeable Instruments of National Policy" (2 Parts), 54 *Yale L. J.* 181, 534 (1945); Edwin Borchard, "Treaties and Executive Agreements—A Reply," 54 *Yale L. J.* 616 (1945); and Craig Mathews, "The Constitutional Power of the President to Conclude International Agreements," 64 *Yale L. J.* 345 (1955).

Act of 1792 authorizing Postmaster General: 1 Stat. 239. *Altman & Co.* v. *United States*, 224 U.S. 583, 601 (1912). Rush and Bagot agreements: Hunter Miller, ed., *Treaties and Other International Acts of the United States of America* (8 vols., Washington, D.C.: Government Printing Office, 1948), II, 645. Partial statutory authority existed for the Rush-Bagot agreements: 3 Stat. 217, sections 2, 4, 6 (Feb. 27, 1816). The statistics for Table 1 are drawn from Elmer Plischke, *Conduct of American Diplomacy*, 3d ed. (Princeton, N.J.: D. Van Nostrand, 1967) for the 1789–1964 period; statistics for the 1965–1970 period were obtained from the State Department, Office of Legal Adviser for Treaty Affairs.

Citations for Court decisions: *United States* v. *Belmont*, 301 U.S. 324 (1937). *United States* v. *Guy W. Capps, Inc.*, 204 F.2d 655, 660; see Arthur E. Sutherland, Jr., "The Bricker Amendment, Executive Agreements, and Imported Potatoes," 67 *Harv. L. Rev.* 281 (Dec. 1953). *Seery* v. *United States*, 127 F. Supp. 601, 606; see Arthur E. Sutherland, Jr., "The Flag, the Constitution, and International Agreements," 68 *Harv. L. Rev.* 1374 (June 1955). *Reid* v. *Covert*, 354 U.S. 1, 16 (1957). Senate resolution on executive agreement with Spain in 1970: S. Res. 469, 91st Cong., 2d Sess.; 116 Cong. Rec. S20014 (daily ed, Dec. 11, 1970); *Spanish Base Agreement*, hearings before the Senate Committee on Foreign Relations, 91st Cong., 2d Sess. (Aug. 26, 1970); and Senate Report No. 1425, 91st Cong., 2d Sess. (Dec. 9, 1970). Executive Agreement with Thailand in 1954–65 is brought out in *United States Security Agreements and Commitments Abroad: Kingdom of Thailand* (Part 3), hearings before the Senate Committee on Foreign Relations

(1969). Bill by Senator Case: S. 4556, 91st Cong., 2d Sess. (Dec. 2, 1970).

Rules and Regulations. President Taft's remark is from his *Our Chief Magistrate and His Powers*, p. 78. The statistics on Executive Orders issued by Roosevelt in the 1933–34 period, as well as the 1934 case where a proceeding lacked a regulation, are taken from Erwin N. Griswold, "Government in Ignorance of the Law—A Plea for Better Publication of Executive Legislation," 48 *Harv. L. Rev.* 198, 198–199, 204 (Dec. 1934). For Court cases on rules and regulations, see *United States* v. *Eliason*, 41 U.S. (16 Pet.) 291, 301 (1842), and *Boske* v. *Comingore*, 177 U.S. 459 (1900). See also *Kurtz* v. *Moffit*, 115 U.S. 487, 503 (1885), and George B. Davis, "Doctor Francis Lieber's Instructions for the Government of Armies in the Field," 1 *Am. J. Int. Law* 13 (Jan. 1907).

The three executive decisions on tax rules and regulations are as follows: shipping ruling story is in *The New York Times*, March 11, 1970, 1:7; the new procedure announced by the Internal Revenue Commissioner is discussed in *The Washington Post*, Nov. 8, 1970, A1:6; and the liberalization of depreciation provisions is covered in *Wkly Comp. Pres. Doc.*, Vol. 7, No. 3, pp. 58–59, and *The Washington Post*, March 13, 1971, C7:1; statutory authority for the latter is at Sec. 167 of the Internal Revenue Code of 1954, 68A Stat. 51. The House Ways and Means Committee altered the depreciation system that had been announced by the President. In reporting out the Revenue Act of 1971, the Committee changed the depreciation rules so that business taxes would be decreased by an estimated $1.9 billion in calendar year 1972 and by $2.4 billion in calendar year 1973. House Report No. 533, 92d Cong., 1st Sess., p. 7 (Sept. 29, 1971).

Proclamations. See Hans Aufricht, "Presidential Proclamations and the British Tradition," 5 *J. Pol.* 142 (May 1943). Example of Presidential proclamations being upheld by the Supreme Court: *Jenkins* v. *Collard*, 145 U.S. 546, 560–561 (1892). The 1907 proclamations by Teddy Roosevelt are discussed in *The Works of Theodore Roosevelt*, XX, 394ff, while the proclamations themselves, giving description of sites, can be found in 35 Stat. 2119ff. Roosevelt's tactic in protecting forest land in the Northwest is recounted in *The Works of Theodore Roosevelt*, XX, 395–396.

Executive Orders. For general studies on Executive Orders, as well as on other forms of administrative legislation, see Robert B. Cash, "Presidential Power: Use and Enforcement of Executive Orders," 39 *Notre Dame Lawyer* 44 (Dec. 1963), and William D. Neighbors, "Presidential Legislation by Executive Order," 37 *U. Colo. L. Rev.* 105 (Fall 1964). Roosevelt's actions from 1941 to 1943 are cited as follows: Executive Order [hereafter E.O.] 8773, 6 Fed. Reg. 2777 (June 9, 1941); E.O. 8868, 6 Fed. Reg. 4349 (Aug. 23, 1941); E.O. 8928, 6 Fed. Reg. 5559 (Oct. 30, 1941); E.O. 9220, 7 Fed. Reg. 6413 (Aug. 13, 1942); E.O.

9225, 7 Fed. Reg. 6627 (Aug. 19, 1942); E.O. 9340, 8 Fed. Reg. 5695 (May 1, 1943); see also John L. Blackman, Jr., *Presidential Seizure in Labor Disputes* (Cambridge: Harvard University Press, 1967).

Equal employment policy, contained in Executive Orders from 1941 to 1965: E.O. 8802, 6 Fed. Reg. 3109 (June 25, 1941); E.O. 10308, 16 Fed. Reg. 12303 (Dec. 3, 1951); E.O. 10479, 18 Fed. Reg. 4899 (Aug. 13, 1953); E.O. 10925, 26 Fed. Reg. 1977 (March 6, 1961); E.O. 11246, 30 Fed. Reg. 12319 (Sept. 24, 1965). The Comptroller General decision issued after Kennedy's Executive Order is at 40 Comp. Gen. 593, Dec. B-145475 (April 21, 1961). See also James E. Remmert, "Executive Order 11,246: Executive Encroachment," 55 *Am. Bar Asso. J.* 1037 (Nov. 1969), and Ruth H. Morgan, *The President and Civil Rights: Policy-Making by Executive Order* (New York: St. Martin's Press, 1970).

The Comptroller General decision issued during the Nixon Administration is 49 Comp. Gen. 59, Dec. B-163026 (Aug. 5, 1969), reprinted at 115 Cong. Rec. S9176–9179 (daily ed., Aug. 5, 1969). Announcement by Secretary of Labor is at 115 Cong. Rec. S9954 (daily ed., Aug. 13, 1969). Attorney General's opinion: 42 Op. A.G., No. 37 (Sept. 22, 1969), reprinted at 115 Cong. Rec. S11318 (daily ed., Sept. 25, 1969). The Senate subcommittee report in April 1971 is *Congressional Oversight of Administrative Agencies: The Philadelphia Plan*, Report of the Senate Judiciary Committee made by its Subcommittee on Separation of Powers, Senate Committee Print, 92d Cong., 1st Sess., p. 13 (1971). The Court of Appeals decision is reprinted at 117 Cong. Rec. S5998 (daily ed., April 30, 1971). On October 12, 1971, in *Contractors Association of Eastern Pennsylvania* v. *Hodgson,* the Supreme Court let stand the Court of Appeals ruling that had upheld the constitutionality of the Philadelphia Plan.

For an example where a court upholds the legality of an Executive Order, see *State ex rel. Kaser* v. *Leonard,* 102 P.2d 197, 129 A.L.R. 1125, 1136 (1940). Executive Orders struck down: *Little* v. *Barreme,* 2 Cr. 170 (1804); *United States* v. *Symonds,* 120 U.S. 46 (1887); *Panama Refining Co.* v. *Ryan,* 293 U.S. 388, 433 (1935); and *Youngstown Co.* v. *Sawyer,* 343 U.S. 579 (1952). On numbering of Executive Orders, see *Presidential Executive Orders,* comp. by W.P.A. Historical Records Survey (2 vols., New York: Hastings House, 1944), p. viii. Estimates of unnumbered Orders: *Executive Orders and Proclamations: A Study of a Use of Presidential Powers,* printed for the use of the House Committee on Government Operations, 85th Cong., 1st Sess., p. 37 (Dec. 1957); for a partial list of unnumbered Orders, see *List and Index of Presidential Executive Orders (Unnumbered Series), 1789–1941,* The New Jersey Historical Records Survey, Work Projects Administration (Newark, N.J., 1943).

Another controversial Executive Order, challenged by Members of Congress as a usurpation of legislative authority, is Executive Order

11605, issued by President Nixon on July 2, 1971. The Order expands the power of the Subversive Activities Control Board, which was established by statute in 1950. A resolution submitted by Senator Ervin declared that the President had no power "to alter by executive order the content or effect of legislation enacted by Congress." 117 Cong. Rec. S13511 (daily ed., Aug. 6, 1971). Executive Order 11605 is printed in *Wkly Comp. Pres. Doc.*, Vol. 7, No. 28, p. 1026 (July 12, 1971). See also 117 Cong. Rec. S12211 (daily ed., July 27, 1971) and 117 Cong. Rec. H7178–7185 (daily ed., July 27, 1971).

Bill-drafting and Central Clearance. Gallatin's activity: Henry Adams, *History of the United States of America* (9 vols., New York: Scribner's, 1889–91), I, 238–272. Jefferson's draft for "the useful arts" is mentioned in Ralph Volney Harlow, *The History of Legislative Methods in the Period Before 1825* (New Haven: Yale University Press, 1917), p. 135. Broadside drafted by Jefferson: his *Writings*, VI, 168. Jefferson's bill-drafting as President: *ibid.*, VIII, 275n, 333, 403n, 424; IX, 69, 190n. Instruction to Gallatin: Henry Adams, ed., *The Writings of Albert Gallatin* (3 vols., New York: Antiquarian Press, 1960), I, 380. Judicial bill-drafting: Felix Frankfurter and James M. Landis, *The Business of the Supreme Court: A Study in the Federal Judicial System* (New York: Macmillan, 1928), pp. 36, 260–280.

Taft's 1912 suggestion for Cabinet officers: Richardson, *Messages and Papers*, XV, 7811 (Dec. 19, 1912). Central clearance development is described by Carl R. Sapp, "Executive Assistance in the Legislative Process," 6 *Pub. Ad. Rev.* 10 (Winter 1946), and Richard E. Neustadt, "Presidency and Legislation: The Growth of Central Clearance," 48 *Am. Pol. Sci. Rev.* 641 (Sept. 1954). A later study by Robert Gilmour discusses White House intervention in the central clearance process. The White House has "taken over from Management and Budget on legislative matters of 'any real importance.' . . . OMB no longer has the monopoly claim on clearance decisions held by the Bureau of the Budget in the 1950's." According to Gilmour, all three Presidents of the 1960s short-circuited the normal clearance channels in order to put a personal stamp on high-priority legislation. Robert S. Gilmour, "Central Legislative Clearance: A Revised Perspective," 31 *Pub. Ad. Rev.* 150 (March/April 1971). The same point is developed by Allen Schick, "The Budget Bureau That Was: Thoughts on the Rise, Decline, and Future of a Presidential Agency," 35 *Law & Contemp. Prob.* 519, 525–528 (Summer 1970). While it is no doubt true that the White House has greater influence in central clearance, it is doubtful that the Budget Bureau ever enjoyed a "monopoly claim" on clearance decisions.

Remark by senior Republican chairman in 1953: Richard E. Neustadt, "Presidency and Legislation: Planning the President's Program," 49 *Am. Pol. Sci. Rev.* 980, 1015 (1955). The 50 to 80 percent range for executive-originated legislation comes from John M. Pfiffner and Robert Prethus, *Public Administration*, 5th ed. (New York: The Ronald Press, 1967), p. 51, and Samuel P. Huntington, "Congressional Responses in the Twentieth Century," in *The Congress and America's Future*, ed. David B. Truman (Englewood Cliffs: Prentice Hall, 1965), p. 23. For an example of how Congress influences legislation by "anticipated response" (a calculation on the part of executive agencies as to what Congress will accept), as well as other forms of legislative influence, see John F. Manley, *The Politics of Finance: The House Committee on Ways and Means* (Boston: Little, Brown and Co., 1970), pp. 322–379.

3. DELEGATION OF POWER

Of the dozens of studies that have appeared on the delegation of legislative power to the executive branch, three particularly good ones are by Stephen A. Foster, "The Delegation of Legislative Power to Administrative Officers," 7 *Ill. L. Rev.* 397 (Feb. 1913); John B. Cheadle, "The Delegation of Legislative Functions," 27 *Yale L. J.* 892 (May 1918); and O. Douglas Weeks, "Legislative Power Versus Delegated Legislative Power," 25 *Geo. L. J.* 314 (Jan. 1937). See also Robert L. Farrington, *The Limitations Upon the Delegation of Power by the Federal Legislature* (Ph.D. dissertation, Catholic University, 1941), and Louis L. Jaffe, "Delegation of Legislative Power," chapter 2 of his *Judicial Control of Administrative Action* (Boston: Little, Brown, 1965), pp. 28–86. Most of the material in my chapter appeared earlier in Louis Fisher, "Delegating Power to the President," *J. Public Law*, Vol. 19, No. 2 (1970).

For two studies on the origin and meaning of the maxim *delegata potestas non potest delegari* (delegated power cannot be delegated), see Patrick W. Duff and Horace E. Whiteside, "Delegata Potestas Non Potest Delegari: A Maxim of American Constitutional Law," 14 *Corn. L. Q.* 168 (Feb. 1929), and also Horst P. Ehmke, " 'Delegata Potestas Non Potest Delegari,' A Maxim of American Constitutional Law," 47 *Corn. L. Q.* 50 (Fall 1961). Duff and Whiteside attribute the maxim to a transcriptional error committed by a sixteenth century printer. An earlier version of the maxim suggests that it was not intended to prohibit delegation but merely to indicate that delegation by the King did not diminish the power residing in his office. On the other hand, Ehmke argues that the maxim is rooted in the writings of John Locke and in Anglo-American common law.

The three Court cases cited at the beginning of the chapter are *Wayman* v. *Southard*, 10 Wheat. 1, 46 (1825); *Field* v. *Clark*, 143 U.S. 649, 692 (1891); and *S. W. Hampton, Jr. & Co.* v. *United States*, 276 U.S. 394, 406 (1928). Author of syllogism is Robert E. Cushman, *The*

Independent Regulatory Commissions (New York: Oxford University Press, 1941), p. 429.

Reasons for Delegating Power

Continuity in Office. John Locke, *Second Treatise*, §153. Recommendation at Philadelphia Convention: Farrand, *Records*, I, 67. Resolution and statutes in 1794: *Annals*, I, 530, and 1 Stat. 372, 400, 401. Act in 1798 and delegate's description of commercial advantages the following year: 1 Stat. 566, and *Annals*, 5th Cong., 2756–2757. Statute in 1806: 2 Stat. 411. Debate on Jefferson's embargo: *Annals*, 10th Cong., 1st Sess., Vol. 2, pp. 2125, 2142, 2202, 2203; April 22, 1808 statute is at 2 Stat. 490. Comment by Senator Giles: *Annals*, 10th Cong., 2d Sess., 259–260.

Flexibility of Timing. Blackstone, *Commentaries*, Book 1, *270. Statutes in 1799 and 1806: 1 Stat. 615 and 2 Stat. 352. *Brig Aurora* v. *United States*, 11 U.S. (7 Cr.) 382, 386 (1813). Pennsylvania case in 1873 is *Locke's Appeal*, 72 Pa. St. 491, 498–499. Court decision on 1922 flexible tariff provision: *Hampton & Co.* v. *United States*, 276 U.S. 394, 407 (1928).

Channel for Foreign Communication. Locke, *Second Treatise*, §146; Blackstone, *Commentaries*, Book 1, *252. Proposals at the Philadelphia Convention: Farrand, *Records*, II, 185, 336–337. Letter by Jefferson, his *Writings*, VI, 451. Logan Act: 1 Stat. 613; resolution is cited at *Annals*, 5th Cong., 2489; see Charles Warren, *History of Laws Prohibiting Correspondence with a Foreign Government and Acceptance of a Commission*, Senate Document No. 696, 64th Cong., 2d Sess. (Jan. 29, 1917). Statutes in 1822 and 1845: 3 Stat. 681 and 5 Stat. 748. Commercial statutes at the end of the nineteenth century and characterization by Senator of President's economic weapon: 24 Stat. 475 (1887), 27 Stat. 267 (1892), and 18 Cong. Rec. 938 (Jan. 24, 1887).

Joint resolutions in 1912 and 1922: 37 Stat. 630 and 42 Stat. 361; *United States* v. *Curtiss-Wright*, 299 U.S. 304, 319, 320 (1936). Joel Francis Paschal, *Mr. Justice Sutherland: A Man Against the State* (Princeton: Princeton University Press, 1951), p. 93. George Sutherland, *Constitutional Power and World Affairs* (New York: Columbia University Press, 1919). See Edwin Borchard, "Shall the Executive Agreement Replace the Treaty?," 38 *Am. J. Int. Law* 637, 641–642 (Oct. 1944), and David M. Levitan, "The Foreign Relations Powers: An Analysis of Mr. Justice Sutherland's Theory," 55 *Yale L. J.* 467, 471–475 (April 1946). Legislation on interest equalization tax and Presidential actions: 81 Stat. 145 (July 31, 1967), 85 Stat. 13 (April 1, 1971), *Wkly Comp. Pres. Doc.*, Vol. 3, No. 35, pp. 1232, 1233–1234 (Aug. 28, 1967), and *Public Papers of the Presidents, 1969*, p. 267 (April 4, 1969).

National Representative. Remarks by Gouverneur Morris and Madison: Farrand, *Records*, II, 52, 81. Polk: Richardson, *Messages and*

Papers, VI, 2515 (Dec. 5, 1848). Philip Wright, *Tariff-Making by Commission* (Washington, D.C.: The Rawleigh Tariff Bureau, 1930), p. 29. Senators Walsh and La Follette: 72 Cong. Rec. 5669, 5977 (March 20–24, 1930). Raymond A. Bauer, Ithiel de Sola Pool, and Lewis Anthony Dexter, *American Business and Public Policy: The Politics of Foreign Trade* (New York: Atherton Press, 1963), p. 37.

Edward S. Corwin, *The Twilight of the Supreme Court* (New Haven: Yale University Press, 1934), p. 178. Senator Reed: 75 Cong. Rec. 9644 (May 5, 1932). Representative Griffin: 77 Cong. Rec. 207 (March 11, 1933). Senator Tydings: 77 Cong. Rec. 270 (March 13, 1933). Postal and Revenue Salary Act of 1967: 81 Stat. 642, Sec. 225 (Dec. 16, 1967); Representative Holifield: 113 Cong. Rec. 28644 (Oct. 11, 1967).

Fact-finding and Coordination. Statutes on forest reservations: 26 Stat. 1103 (1891); 30 Stat. 35 (1897); and 33 Stat. 628 (1905). *United States* v. *Grimaud,* 220 U.S. 506, 516 (1911); see companion case, *Light* v. *United States,* 220 U.S. 523 (1911) and also *Grisar* v. *McDowell,* 6 Wall. 363 (1867) for earlier precedents. *Buttfield* v. *Stranahan,* 192 U.S. 470, 496 (1904). For discretionary authority over the height of bridges, see *Union Bridge Co.* v. *United States,* 294 U.S. 364, 386 (1907) and *Monongahela Bridge* v. *United States,* 216 U.S. 177 (1910).

The "Hot Oil" case is *Panama Refining Co.* v. *Ryan,* 293 U.S. 388, 421 (1935). For the due process aspect of this case, see John D. McGowan, "An Economic Interpretation of the Doctrine of Delegation of Governmental Powers," 12 *Tulane L. Rev.* 179, 192 (1938). Elimination of the criminal offense clause from the code is cited by Carl Brent Swisher, *American Constitutional Development,* 2d ed. (Cambridge: Houghton Mifflin, 1954), pp. 925–930. Cardozo's remark about discretion being "canalized" is on page 440 of *Panama Refining* decision. His "delegation running riot" is at *Schechter Corp.* v. *United States,* 295 U.S. 495, 553 (1935).

Cartoon on the Schechter case is reprinted in James MacGregor Burns, *Roosevelt: The Lion and the Fox* (New York: Harcourt, Brace & World, 1956), p. 310. Editorial in *The New York Times* appears on page 24 of May 28, 1935 edition. Marriner Eccles, *Beckoning Frontiers* (New York: Alfred A. Knopf, 1951), pp. 125–126, but see also J. M. Clark, "Economics and the National Recovery Administration," 24 *Am. Econ. Rev.* 11 (March 1934), and Arthur Robert Burns, "The First Phase of the National Industrial Recovery Act, 1933," 49 *Pol. Sci. Q.* 161 (June 1934).

Delegation after 1935 was upheld in *Currin* v. *Wallace,* 306 U.S. 1, 15 (1939); *Mulford* v. *Smith,* 307 U.S. 38, 49 (1939); *U.S.* v. *Rock Royal Co-op,* 307 U.S. 533 (1939); *H. P. Hood & Sons* v. *U.S.,* 307 U.S. 588 (1939); *Sunshine Coal Co.* v. *Adkins,* 310 U.S. 381, 398 (1940); and *Opp Cotton Mills* v. *Administrator,* 312 U.S. 126, 145 (1941). See Charles B.

Nutting, "Congressional Delegations Since the Schechter Case," 14 *Miss. Law J.* 350 (April 1942). Federal Pay Comparability Act of 1970: 84 Stat. 1946; Federal Salary Act of 1967: 81 Stat. 634; Senator McGee's remarks: 116 Cong. Rec. S21563 (daily ed., Dec. 30, 1970).

National Emergencies. John Locke, *Second Treatise,* Ch. XIV. Convention debate on "make war": Farrand, *Records,* II, 318–319. Report by the Senate Foreign Relations Committee: *National Commitments,* Senate Report No. 129, 91st Cong., 1st Sess., pp. 15–16 (April 16, 1969). Member of Congress saying "How the hell do we know . . . ?": Lewis Anthony Dexter, "Congressmen and the Making of Military Policy," reprinted in *New Perspectives on the House of Representatives,* 2d ed., Robert L. Peabody and Nelson W. Polsby, eds. (Chicago: Rand McNally, 1969), p. 185. William E. Leuchtenburg, "The New Deal and the Analogue of War," in *Change and Continuity in Twentieth-Century America,* ed. John Braeman *et al* (Ohio State University Press, 1964), p. 99. Roosevelt's inaugural address and bank holiday proclamation: *Public Papers,* Vol. II, 1933, pp. 14–15, 25. "House is burning down" exclamation is from James MacGregor Burns, *Roosevelt: The Lion and the Fox,* p. 167. Johnson's "war on poverty" speech: *Public Papers of the Presidents, 1963–64,* I, 114; see also p. 380. "War on crime": *Public Papers of the Presidents, 1967,* I, 313. See J. Malcolm Smith and Cornelius Cotter, *Powers of the President During Crisis* (Washington, D.C.: Public Affairs Press, 1960).

Checks on Arbitrary Executive Actions

The subdelegation case is *French* v. *Weeks,* 259 U.S. 326 (1922). The Court also said, in *United States* v. *Chemical Foundation,* 272 U.S. 1 (1926), that "Obviously all the functions of his great office cannot be exercised by the President in person." See Glendon A. Schubert, Jr., "Judicial Review of the Subdelegation of Presidential Power," 12 *J. Pol.* 668 (Nov. 1950); Eli G. Nobleman, "The Delegation of Presidential Functions: Constitutional and Legal Aspects," *The Annals,* pp. 134–143 (Sept. 1956); and Nathan Grundstein, *Presidential Delegation of Authority in Wartime* (Pittsburgh: University of Pittsburgh Press, 1961). Statement by President Truman on administrative burdens is from Glendon A. Schubert, Jr., "The Presidential Subdelegation Act of 1950," 13 *J. Pol.* 647, 652–653 (Nov. 1951). For the subdelegation act, and current law, see 64 Stat. 419 (Aug. 8, 1950) and 3 U.S.C. §301; for delegation by departmental heads, see 5 U.S.C. §22a.

Statutory Guidelines. Theodore J. Lowi, *The End of Liberalism* (New York: W. W. Norton, 1969), p. 298; see also Maurice H. Merrill, "Standards—A Safeguard for the Exercise of Delegated Power," 47 *Neb. L. Rev.* 469 (May 1968). Material quoted from Kenneth Culp Davis is from his *Discretionary Justice: A Preliminary Inquiry* (Baton

Rouge: Louisiana State University Press, 1969), p. 49, but see also p. 58 and his article "A New Approach to Delegation," 36 *U. Chi. L. Rev.* 713 (Summer 1969).

Procedures for Administrative Action. Administrative Procedure Act: 60 Stat. 237 (June 11, 1946); see Foster H. Sherwood, "The Federal Administrative Procedure Act," 41 *Am. Pol. Sci. Rev.* 271 (April 1947); Frederick F. Blachly and Miriam E. Oatman, "Sabotage of the Administrative Process," 6 *Pub. Ad. Rev.* 213 (Summer 1946); and Victor S. Netterville, "The Administrative Procedure Act: A Study in Interpretation," 20 *G.W. L. Rev.* 1 (Oct. 1951). Administrative Conference established in 1964: 78 Stat. 616, sec. 6. Proposal to include representation for the poor is included in Administrative Conference of the United States, *1969 Annual Report* (Jan. 1970), p. 31.

Judicial review of administrative discretion was the topic of an extended discussion between Raoul Berger and Kenneth Culp Davis: Berger, "Administrative Arbitrariness and Judicial Review," 65 *Colum. L. Rev.* 55 (Jan. 1965); Berger, "Administrative Arbitrariness—a Reply to Professor Davis," 114 *U. Pa. L. Rev.* 783 (April 1968); Davis, "Administrative Arbitrariness—A Final Word," 114 *U. Pa. L. Rev.* 814 (April 1966); Berger, "Administrative Arbitrariness—A Rejoinder to Professor Davis' 'Final Word'," 114 *U. Pa. L. Rev.* 816 (April 1966); Davis, "Administrative Arbitrariness—A Postscript," 114 *U. Pa. L. Rev.* 823 (April 1966); Berger, "Administrative Arbitrariness: A Sequel," 51 *Minn. L. Rev.* 601 (March 1967); Davis, "Administrative Arbitrariness is Not Always Reviewable," 51 *Minn. L. Rev.* 643 (March 1967); Berger, "Administrative Arbitrariness: A Synthesis," 78 *Yale L. J.* 965 (May 1969).

Congressional Oversight. For the waiting-period requirement, see "'Laying on the Table'—A Device for Legislative Control Over Delegated Powers," 65 *Harv. L. Rev.* 637 (1952). On reporting, see J. Malcolm Smith and Cornelius P. Cotter, "Administrative Accountability: Reporting to Congress," 10 *West. Pol. Q.* 405 (June 1957). Provision for legislative members participating in tariff bargaining sessions can be found at section 243 of the Trade Expansion Act of 1962, 76 Stat. 878.

Washington denying the House papers on Jay Treaty: Richardson, *Messages and Papers,* I, 186; for a detailed listing of previous actions where the President has invoked the right of "executive privilege," see *The Power of the President to Withhold Information from the Congress,* compiled by the Subcommittee on Constitutional Rights of the Senate Committee on the Judiciary, 85th Cong., 2d Sess. (1958). Senator Case bill: S. 4556, 91st Cong., 2d Sess. (Dec. 2, 1970); Senator Ervin bill: S. 2027, 92d Cong., 1st Sess. (June 9, 1971); Senator Chiles bill: S. 1334, 92d Cong., 1st Sess. (March 23, 1971). Recommendation by Senate Foreign Relations Committee is included in *National Commit-*

ments, Senate Report No. 129, 91st Cong., 1st Sess., p. 33 (April 16, 1969).

For discussion on the merits of the legislative veto procedure, see Joseph Cooper, "The Legislative Veto: Its Promise and its Perils," 7 *Public Policy* 128 (1956) and the exchange between Professor Cooper and Peter Schauffler in *Public Policy,* Vol. 8 (1957), pp. 296–335. For further discussion on the legislative-veto and committee-veto procedures, see *Separation of Powers,* hearings before the Senate Judiciary Committee, 91st Cong., 1st Sess. (1967), especially pp. 113ff. The development of the legislative veto is covered by Joseph P. Harris, *Congressional Control of Administration* (Washington, D.C.: Brookings Institution, 1964), ch. 8.

1939 debate on legislative veto is from Buckwalter, "The Congressional Concurrent Resolution: A Search for Foreign Policy Influence," 14 *Midwest J. Pol. Sci.* 434, 438–440 (1970). On the objectives of concurrent resolutions, see Cornelius P. Cotter and J. Malcolm Smith, "Administrative Accountability to Congress: The Concurrent Resolution," 9 *West. Pol. Q.* 955 (Dec. 1956); see also Robert W. Ginnane, "The Control of Federal Administration by Congressional Resolutions and Committees," 66 *Harv. L. Rev.* 569 (Feb. 1953).

Eisenhower's opposition to the committee veto: *Public Papers of the Presidents, 1955,* p. 688; Johnson's opposition: *Public Papers of the Presidents, 1965,* II, p. 861, and 111 Cong. Rec. 12639 (1965). For Johnson's withholding of funds because of committee-veto provision, see *Public Papers of the Presidents, 1966,* II, pp. 907, 1082, and Louis Fisher, "The Politics of Impounded Funds," 15 *Admin. Sci. Q.* 361, 374 (Sept. 1970). Congressional duty of "continuous watchfulness" appears at 60 Stat. 832 (Aug. 2, 1946). Comptroller General's responsibility under 1946 Act is included in section 206, 60 Stat. 837. 1970 mandate for Comptroller General is in section 204 of the Legislative Reorganization Act, 84 Stat. 1168.

4. SPENDING POWERS

Development of Executive Budget

The main steps leading to the adoption of a Presidential budget in 1921 have been described elsewhere. For example, see Henry Jones Ford, "Budget Making and the Work of Government," *The Annals,* Vol. LXII (Nov. 1915); Gustavus A. Weber, *Organized Efforts for the Improvement of Methods of Administration in the United States* (New York: D. Appleton, 1919); Frederick A. Cleveland and Arthur Eugene Buck, *The Budget and Responsible Government* (New York, Macmillan, 1920); and Lewis H. Kimmel, *Federal Budget and Fiscal Policy,*

1789–1958 (Washington, D.C.: The Brookings Institution, 1959). What I have done is to emphasize some neglected aspects of this development: (1) the rigid concepts of the separation doctrine which delayed the adoption of an executive budget; (2) budgetary accomplishments of executives between Hamilton and Taft, particularly Albert Gallatin and James K. Polk; (3) reassertion of legislative budget control in the context of President Jackson's struggle with the national bank and the subsequent pledge by his Whig successors that there be a complete separation between the sword and the purse; (4) the emergent role of the President after the Civil War as "protector of the purse"; and (5) a focus on the recurrent deficits between 1900 and 1921 to explain the cyclical interest shown toward budgetary reform.

Establishing the Treasury Department. Debates on creation of the Treasury Department: *Annals,* 1st Cong., 1–2 Sess., pp. 592–594, 604–607 (June 25, 1789); statute: 1 Stat. 65. Acts creating the Departments of Foreign Affairs and War: 1 Stat. 28, 49. Members objecting to heads of departments originating or influencing legislation: *Annals,* 2d Cong., 1–2 Sess., pp. 703–708 (Nov. 20, 1792). For legislative attacks on Hamilton in 1793 and 1794, see *Annals,* 2d Cong., 1–2 Sess., pp. 899–963 (Feb. 28 to March 1, 1793); *ibid.,* 3d Cong., 1–2 Sess., p. 458 (Feb. 19, 1794); *ibid.,* pp. 463–466 (Feb. 24, 1794); *ibid.,* p. 954 (Dec. 2, 1794); and Broadus Mitchell, *Alexander Hamilton* (2 vols., New York: Macmillan, 1957–1962), II, 245–286. Remark by Fisher Ames is from Henry Jones Ford, "Budget Making and the Work of Government," *The Annals,* American Academy of Political and Social Science, p. 7 (1915). See Patrick J. Furlong, "The Origins of the House Committee of Ways and Means," 25 *Wm. & Mary Q.* 587 (Oct. 1968), and *History of the Committee on Finance, United States Senate,* Senate Document No. 57, 91st Cong., 2d Sess., pp. 14ff. (March 5, 1970).

Gallatin's budget policy: Henry Adams, ed., *The Writings of Albert Gallatin* (3 vols., Antiquarian Press, 1960), I, 24–26; Henry Adams, *History of the United States of America* (9 vols., New York: Scribner's, 1889–1891), I, 239–240, 241–272; IV, 156–157, 366–367; VI, 126–127, 157–158; and Henry Adams, *Life of Albert Gallatin* (Philadelphia: J. B. Lippincott, 1879), pp. 167–175.

Executive Control, 1812–1861. Experiences of Madison and Monroe are described by Leonard D. White, *The Jeffersonians: A Study in Administrative History, 1801–1829* (New York: Macmillan, 1951), pp. 68–69. On the Monroe-Crawford confrontation, see *Memoirs of John Quincy Adams,* Charles Francis Adams, ed., (12 vols., Philadelphia: J. B. Lippincott, 1874–77), VII, 81; see also VI, 388, 390, 394, 439. For J. Q. Adams's own performance on budget estimates, see *Memoirs of John Quincy Adams,* VII, 359 and also VII, 195, 247.

Defense of Andrew Jackson for removing Treasury Secretaries: Richardson, *Messages and Papers,* III, 1301 (April 15, 1834). Positions taken by Harrison and Tyler, *ibid.,* IV, 1867–1868 (March 4, 1841) and

1890–1891 (April 9, 1841); see also IV, 1939–1940 (Dec. 7, 1841). Polk's warning to bureau chiefs concerning estimates: *Diary of James K. Polk*, I, 48. For Jesup incident, see *ibid.*, III, 125–142. Other budget actions: *ibid.*, III, 213–221; IV, 165–181.

Splintering of Committee Structure. Creation of Senate Appropriations: *Committee on Appropriations: United States Senate*, 100th Anniversary, 1867–1967, Senate Document No. 21, 90th Cong., 1st Sess., pp. 4ff (1967). History of House Appropriations, concentrating mainly on the committee chairmen between 1865 and 1941: *A History of the Committee on Appropriations: House of Representatives*, by Edward T. Taylor, House Document No. 299, 77th Cong., 1st Sess. (1941). Reminder to the House Appropriations Committee concerning the tendency to extravagance: Cong. Globe, 38th Cong., 2d Sess., p. 1312 (March 2, 1865).

House Appropriations accused of introducing legislation: see speech by Rep. George H. Mahon on the 100th anniversary of the Committee, 111 Cong. Rec. 3960–3961 (March 2, 1965). Reduction of Committee's power: 7 Cong. Rec. 18–26 (Dec. 4, 1877); 10 Cong. Rec. 200, 663, 1261 (1880); 15 Cong. Rec. 196, 214–216 (1883); 10 Cong. Rec. 683–686 (Feb. 3, 1880). Explanation of retaliation against Randall: *The National Budget*, by Joseph G. Cannon, House Document No. 264, 66th Cong., 1st Sess., pp. 11–15 (1919). Report from Francis Wharton: Leonard D. White, *The Jacksonians* (New York: Macmillan, 1954), p. 27.

"Protector of the Purse." Polk vetoing river and harbor legislation: Richardson, *Messages and Papers*, V, 2314 (Aug. 3, 1846), and *ibid.*, VI, 2463 (Dec. 15, 1847). Striking out smuggled projects from estimates: *Diary of James K. Polk*, IV, 190. Arthur's remark in vetoing 1882 bill: Richardson, *Messages and Papers*, X, 4708 (Aug. 1, 1882); passed over his veto, 22 Stat. 191 (Aug. 2, 1882). Thomas Nast cartoon on Arthur: *Harper's Weekly*, Aug. 12, 1882, p. 497.

Pension frauds in 1835 and 1853: Leonard D. White, *Jacksonians*, p. 413. The period after the Civil War, in the caustic language of Talcott Powell, ushered in "a new era of rapacity and fraud" and the "tragic debauching of the patriotic motives of citizen soldiers by as swinish a group of politicians and parasitical pension agents as the world has even seen"; *Tattered Banners* (New York: Harcourt, Brace, 1933), p. 130. Member of the House in 1886: 17 Cong. Rec. 7764–7765 (July 30, 1886). Comments from Charles Francis Adams: Henry F. Pringle, *The Life and Times of William Howard Taft* (2 vols., Farrar & Rinehart, 1939), II, 641. Statistics for pension outlays from 1870 to 1900: William H. Glasson, *Federal Military Pensions in the United States* (New York: Oxford University Press, 1918), p. 123. Revolutionary War benefit paid out in 1906: *History of the Committee on Finance: United States Senate*, Senate Document No. 91–57, 91st Cong., 2d Sess., p. 78 (1970). Statistics on Cleveland's vetoes: *Presidential Ve-*

toes, 1789–1968, compiled by the Senate Library (Washington, D.C.: Government Printing Office, 1969), pp. 31–56. Cleveland receiving 240 pension bills on one day: Richardson, *Messages and Papers,* X, 5001–5002 (May 8, 1886); some sarcastic vetoes in 1886: *ibid.,* X, 5028 and 5033–5034 (June 23, 1886); forty-three vetoes delivered from June 21 to June 23. Thomas Nast cartoon of Cleveland: *Harper's Weekly,* July 3, 1886, p. 421. Effect of pension policies on 1888 election: William H. Glasson, *Federal Military Pensions,* pp. 225–228, 279. Cleveland after 1892: Richardson, *Messages and Papers,* XII, 5978 (Dec. 3, 1894); XIII, 6169 (Dec. 7, 1896); XIII, 6186 (Feb. 22, 1897).

Studies on Economy and Efficiency. Budget surpluses and deficits obtained from U.S. Bureau of the Census, *Historical Statistics of the United States of America, Colonial Times to 1957* (Washington, D.C.: Government Printing Office, 1960), Series Y 254–257, p. 711; yearly shifts in revenue and expenditure are taken from the *Annual Reports of the Secretary of the Treasury on the State of the Finances.* Material on Teddy Roosevelt is from *Letters of Theodore Roosevelt,* Elting E. Morison, ed. (8 vols., Cambridge: Harvard University Press, 1951–54), IV, 1201–1202; *Works of Theodore Roosevelt,* Executive Edition (8 vols., New York: Collier, 1914), IV, 696; see Richardson, *Messages and Papers,* XIV, 6988–6990 (Dec. 5, 1905), and Oscar Kraines, "The President Versus Congress: The Keep Commission, 1905–1909: First Comprehensive Presidential Inquiry into Administration," 23 *West. Pol. Q.* 5 (March 1970). See also Kraines' study on "The Cockrell Committee, 1887–1889: First Comprehensive Congressional Investigation into Administration," 4 *West. Pol. Q.* 583 (Dec. 1951).

Deficit forecast for fiscal 1910: *Annual Report of the Secretary of the Treasury,* 1908/09, p. 25. Grant of power in 1909 to Secretary of the Treasury, 35 Stat. 1027, sec. 7. Taft's scrutiny of budget estimates: *Annual Report of the Secretary of the Treasury,* 1908/09, p. 5; 1909/10, p. 1. Appropriation of $100,000 in 1910: 36 Stat. 703. Commission's report on national budget: *The Need for a National Budget,* House Document No. 854, 62d Cong., 2d Sess., p. 138 (June 27, 1912). Act of August 23, 1912 directing administrative personnel to prepare estimates as required by law: 37 Stat. 360, 415. Taft insisting on two sets of estimates: Frederick A. Cleveland, "The Federal Budget," *Proceedings of the Academy of Political Science,* Vol. III, pp. 167–168 (1912–13). Dust accumulating on commission study: William Howard Taft, *Our Chief Magistrate and His Powers* (New York: Columbia University Press, 1916), pp. 64–65; for model budget transmitted to Congress: 49 Cong. Rec. 3985ff (Feb. 26, 1913). Rep. J. Swager Sherley, soon to be Fitzgerald's successor as chairman of the House Appropriations Committee, was the only legislator to express support, 49 Cong. Rec. 4349ff (Feb. 28, 1913).

Budget and Accounting Act of 1921. Wilson's initial interest in budget reform: Ray Stannard Baker, ed., *Woodrow Wilson: Life and*

Letters (8 vols., New York: Doubleday, Doran, 1927–29), VII, 291–292 (Wilson to Rep. Fitzgerald); see also IV, 212 (Jan. 30, 1913). Fitzgerald's recommendations for budget reform: William Franklin Willoughby, *The Problem of a National Budget* (New York: D. Appleton, 1918), pp. 146–149. Platforms of three major parties: Edward Stanwood, *A History of the Presidency* (2 vols., Boston: Houghton Mifflin, 1898–1916), II, 344–345, 349, 358. Position of the Institute for Government Research: Willoughby, *op. cit.*, p. 29. Wilson's message in December 1917: Israel, *State of the Union Messages*, III, 2588. Senator Kenyon introduced S.J. Res. 121 for budget commission: 56 Cong. Rec. 705, 10097, 11188, 11317–11321; Rep. Barnhart introduced resolution (H. Res. 289) for extra copies of budget study: 56 Cong. Rec. 4143, 4144. McCormick's proposals: *Plan for a National Budget System*, House Document No. 1006, 65th Cong., 2d Sess. (March 27, 1918).

Cannon's warning: *The National Budget*, House Document No. 264, 66th Cong., 1st Sess., pp. 28–29 (1919). Edward Fitzpatrick, *Budget Making in a Democracy* (New York: Macmillan, 1918); pp. viii–ix, 117. Wilson's cable to Sherley: *The New York Times*, Feb. 12, 1919, 7:3. Wilson waiting for Senate action on peace treaty: David Houston, *Eight Years With Wilson's Cabinet* (2 vols., Garden City, N.Y.: Doubleday, Page, 1926), II, pp. 7–8. House report in 1919: *National Budget System*, House Report No. 362, 66th Cong., 1st Sess., p. 5 (Oct. 8, 1919). Wilson's support on December 2: Israel, *State of the Union Messages*, III, 2599. The Senate version of a national budget had placed the budget bureau in the Treasury Department rather than directly under the President. The conference committee reached an imaginative compromise by placing the budget bureau "directly under the control of the President" but then making the Secretary of the Treasury the budget director. Senate version: *National Budget System*, Senate Report No. 524, 66th Cong., 2d Sess. (April 13, 1920); conference report: *National Budget System, Conference Report*, House Report No. 1044, 66th Cong., 2d Sess. (May 26, 1920). Wilson veto: Richardson, *Messages and Papers*, XVII, 8851 (June 4, 1920). Budget and Accounting Act: 42 Stat. 20 (June 10, 1921).

Centralization of Budget Controls. House consolidation: Richard F. Fenno, Jr., *The Power of the Purse: Appropriations Politics in Congress* (Boston: Little, Brown, 1966), pp. 9–10, 45–46. Senate consolidation: Stephen Horn, *Unused Power: The Work of the Senate Committee on Appropriations* (Washington, D.C.: The Brookings Institution, 1970), pp. 57–60. Norm of reciprocity: Fenno, *The Power of the Purse*, pp. 162–163.

Circular issued by Dawes in 1921: U.S. Bureau of the Budget, "First Budget Regulations," Circular No. 4 (July 1, 1921). Economy Act of 1933: 48 Stat. 8; Executive Order 6166: 77 Cong. Rec. 5708 (June 10, 1933); 5 U.S.C. §132, sections 16 and 20 (1934 ed.). Reorganization Act of 1939 and transfer of Budget Bureau to the Executive Office of the President: 53 Stat. 561, 1423. March 1970 proposal for Office of Management and Budget: *Wkly Comp. Pres. Doc.,* Vol. 6, No. 11, p. 353 (March 12, 1970). Disapproval by House Government Operations Committee: House Report. No. 1066, 91st Cong., 2d Sess., p. 10 (May 8, 1970). For debate and vote on Reorganization Plan No. 2 of 1970, which established the OMB, see 116 Cong. Rec. H4312–4346 (daily ed., May 13, 1970).

Spending Ceilings. Employment Act of 1946: 60 Stat. 23, sec. 4(c). Congress tried several techniques in the postwar years to place restrictions on Federal spending. As part of the Legislative Reorganization Act of 1946, a joint committee was formed to prepare a "legislative budget" and to prescribe a ceiling on expenditures. The work of the joint committee, consisting of 102 members from the taxing and spending committees of each house, was hampered by friction between the two houses, disputes between taxing and spending committees, and by intraparty wrangling. Moreover, this new procedure conflicted with the established practice of having separate appropriations subcommittees review the President's budget to decide the level of funding. Thus, the Legislative Budget prematurely set a ceiling before the subcommittees could complete their work. It was abandoned by Congress after three unsuccessful efforts. See Avery Leiserson, "Coordination of Federal Budgetary and Appropriations Procedures under the Legislative Reorganization Act of 1946," 1 *Natl Tax J.* 118 (June 1948), and Clinton Fielder, "Reform of the Congressional Legislative Budget," 4 *Natl Tax J.* 65 (March 1951).

A new legislative approach appeared in 1950. Instead of handling appropriations by separate bills, the House Appropriations Committee reported out a single-package ("omnibus") appropriation bill. In addition to making selective cuts in the President's budget, the House considered a proposal by Congressman Thomas to authorize the President to cut out an additional $500 million, subject to two guidelines: (1) reductions would not apply to military programs and (2) no domestic program could be cut by more than 15 percent. Clarence Cannon, chairman of the House Appropriations Committee, criticized this as an abdication of legislative responsibility. Congressman Keefe charged that the prospect of turning over to the President the responsibility for making reductions was "a monstrous display of congressional incompetence, to say the least." 96 Cong. Rec. 6812, 6814 (May 10, 1950). The Thomas proposal was amended by Congressman Taber to exert greater congressional control. The Senate later passed its own version of a plan whereby the President could reduce the budget. 96 Cong. Rec. 6815, 6844, 11547–11695. The conference committee simply directed the President to cut the budget by not less than $550 million, without impairing the national defense. President Truman fulfilled the statutory directive by placing $573 million in reserve, including $343 million in appropriations, $119 million in contract authority, and $110 million in authority to borrow from the Treasury. 64 Stat. 595, sec. 1214 (Sept. 6, 1950); House Document No. 182, 82d Cong., 1st Sess. (June 27, 1951). See Dalmas H. Nelson, "The Omnibus Appropriations Act of 1950," 15 *J. Pol.* 274 (May 1953), and John Phillips, "The Hadacol of the Budget Makers," 4 *Natl Tax J.* 255 (Sept. 1951).

Authority to set aside funds, from the 1950 omnibus appropriations act: 64 Stat. 765, sec. 1211; 31 U.S.C. §665(c). Mahon statement to the House in 1967: 113 Cong. Rec. 29282 (Oct. 18, 1967). Democratic-Republican vote in 1967 on the $5 billion cut: *Cong. Q. Wkly Report,* Oct. 20, 1967, p. 2150. Conference report: House Report No. 1011, 90th Cong., 1st Sess., p. 4 (Dec. 7, 1967). For statutory language and congressional and executive budget cuts, see 81 Stat. 662 (Dec. 18, 1967), and *Public Papers of the Presidents, 1967,* II, p. 1174 (Dec. 19, 1967).

Figures for the Revenue and Expenditure Control Act of June 1968 are from a joint statement by Treasury Secretary Kennedy and Budget Director Mayo, 115 Cong. Rec. E6374 (daily ed., July 29, 1969): for language of Act: 82 Stat. 271, sec. 202 (June 28, 1968). Spending ceiling for fiscal 1970: 83 Stat. 82, sec. 401 (July 22, 1969); ceiling was later raised by Congress to $197.8 billion: 84 Stat. 405, sec. 401 (July 6, 1970). Spending ceiling for fiscal 1971: 84 Stat. 406, sec. 501 (July 6, 1970). Omitting the borrowed trust fund surpluses would give an estimated $30.2 billion deficit for fiscal 1971; 117 Cong. Rec. H8152 (daily ed., Aug. 6, 1971). For further details on spending controls and anti-inflation policy, see Louis Fisher, "The Politics of Impounded Funds," 15 *Admin. Sci. Q.* 361, 369–373 (Sept. 1970). Aaron Wildavsky, *The Politics of the Budgetary Process* (Boston: Little, Brown, 1964), covers the strategies and games played by the executive and legislative branches in formulating the budget.

Congress did not adopt a spending ceiling for fiscal 1972. As Representative Evins told an Office of Management and Budget official: "The Congress feels that they don't want to give you a flexible ceiling which you could use as a tool to freeze and impound funds as you did in the past." *Public Works for Water and Power Development and Atomic Energy Commission Appropriations* (Part 6), hearings before the House Committee on Appropriations, 92d Cong., 1st Sess., p. 13 (1971).

Executive Spending Discretion

The only thorough study of executive spending discretion is by Lucius Wilmerding, Jr., *The Spending Power: A History of the Efforts of Congress to Control Expenditures* (New Haven: Yale University Press, 1943). Valuable sections can be found in Elias Huzar, *The Purse and the Sword: Control of the Army by Congress through Military Appropriations, 1933–1950* (Ithaca, N.Y.: Cornell University Press, 1950), while an excellent compilation of documents has been prepared by Fred Wilbur Powell, *Control of Federal Expenditures: A Documentary History: 1775–1894* (Washington, D.C.: The Brookings Institution, 1939). For a more detailed and current discussion of executive spending discretion, see Louis Fisher, "Presidential Spending Discretion and Congressional Controls," *Law & Contemp. Prob.*, to be published in 1972.

Lump-sum Appropriations. Appropriation act of 1789: 1 Stat. 95 (Sept. 29, 1789): acts for 1790 and 1791: 1 Stat. 104 (March 26, 1790) and 1 Stat. 190 (Feb. 11, 1791). Appropriation act of Dec. 23, 1791: 1 Stat. 226; for 1793: 1 Stat. 325, 327. Jefferson to Congress in 1801: Richardson, *Messages and Papers,* I, 317 (Dec. 8, 1801); Hamilton's critique: Hamilton, *Works,* VII, 256–257.

Quotation from Gallatin: *The Writings of Albert Gallatin* (Adams ed.), III, 117; quotation from Jefferson: *Writings* (Washington ed.), IV, 529–530, 533. See also *The Writings of Albert Gallatin* (Adams ed.), I, 68, 73–74; Henry Adams, *The Life of Albert Gallatin* (New York: Peter Smith, 1943), p. 157; compare Gallatin's breakdown of War Department figures with earlier statutes on military spending: 1 Stat. 228, 328, 342, 438, 493, 508, 563, 742; 2 Stat. 66.

Civil War act: 12 Stat. 344 (1862); World War I acts: 40 Stat. 28, 182 (1917). Appropriation of $950 million in 1934: 48 Stat. 351; Emergency Relief Appropriation Act of 1935; 49 Stat. 115. Appropriations for World War II: 57 Stat. 209, 357 (1943). For financing of Manhattan Project, see Joe Martin, *My First Fifty Years in Politics* (New York: McGraw-Hill, 1960), pp. 100–101, and Leslie R. Groves, *Now It Can Be Told: The Story of the Manhattan Project* (New York: Harper & Bros., 1962), pp. 360–361. The "writer" informed about the $800 million is Elias Huzar, *The Purse and the Sword,* p. 338. AEC appropriations in 1970: 84 Stat. 890; see Michael W. Kirst, *Government Without Passing Laws: Congress' Nonstatutory Techniques for Appropriations Control* (Chapel Hill: University of North Carolina Press, 1969).

Contingency Funds. Emergency funds during World War II: for national security and defense, 54 Stat. 297, 377; 55 Stat. 94, 818; 56 Stat. 705, 995, and for defense housing, 55 Stat. 14, 198, 818. Creation of Peace Corps: 26 Fed. Reg. 1789 (March 1, 1961); appropriations: 75 Stat. 721 (Sept. 30, 1961); interim financing of Peace Corps explained in House Report No. 1115, 87th Cong., 1st Sess., p. 66 (Sept. 5, 1961). Foreign assistance acts: 75 Stat. 717 (1961), and 76 Stat. 1163 (1962). Emergency Fund for Southeast Asia: 79 Stat. 872 (1965). Disaster relief acts: 64 Stat. 1109 (1950); 80 Stat. 1316 (1966); 84 Stat. 1744 (1970). The number of declarations and total allocations were obtained from the Office of Emergency Preparedness; figures include actions by the Housing and Home Finance Agency in 1951–52 when it administered disaster relief programs.

Free World Forces. Expression of gratitude by President Johnson in 1966 for Philippine civic action group: *Public Papers of the Presidents, 1966*, II, 1029 (Sept. 15, 1966). Hearings by the Symington Subcommittee: *United States Security Agreements and Commitments Abroad: The Republic of the Philippines* (Part 1), hearings before the Senate Foreign Relations Committee, 91st Cong., 1st Sess., pp. 261, 358 (1969). Denial by Philippine Government and GAO investigation: *The New York Times*, Nov. 20, 1969, 13:1, and 116 Cong. Rec. S4453 (daily ed., March 25, 1970). Thai agreement in 1967 and GAO report: *United States Security Agreements and Commitments Abroad: Kingdom of Thailand* (Part 3), hearings before the Senate Foreign Relations Committee, 91st Cong., 1st Sess., pp. 624–5, 657 (1969), and 116 Cong. Rec. S19743 (daily ed., Dec. 9, 1970). The Foreign Ministry of Thailand denied that the United States had offered payments to induce Thailand to send armed forces to Vietnam; *The New York Times*, Dec. 16, 1969, 10:1. Subsidies to South Korea: *United States Security Agreements and Commitments Abroad: Republic of Korea* (Part 6), hearings before the Senate Foreign Relations Committee, 91st Cong., 2d Sess., pp. 1529–1547 (1970).

Covert financing has also been used to finance, through the Central Intelligence Agency, such activities as military operations in Laos and the broadcasting of American information to Eastern Europe. With regard to the former, see remarks of Senator Case, 117 Cong. Rec. S7503 (daily ed., May 20, 1971); *The Washington Post*, May 22, 1971, A17:1; and *Laos: April 1971*, A Staff Report Prepared for the Use of the Subcommittee on U.S. Security Agreements and Commitments Abroad of the Senate Foreign Relations Committee, 92d Cong., 1st Sess., p. 3 (Aug. 3, 1971). For CIA financing of Radio Free Europe and Radio Liberty, see 117 Cong. Rec. S130 (daily ed., Jan. 25, 1971); S. 18, 92d Cong., 1st Sess. (Jan. 25, 1971); *The New York Times*, May 24, 1971, 5:1; and 117 Cong. Rec. S12756 (Aug. 2, 1971).

Transfers between Classes. For debate on the Giles resolutions, see *Annals*, 2d Cong., pp. 890, 899–902 (Feb. 22, 1793). Role of Jefferson and Hamilton in these resolutions: Jefferson, *Writings*, VI, 168, and Broadus Mitchell, *Alexander Hamilton* (2 vols., New York: Macmillan, 1957–62), II, 260–263. Congressman Bayard during Jefferson's Administration: *Annals*, 7th Cong., 1st Sess., p. 320 (Dec. 14, 1801). Secretary Crawford: *Annals*, 14th Cong., 2d Sess., pp. 420–421 (Jan. 6, 1817). Transfer authority from 1820 to 1848: 3 Stat. 568; 4 Stat. 558, 742; 5 Stat. 78, 223, 533; 9 Stat. 101, 171; 1860 statute: 12 Stat. 81, sec. 2; 1868 statute: 15 Stat. 36, sec. 2. Economy Act of 1932: 47 Stat. 411, sec. 317 (June 30, 1932); see Wilmerding, *The Spending Power*, pp. 180–184. Lend Lease Act: 55 Stat. 54 (March 27, 1941). Military appropriations in 1943: 57 Stat. 367, sec. 3 (July 1, 1943).

Aid to Cambodia. Current law on transfers: 31 U.S.C. §628. Transfer of funds to Cambodia: *Supplemental Foreign Assistance Authorization, 1970*, hearings before the Senate Foreign Relations Committee, 91st Cong., 2d Sess., pp. 2, 78 (1970); 76 Stat. 442, sec. 610 (Sept. 4, 1961); 22 U.S.C. §2360(a).

Reprograming. Defense Department reprograming by the Kennedy Administration: *Department of Defense Reprograming of Appropriated Funds: A Case Study,* House Committee on Armed Services, 89th Cong., 1st Sess., p. 32 (July 8, 1965). Insistence on semi-annual reporting: House Report No. 493, 84th Cong., 1st Sess., p. 8 (May 5, 1955). Request for more frequent reporting: House Report No. 408, 86th Cong., 1st Sess., p. 20 (May 28, 1959). House request for immediate revision of reprograming procedure: House Report No. 1607, 87th Cong., 2d Sess., p. 21 (April 13, 1962). Response by Defense Department in 1963: *Department of Defense Directive,* "Reprogramming of Appropriated Funds," No. 7250.5 (March 4, 1963). Chiles bill: S. 1333, 92d Cong., 1st Sess. (March 23, 1971).

Current procedures for defense reprograming are spelled out in *Department of Defense Directive,* "Reprogramming of Appropriated Funds," No. 7250.5 (May 21, 1970), and *Department of Defense Instruction,* "Implementation of Reprogramming of Appropriated Funds," No. 7250.10 (April 1, 1971). The *Directive* is misleading in that it describes "prior approval" by the committees as follows: in the event that the Secretary of Defense is not informed of approval or disapproval within 15 days of receipt by the committees of a reprograming request, it is assumed that there is no objection to the implementation of the proposed reprograming (p. 3). In actual fact, prior approval means *explicit* committee approval, no matter how long it takes.

Transfers in Time. Restriction in 1795: 1 Stat. 433, sec. 16 (March 3, 1795). Monroe's action in 1819: *Annals,* 16th Cong., 1st Sess., pp. 807–809 (Dec. 28, 1819); see Wilmerding, *The Spending Power,* pp. 83–94. 1820 statute: 3 Stat. 567, sec. 1 (May 1, 1820). 1852 statute and Attorney General opinions: 10 Stat. 98, sec. 10 (Aug. 31, 1852); 7 Op. A.G. 1, 14 (1854). Statutes in 1870 and 1874: 16 Stat. 230 (July 12, 1870), and 18 Stat. 85 (June 20, 1874). Current law on no-year money for public works and public buildings: 31 U.S.C. §§635, 682. Fiscal 1970 no-year funds for Defense Department: 83 Stat. 475–479 (Dec. 29, 1969); closer control on DOD carryover balances in fiscal 1971 appropriation bill: 84 Stat. 2037 (Jan. 11, 1971). According to Article I, Section 8 of the Constitution, appropriations to raise and support armies shall not be for a longer term than two years. Yet no-year financing for military procurement has been upheld in several opinions by the Attorney General. A 1904 opinion argued that to raise and support an army was one thing; to equip it was another. The constitutional prohibition applied only to the first. If that reasoning seems a little less than profound, the opinion advances a second argument, namely, that the power to arm and equip armies follows from the power to declare war, to raise and support armies, to provide forts, magazines, and arsenals, and to levy and collect taxes to provide for the common defense.

25 Op. A.G. 105 (Jan. 2, 1904), but see also 40 Op. A.G. 555 (Jan. 8, 1948).

Speeding up Expenditures. Anti-recession actions by Eisenhower Administration in 1958: Wilfred Lewis, Jr., *Federal Fiscal Policy in the Postwar Recessions* (Washington, D.C.: The Brookings Institution, 1962), pp. 221–227; anti-recession actions by Kennedy Administration in 1961: *ibid.*, pp. 250–273; also, *Public Papers of the Presidents, 1961*, p. 41, and *Economic Report of the President, 1962*, p. 98.

Impoundment. For author's analysis of legal issue, see Louis Fisher, "Funds Impounded by the President: The Constitutional Issue," 38 *G.W. L. Rev.* 124 (Oct. 1969); the writer who states that the President "can and may" withhold expenditures is Arthur Selwyn Miller, "Presidential Power to Impound Appropriated Funds: an Exercise in Constitutional Decision-Making," 43 *N.C. L. Rev.* 502, 533 (1965). Articles asserting unconstitutionality of impoundment: John H. Stassen, "Separation of Powers and the Uncommon Defense: The Case Against Impounding of Weapons System Appropriations," 57 *Geo. L. J.* 1159 (1969); Gerald W. Davis, "Congressional Power to Require Defense Expenditures," 33 *Fordham L. Rev.* 39 (1964); and Robert E. Goostree, "The Power of the President to Impound Appropriated Funds: With Special Reference to Grants-in-aid to Segregated Activities," 11 *Am. U. L. Rev.* 32 (1962).

Statutory basis for withholding funds includes Title VI of the 1964 Civil Rights Act, 42 U.S.C. § 2000d-1; welfare payment standards, 81 Stat. 898 (Jan. 2, 1968); for threats by the Department of Health, Education and Welfare during 1971 to cut off relief funds from California, Indiana, Nebraska, and Arizona, see *The Washington Post,* Jan. 9, 1971, A2; *The New York Times,* Jan. 20, 1971, 15:1; *The Washington Post,* Jan. 28, 1971, A18; *The New York Times,* March 29, 1971, 19:1; and *The New York Times,* April 1, 1971, 24:3. Revenue and Expenditure Control Act of 1968: 82 Stat. 271.

Authority of President to set aside funds for contingencies or to effect savings: 31 U.S.C. § 665(c)(2). Suspension of mortgage-subsidy program is described in *The Washington Post,* Jan. 15, 1971, A2; for impoundment of antimissile funds, see *Public Papers of the Presidents, 1960–61,* pp. 54–55, 414. Statement of Congressman Mahon is in letter to Senator Sam J. Ervin, Jr., Feb. 25, 1969; copy obtained from Mr. Eugene B. Wilhelm, staff assistant, House Committee on Appropriations. For withholding of B-70 funds and other impoundment disputes, see Louis Fisher, "The Politics of Impounded Funds," 15 *Admin. Sci. Q.* 361 (Sept. 1970). Statement by Senator Thomas on impoundment of Air Force funds appears at 95 Cong. Rec. 14355 (Oct. 12, 1949); see also exchange between Senators Ferguson and Saltonstall at page 14855 (Oct. 18, 1949), and my discussion in "The Politics of Impounded Funds," pp. 366–367. Explanation by Secretary Romney: *Withholding of Funds for Housing and Urban Development Programs, Fiscal Year*

1971, hearings before the Senate Committee on Banking, Housing and Urban Affairs, 92d Cong., 1st Sess., pp. 163, 165 (1971).

For withholding of funds in 1966–1967, see Fisher, "The Politics of Impounded Funds," *op. cit.,* pp. 370–371. Remark by Cabinet officer (HEW Secretary Richardson) in 1970: *The Washington Post,* Oct. 23, 1970, A6. Dispute on Model Cities funds in 1971: *The New York Times,* Feb. 12, 1971, 1:6 and 31:2; Feb. 19, 1971, 20:7. March 1971 hearings by Senate Subcommittee on Separation of Powers: *Executive Impoundment of Appropriated Funds,* hearings before the Senate Judiciary Committee, 92d Cong., 1st Sess. (1971); Ervin bill: S. 2027, 92d Cong., 1st Sess. (June 9, 1971). Legal memorandum is by William H. Rehnquist, Assistant Attorney General, Office of Legal Counsel, Dec. 1, 1969; placed in the Congressional Record, Vol. 116, pp. S158–160 (daily ed., Jan. 20, 1970).

On September 27, 1971, Senator Ervin introduced a stronger bill (S. 2581) to provide that an impoundment action by the President shall cease at the end of 60 calendar days unless Congress approves the action by concurrent resolution. The bill was stronger in two aspects. It provided for affirmative approval instead of a resolution of disapproval, and it relied on a concurrent resolution (which cannot be vetoed) instead of a joint resolution (which requires the President's signature).

Unauthorized Commitments. In 1803, Congress appropriated $2 million to be applied toward the purchase of New Orleans and the Floridas; *Annals,* 7th Cong., 2d Sess., pp. 370–371, and 2 Stat. 202 (Feb. 26, 1803). When France offered to sell the whole of Louisiana, Jefferson's agents in Paris accepted the offer. Uneasy about the constitutionality of this agreement, Jefferson explained to Congress that the provisional appropriation seemed to him to convey "the sanction of Congress to the acquisition proposed." Richardson, *Messages and Papers,* I, 346 (Oct. 17, 1803). Congress subsequently passed a supplemental appropriation to cover the full price of the Louisiana Territory; 2 Stat. 245, 247 (Nov. 10, 1803). For negotiations with France, see Henry Adams, *History of the United States of America,* II, ch. II. The *Chesapeake* incident is described at Richardson, *Messages and Papers,* I, 416 (Oct. 27, 1807).

For Lincoln's action, see Richardson, *Messages and Papers,* VII, 3279 (May 26, 1862); Lincoln's use of funds to employ secret agents was upheld by the Supreme Court in *Totten, Administrator* v. *United States,* 92 U.S. (2 Otto.), 105, 106 (1875). Teddy Roosevelt describes the fleet issue in his autobiography; *The Works of Theodore Roosevelt,* XX, 552–553. A less successful effort involved Roosevelt's habit of appointing extralegal, unsalaried commissions to study social and economic issues. To publish the findings of one of his commissions he asked Congress for $25,000. Not only did Congress refuse, it enacted a prohibition against the appointment of commissions without legislative authority. Roosevelt said that Congress had no right to issue such an order and that he would ignore it. But he did not get the money. A private organization had to publish the study; *ibid.*, XX, 416–417.

The initiative by John B. Floyd was decided in *The Floyd Acceptances,* 74 U.S. (7 Wall.) 666 (1868); for an earlier decision in which the Supreme Court upheld the need for executive spending discretion, see *United States* v. *Macdaniel,* 32 U.S. (7 Pet.) 1, 14 (1833). 1820 statute: 3 Stat. 567, sec 6 (May 1, 1820). Report by Secretary of the Navy: U.S. Congress, *American State Papers,* Class VI, Naval Affairs, Vol. II, p. 101. Gilmer Committee: House Report No. 741, 27th Cong., 2d Sess., pp. 17–18 (May 23, 1842). Unauthorized commitments of postal revenue funds in the 1830s are discussed in Leonard D. White, *The Jacksonians* (New York: Macmillan, 1954), pp. 265–266, and Senate Report No. 422, 23d Cong., 1st Sess. (June 9, 1834). Unauthorized commitments of custom revenue funds are criticized in House Report No. 756, 27th Cong., 2d Sess., p. 6 (May 25, 1842).

Cambodia and the C-5A. Contemporary regulations on unauthorized commitments: 31 U.S.C. §665(a). Secretary Rogers' explanation of Cambodian commitment: *Supplemental Foreign Assistance Authorization, 1970,* hearings before the Senate Foreign Relations Committee, 91st Cong., 2d Sess., p. 27 (1970). In an interview with a Washington reporter, the Cambodian foreign minister said that he felt there was an unwritten treaty between the two countries: "I am convinced that there really is a moral obligation of the United States to help. We are confident that the United States will continue to help us." *The Sunday Star,* May 23, 1971, A-5; interview with Henry Bradsher. With regard to the C-5A cost overrun, the 1958 statute is 72 Stat. 972 (Aug. 28, 1958); 50 U.S.C. §1433. The Defense Department contended that enactment of the law "would cause no apparent increase in the budgetary requirement of the Department of Defense," but no such restriction appeared in the act; House Report No. 2232, 85th Cong., 2d Sess., p. 2 (July 18, 1958). For Truman's proclamation, see *Public Papers of the Presidents, 1950,* p. 756.

5. TAXING POWERS

Tariff Powers

General studies on U.S. tariff policy include: John Dean Goss, "The History of Tariff Administration in the United States from Colonial Times to the McKinley Administrative Bill," *Studies in History, Economics and Public Law,* Columbia University, Vol. I, No. 2 (1891); F. W. Taussig, *The Tariff History of the United States,* 8th rev. ed. (New York: G. P. Putnam's, 1931); Percy W. Bidwell, *Tariff Policy of the United States* (New York, 1933); U.S. Tariff Commission, *The Tar-*

iff and Its History (Washington, D.C.: Government Printing Office, 1934); Lawrence H. Chamberlain, *The President, Congress and Legislation* (New York: Columbia University Press, 1946), ch. III; Joe R. Wilkinson, *Politics and Trade Policy* (Washington, D.C.: Public Affairs Press, 1960); Raymond A. Bauer, Ithiel de Sola Pool, and Lewis Anthony Dexter, *American Business and Public Policy: The Politics of Foreign Trade* (New York: Atherton Press, 1963); William B. Kelly, Jr., ed., *Studies in United States Commercial Policy* (Chapel Hill: University of North Carolina Press, 1963); Paul H. Douglas, *America in the Market Place: Trade, Tariffs and the Balance of Payments* (New York: Holt, Rinehart and Winston, 1966); and Bela Balassa, *Trade Liberalization Among Industrial Countries* (New York: McGraw-Hill, 1967).

Woodrow Wilson's idea of two price tags: Woodrow Wilson, *The New Freedom*, ed. William Bayard Hale (New York: Doubleday, Page, 1918), pp. 150–160. Customs revenue figures from 1837 to 1916 come from Seymour Harris, "Fiscal Policy," *American Economic History*, ed. Seymour Harris (New York: McGraw-Hill, 1961, p. 134.

Development of Protective Tariff. Washington address to Congress: Richardson, *Messages and Papers,* I, 57 (Jan. 8, 1790); tariff act of 1789: 1 Stat. 24 (July 4, 1789). Hamilton's Report on Manufactures: Alexander Hamilton, *Papers on Public Credit, Commerce, and Finance,* Samuel McKee, Jr., ed. (Indianapolis: Bobbs-Merrill, 1957), p. 234. Trade acts passed in 1815, 1823, and 1824: 3 Stat. 224 (March 3, 1815); 3 Stat. 740, sec. 3 (March 1, 1823); 4 Stat. 2, sec. 4 (Jan. 7, 1824). Presidents from J. Q. Adams to Hayes who issued proclamations under the 1824 act, as amended: Adams: 4 Stat. 815; Jackson: 4 Stat. 814, 816; 11 Stat. 781, 782; Polk: 9 Stat. 1001; Fillmore: 9 Stat. 1004; Buchanan: 11 Stat. 795; Lincoln: 13 Stat. 739; Johnson: 14 Stat. 818, 819; Grant: 16 Stat. 1127, 1130, 1137; 17 Stat. 954, 956, 957; Hayes: 21 Stat. 800.

Tariff Act of 1890: 26 Stat. 612, sec. 3; *Field* v. *Clark,* 143 U.S. 649, 656–9, 691 (1892). In time of war, American military commanders have collected duties without legislative authority. During the Mexican war, military commanders established a customhouse at Tampico and collected duties. The Supreme Court, in *Fleming* v. *Page,* 9 How. 603, 616 (1850), upheld the action, admitting that duties were exacted not as prescribed by law but rather by the President in his capacity as commander in chief. During the war with Spain in 1898, American military commanders occupied Puerto Rico and continued to collect duties on imports from the United States. Although no legislative authority justified their actions, the Supreme Court declared that "the laws of war" authorized this taking of revenue: "The government must be carried on, and there was no one left to administer [Puerto Rico's] functions but the military forces of the United States. Money is requisite for that purpose, and money could only be raised by order of the military commander." *Dooley* v. *United States,* 182 U.S. 222, 230 (1901).

Dingley Tariff Act of 1897: 30 Stat. 151; for Section 4 actions, see Harold U. Faulkner, *The Decline of Laissez Faire, 1897–1917* [volume VII of *The Economic History of the United States*] (New York: Rinehart, 1951), p. 65. Republican platform of 1908: Kirk H. Porter and Donald Bruce Johnson, comp., *National Party Platforms, 1840–1968* (Urbana, University of Illinois Press, 1970), p. 158. Payne-Aldrich Tariff Act of 1909: 36 Stat. 82, sec. 2 (Aug. 5, 1909); Taft's recommendation of permanent tariff commission: Israel, *State of the Union Messages*, III, 2389 (Dec. 6, 1910). Democrats regarding tariff board as "an impudent attempt . . .": Philip G. Wright, *Tariff-Making by Commission* (Washington, D.C.: The Rawleigh Tariff Bureau, 1930), p. 9.

Flexible Tariffs. Taft saying "Flat tariffs are out of date": Israel, *State of the Union Messages,* III, 2461, 2497. Arthur S. Link, *Woodrow Wilson and the Progressive Era, 1900–1917* (New York: Harper & Row, 1954), p. 42; 50 Cong. Rec. 1802–1817 (May 29, 1913). Further discussion on the Underwood Tariff Act of 1913: Arthur S. Link, *Woodrow Wilson and the Progressive Era,* pp. 35–43, and Arthur S. Link, *Wilson: The New Freedom* (Princeton: Princeton University Press, 1956), pp. 177–197. Wilson warning against a revival of protectionist legislation: Israel, *State of the Union Messages,* III, 2600.

Republican Platform of 1920: Porter and Johnson, *National Party Platforms,* p. 230. For an evaluation of Section 317 of the Fordney-McCumber Tariff Act of 1922, empowering the President to place additional duties on products from countries that discriminated against the U.S., see Wallace McClure, "A New American Commercial Policy," *Studies in History, Economics and Public Law,* Columbia University, Vol. CXIV, No. 2 (1924). Senator McCumber, telling colleagues that it was the "very worst time" to formulate a tariff measure: 62 Cong. Rec. 5763 (April 20, 1922). McCumber claiming tariff provision was temporary: 62 Cong. Rec. 11155 (Aug. 10, 1922). *Hampton & Co.* v. *United States,* 276 U.S. 394, 395–400, 407 (1928). Additional court decisions on Presidential tariff actions: Glendon A. Schubert, Jr., *The Presidency in the Courts* (Minneapolis: University of Minnesota Press, 1957), ch. 5.

"Scientific" Tariff-Making. Philip G. Wright, *Tariff-Making by Commission,* pp. 17–29; see also Catherine Hackett, "The Failure of the Flexible Tariff: 1922–1927," *The New Republic,* Vol. LI, No. 660, pp. 244–247 (July 27, 1927); E. Pendleton Herring, "The Political Context of the Tariff Commission," 49 *Pol. Sci. Q.* 421 (Sept. 1934); and *The New York Times,* Dec. 30, 1925, 1:3, and March 25, 1926, 10:1. Senator Smoot's prediction: 62 Cong. Rec. 11192–3 (Aug. 10, 1922). For tariff rate adjustments by Presidents Harding, Coolidge, and Hoover, see J. Marshall Gerstling, *The Flexible Provisions in the United States Tariff, 1922–1930* (Philadelphia, 1932), pp. 173, 184–5.

Senators objecting to flexible tariff formula: *Tariff Bill: Views of the Minority,* Senate Report No. 595, Part 2, 67th Cong., 2d Sess., p. 7 (April 20, 1922). Study by Tariff Commission on butter: Philip G. Wright, *Tariff-Making by Commission,* p. 32. Other critiques on cost-of-production formula: F. W. Taussig, *Free Trade, the Tariff and Reciprocity* (New York: Macmillan, 1920), ch. VII; Thomas Walker Page, *Making the Tariff in the United States* (New York: McGraw-Hill, 1924), pp. 73–99; John Lee Coulter, "The Tariff Commission and the Flexible Clause," *Proceedings of the Academy of Political Science*, Vol. XV, No. 3 (June 1933), pp. 42–47; and John Day Larkin, *The President's Control of the Tariff* (Cambridge: Harvard University Press, 1936), pp. 103–150.

Hoover's request for limited revision of tariff structure in April 1929: 71 Cong. Rec. 42 (April 16, 1929); see his *Memoirs*, II, 293. Criticism of Smoot-Hawley by Senator La Follette and others: 72 Cong. Rec. 5976–7 (March 24, 1930). E. E. Schattschneider, *Politics, Pressures and the Tariff* (New York: Prentice-Hall, 1935), p. 13; additional material on the 1930 tariff act, including extensive references, can be found in Harris Gaylord Warren, *Herbert Hoover and the Great Depression* (New York: Oxford University Press, 1959), ch. 7.

Reciprocal Trade Agreements. Roosevelt's first Inaugural Address: *Public Papers*, II, 14 (March 4, 1933). Section 3(e) of the NIRA: 48 Stat. 196–197 (June 16, 1933). Section 15(e) of the AAA: 48 Stat. 40 (May 12, 1933). Roosevelt's interest in tariff cuts in April 1933: Herbert Feis, *1933: Characters in Crisis* (Boston: Little, Brown, 1966), p. 112. Fireside chat of May 7 and appeal on May 16: Roosevelt, *Public Papers*, II, 167, 186. Background on "The Economics of Nationalism" is provided by Arthur M. Schlesinger, Jr., *The Coming of the New Deal* (Boston: Houghton Mifflin, 1959), ch. 11–15. Roosevelt's message to the London Conference: Roosevelt, *Public Papers*, II, 264. An insider's account of the Conference appears in Feis, *1933*, pp. 169–258. Roosevelt's equivocation on world trade during 1933–34 period is covered by Henry J. Tasca, *The Reciprocal Trade Policy of the United States* (Philadelphia: University of Pennsylvania Press, 1938), pp. 16–28.

Creation of Export-Import Bank: Roosevelt, *Public Papers*, III, 76. Representative Hill on flexible tariffs: 78 Cong. Rec. 5514 (March 27, 1934). Roosevelt's request for reciprocal trade authority: Roosevelt, *Public Papers*, III, 113–115; reciprocal trade act of 1934: 48 Stat. 943. Presidential actions from 1934 to 1940: Grace Beckett, *The Reciprocal Trade Agreements Program* (New York: Columbia University Press, 1941), Appendix IV, p. 24; see also Lloyd C. Gardner, *Economic Aspects of New Deal Diplomacy* (Madison: University of Wisconsin Press, 1964), pp. 3–46. Lend-Lease agreements: *Documents on American Foreign Relations*, IV, 237, and Julius Pratt, *Cordell Hull*, Vol. XII, pp. 134–137, of *The American Secretaries of State and Their Diplomacy*, Robert W. Ferrell, ed. (New York: Cooper Square Publishers, 1964); see the entire Chapter 5 of Volume XII for Pratt's treatment of "The Trade Agreements Program."

Reference to 1954 President's Commission on Foreign Economic

Policy is from Harry Magdoff, *The Age of Imperialism: The Economics of U.S. Foreign Policy* (New York: Modern Reader Paperbacks, 1969), pp. 49–50, but see entire section from pages 45 to 54; see also Percy W. Bidwell, *Raw Materials: A Study of American Policy* (New York: Harper & Bros., 1958). Voting figures for Table 3 are taken from *Congressional Quarterly Almanacs*. Figures from 1934 through 1949 come from *Volume 7–1951*, p. 215; 1951 figures for the Senate are on page 259; for 1953: *Volume IX*, p. 252; for 1954: *Volume X*, pp. 292, 296; for 1955: *Volume XI*, pp. 123, 138; for 1958: *Volume XIV*, pp. 388, 448. See Richard A. Watson, "The Tariff Revolution: A Study of Shifting Party Attitudes," 18 *J. Pol.* 678 (Nov. 1956).

Multilateral Bargaining. Background on GATT: Gerard Curzon, *Multilateral Commercial Diplomacy* (London: Michael Joseph Ltd., 1965). Statistics for Table 4 come from *Historical Statistics of the United States: Colonial Times to 1957* (Government Printing Office, 1960), p. 539; *Historical Statistics of the United States: Continuation to 1962 and Revisions* (Government Printing Office, 1965), p. 75. Legislative restrictions on President's bargaining authority, from 1948 to 1958: 62 Stat. 1053, sec. 3(a) (June 26, 1948); 63 Stat. 697 (Sept. 26, 1949); 65 Stat. 72, sec. 6 (June 16, 1951); 69 Stat. 162, sec. 7 (June 21, 1955); 72 Stat. 673 (Aug. 20, 1958). Background on U.S. escape clauses, going back to 1935, is covered by S. M. Finger, "The Escape Clause in U.S. Commercial Practice: Its Impact on International Economic Relations," 6 *Public Policy* 265 (1955).

The Kennedy Round. Kennedy to Congress: *Public Papers of the Presidents, 1962*, p. 68 (Jan. 25, 1962). His addresses in May and July, 1962: *ibid.*, pp. 409, 537. Trade Expansion Act of 1962: 76 Stat. 872 (Oct. 11, 1962); see Stanley D. Metzger, "The Trade Expansion Act of 1962," 51 *Geo. L. J.* 425 (Spring 1963) and his *Trade Agreements and the Kennedy Round* (Fairfax, Va.: Coiner Publications, 1964). Accomplishments of the Kennedy Round are evaluated in U.S. Tariff Commission, *Operation of the Trade Agreements Program*, TC Publication 287 (1969), pp. 236–263. For analyses of the Kennedy Round see John W. Evans, *U.S. Trade Policy* (New York: Harper & Row, 1967); Ernest H. Preeg, *Traders and Diplomats* (Washington, D.C.: The Brookings Institution, 1970); and Thomas B. Curtis and John Robert Vastine, Jr., *The Kennedy Round and the Future of American Trade* (New York: Praeger Publishers, 1971).

If doctoral dissertations are any indication, we can expect a number of new articles and books on Presidential tariff powers; see Diane Monson, *Interests and Tariff Policy: A Case Study of the Trade Expansion Act of 1962* (Ph.D. dissertation, New York University, 1963); Robert Wesley Barrie, *Congress and the Executive: The Making of U.S. Foreign Trade Policy* (Ph.D. dissertation, University of Minnesota, 1968); and Graeme William Starr, *The Politics of the U.S. Trade Expansion Program, 1962–1969* (Ph.D. dissertation, West Virginia University, 1969). The latter argues that protectionist trends were evident in the politics of the Trade Expansion Act.

Nontariff Barriers. The figure of 276 nontariff barriers comes from Donald R. Wilson, "Nontariff Barriers to International Trade: A Survey of Current Problems," 18 *J. Public Law* 403, 404 (1969), but see also Craig Mathews, "Non-Tariff Import Restrictions: Remedies Available in United States Law," 62 *Mich. L. Rev.* 1295 (June 1964); Mark S. Masses, "Non-Tariff Barriers as an Obstacle to World Trade," Reprint 97 (Washington, D.C.: The Brookings Institution, 1965); William B. Kelly, Jr., "Nontariff Barriers," in *Studies in Trade Liberalization*, ed. Bela Balassa (Baltimore: Johns Hopkins Press, 1957), pp. 265–314; and Committee for Economic Development, *Nontariff Distortions of Trade* (Sept. 1969).

Presidents Johnson and Nixon urging repeal of the ASP system: *Public Papers of the Presidents, 1968–69,* I, 649 (May 28, 1968) and *Public Papers of the Presidents, 1969,* 942 (Nov. 18, 1969). Labor's position toward foreign subsidiaries and multinationals is contained in testimony by Andrew A. Biemiller, Director, Department of Legislation, AFL-CIO, *Tariff and Trade Proposals* (Part 4), hearings before the House Ways and Means Committee, 91st Cong., 2d sess., pp. 1001–1015 (May 19, 1970). President Nixon's pledge of support to the textile industry: *Nixon on the Issues* (New York: Nixon-Agnew Campaign Committee, 1968), p. 135. Nixon denouncing voluntary textile quota agreement: *Wkly Comp. Pres. Doc.,* Vol. 7, No. 11, pp. 466–467 (March 11, 1971); see editorial column by James J. Kilpatrick, Washington *Sunday Star,* March 28, 1971, reprinted at 117 Cong. Rec. S4491 (daily ed., April 1, 1971). Mills' role in establishing voluntary curb on Italian shoes exports: *The Washington Post,* July 13, 1971, A1, and *The Evening Star,* July 21, 1971, A-9. Surcharge in August 1971: *Wkly Comp. Pres. Doc.,* Vol. 7, No. 34, p. 1174 (Aug. 15, 1971). On October 15, 1971, the Japanese government entered into a three-year pact with the United States to limit its shipment of textiles and apparel to the American market.

Confrontation between President Nixon and Bethlehem Steel: *The Washington Post,* Jan. 13, 1971, 1:1. Farm product quotas discussed in U.S. Department of Agriculture, Foreign Agricultural Service, *Import Controls Under Section 22 of the Agricultural Adjustment Act, As Amended* (Oct. 1969). The International Coffee Agreement Act was extended on January 12, 1971: 84 Stat. 2077. Meat import quotas: 78 Stat. 594 (Aug. 22, 1964); regarding Nixon's proclamation, increasing meat quota, see *Wkly Comp. Pres. Doc.,* Vol. 6, No. 27, p. 857 (June 30, 1970). Sugar quotas: 74 Stat. 330 (July 6, 1960); Eisenhower's action: *Public Papers of the Presidents, 1960–61,* p. 562 (July 6, 1960); and 77 Stat. 386 (Dec. 16, 1963); see also U.S. Department of Agriculture, Agricultural Stabilization and Conservation Service, *The United States Sugar Program,* p. 4 (Dec. 1966). Background on oil quotas:

Congressional Quarterly, Inc., *Congress and the Nation, 1945–1964*, pp. 976–977, and *Congressional Quarterly Almanac, 1970*, pp. 895–899. Nixon's action on his Cabinet Task Force on Oil Imports: *Wkly Comp. Pres. Doc.*, Vol. 6, No. 8, p. 247 (Feb. 20, 1970). Regarding administrative actions to relieve the pressure of import competition on domestic industries, see article by Frank V. Fowlkes, *National Journal*, Vol. 3, No. 30, pp. 1544–1550 (July 24, 1971).

Standby Tax Controls

Kennedy's determination expressed in *The New York Times*, Dec. 24, 1960, 5:1. Background information on his economic policies: Edwin Kuh, "Economic Problems of the Kennedy Administration," 32 *Pol. Q.* 183 (1962); Seymour E. Harris, *Economics of the Kennedy Years* (New York: Harper & Row, 1964); Bernard Nossiter, *The Mythmakers: An Essay on Power & Wealth* (Boston: Houghton Mifflin, 1964); Edward S. Flash, Jr., *Economic Advice and Presidential Leadership* (New York: Columbia University Press, 1965); E. Ray Canterbury, *Economics on a New Frontier* (Belmont, Calif.: Wadsworth, 1968); and Jim F. Heath, *John F. Kennedy and the Business Community* (Chicago: University of Chicago Press, 1969).

Employment Act of 1946. John Maynard Keynes, *General Theory of Employment, Interest, and Money* (New York: Harcourt, Brace, 1936), pp. 9, 380. William H. Beveridge, *Full Employment in a Free Society* (New York: W. W. Norton, 1945), pp. 15, 20; for other differences with Keynes, see pp. 23, 26. Economic Bill of Rights: *Public Papers and Addresses of Franklin D. Roosevelt*, 1944–45 Volume, p. 41 (Jan. 11, 1944). Text of the Full Employment Bill of 1945 and its eventual transformation into the Employment Act of 1946 (60 Stat. 23): Stephen Kemp Bailey, *Congress Makes a Law* (New York: Columbia University Press, 1950), Ch. 7. A superb account of full-employment policies from Herbert Hoover to Lyndon Johnson is provided by Herbert Stein, *The Fiscal Revolution in America* (Chicago: University of Chicago Press, 1969). A recent description of the technical and institutional considerations of tax policy appears in Lawrence C. Pierce, *The Politics of Fiscal Policy Formation* (Pacific Palisades, Calif.: Goodyear Publishing Co., 1971).

Truman's interpretation of the Employment Act: 1953 *Economic Report*, p. 8; 1947 *Economic Report* (July), p. 37; and 1950 *Economic Report* (Jan.), p. 99. Eisenhower emphasizing the promotion of free enterprise: 1958 *Economic Report*, p. 5; describing 1953–54 recovery: Dwight D. Eisenhower, *Mandate for Change, 1953–1956* (Garden City, N.Y.: Doubleday, 1963), p. 486; see also 1954 *Economic Report*, pp. 111–114; 1955 *Economic Report*, pp. 1–6; 1957 *Economic Report*, pp. 1–3; and 1961 *Economic Report*, p. 54.

Truman emphasizing balanced economy over balanced budget:

1949 *Economic Report* (Jan.), CEA Report, p. 38; and 1949 *Economic Report* (July), p. 8. Truman advocating tax adjustments: 1948 *Economic Report* (Jan.), p. 10. Eisenhower did not adhere rigidly to the concept of a balanced budget. For instance, a balanced budget did not necessarily override all other goals during a recession (Wilfred Lewis, *Federal Fiscal Policy in the Postwar Recessions*, Washington, D.C., The Brookings Institution, 1962, p. 146), nor should it take priority over national security or essential government programs (Robert J. Donovan, *Eisenhower: The Inside Story*, New York, Harper & Bros., 1956, p. 353). Moreover, the use of a budget surplus in time of prosperity, in order to reduce the public debt, would "signify with unmistakable clarity that our democracy is capable of self-discipline" (1956 *Economic Report*, p. v). Yet a balanced budget was generally emphasized; *e.g.*, 1959 *Economic Report*, p. vi. Eisenhower disapproving of tax adjustments as countercyclical device: 1959 *Economic Report*, p. iv; 1961 *Economic Report*, pp. 59–60.

Other comparisons between the Truman and Eisenhower Administrations in executing the Employment Act of 1946: Flash, *Economic Advice and Presidential Leadership;* Edwin G. Nourse, *Economics in the Public Service: Administrative Aspects of the Employment Act* (New York: Harcourt, Brace, 1953); Corrine Silverman, "The President's Economic Advisers," Inter-University Case Program #48 (Indianapolis: Bobbs-Merrill, 1959); Paul S. Strayer *et al*, "Stabilizing the Economy—the Employment Act of 1946 in Operation," 40 *Am. Econ. Rev.* 144 (1950); Warren Cikins, "The Council of Economic Advisers: Political Economy at the Crossroads," 4 *Public Policy* 94 (1953); Ronald C. Hood, "Reorganizing the Council of Economic Advisers," 69 *Pol. Sci. Q.* 413 (Sept. 1954); Onofre Dizon Corpus, "The Role of the President's Economic Adviser(s)," 6 *Public Policy* 209 (1955); and Reuben E. Slesinger, ed., *National Economic Policy: The Presidential Reports* (Princeton: D. Van Nostrand, 1968).

Countercyclical Record, 1945–1960. Decline in real GNP during recessions: Lewis, *Federal Fiscal Policy in the Postwar Recessions*, p. 4; length of recovery period: Geoffrey H. Moore and Julius Shiskin, *Indicators of Business Expansions and Contractions* (New York: National Bureau of Economic Research, 1967), p. 113. Wilfred Lewis (pp. 277ff) arrived at an estimate of $109 billion by making interpolations between the prerecession peak and the final quarter of recovery. That measured the loss produced by the dips in the economy, but the economy itself was operating below its full employment potential. Thus, onto the four recession dips, Howard Pack added the layer of gross national product that corresponded to underemployment and arrived at a figure of $156 billion; *Formula Flexibility: A Quantitative Appraisal* (Ph.D. dissertation, Massachusetts Institute of Technology, 1964), pp. 1–6. In various estimates Walter Heller put the postwar loss of output as high as $200 billion or more: *Public Works Acceleration*, hearings before the Senate Committee on Public Works, 87th Cong., 2d Sess., p. 101 (1962), and *January 1962 Economic Report of the President,* hearings before the Joint Economic Committee, 87th Cong., 2d Sess., p. 3 (1962).

Recession of 1948–49: H. A. Holmans, *United States Fiscal Policy, 1945–1959* (New York: Oxford University Press, 1961), p. 100. Recession of 1953–54: Paul A. Samuelson, "The Economic of Eisenhower: A Symposium," Part III, 38 *Rev. Econ. & Stat.* 371, 372 (1956); see also Edwin L. Dale, Jr., *Conservatives in Power: A Study in Frustration* (New York: Doubleday, 1960), pp. 139–140. With regard to 1957–58 recession, see Lewis, *Federal Fiscal Policy in the Postwar Recessions,* pp. 188ff and 233; Richard E. Neustadt, *Presidential Power* (New York: John Wiley, 1960), pp. 107ff; and Holmans, *United States Fiscal Policy, 1945–1959,* pp. 259ff.

Kennedy Standby Proposals. Heller revealing preference: *The New York Times,* Dec. 24, 1960, 5:1. Kennedy's reference to repairing roof while sun shines: *Public Papers of the Presidents, 1962,* p. 6. Standby proposals described in 1962 *Economic Report,* pp. 18ff. Kennedy characterizing standby proposals as greatest steps forward in stabilization policy since Employment Act: *Public Papers of the Presidents, 1962,* p. 43. Reuss: Joint Economic Committee, *1962 Joint Economic Report,* 87th Cong., 2d Sess., p. 112. McCracken: *U.S. News & World Report,* June 18, 1962, p. 69.

Douglas-Bolling bill: S. 2913, H.R. 7766, 83d Cong., 2d Sess. (Feb. 8, 1954). Stand-by Anti-Recession Act of 1960: S. 3471, 86th Cong., 2d Sess. (May 3, 1960); Senators Joseph S. Clark, Eugene J. McCarthy, Pat McNamara, Jennings Randolph, Vance Hartke, and Gale W. McGee. Kennedy's letter to Clark: *The New York Times,* Aug. 23, 1961, 29:1; address to AFL-CIO: *Public Papers of the Presidents, 1961,* p. 790.

Alvin Hansen, *Economic Policy and Full Employment* (New York: McGraw-Hill, 1947), p. 141; Albert G. Hart, *Money, Debt, and Economic Activity* (Englewood Cliffs, N.J.: Prentice-Hall, 1948), pp. 490ff; see also Walter P. Egle, *Economic Stabilization* (Princeton: Princeton University Press, 1952), pp. 177ff. Patman bill: H.R. 12360, 86th Cong., 2d Sess. (May 24, 1960); Udall bills: H.R. 9813 and 9814, 87th Cong., 2d Sess. (Jan. 22, 1962). Joint Economic Committee, *Employment, Growth, and Price Levels,* 86th Cong., 2d Sess., p. 21 (Jan. 26, 1960), and also *1961 Joint Economic Report,* p. 31. Samuelson Task Force proposal cited in *U.S. News & World Report,* Jan. 16, 1961, p. 87.

Commission on Money and Credit, *Money and Credit: Their Influence on Jobs, Prices, and Growth* (Englewood Cliffs, N.J.: Prentice-Hall, 1961), pp. 136–137. Wallich-Balassa article: "New Look at Money and Credit," 39 *Harv. Bus. Rev.* 70, 72 (Nov.–Dec. 1961). Commission considering tax discretion necessary adjunct of Employment Act: *Money and Credit: Their Influence on Jobs, Prices, and Growth,* p. 136. Wilde, Nathan, and Samuelson: *Review of Report of the Commis-*

sion on Money and Credit, hearings before the Joint Economic Committee, 87th Cong., 1st Sess., pp. 11, 167, 449 (1961). Testimony by Gurley, Musgrave, and Hansen: *January 1962 Economic Report of the President*, hearings before the Joint Economic Committee, 87th Cong., 2d Sess., pp. 460, 461, 615; McCracken and Pechman: *State of the Economy and Policies for Full Employment*, hearings before the Joint Economic Committee, 87th Cong., 2d Sess., pp. 207, 220 (1962).

Congressional Response. Curtis: *State of the Economy and Policies for Full Employment*, hearings before the Joint Economic Committee, 87th Cong., 2d Sess., p. 226 (1962). Mills: *The New York Times*, Jan. 12, 1962, 13:7-8; Heller: *January 1962 Economic Report of the President*, hearings before the Joint Economic Committee, 87th Cong., 2d Sess., p. 28. Kennedy denying that Congress would be delegating tax power: *Public Papers of the Presidents, 1962*, p. 371. Ways and Means entry in calendar: House Committee on Ways and Means, *Final Calendar*, 87th Cong., p. 10 (Jan. 3, 1963). Byrd: *The New York Times*, Jan. 12, 1962, 14:1; Keating: *The New York Times*, Feb. 7, 1962, 49:6; Minority Views: *1962 Joint Economic Report*, pp. 129-130. Eisenhower: "Are We Headed in the Wrong Direction?," *Sat. Eve. Post*, Aug. 11, 1962, pp. 19-22, and *The New York Times*, Sept. 23, 1962, 66:5, and Oct. 11, 1962, 34:3-5.

1963 *Economic Report*, p. xxi. Smathers to Heller: *Revenue Act of 1963* (Part 4), hearings before the Senate Committee on Finance, 88th Cong., 1st Sess., p. 1601 (1963). 1964 *Economic Report*, p. 41; 1965 *Economic Report*, p. 11; 1966 *Economic Report*, p. 18. Bach *et al* in *Fiscal Policy Issues of the Coming Decade*, hearings before the Joint Economic Committee, 89th Cong., 1st Sess., pp. 7, 44, 58, 140 (1965). Wallich: *Tax Changes for Shortrun Stabilization*, hearings before the Joint Economic Committee, 89th Cong., 2d Sess., p. 77 (1966); Wallich recommended this earlier in "Tout Comme Chez Nous," 44 *Rev. Econ. & Stat.* 11 (1962) and in *January 1962 Economic Report of the President*, hearings before the Joint Economic Committee, p. 621. Republic Party statement: press release by Senator Everett M. Dirksen, March 10, 1966. Nourse: *Twentieth Anniversary of the Employment Act of 1946: An Economic Symposium*, hearing before the Joint Economic Committee, 89th Cong., 2d Sess., p. 91 (1966), and Supplement to Hearing on *Twentieth Anniversary of the Employment Act of 1946: An Economic Symposium*, 89th Cong., 2d Sess., pp. 120ff (1966).

Prospects for Standby Tax Powers. Shoup: *Review of Report of the Commission on Money and Credit*, hearings before the Joint Economic Committee, 87th Cong., 1st Sess., p. 180 (1961). Joint Economic Committee report: *Tax Changes for Shortrun Stabilization*, 89th Cong., 2d Sess., p. 16 (May 27, 1966). See Howard Pack, *Formula Flexibility: A Quantitative Appraisal* (Ph.D. dissertation, Massachusetts Institute of Technology, 1964), as well as his article under the same title in *Studies in Economic Stabilization*, ed. Albert Ando *et al* (Washington,

D.C.: The Brookings Institution, 1968), pp. 5–38. Peter W. Rodman discusses the merits of formula flexibility in "Tax Adjustments for Economic Stability and Growth: Proposals for Reform of the Legislative Process," 5 *Harv. J. on Leg.* 265, 287–289 (Jan. 1968).

Joseph W. Barr, former Under Secretary of the Treasury, rejected the inevitability of long time lags between Presidential requests and congressional action. "That theory is no longer valid," he said. "The Congress right now is demonstrating—as it did with the swift enactment of the excise tax legislation in 1965—that tax policy is an effective economic weapon which can be brought into play both responsibly and responsively without protracted delays" (press release, speech to the National League of Insured Savings Association, Feb. 22, 1966; see *The New York Times,* Feb. 23, 1966). Another high-ranking official in the Treasury Department, Assistant Secretary Stanley S. Surrey, pointed to the quick legislative action on the Tax Adjustment Act of 1966 and the attitudes expressed at the March 1966 hearings on short-run tax changes as evidence that there was little point in seeking Presidential tax discretion (press release, speech to the Tax Executive Institute, March 23, 1966). Phillip Michael Simpson, in *Macro-Economic Decision-Making: The 1964 and 1968 Revenue Acts* (Ph.D. dissertation, University of Arizona, 1971), proposes that a commission composed of representatives from the executive and legislative branches be empowered to alter tax rates for macro-economic manipulation, with the President and Congress having ultimate veto power over commission actions.

"Senator McCarthy Urges Responsive Fiscal, Monetary Program," press release, March 12, 1966. Moorhead bill: H.R. 16486, 89th Cong., 2d Sess. (July 25, 1966). Kennedy proposal: "A Program for a Sound Economy," press release, May 12, 1968. Johnson before the Business Council: *Wkly Comp. Pres. Doc.,* Vol. 4, No. 49, p. 1671 (Dec. 4, 1968); also, 1969 *Economic Report,* p. 13. *Fiscal and Monetary Policies for Steady Economic Growth* (Committee for Economic Development, Jan. 1969), p. 68.

In March 1969, Senator Jacob K. Javits recommended that the President be given authority to vary the rate of the surcharge from zero to 10 percent; 115 Cong. Rec. S2398 (daily ed., March 7, 1969). Joint Economic Committee, *1969 Joint Economic Report,* 91st Cong., 1st Cong., p. 102; Republican members are Senators Javits, Jordan, and Percy, and Representatives Widnall, Rumsfeld, Brock, and Conable; Senator Jack Miller expressed his opposition to Presidential tax discretion. Brooke bill: S. 3715, 91st Cong., 2d Sess. (April 14, 1970), discussed at 116 Cong. Rec. S5672 (daily ed., April 14, 1970). Disappointment in monetarism: *The Sunday Star,* Nov. 29, 1970, A1:6. I speculate on the possibility of Republicans supporting Presidential tax discretion in Louis Fisher, "Nixon at the Controls," *The New Leader,* Dec. 16, 1968.

6. PRESIDENTIAL WAR POWERS

General studies include the following: Howard White, "Executive Influence in Determining Military Policy in the United States," *University of Illinois Studies in the Social Sciences,* Vol. XII, Nos. 1–2 (March–June 1924); Clinton Rossiter, *Constitutional Dictatorship: Crisis Government in the Modern Democracies* (Princeton: Princeton University Press, 1948); *The Powers of the President as Commander in Chief of the Army and Navy of the United States,* House Document No. 443, 84th Cong., 2d Sess. (1956); Ernest R. May, ed., *The Ultimate Decision: The President as Commander in Chief* (New York: George Braziller, 1960); Sidney Warren, *The President as World Leader* (Philadelphia: J. B. Lippincott, 1964); and Merlo J. Pusey, *The Way We Go To War* (Boston: Houghton Mifflin, 1969).

Protecting Life and Property

Further details on life-and-property actions, hot pursuits, and limited wars can be found in *The Little Wars of the United States,* Colonel R. Ernest Dupuy and Major General William H. Baumer (New York: Hawthorn Books, 1968). *Durand* v. *Hollins,* 4 Blatch. 451, 454 (1860). Background information and description of the Greytown bombing: Milton Offutt, "The Protection of Citizens Abroad by the Armed Forces of the United States," *Johns Hopkins University Studies in Historical and Political Science,* Series XLIV, No. 4 (1928), pp. 32–34. James Grafton Rogers, *World Policing and the Constitution* (Boston: World Peace Foundation, 1945). Compilation by the Library of Congress: *Background Information on the Use of United States Armed Forces in Foreign Countries,* committee print prepared for the House Committee on Foreign Affairs, 91st Cong., 2d Sess., pp. 50–57 (1970).

The Roosevelt Corollary: Israel, *State of the Union Messages,* II, 2134. His tactics with Colombia: *ibid.,* II, 2101. Draft message to Congress on Colombia: see George E. Mowry, *The Era of Theodore Roosevelt and the Birth of Modern America, 1900–1912* (New York: Harper & Bros., 1958), p. 151. The Thompson-Urrutia Treaty, a treaty "for the Settlement of Differences Arising Out of the Events Which Took Place on the Isthmus of Panama in November, 1903," was ratified in 1922. The original version of the treaty contained an expression of "sincere regret" for the United States action in 1903; see Robert K. Murray, *The Harding Era: Warren G. Harding and His Administration* (Minneapolis: University of Minnesota Press, 1969), p. 340.

Roosevelt intervened in the Dominican Republic in 1904 to set up a fiscal protectorate, while Taft carried on the Roosevelt Corollary by intervening twice in Nicaragua and once each in Honduras and Cuba; Offutt, pp. 104, 107, 109, 111. Wilson's intervention in Tampico and occupation of Veracruz: Robert E. Quirk, *An Affair of Honor: Woodrow Wilson and the Occupation of Veracruz* (University of Kentucky Press, 1962). His doubts about legal authority to intervene in Haiti: Arthur S. Link, *Wilson: The Struggle for Neutrality, 1914–1915* (Princeton: Princeton University Press, 1960), p. 536. His intervention in Dominican Republic: *ibid.*, pp. 543–549. The Pershing Expedition: *ibid.*, pp. 233–234, 456, 467, 489–491; also, see Arthur S. Link, *Wilson: Confusion and Crises, 1915–1916* (Princeton: Princeton University Press, 1964), pp. 196–208, 216–217. Cuban intervention: *Foreign Relations of the United States, 1917* (Government Printing Office, 1926), pp. 350–456. Russian intervention: *Foreign Relations of the United States, 1918: Russia* (Government Printing Office, 1932), and William Appleman Williams, "American Intervention in Russia: 1917–1920," in *Containment and Revolution,* David Horowitz, ed. (Boston: Beacon Press, 1968), pp. 26–75.

Lebanon intervention in 1958: *Public Papers of the Presidents, 1958,* p. 549. Dominican intervention in 1965: *Public Papers of the Presidents, 1965,* II, p. 616. Nixon's explanation for intervening in Cambodia: *Wkly Comp. Pres. Doc.,* Vol. 6, No. 18, p. 597. State Department position on Laotian intervention: *The New York Times,* Feb. 9, 1971, 17:6.

Time Boundaries of "War Period" (1789–1945)

Bas v. *Tingy,* 4 U.S. (4 Dall.) 37, 40 (1800). *Talbot* v. *Seeman,* 1 Cr. 1, 8 (1801). Efforts have been made to suggest that executive war-making is essentially a 20th century phenomenon. For example, Albert H. Putney, "Executive Assumption of the War Making Power," 7 *Natl U. L. Rev.* 1 (May 1927). The record, however, shows otherwise.

Executive Prerogative. Locke, *Second Treatise,* Ch. XIV. Substitution of "declare" for "make" in Constitution: Farrand, *Records,* II, 318. *Little* v. *Barreme,* 6 U.S. (2 Cr.) 170 (1804). Jefferson to Congress: Richardson, *Messages and Papers,* I, 315 (Dec. 8, 1801). Jefferson's position on prerogative: *Writings,* IX, 279. Statutes in 1792 and 1795: 1 Stat. 264, 424. *Martin* v. *Mott,* 12 Wheat. 19, 30–32 (1827). See Charles C. Tansill, "War Powers of the President of the United States with Special Reference to the Beginning of Hostilities," 45 *Pol. Sci. Q.* 1 (1930).

Polk meeting with Cabinet on May 9: *The Diary of James K. Polk,* I, 384–386; notification to Congress on May 11: Richardson, *Messages and Papers,* V, 2287–2293; legislative action: 9 Stat. 9. Censure by House: *Cong. Globe,* 30th Cong., 1st Sess., p. 95 (1848). Lincoln writing to a friend: *The Works of Abraham Lincoln,* Arthur Brooks Lapsley, ed., Federal Edition (8 vols., New York: G. P. Putnam's Sons, 1905–1906), II, 51. His proclamations in April 1861: Richardson, *Messages and Papers*, VII, 3214–3220. *The Prize Cases*, 2 Black 635, 669 (1862). Congress empowering Lincoln to declare when insurrection existed: 12 Stat. 284 (July 31, 1861). *The Protector*, 12 Wall. 700, 702 (1872). Lincoln also issued a proclamation authorizing military trials of citizens in areas where civil courts still operated. In *Ex parte Vallandigham*, 1 Wall. 243 (1864), the Court refused to pass on the constitutionality of his order. Not until after the war was over, and Lincoln dead, did the Court dare challenge the President's war power. In *Ex parte Milligan*, 4 Wall. 2 (1866), it declared that Lincoln had overstepped his constitutional authority in trying civilians by military courts.

McKinley to Congress on April 11, 1898: Richardson, *Messages and Papers*, XIII, 6281–6292. Legislative action on April 20: 30 Stat. 738. Proclamations by McKinley: 30 Stat. 1769, 1770. Cable to Dewey: John D. Long, *The New American Navy* (2 vols., New York: The Outlook Co., 1903), I, 182. Declaration by Congress: 30 Stat. 364. *The Pedro*, 175 U.S. 354, 363 (1899). Opinion by Attorney General in 1914 regarding the closing down of the wireless station: 30 Op. A.G. 291 (1914). For Wilson and the arming of American merchant ships, see Joseph S. Clark, *Congress: The Sapless Branch* (New York: Harper & Row, 1964), pp. 97–98.

List by Attorney General in 1939: *Executive Powers Under National Emergency*, Senate Document No. 133, 76th Cong., 2d Sess. (Oct. 5, 1939). Destroyers-Bases deal: *Public Papers and Addresses of Franklin D. Roosevelt*, 1940 Volume, Vol. 9, p. 391; 39 Op. A.G. 484, 486 (1940). Other actions by Roosevelt in 1941: *Public Papers and Addresses of Franklin D. Roosevelt*, 1941 Volume, Vol. 10, p. 96 (agreement with Denmark), pp. 132–135 (extending naval patrol), p. 194 (unlimited national emergency), p. 255 (agreement with Iceland), p. 205 (seizing plant), p. 217 (freezing assets), pp. 390–391 (shoot-on-sight order). See Louis William Koenig, *The Presidency and the Crisis: Powers of the Office from the Invasion of Poland to Pearl Harbor* (New York: King's Crown Press, 1944).

Waging War. Polk's plans to acquire territory: *The Diary of James K. Polk*, I, 306–307, 396–397, 436–439, 443. His recommendation to Congress: Richardson, *Messages and Papers*, V, 2382–2395 (Dec. 7, 1847). Congress approving actions taken by Lincoln: 12 Stat. 326 (emphasis supplied in text). Delegating power over railroad and telegraph lines and over draft: 12 Stat. 334; 13 Stat. 6. Observation by Senator Spooner: Harold U. Faulkner, *Politics, Reform and Expansion: 1890–1900* (New York: Harper & Row, 1959), p. 234.

Powers delegated to Wilson: 40 Stat. 75 and 225; 286 and 548; 451 and 904; 550, 277, and 279; for other powers exercised by Wilson during World War I, see Clarence A. Berdahl, "War Powers of the Executive in the United States," *University of Illinois Studies in the Social Sciences*, Vol. 9, Nos. 1–2 (1920). Lend-Lease Act: 55 Stat. 37. *United States* v. *Bethlehem Steel*, 315 U.S. 289, 305 (1942). Mobilization authority: 56 Stat. 176; 57 Stat. 163. Emergency Price Control Act of 1942: 56 Stat. 23; *Bowles* v. *Willingham*, 321 U.S. 503, 515 (1944). Roosevelt's message to Congress on inflation control: 88 Cong. Rec. 7044 (Sept. 7, 1942). Inflation controls: 56 Stat. 765; *Yakus* v. *United States*, 321 U.S. 414, 425 (1944). *Lichter* v. *United States*, 334 U.S. 742, 785 (1947).

Demobilization Powers. Roosevelt's announcement in 1942: 88 Cong. Rec. 7044. Executive decrees issued to mark date of suppression of the Civil War: 13 Stat. 763; 14 Stat. 811, 814. *United States* v. *Anderson*, 9 Wall. 56 (1870); see also *The Protector*, 12 Wall. 700, 702 (1872). *Stewart* v. *Kahn*, 11 Wall. 493, 507 (1870). *Hijo* v. *United States*, 194 U.S. 315, 323 (1904). Wilson to Congress on need to retain wartime controls: Israel, *State of the Union Messages*, III, 2591–2592 (Dec. 2, 1918). 1918 act prohibiting liquor traffic: 40 Stat. 1046; *Hamilton* v. *Kentucky Distilleries*, 251 U.S. 146, 161 (1919). Joint resolution ending war on July 2, 1921: 42 Stat. 105. *Commercial Trust* v. *Miller*, 262 U.S. 51, 57 (1923). *Chastleton Corp.* v. *Sinclair*, 264 U.S. 533, 547–548 (1924); see also *United States* v. *Cohen Grocery Co.*, 255 U.S. 81, 88 (1921), where the Court held that "the mere existence of a state of war could not suspend or change the operation upon the power of Congress of the guaranties and limitations of the Fifth and Sixth Amendments as to questions such as we are here passing upon."

Truman seizing bituminous coal mines: E.O. 9728, 11 Fed. Reg. 5593 (May 21, 1946); War Labor Disputes Act: 57 Stat. 163. Proclamation of December 31, 1946: *Public Papers of the Presidents, 1946*, p. 513. The Attorney General had compiled a list of wartime statutes which expired on fixed dates, while others depended upon termination of hostilities, termination of the 1939 and 1941 emergency proclamations, and upon termination of the war; House Document No. 282, 79th Cong., 1st Sess., pp. 49–145 (Sept. 6, 1945). For opinion by Attorney General Tom Clark, regarding the President's power to decide when wartime legislation terminates, see 40 Op. A.G. 421 (Sept. 1, 1945). *Woods* v. *Miller*, 333 U.S. 138, 146 (1948). Repeal of certain powers on July 25, 1947: 61 Stat. 449; see also *Public Papers of the President, 1947*, p. 357; George M. Lhamon, "The War Power Extended," 17 *G.W. L. Rev.* 461 (June 1949); Notes, "Judicial Determination of the End of the War," 47 *Colum. L. Rev.* 255 (March 1947); *Termination of War Controls*, Senate Document No. 5, 80th Cong., 1st Sess. (Jan. 8, 1947); and Theodore French, "The End of the War," 14 *G.W. L. Rev.* 191 (Feb. 1947). Action by Truman on April 28, 1952: *Public Papers of the President, 1952–53*, p. 302.

War Powers, 1945–1971

"Defensive War." Senator Williams: 116 Cong. Rec. S8957 (daily ed., June 12, 1970). Legal memorandum on Korean intervention: *The Department of State Bulletin,* Vol. XXIII, July 31, 1950, p. 173; included in *Background Information on Korea,* House Report No. 2495, 81st Cong., 2d Sess., pp. 61–68 (July 11, 1950). Actions between June 25 and June 27: *United States Security Agreements and Commitments Abroad: Republic of Korea* (Part 6), hearings before the Senate Foreign Relations Committee, 91st Cong., 2d Sess., p. 1522 (1970). Truman's remark to Acheson: Glenn D. Paige, *The Korean Decision* (New York: The Free Press, 1968), p. 188. Dean Acheson, *Present at the Creation: My Years in the State Department* (New York: W. W. Norton, 1969), p. 408. United Nations Participation Act of 1945: 59 Stat. 621. See Arthur V. Watkins, "War By Executive Order," 4 *West. Pol. Q.* 539 (Dec. 1951).

Convenient background material on defense treaties is included in *Global Defense: U.S. Military Commitments Abroad* (Congressional Quarterly Service, Sept. 1969). Legal memorandum on Vietnam: *The Department of State Bulletin,* Vol. LIV, March 28, 1966, p. 485. A distinguished group of international lawyers issued a rebuttal to this memorandum; their statement appears in *The New York Times,* Jan. 15, 1967, p. E9, while the full text of their critique appears in *Vietnam and International Law,* John H. E. Fried, Rapporteur (Flanders, N.J.: O'Hare Books, 1967). See David W. Robertson, "The Debate Among American International Lawyers About the Vietnam War," 46 *Texas L. Rev.* 898 (July 1968); Richard A. Falk, "Law, Lawyers, and the Conduct of American Foreign Relations," 78 *Yale L. J.* 919 (May 1969); Stuart S. Malawer, "The Vietnam War Under the Constitution: Legal Issues Involved in the United States Military Involvement in Vietnam," 31 *U. Pittsburgh L. Rev.* 205 (Winter 1969).

Policy statements and communiqués on Philippines: *United States Security Agreements and Commitments Abroad: The Republic of the Philippines* (Part 1), hearings before the Senate Foreign Relations Committee, 91st Cong., 1st Sess., pp. 6–7 (1969). Warning on quasi-commitment nature of bases agreements elsewhere: *National Commitments,* Senate Report No. 129, 91st Cong., 1st Sess., p. 28 (April 16, 1969). Kennedy announcing troops to Thailand: *Public Papers of the Presidents, 1962,* p. 396 (May 15, 1962). His statement regarding missile sites in Cuba: *ibid.,* p. 485 (Oct. 22, 1962). Johnson maintaining that threat in Southeast Asia was threat to United States: *Public Papers of the Presidents, 1963–1964,* II, p. 931 (Aug. 5, 1964). Lausche: 110 Cong. Rec. 18084 (Aug. 5, 1964). Enlarged objectives in Korea: *The Department of State Bulletin,* Vol. XXIII, July 3, 1950, p. 5, and Martin Lichterman, "To the Yalu and Back," in *American Civil-Military*

Decisions, Harold Stein, ed. (Birmingham: University of Alabama Press, 1963).

U.S.-Thailand contingency plan: 115 Cong. Rec. S9503–9505 (daily ed., Aug. 8, 1969); 115 Cong. Rec. S14161 (daily ed., Nov. 12, 1969); *The New York Times,* Aug. 13, 1969, 4:4 and Aug. 21, 1969, 5:1. Military negotiations in Spain: articles by Flora Lewis and Warren Unna in *The Washington Post,* Feb. 25, 1969, both of which are reprinted at 115 Cong. Rec. S1898 (daily ed., Feb. 25, 1969). Symington Subcommittee hearings on Laotian involvement: *United States Security Agreements and Commitments Abroad: Kingdom of Laos* (Part 2), hearings before the Senate Foreign Relations Committee, 91st Cong., 1st Sess., pp. 433–434 (1969). See W. Taylor Reveley III, "Presidential War-Making: Constitutional Prerogative or Usurpation?," 55 *Va. L. Rev.* 1243 (1969), and Notes, "Congress, the President, and the Power to Commit Forces to Combat," 81 *Harv. L. Rev.* 1771 (1967–1968).

Legal Limits. C. & S. Airlines v. *Waterman Corp.,* 333 U.S. 103, 111 (1948). "Political questions" respecting boundaries [*Foster* v. *Neilson,* 2 Pet. 253 (1829) and *Williams* v. *Suffolk Insurance Co.,* 13 Pet. 415 (1839)], recognition [*Rose* v. *Himely,* 4 Cr. 241 (1808) and *Gelston* v. *Hoyt,* 3 Wheat. 246 (1818)], envoys [*Ex parte Hitz,* 111 U.S. 766 (1884)], and foreign agreements [*Doe* v. *Braden,* 16 How. 635 (1853)]. For an excellent treatment of the issue of national security versus individual freedoms, see Chapter 12 of David Fellman's *The Defendant's Rights* (New York: Rinehart & Co., 1958). *Baker* v. *Carr,* 369 U.S. 186, 211 (1962). *United States* v. *Robel,* 389 U.S. 258, 263–264 (1967). In *Kennedy* v. *Mendoza-Martinez,* 372 U.S. 144, 164–165 (1963), Justice Goldberg, writing for the Court, regarded it as "fundamental that the great powers of Congress to conduct war and to regulate the Nation's foreign relations are subject to the constitutional requirements of due process."

Ludecke v. *Watkins,* 335 U.S. 160 (1948). *Knauff* v. *Shaughnessy,* 338 U.S. 537, 551 (1950). Mrs. Knauff eventually allowed to enter country: Walter Gellhorn, *Individual Freedom and Governmental Restraints* (Baton Rouge: Louisiana State University Press, 1956), p. 36. *Shaughnessy* v. *Mezei,* 345 U.S. 206, 228 (1953); see Gellhorn, p. 37, for aftermath of Mezei case. Another case involving exclusion of aliens: *Harisiades* v. *Shaughnessy,* 342 U.S. 580 (1952). The loyalty cases discussed are as follows: *Peters* v. *Hobby,* 349 U.S. 331 (1955); *Cole* v. *Young,* 351 U.S. 536, 546 (1956); *Greene* v. *McElroy,* 360 U.S. 474 (1959). Other decisions in the 1950s in which the Court placed curbs on arbitrary administrative actions in dismissing so-called loyalty risks include *Service* v. *Dulles,* 354 U.S. 363 (1957) and *Vitarelli* v. *Seaton,* 359 U.S. 535 (1959).

Background information on the political use of passport refusal: Leonard B. Boudin, "The Constitutional Right to Travel," 56 *Colum. L. Rev.* 47, 60 (1956); Note, "'Passport Denied': State Department

Practice and Due Process," 3 *Stanford L. Rev.* 312 (1951); Note, "Passport Refusals for Political Reasons: Constitutional Issues and Judicial Review," 61 *Yale L. J.* 171 (1952). See also Leonard B. Boudin, "The Right to Travel," in *The Rights of Americans: What They Are—What They Should Be,* Norman Dorsen, ed. (New York: Pantheon Books, 1971), pp. 381–398. Cases discussed: *Kent* v. *Dulles,* 357 U.S. 116 (1958); *Aptheker* v. *Secretary of State,* 378 U.S. 500, 517 (1964); *United States* v. *Laub,* 385 U.S. 475 (1967); *Lynd* v. *Rusk,* 389 F. 2d 940 (1967). In *Zemel* v. *Rusk,* 381 U.S. 1 (1965), the Court upheld a statute authorizing the Secretary of State to refuse to validate the passports of U.S. citizens for travel to Cuba. In response to the charge that the statute lacked adequate standards for executive action, the Court called upon the *Curtiss-Wright* precedent to argue that the changeable nature of international relations made it necessary for Congress to "paint with a brush broader than that it customarily wields in domestic areas" (p. 17). When the State Department, acting on the basis of a 1926 statute, refused to renew an individual's passport on the grounds that he had lost his citizenship by voting in a foreign election, the Court held in *Afroyim* v. *Rusk,* 387 U.S. 253 (1967), that Congress had no power to divest a person of his citizenship unless he voluntarily renounces it. See Donald K. Duvall, "Expatriation Under United States Law. *Perez* to *Afroyim:* The Search for a Philosophy of American Citizenship," 56 *Va. L. Rev.* 408 (April 1970). On April 5, 1971, the Court upheld (5 to 4) the constitutionality of a Federal law that strips certain foreign-born American citizens if they fail to live in the United States for at least five years before their 28th birthdays; *Rogers* v. *Bellei,* 401 U.S. 815.

In 1967 the Court refused to review a case in which an individual, who maintained that the Vietnam war was in violation of various treaties signed by the United States, was sentenced to five years imprisonment for not reporting for induction; *Mitchell* v. *United States,* 386 U.S. 972 (1967). In another case that year, three Army privates sought to prevent the Army from transferring them to Vietnam, claiming that the American presence there had no legal standing. Again the Supreme Court refused to hear the case; *Mora* v. *McNamara,* 389 U.S. 934 (1967). The next year the Court declined to hear a case on the question of whether there could be conscription in the absence of a declaration of war; *Holmes* v. *United States,* 391 U.S. 936 (1968). Also in 1968, the Court rejected a hearing on the Government's right to send citizens abroad to fight a war which Congress had not declared; *McArthur* v. *Clifford,* 393 U.S. 1002 (1968). A group of 113 Army reservists from the Cleveland area later challenged the President's authority under a 1966 statute to call up reservists in the absence of a declaration of war or national emergency by Congress, contending that the law was an unconstitutional delegation of legislative power to the President. The Court refused to hear the case; *Morse* v. *Boswell,* 393

U.S. 1052 (1969). On November 9, 1970, the Court refused to hear a case from Massachusetts contesting the legality of the war; *Massachusetts* v. *Laird*, 400 U.S. 886 (1970). On October 12, 1971, in *Orlando* v. *Laird*, the Supreme Court let stand a lower court's ruling that the Vietnam war was constitutional in the sense that Congress had impliedly approved the war by adopting the Gulf of Tonkin Resolution, appropriating money to support the war, and approving successive draft bills.

Justice Douglas's remark is from *McArthur* v. *Clifford*, 393 U.S. 1002 (1968). For Justice Black's statement, see *New York Times Co.* v. *United States*, 29 L Ed 2d 822, 828 (June 30, 1971). A number of excellent articles have appeared recently on the Court's role in the Vietnam war: Lawrence R. Velvel, "The War in Viet Nam: Unconstitutional, Justiciable, and Jurisdictionally Attackable," 16 *U. Kans. L. Rev.* 449 (1968); Warren F. Schwartz and Wayne McCormack, "The Justiciability of Legal Objections to the American Military Effort in Vietnam," 46 *Texas L. Rev.* 1033 (Nov. 1968); Louis Henkin, "Forward: On Drawing Lines," 82 *Harv. L. Rev.* 63, 88–89 (1968–1969;; Louis Henkin, "Viet-Nam in the Courts of the United States: 'Political Questions'," 63 *Am. J. Int. Law* 284 (1969); Michael E. Tigar, "Judicial Power, the 'Political Question Doctrine,' and Foreign Relations," 17 *UCLA L. Rev.* 1135 (June 1970); and Leonard G. Ratner, "The Coordinated Warmaking Power—Legislative, Executive, and Judicial Roles," 44 *So. Cal. L. Rev.* 461 (Winter 1971). See also the Special Issue on *United States Intervention in Cambodia: Legal Analyses of the Event and its Domestic Repercussions*, 50 *B.U.L. Rev.* (Spring 1970).

7. CONGRESS AND THE WAR POWER

Most of the material in this chapter first appeared in Louis Fisher, "Congress and the War Power," a paper presented to the Center for the Study of Democratic Institutions, Santa Barbara, California, on July 28, 1971.

A number of studies and compilations questioning the scope of executive influence in foreign affairs have appeared in recent years. These include: *U.S. Commitments to Foreign Powers*, hearings before the Senate Foreign Relations Committee, 90th Cong., 1st Sess. (1967); *Resolved: That Executive Control of United States Foreign Policy Should be Significantly Curtailed*, A Collection of Excerpts and Bibliography Relating to the National Collegiate Debate Topic, 1968–1969, House Document No. 298, 90th Cong., 2d Sess. (1968); *The President's Powers in the Field of Foreign Policy—Should They Be Curtailed?*, College Debate Series (Washington, D.C.: American Enterprise Institute, Oct. 31, 1968); *What Should Be the United States Military Commitment to Foreign Countries?*, A Collection of Excerpts and Bibliography Relating to the National High School Debate Topic, 1969–1970, Senate Document No. 91–16, 91st Cong., 1st Sess. (1969); *Global Defense: U.S. Military Commitments Abroad* (Washington, D.C.: Congressional Quarterly Service, Sept. 1969); *Congress, the President, and the War Powers*, hearings before the House Committee on Foreign Affairs, 91st Cong., 2nd Sess. (1970); John C. Stennis, J. William Fulbright, *The Role of Congress in Foreign Policy* (Washington, D.C.: American Enterprise Institute, 1971).

Professor Corwin's phrase is from his article "The President's Power," *The New Republic* (Jan. 29, 1951). For Schlesinger's change from support of Presidential war powers to a critic, compare his letter to *The New York Times*, Jan. 9, 1951, with his remarks in *Congress and the Presidency: Their Role in Modern Times* (Washington, D.C.: American Enterprise Institute, 1967), p. 28. The latter contains his views expressed in 1966 during the Rational Debate Seminars. Compare Commager's article "Presidential Power: The Issue Analyzed," *New York Times Magazine*, Jan. 14, 1951, with his testimony before the Senate Committee on Foreign Relations, hearings on *Changing American Attitudes Toward Foreign Policy*, 90th Cong., 1st Sess., p. 21 (1967). For March 1969 conference, see "The Power of the Pentagon," *The Progressive* (June 1969), and *American Militarism: 1970*, ed. Erwin Knoll and Judith Nies McFadden (New York: The Viking Press, 1969). J. William Fulbright, "American Foreign Policy in the 20th Century Under an 18th-Century Constitution," 47 *Corn. L. Q.* 1, 2 (Fall 1961).

Executive Qualities Reexamined

Holbert N. Carroll, *The House of Representatives and Foreign Affairs* (Boston: Little, Brown, 1966), p. 20. Senator Clark: *U.S. Commitments to Foreign Powers*, hearings before the Senate Foreign Relations Committee, 90th Cong., 1st Sess., p. 105 (1967); reaction to President Nixon's June 1969 address: *The New York Times*, June 12, 1969, 1:7. Nixon to Saxbe: *Wkly Comp. Pres. Doc.*, Vol. 6, No. 14, p. 467 (April 1, 1970). Church: 116 Cong. Rec. S6333 (daily ed., April 30, 1970). Cook: 116 Cong. Rec. S7203 (daily ed., May 15, 1970).

"Unity." Samuel P. Huntington, "Strategic Planning and the Political Process," 38 *Foreign Affairs* 285, 291–2 (Jan. 1960). Arthur Maass, in studying how the Budget Bureau conferences resolved policy and legislative disputes, concluded that the conferences "avoid the basic issues and compromise, through a game of give and take . . ."; from his article "In Accord With the Program of the President?," 4 *Public Policy* 77, 81 (1953). For a recent criticism of fragmentation in foreign policy-making, see John Franklin Campbell, "What Is To Be Done?:

Gigantism in Washington," 49 *Foreign Affairs* 81 (Oct. 1970). The separation that exists between the White House and the executive departments is studied by Thomas E. Cronin, *" 'Everybody Believes in Democracy Until He Gets to the White House . . .': An Examination of White House-Departmental Relations,"* 35 *Law & Contemp. Prob.* 573 (Summer 1970).

Kissinger's remark is from *No More Vietnams?*, Richard M. Pfeffer, ed. (New York: Harper & Row, 1968), p. 11. Schultze testimony: *The Military Budget and National Economic Priorities* (Part 1), hearings before the Joint Economic Committee, 91st Cong., 1st Sess., p. 72 (1969). Regarding less scrutiny given to military spending, see *ibid.*, p. 54; 115 Cong. Rec. E2242 (daily ed., March 20, 1969); and 115 Cong. Rec. E5466 (daily ed., July 1, 1969).

"National Interest." Air Force colonel testimony: *Government Procurement and Contracting* (Part 4), hearings before the House Committee on Government Operations, 91st Cong., 1st Sess., pp. 1179–83. Robert H. Charles, Assistant Secretary of the Air Force, conceded that this had been a factor in suppressing the information on the C-5A; *The New York Times*, May 3, 1969, 19:1. Air Force officers who had worked on Minuteman: *The Military Budget and National Economic Priorities* (Part 2), hearings before the Joint Economic Committee, 91st Cong., 1st Sess., p. 503 (1969); also, 115 Cong. Rec. S7089 (daily ed., June 25, 1969). Top-ranking procurement official is Gordon W. Rule: *The Military Budget and National Economic Priorities,* p. 510, but see also p. 504. Hubert H. Humphrey, "The Senate in Foreign Policy," 37 *Foreign Affairs* 525 (July 1959). Former members of the Johnson Administration, such as Townsend Hoopes and George E. Reedy, describe the President as losing touch with the public, drawing sustenance and advice from a narrow circle of friends and well-wishers: Townsend Hoopes, *The Limits of Intervention: An inside account of how the Johnson policy of escalation in Vietnam was reversed* (New York: David McKay, 1969); George E. Reedy, *The Twilight of the Presidency* (New York: World Publishing Co., 1970).

"Expertise." Skepticism of Senate Foreign Relations Committee: *National Commitments,* Senate Report No. 129, 91st Cong., 1st Sess., p. 16 (1969). On the reliability of executive statements, see *Civilian Casualty and Refugee Problems in South Vietnam,* hearings before the Senate Committee on the Judiciary, 90th Cong., 2d Sess. (May 9, 1968); and compare the following accounts of the Tonkin Gulf incident: *Southeast Asia Resolution,* joint hearing before the Senate Committees on Foreign Relations and Armed Services, 88th Cong., 2d Sess. (Aug. 6, 1964), versus *The Gulf of Tonkin: The 1964 Incidents,* hearing before the Senate Committee on Foreign Relations, 90th Cong., 2d Sess. (Feb. 20, 1968). Bingham's story: "Can Military Spending be Controlled?," 48 *Foreign Affairs* 51, 59–60 (Oct. 1969). Proxmire's disclosure: 115 Cong. Rec. S5253 (daily ed., May 16, 1969).

GAO study in 1967 on use of Government plant and equipment: *Economy in Government Procurement and Property Management,* hearings before the Joint Economic Committee, 90th Cong., 1st Sess., pp. 1–68 (1967). Small-parts procurement: House Committee on Armed Services, report on *Defense Procurement Policies, Procedures, and Practices: Part II—Small Purchases,* 90th Cong., 2d Sess., pp. 20, 24 (Jan. 22, 1968); see also General Accounting Office, *Requirements Contracting and Other Aspects of Small Purchases in the Department of Defense,* Report No. B-162394 (Feb. 5, 1969). McGee incident: 115 Cong. Rec. S4461 (daily ed., May 1, 1969); see General Accounting Office, *Investigation in Thailand of the Systems for Distributing Petroleum, Oil, and Lubricants and for Processing Related Documentation,* Report No. B-163928 (Jan. 9, 1969). Fitzgerald incident: *Economics of Military Procurement,* hearings before the Joint Economic Committee (Part 1), 90th Cong., 2d Sess., p. 201 (Nov. 13, 1968); Joint Economic Committee, report on *The Economics of Military Procurement,* 91st Cong., 1st Sess., pp. 24ff (May 1969); Fitzgerald's speech, after his dismissal, placed in the *Congressional Record,* Vol. 116, p. E3372 (daily ed., April 20, 1970); *The Dismissal of A. Ernest Fitzgerald by the Department of Defense,* hearings before the Joint Economic Committee, 91st Cong., 1st Sess. (1969).

Safeguard ABM System

The material in this section is drawn from Louis Fisher, "ABM: A Case Study in Deception," *The Progressive* (Nov. 1969). For examples of early Administration opposition to an ABM system, see *Department of Defense Appropriations for 1959,* hearings before the House Committee on Appropriations, 85th Cong., 2d Sess., p. 356 (1958); *Department of Defense Appropriations for 1960* (Part 1), hearings before the House Committee on Appropriations, 86th Cong., 1st Sess., p. 133 (1959); *Public Papers of the Presidents, 1960–61,* pp. 54–55, 414; *Public Papers of the Presidents, 1962,* p. 896 (Dec. 17, 1962); *Public Papers of the Presidents, 1963,* p. 238 (March 6, 1963). September 1967 announcement by McNamara: *The New York Times,* Sept. 19, 1967, and Robert S. McNamara, *The Essence of Security* (New York: Harper & Row, 1968), p. 165.

Wiesner's observation: *Anti-Ballistic Missile: Yes or No?,* a Special Report from the Center for the Study of Democratic Institutions (New York: Hill & Wang, 1969), p. 6. Nixon's announcement to proceed with Safeguard: *Wkly Comp. Pres. Doc.,* Vol. 5, No. 11, p. 401 (March 14, 1969). Rogers: *Briefing by Secretary of State William P. Rogers,* hearing before the Senate Foreign Relations Committee, 91st Cong., 1st Sess., p. 25 (March 27, 1969).

First-strike Capability. Fulbright: *Strategic and Foreign Policy Implications of ABM Systems* (Part I) [hereafter referred to as *Gore Sub-*

committee Hearings], hearings before the Senate Committee on Foreign Relations, 91st Cong., 1st Sess., p. 183. Laird warning: *ibid.*, p. 196. Rogers: *The Department of State Bulletin*, Vol. LX, No. 1557, p. 363. Gore and Fulbright disclosure: *Gore Subcommittee Hearings* (Part II), pp. 492, 528. Laird before House Appropriations: *Safeguard Antiballistic Missile System*, 91st Cong., 1st Sess., p. 7 (1969). Estimate of U.S. Intelligence Board: *Intelligence and the ABM*, hearings before the Senate Committee on Foreign Relations, 91st Cong., 1st Sess., p. 64 (1969). Laird's appearance on June 23: *ibid.*, pp. 7, 46, 59.

Thick or Thin System? Nixon claiming Safeguard was not provocative: *Wkly Comp. Pres. Doc.*, Vol. 5, No. 11, p. 401 (March 14, 1969). Referring to Kosygin statement: *ibid.*, p. 404. Laird before House Appropriations: *Safeguard Antiballistic Missile System*, hearings before House Committee on Appropriations, 91st Cong., 1st Sess., p. 11 (May 22, 1969). Foster: *U.S. News & World Report*, Nov. 30, 1970. p. 26; reprinted at 116 Cong. Rec. E9900 (daily ed., Nov. 25, 1970). Nixon pointing to city protection from Chinese attack: *Wkly Comp. Pres. Doc.*, Vol. 5, No. 16, p. 572 (April 18, 1969). Packard before newsmen: 115 Cong. Rec. E2127, E2139 (daily ed., March 18, 1969). Laird: *Authorization for Military Procurement, Research and Development, Fiscal Year 1970, and Reserve Strength* (Part 1), hearings before the Senate Committee on Armed Services, 91st Cong., 1st Sess., p. 97 (March 19, 1969). See also Foster's testimony, *ibid.*, p. 205 (March 20, 1969), where he said it was not possible "with current technology" to provide heavy defense for U.S. cities. Exchange between Senator McIntyre, General Betts, and Mr. Poor: *ibid.*, p. 532 (March 27, 1969). Hornig: *Gore Subcommittee Hearings* (Part II), p. 539.

Independent Analysis. Fulbright's question to Packard: *Gore Subcommittee Hearings* (Part I), p. 307 (March 26, 1969). Panofsky's testimony: *ibid.*, pp. 327–328, 334. Scientists consulted on March 17: *ibid.*, p. 308. Packard on scientists' "objectivity": *ibid.*; Gore: *ibid.*, p. 121. Packard on York and York's reply: *ibid.*, p. 312. The extent to which the Administration was open to outside opinion is reflected by the abortive plan to appoint Franklin A. Long head of the National Science Foundation. President Nixon announced April 18 that Dr. Long was being dropped from consideration because of his opposition to the ABM. The White House staff, said the President, felt that Long's appointment "would not be in the best interests of the overall administration position" and would be "misunderstood"; *Wkly Comp. Pres. Doc.*, Vol. 5, No. 16, p. 573 (April 18, 1969). The President was widely censured for letting a matter of Administration policy interfere with the appointment of an NSF official. In a meeting with scientists from the NSF and from the National Academy of Sciences, the President conceded that Long's ABM position should not have been a factor in the nomination. Nixon contacted the scientist to see if he might like to be reconsidered for the post; Long refused the offer because he did not want the issue reopened. See *Cong. Q. Wkly Rep.*, Vol. XXVII, No. 20, p. 724 (May 16, 1969). This unhappy incident can be put in larger perspective by recalling a 1968 campaign statement. In order to close the credibility gap, Mr. Nixon said "we should bring dissenters into policy discussions, not freeze them out . . . The lamps of enlightenment are lit by the spark of controversy; their flame can be snuffed out by the blanket of consensus." *Nixon on the Issues* (New York: Nixon-Agnew Campaign Committee, 1968), p. 79.

Command and Control. York: *Gore Subcommittee Hearings* (Part I), p. 78. Packard: *ibid.*, pp. 265–268. Packard later explaining timing dilemma: *Military Posture* (Part 1), hearings before the House Committee on Armed Services, 91st Cong., 1st Sess., p. 1968 (1969). Recommendation that decision be delegated to Army officers: *ibid.*, pp. 1967–1974. Chief counsel: *Military Posture* (Part 1), hearings before the House Committee on Armed Services, 91st Cong., 2d Sess., p. 7092 (1970).

Cost Estimates. Original estimate of $6–7 billion: *Wkly Comp. Pres. Doc.*, Vol. 5, No. 11, p. 408 (March 14, 1969). DMS estimate: 115 Cong. Rec. S4760 (daily ed., May 8, 1969). Laird: *Safeguard Antiballistic Missile System,* hearings before the House Committee on Appropriations, 91st Cong., 1st Sess., pp. 27–29 (May 22, 1969). Leaving out the cost of warheads, the *St. Louis Post-Dispatch* said, was "something like pricing a Cadillac without the engine"; 115 Cong. Rec. S6777 (daily ed., June 19, 1969). Studies by Institute of Defense Analysis, *et al:* 115 Cong. Rec. S8688–8690 (daily ed., July 28, 1969); *The New York Times,* July 18, 1969, 1:1, July 26, 1969, 1:6, July 29, 1969, 5:1, and July 31, 1969, 8:4.

Senator Smith to Laird: *Authorization for Military Procurement, Research and Development, Fiscal Year 1970, and Reserve Strength* (Part 1), hearings before the Senate Committee on Armed Services, 91st Cong., 1st Sess., pp. 122–123 (March 19, 1969). Laird two months later: *Safeguard Antiballistic Missile System, op. cit.,* pp. 21–22 (May 22, 1969). Starbird: *Department of Defense Appropriations for 1970* (Part 6), hearings before the House Committee on Appropriations, 91st Cong., 1st Sess., p. 199 (1969). Other alterations suggested by Packard: *Military Posture* (Part 1), hearings before the House Committee on Armed Services, 91st Cong., 1st Sess., p. 1960 (1969). Other modifications proposed and tested: *Military Posture* (Part 1), hearings before the House Committee on Armed Services, 91st Cong., 2d Sess., pp. 7073–7076, 7081, 7086, 7099 (1970). Redesign of computer program: *Department of Defense Appropriations for 1971: Safeguard Antiballistic Missile System* (Part 4), hearings before the House Committee on Appropriations, 91st Cong., 2d Sess., p. 72 (1970). Terminal guidance: *ibid.*, p. 106.

Cost increase of $1.6 billion: *ibid.*, p. 33. $200 million estimate for smaller radars: House Report No. 1022, 91st Cong., 2d Sess., p. 87

(April 24, 1970). Cost of warheads for improved Spartans: *Military Posture* (Part 1), hearings before the House Committee on Armed Services, 91st Cong., 2d Sess., p. 7098, but see also discussion on pages 7098–7102 (1970). Cost increase from 1970 to 1971: *Department of Defense Appropriations for 1972* (Part 2), hearings before the House Committee on Appropriations, 92d Cong., 1st Sess., pp. 184–186 (1971). Warning by system manager on inflation allowance: *ibid.*, p. 186. $135 million annual operating costs for three sites: *Fiscal Year 1972 Authorization for Military Procurement, Research and Development, Construction and Real Estate Acquisition for the Safeguard ABM, and Reserve Strengths,* hearings before the Senate Committee on Armed Services, 92d Cong., 1st Sess., p. 1480 (April 19, 1971).

Safeguard expansion plan announced on January 30, 1970: *Wkly Comp. Pres. Doc.,* Vol. 6, No. 5, p. 95. Explanation in 1969 of "phased" program: *Wkly Comp. Pres. Doc.,* Vol. 5, No. 11, p. 408 (March 14, 1969). Foster's argument: 115 Cong. Rec. E3870 (daily ed., May 17, 1969). Progress on two sites by early 1970: *Military Posture* (Part 1), hearings before the House Committee on Armed Services, 91st Cong., 2d Sess., p. 7082 (March 9, 1970).

Legislative Influence in Foreign Policy

Coudert's resolution: 97 Cong. Rec. 34 (Jan. 3, 1951). Wherry's resolution: *ibid.*, p. 94 (Jan. 8, 1951). Resolution passed by Senate: *ibid.*, pp. 2363, 3282 (March 14 and April 4, 1951). Bricker Amendment and substitute: 99 Cong. Rec. 156 (Jan. 7, 1953); 100 Cong. Rec. 2349–2358 (Feb. 26, 1954).

National Commitments Resolution. Fulbright's resolution on national commitments in 1967: S. Res. 151, 90th Cong., 1st Sess. (July 31, 1967). Reported out of committee in November as S. Res. 187, 90th Cong., 1st Sess. (1967). See *National Commitments,* Senate Report No. 797, 90th Cong., 1st Sess. (1967). Reintroduced by Fulbright in 1969 as S. Res. 85, 91st Cong., 1st Sess. (Feb. 4, 1969); adopted: 115 Cong. Rec. S7153 (daily ed., June 25, 1969). Fulbright expressing hope concerning change of attitudes: 115 Cong. Rec. S6829 (June 16, 1969). His remarks when introducing resolution: 115 Cong. Rec. S1238 (Feb. 4, 1969). Statement by Senate Foreign Relations Committee on resolution's effect on existing treaties, etc.: *National Commitments,* Senate Report No. 129, 91st Cong., 1st Sess., p. 6 (1969). On August 2, 1971, the House passed another War Powers Resolution under suspension of the rules. The 1971 resolution was similar to the one passed by the House in 1970.

Senator Javits and other Members of Congress have proposed legislation to define the President's war-making powers. These proposals would spell out certain situations in which the President could take action prior to congressional authorization (repelling sudden attacks, protecting life and property, etc.). Presidential action would then have to cease, within a fixed period of time (30 days, for example), unless Congress specifically granted the President new powers. The objections to such proposals are three. First, the categories are ambiguous. Presidents have used force to promote their own policies, justifying their actions under the cloak of life-and-property actions, "defensive war," and other vague categories. Thus, in what purports to be a restriction on the powers of the President, Congress may actually widen those powers by permitting him to take action under ill-defined categories. Second, as the 30-day deadline approaches, Congress is very likely to "rally around the President" rather than critically deliberate on the wisdom of his actions. Once again the power of the President would be broadened. And thirdly, by passing such proposals Congress may very well conclude that it had discharged its responsibility for "reassertion," whereas it is the daily grind of overseeing and scrutinizing Administration policies that is needed.

Reassertion of Legislative Authority. The phrase "a process of commitment by accretion" comes from *National Commitments,* Senate Report No. 129, 91st Cong., 1st Sess., p. 26 (1969). Cooper: 115 Cong. Rec. S10732 (daily ed., Sept. 17, 1969). Special Foreign Assistance Act of 1971: 84 Stat. 1943 (Jan. 5, 1971). For Symington Subcommittee materials, see the hearings conducted by the Senate Foreign Relations Committee in 1969 and 1970 and *Security Agreements and Commitments Abroad,* report to the Senate Foreign Relations Committee (Dec. 21, 1970).

Mansfield: 115 Cong. Rec. S15164 (daily ed., Dec. 1, 1969). Mathias: S.J. Res. 166, 91st Cong., 1st Sess. (Dec. 8, 1969). Tonkin repeal: 84 Stat. 2055, sec. 12 (Jan. 12, 1971). Chiles: S.J. Res. 70, 92d Cong., 1st Sess. (March 11, 1971). Case: 116 Cong. Rec. S19190 (daily ed., Dec. 2, 1970), S. 4556, 91st Cong., 2d Sess.; reintroduced as S. 596, 92d Cong., 1st Sess. (Feb. 4, 1971). Rep. Morse is sponsoring a similar measure in the House on executive agreements: 117 Cong. Rec. H254 (daily ed., Jan. 29, 1971), H.R. 2503, 92d Cong., 1st Sess. Cranston: 115 Cong. Rec. S5670–5672 (daily ed., May 27, 1969).

The McGovern-Hatfield Amendment, designed to force the Administration to withdraw U.S. troops from Indochina by a certain date, was defeated on two occasions: on September 1, 1970, by a 39 to 55 vote, and on June 16, 1971, by 42 to 55. Considering the bold design of that measure, those votes represented a remarkable show of strength by Senate critics of the war.

Structural and Procedural Reforms. James A. Robinson, *Congress and Foreign Policy-Making,* rev. ed. (Homewood, Ill.: The Dorsey Press, 1967), p. 176. Dirksen: Douglas Cater, *Power in Washington* (New York: Vintage Books, 1965), p. 158. Metcalf: 116 Cong. Rec. S17158 (daily ed., Oct. 6, 1970). Legislative Reorganization Act of 1970: 84 Stat. 1164, Sec. 132 (Oct. 26, 1970). Statistics on roll calls and quorum calls obtained from Clerk of the House. A possible procedure for electronic voting is described in letter from Rep. Friedel to House Members, 116 Cong. Rec. H10862 (daily ed., Nov. 25, 1970). Electronic voting was authorized by Section 121 of the Legislative Reorganization Act of 1970; Senators not hearing one another during Tonkin debate: 110 Cong. Rec. 18406, 18407, 18408 (Aug. 6, 1964). Senator Murphy: 115 Cong. Rec. S735 (daily ed., Jan. 22, 1969).

Observations by Udall, Proxmire, and Goldwater: *The Military Budget and National Economic Priorities* (Part 1), hearings before the Joint Economic Committee, 91st Cong., 1st Sess., pp. 258, 268; *ibid.* (Part 2), p. 471. Members of Congress for Peace Through Law submitted its first analysis of the military budget in 1969: 115 Cong. Rec. S10082–10100 (daily ed., Sept. 3, 1969). See *The Economics of Defense: A Bipartisan Review of Military Spending,* Members of Congress for Peace Through Law, Military Spending Committee (New York: Praeger Publishers, 1971). Two works by members of the Brookings Institution include *Setting National Priorities: The 1971 Budget* and *Setting National Priorities: The 1972 Budget.* Mikva: 115 Cong. Rec. H9440 (daily ed., Oct. 13, 1969), H.R. 14318, 91st Cong., 1st Sess.; H.R. 3641, 92d Cong., 1st Sess. (Feb. 4, 1971).

APPENDIX: HISTORICAL AND PHILOSOPHICAL BACKGROUND ON THE SEPARATION DOCTRINE

John Adams' quote is from Gordon S. Wood, The *Creation of the American Republic, 1776–1787* (Chapel Hill: University of North Carolina Press, 1969), p. 6. General works in the area of the separation doctrine include William Bondy, "The Separation of Governmental Powers in History, in Theory, and in the Constitution," *Studies in History, Economics, and Public Law,* Vol. V, No. 2 (Columbia University, 1896); John A. Fairlie, "The Separation of Powers," 21 *Mich. L. Rev.* 393 (1923); Malcolm P. Sharp, "The Classical Doctrine of the 'Separation of Powers'," 2 *U. Chi. L. Rev.* 385 (April 1935); Lawrence Meyer Levin, *The Political Doctrine of Montesquieu's Esprit des Lois: Its Classical Background* (New York: Columbia University Press, 1936); Reginald Parker, "Separation of Powers Revisited," 49 *Mich. L. Rev.* 1009 (May 1951); Reginald Parker, "The Historic Basis of Administrative Law: Separation of Powers and Judicial Supremacy," 12 *Rutgers L. Rev.* 449 (Spring 1958).

Mixed Government

Plato, *Laws,* Bk. III, Steph. 693. Aristotle, *Politics,* Bk. IV. Polybius, *Histories,* Bk. VI, 10. Machiavelli, *Discourses,* Bk. One, Ch. II.

Locke, *Two Treatises of Civil Government*, Book II, §§107, 143; for sharing of powers between Locke's legislature and executive, see *ibid.*, §§153, 156. Quote from Maitland is from Kenneth Culp Davis, *Handbook on Administrative Law*, Hornbook Series (St. Paul, Minn.: West Publishing Co., 1951), p. 28. Walter Bagehot, *The English Constitution and Other Political Essays* (New York: D. Appleton, 1895), p. 78.

The British Model

Coke's statement in 1605: J. R. Tanner, *English Constitutional Conflicts of the Seventeenth Century, 1603–1689* (Cambridge, England: Cambridge University Press, 1961), pp. 35–36. Coke two years later: W. B. Gwyn, *The Meaning of the Separation of Powers*, Tulane Series in Political Science, Vol. IX (The Hague, Netherlands: Martinus Nijhoff, 1965), p. 6. For Dr. Bonham's case, see Edward S. Corwin, *The 'Higher Law' Background of American Constitutional Law* (Ithaca: Cornell University Press, 1955), pp. 40–57.

John Lilburne's experience: William Haller, ed., *Tracts on Liberty in the Puritan Revolution, 1638–1647* (3 vols., New York: Columbia University Press, 1933–34), III, 289. Experiences of Philip Hunton and John Sadler: Francis D. Wormuth, *Origins of Modern Constitutionalism* (New York: Harper & Bros., 1949), pp. 53, 61. Clement Walker's experience is described by Max Radin, "The Doctrine of the Separation of Powers in Seventeenth Century Controversies," 86 *U. Pa. L. Rev. & Am. L. Reg.* 842, 852–855 (June 1938). Clayton Roberts, *The Growth of Responsible Government in Stuart England* (Cambridge, England: Cambridge University Press, 1966), p. 145, but see also pp. 145–154. Other arguments put forth to justify a separation of powers between King and Parliament: Gwyn, *The Meaning of the Separation of Powers*, Ch. IV.

For troubles of George I, see Wolfgang Michael, *England Under George I* (2 vols., London; MacMillan and Co., Ltd., 1936–1939), especially Bonet's description at I, 374–375: *Le comte de Nottingham se trouve d'ailleurs fort embarrassé par cette ignorance de la langue, en ce qu'il est obligé par sa charge de président de conseil de rendre à Sa Majesté compte des matières qui s'y agitent, et qu'il est très difficile de trouver toujours sur le champ des termes propres pour explique chaque chose, ou les lois du pays qui en sont la règle. Cela fait que Sa Majesté donne souvent son consentement à des choses qu'il n'entend pas bien, et dont il ne comprend pas toutes les raisons.* See also J. H. Plumb, *Sir Robert Walpole* (2 vols., Boston: Houghton Mifflin, 1956–1961), I, 203. Gouverneur Morris' reference to "the real King, the Minister" is from Farrand, *Records*, II, 104. Rapin de Thoyras, *The History of England*, trans. by N. Tindal, 3d ed. (5 vols., London, 1743), I, iv–v; II, 796.

Influence of Montesquieu

Background information on the state of English politics during Montesquieu's visit to London: see Walter Sichel, *Bolingbroke and His Times* (2 vols., London: James Nisbet & Co., Ltd., 1901–1902); Charles Bechdolt Realey, "The Early Opposition to Sir Robert Walpole, 1720–1727," *Bulletin U. Kansas,* Vol. XXXII, No. 8 (1931); F. T. H. Fletcher, *Montesquieu and English Politics (1750–1800),* (London: Edward Arnold & Co., 1939); Robert Shackleton, "Montesquieu, Bolingbroke, and the Separation of Powers," 3 *French Studies* 25 (1949); and Robert Shackleton, *Montesquieu: A Critical Biography* (New York: Oxford University Press, 1961).

Bolingbroke's periodical versus the *London Journal:* Shackleton, *Montesquieu: A Critical Biography,* p. 299. Oliver Wendell Holmes, *Collected Legal Papers* (New York: Harcourt, Brace and Howe, 1920), p. 263. Montesquieu's reliance on balance between distinct social classes: *The Spirit of the Laws,* I, 155–156, and Francis G. Wilson, "The Mixed Constitution and the Separation of Powers," 15 *Southwestern Soc. Sci. Q.* 14 (June 1934). Montesquieu's conception of judiciary: *The Spirit of the Laws,* I, 153, 156. Safety of people supreme goal: *ibid.,* II, 78. Need to move in concert: *ibid.,* I, 160. Favoring single executive: *ibid.,* I, 156. Legislature exercising judicial functions: *ibid.,* I, 158ff. Powers counterpoised: *ibid.,* I, 62. Axiom of power checking power: *ibid.,* I, 150: French is from *Oeuvres Complète* (2 vols., Librairie Gallimard, 1951), II, 395.

Legislature prohibited from impeaching executive: *The Spirit of the Laws,* I, 158. Madison: Farrand, *Records,* II, 65, 550–551. Power of Montesquieu's "senate" to reject bills relating to supplies: *The Spirit of the Laws,* I, 156. Opposing executive participation in the legislative process, except for veto: *ibid.,* I, 159–160. Warning against foreign maxims: *ibid.,* II, 78. See also William G. Hastings, "Montesquieu and Anglo-American Institutions," 13 *Ill. L. Rev.* 419 (Dec. 1918); James T. Bland, "Montesquieu and the Separation of Powers," 12 *Ore. L. Rev.* 175 (1933); Mitchell Franklin, "The Passing of the School of Montesquieu and its System of Separation of Powers," 12 *Tulane L. Rev.* 1 (1937); Paul Merrill Spurlin, *Montesquieu in America, 1760–1801* (Baton Rouge: Louisiana State University Press, 1940); and Charles Morgan, *The Liberty of Thought and the Separation of Powers: A Modern Problem Considered in the Context of Montesquieu* (London: Oxford University Press, 1948).

Colonial Developments

Development of separated powers in Virginia and other colonies: Benjamin F. Wright, Jr., "The Origins of the Separation of Powers in

America," *Economica*, Vol. XIII, No. 40, pp. 171–172 (1933). Massachusetts in the 1640s and in 1679: M. J. C. Vile, *Constitutionalism and the Separation of Powers* (London: Oxford University Press, 1967), pp. 123–125. Massachusetts in 1723: *ibid.*, p. 128. Massachusetts in 1742: William S. Carpenter, "The Separation of Powers in the Eighteenth Century," 22 *Am. Pol. Sci. Rev.* 32, 37 (Feb. 1928). Massachusetts constitution: Francis Newton Thorpe, ed., *The Federal and State Constitutions, Colonial Charters, and Other Organic Laws* (7 vols., Washington, D.C.: Government Printing Office, 1909), III, 1893, 1897, 1902, 1904, 1905. New Hampshire constitution: *ibid.*, IV, 2457 (Art. XXXVII).

"Intent" of the Framers

For an analysis of the views of John Adams, Jefferson, and Madison on divided powers, not only within the Federal Government but between it and the states, see Samuel P. Huntington, "The Founding Fathers and the Division of Powers," in *Area and Power: A Theory of Local Government*, ed. by Arthur Maass (Glencoe, Ill.: The Free Press, 1959). The material in this section appeared earlier in Louis Fisher, "The Efficiency Side of Separated Powers," *J. Am. Studies* (August 1971).

George Washington. July 10, 1775 report: *Writings*, III, 324. Letter ten days later: *ibid.*, 350. Letter to Washington regarding "vapid desultory habit": Burnett, *Letters*, III, 283. Washington feeling like an alien: *Writings*, XVI, 28. Washington to Duane in 1780: *ibid.*, XX, 117. Criticism of boards: *ibid.*, XXI, 14. Other letters during the winter of 1780–81: *ibid.*, XX, 371–374; XXI, 164. Hope for "system order and oeconomy": *ibid.*, XXI, 248; see *ibid.*, 181. Letter to Sullivan: *ibid.*, XXII, 71. Letter to Duane regarding Capt. Huddy: *ibid.*, XXV, 222. Regretting resignation of Robert Morris: *ibid.*, XXVI, 200. To Knox: *ibid.*, XXIX, 153. Separation of powers a search for more effective government: *ibid.*, XXX, 300–301.

Alexander Hamilton. Stating preference for single executives in winter of 1779–1780: *Papers*, II, 246n. Suggestions during fall of 1780: *ibid.*, 404–405; see also II, 554, 604–605. Resolution drafted in July 1783: *ibid.*, III, 420–421. Regret at Morris resignation: *ibid.*, 320. Speech at New York ratifying convention: *ibid.*, V, 95. For Antifederalist objections to the mixture of President and Senate in the treaty-making power, see Morton Borden, ed., *The Antifederalist Papers* (East Lansing: Michigan State University Press, 1965), pp. 214–215. Hamilton in later years describing departments and powers as "essentially" distinct: *Works*, VIII, 333 (1802).

John Jay. To Washington in 1779: *Correspondence*, I, 209. Complaint from Spain: *ibid.*, 440–441. Dismay at Morris resignation: *ibid.*,

III, 65. Restating preference for single executives: *ibid.*, 141–142. To Jefferson in 1786, regarding legislative inaction on his reports: *ibid.*, 210. To Jefferson in December 1786: *ibid.*, 223. To Washington: *ibid.*, 227. To Jefferson on inconvenience of system: *ibid.*, 231–232. To John Adams: *ibid.*, 234. Public address to New York citizens: Paul Leicester Ford, ed., *Pamphlets on the Constitution of the United States* (Brooklyn, N.Y., 1888), pp. 75, 77.

Thomas Jefferson. On "173 despots": *Writings*, III, 223. Comparison between 1776 and 1783 drafts for a constitution: *Papers*, I, 358–360; VI, 298–302. Difficulty in obtaining quorum for Continental Congress: *ibid.*, VI, 388; other letters at VI, 419, 432, 437, 469, 569. "Rational and necessary" to create independent executive and judicial branches: *ibid.*, VII, 293. Proposal for separate executive during summer 1784 recess: *ibid.*, VI, 516–529. Edmund C. Burnett, "The Committee of the States, 1784," *Report*, American Historical Association, I, 141, 158 (1913). Letter from France in 1786: *Papers*, X, 603. Congress waiting until "last extremeties": *ibid.*, XI, 679; see also XI, 480 and XII, 34. To John Adams: *ibid.*, XII, 189. Reaction to Constitution: *ibid.*, XII, 440 and XIV, 650. Stricter view of separated powers when Federalists were in power: *Writings*, VI, 102, 108, 143; VII, 108, 170.

John Adams. Continental Congress "slow as snails": Burnett, *Letters*, I, 47, 67. Delegates displaying oratorical abilities: *ibid.*, p. 81; see also No. 134 at p. 95 and No. 150 at p. 107. Turnover in membership: *ibid.*, II, 260. Views during winter of 1775–1776: *Works*, IV, 196; see pp. 186, 205–206. Danger of executive being run down like a hare: *ibid.*, IX, 506. Draft for Massachusetts Constitution of 1780: *ibid.*, IV, 230–231. Fear of blood being shed: *ibid.*, IX, 623. For description of the writing of *A Defence*, see Zoltán Haraszti, *John Adams & The Prophets of Progress* (Cambridge: Harvard University Press, 1952), pp. 155–156, and Page Smith, *John Adams* (2 vols., New York: Doubleday, 1962), II, 690–702. Tripartite system as "political trinity in unity": *Works*, VI, 128; see Correa Moylan Walsh, *The Political Science of John Adams* (New York: G. P. Putnam's, 1915), p. 15. Shifting between theoretical and pragmatic positions: *Works*, IV, 579. String of sentences on separation between legislature and executive: *ibid.* Explanation of response to Turgot: *ibid.*, IX, 572–573. Learning of plan to establish a Secretary for Foreign Affairs: *ibid.*, VII, 343. Pleasure in learning of Livingston's election: *ibid.*, 510. Willingness to help: *ibid.*, 660. Need for more blending between President and Congress: *ibid.*, VI, 432–433. Corruption first introduced in legislatures: *ibid.*, IX, 302.

James Madison. To Jefferson in March 1780: *Papers*, II, 6. Supporting single executives in 1781: *ibid.*, 19–20. Defense of Robert Morris: *ibid.*, III, 179 and IV, 313. Instead of the word "specious," cited in the latter reference, Madison actually used "suspicious" in his letter to Edmund Randolph, June 4, 1782, *Papers of James Madison*, The Library of Congress. Explanation of Livingston's resignation and defense of Jay's insistence: *Writings,* II, 127–128. Suggestions for Kentucky constitution: *ibid.,* 169. Recommendation at Philadelphia Convention that judiciary be introduced in business of legislation: Farrand, *Records,* I, 108, 139.

TABLE OF CASES

INDEX